BUILT IN BOSTON

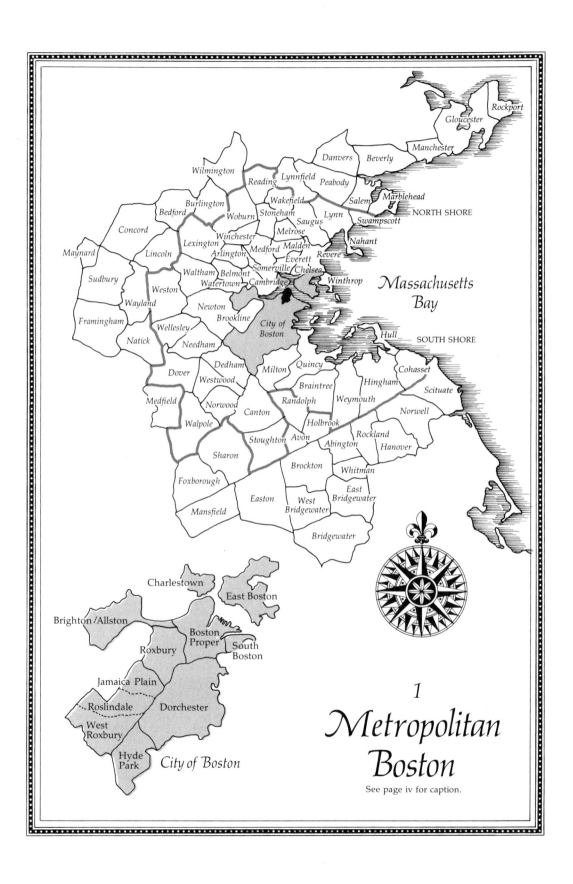

Rockport

Gloucester

Manchester

Danvers   Beverly

Wilmington   Lynnfield   Peabody

Reading

Burlington   Wakefield   Salem   Marblehead

Bedford   Woburn   Stoneham   Lynn   NORTH SHORE

Concord   Winchester   Saugus   Swampscott

Lexington   Melrose   Nahant

Maynard   Lincoln   Arlington   Medford   Malden

Waltham   Belmont   Everett   Revere

Sudbury   Somerville   Chelsea

Weston   Watertown   Cambridge   Winthrop

Wayland   Newton   Massachusetts
Bay

Framingham   Brookline   City of
Boston

Wellesley   Hull   SOUTH SHORE

Natick   Needham

Dedham   Quincy   Cohasset

Dover   Milton   Hingham   Scituate

Medfield   Westwood   Braintree   Weymouth

Norwood   Randolph   Norwell

Walpole   Canton   Holbrook   Rockland

Stoughton   Avon   Hanover

Sharon   Abington

Brockton   Whitman

Foxborough

East
Bridgewater

Mansfield   Easton   West
Bridgewater

Bridgewater

Charlestown

East Boston

Brighton/Allston

Boston
Proper   South
Boston

Roxbury

Jamaica Plain

Roslindale   Dorchester

West
Roxbury

Hyde
Park   City of Boston

1

Metropolitan
Boston

See page iv for caption.

DOUGLASS SHAND-TUCCI

Built in Boston

CITY AND SUBURB

1800–1950

with a foreword by

WALTER MUIR WHITEHILL

and a new preface by the author

THE UNIVERSITY OF MASSACHUSETTS PRESS

AMHERST

Copyright © 1978, 1988 by Douglass Shand-Tucci
All rights reserved
Printed in the United States of America
LC 88-14151
ISBN 0–87023–649–0

Library of Congress Cataloging-in-Publication Data

Shand-Tucci, Douglass, 1941–
    Built in Boston:city and suburb, 1800–1950 /
Douglass Shand-Tucci ; with a foreword by
Walter Muir Whitehill and a new preface
by the author.
        p.   cm.
    Reprint. Originally published: Boston : New
York Graphic Society, 1978.
    Bibliography: p.
    Includes index.
    ISBN 0–87023–649–0 (pbk. : alk. paper).
    1. Architecture, Modern—19th century—
Massachusetts—Boston. 2. Architecture,
Modern—20th century—Massachusetts—
Boston. 3. Boston (Mass.)—Buildings, struc-
tures, etc. 4. Architecture, Modern—19th
century—Massachusetts—Boston Metropolitan
Area. 5. Architecture, Modern—20th century—
Massachusetts—Boston Metropolitan Area.
6. Architecture—Massachusetts—Boston
Metropolitan Area. I. Title.
NA735.B7S53   1988
720'.9744'61—dc19   88–14151
                                   CIP

British Library Cataloguing in Publication data are
available.

The quotation on pages 57 and 60 is from
Bainbridge Bunting, *Houses of Boston's Back Bay,* The
Belknap Press of Harvard University Press. ©
Copyright 1967 by the President and Fellows of
Harvard College. The clerihew on page 183 is from
About Boston: Sight, Sound, Flavor and Inflection by
David McCord. Copyright 1948 by David McCord.
Reprinted by permission of Little, Brown and
Company.

MAP 1, the frontispiece, was prepared from one
entitled "The Four Bostons" which appeared in the
tercentenary history, *Fifty Years of Boston* (1930).
The black area shows Boston Proper—the seventeenth-century peninsular town subsequently enlarged by landfill. This area, including Beacon Hill
and the North End, was by 1900 the downtown
commercial and cultural hub of the metropolis
shown in this map. The gray area shows the City
of Boston—sections added by landfill and also
those cities and towns annexed by 1930, the
boundaries of which are shown in the lower left-
hand corner. Within the heavy line are the inner
suburbs of Metropolitan Boston, many of which
(though not annexed to the City of Boston) had by
1930 surrendered certain responsibilities such as
water supply to metropolitan government. Beyond
the heavy line are the outer suburbs, the further-
most cities and towns of the Boston Metropolitan
District as defined by the U.S. Bureau of the
Census in 1930.

MAP 2, on page xxviii, is a street map showing
Boston Proper and some of the neighborhoods
dealt with in this book.

In Memoriam
WALTER MUIR WHITEHILL
1905–1978

ACKNOWLEDGMENTS

SEVERAL FRIENDS and colleagues have helped in the preparation of this book in a variety of ways: particularly Wheaton Holden, with whom I talked about both the Shingle Style and the Chicago School; Robert Bell Rettig, who has continued to encourage my interest in multifamily housing; Cynthia Zaitzevsky, whose tour of those parts of Jamaica Plain she judged comparable to Dorchester proved of great benefit; and Leland Roth, who discussed with me his work on Charles Follen McKim and first prompted my reflection that McKim and Ralph Adams Cram were two sides of the same coin. The late Walter Muir Whitehill acted as my reader.

I am also indebted to a number of people for a wide miscellany of kindnesses: Mr. and Mrs. Laurence Etter; William N. McCarthy; Lawrence G. Driscoll; William Smith; Mrs. Nicholas Hume; Walter Carney; Frederic Detweiller; John T. Doran; Eugene Kennedy; and John B. Carney. Florence Connolly, Curator of Fine Arts of the Boston Public Library, and Theresa Cederholm of the same department both helped in a multitude of ways, as did Thomas Parker, Director of the Bostonian Society, Rodney Armstrong, Director of the Boston Athenaeum, Heath Aldridge of the Brookline Planning Department, Victoria L. DiStefano of the Cambridge Historical Commission, Deborah A. Gribbon of the Gardner Museum, and Donald Tirabassi of the Colonial Theatre. So also did my typists, Doris Haskell and Mary Nadler.

The staffs of many institutions were also helpful, including those of the Boston Athenaeum; the Bostonian Society; the President's Office at Boston University; the State Street Bank and Trust Company; St. John's Seminary; the Library of the Society for the Preservation of New England Antiquities; the *Boston Herald-American*; and the Boston Building Department and those of Brookline and Newton particularly.

Many of the photographs and drawings were prepared especially for this book. Ron Havern and Leslie Larson, two good friends who are also excellent photographers have greatly enlivened it visually. The value of John Tankard's drawings and Ann Lampton Curtis's maps is self-evident. Jonathan Goell's photographs are, as always, distinguished. I am also grateful to Richard Cheek, whose work I have long admired, for allowing me to reproduce several of his photographs.

Finally, there are those people without whom there would have been either no book or at least a much poorer book — the staff of the New York Graphic Society and Little, Brown and Company. My editor, Robin Bledsoe, whose idea this book was, has been more than painstaking; she has been unfailingly stimulating throughout its preparation. I am also grateful to Tim Hill, Editor-in-Chief of New York Graphic Society, and to Betsy Pitha of Little, Brown's copyediting department for her always careful perusal of both manuscript and galleys. The designer, Barbara Bell Pitnof, has endowed the book with a considerable distinction.

All these good people have made the writing of this book a positive pleasure. My only comparable debt is to my mother, Geraldine Groves Tucci, who typed and proofread the first handwritten drafts, which no one else could have understood.

Contents

MAP 1, Metropolitan Boston, is the frontispiece.

MAP 2, Boston Proper & Environs, is on page xxviii.

Preface to the
Paperback Edition

THE LATE SIR JOHN BETJEMAN, whose passion for Victorian and Edwardian architecture was a light in the darkness for many of my generation, once kindly invited me to stay to luncheon after a marvelous morning's talk at his London house, to which I had been asked through the good offices of my kinsman Bruce Shand. Struck by how remarkably alike were our responses to everything from the rigors of boarding school to the intricacies of High Church Anglican ceremonial, I was not surprised that this was even more the case with architecture. I remember particularly one remark of the Queen's Poet Laureate, his eyes twinkling: "I do love architecture," he said, "don't you? It never answers back."

How very true, and thank goodness for it. I think of my own architectural "first loves" — the Radcliffe Camera at Oxford, King's College Chapel at Cambridge, the Abbey Room of the Boston Public Library, all pictured on my desk as I write; the nave of St. John the Divine in New York, the Viceroy's House at Delhi (photographs of which hang on the wall facing me in my study); Palace Square in Leningrad, the Royal Pavilion in Brighton, London's House of Lords and St. Cyprian's, Clarence Gate, and St. Paul's and Westminster cathedrals; the M.I.T. Chapel; the steep Baroque vistas of Prague and of Rome; so much of Venice; at least a half dozen English country houses; seemingly *all* of Paris and Oxford; and yes, Beacon Hill and Harvard Yard and Lowell House and the exquisite small church of All Saints in Peterborough, New Hampshire. One may stand in such places as these, even if only in memory or imagination, pouring out one's heart in the most extraordinary way toward something that — in just the same key — will always give back more than one could have imagined. Only music, perhaps (certainly not poetry, which so often has a mind of its own), seems to me to yield so immediately and profoundly to such outpouring in so personally and intensely fulfilling a way as does architecture.

That is why, ten years ago, I wrote *Built in Boston* — with this difference: that I felt then incredibly frustrated because so many of the buildings that moved me seemed to move no one else. Despite the books that had got me going, so to speak, as an undergraduate in the late 1960s — Walter Muir Whitehill's *Topographical History of Boston, Houses of Boston's Back Bay* by Bainbridge Bunting, the early *Survey of Cambridge Architecture* volumes, and Sam Bass Warner's *Streetcar Suburbs* — few people at that time were really very interested in the Harvard Houses or the architecture of the streetcar suburbs or apartment houses, or even in the work of Ralph Adams Cram. And almost no one had yet been intrigued by movie palaces or by three-deckers or by Colonial Revival suburban houses.

There were some kindred spirits: John Coolidge at Harvard, Walter Whitehill, Frank Moloney at the Boston Public Library, Robert Bell Rettig, Margaret Henderson Floyd, William Morgan at Princeton, Wheaton Holden, and George R. Ursul. But not many. And how could it have been otherwise, given the sorry state of so much American cultural and art history then? Truly, it is no exaggeration to say that *Built in Boston* was born of my outrage that the architectural history not just of Boston but of America had been so distorted and misrepresented by art historians who in my youth were writing not history but polemics.

This was an easy distinction for me to make in 1978, fresh as I was from the rigors of Elliott Perkins's Harvard History Department (where the name of Samuel Eliot Morison could still be invoked without risk). For the History Department was a very different place from the Fogg Museum and the Fine Arts Department, where it seemed to me that even the most distinguished art historians might know much more than I of art but assuredly knew much less of how to write history. Having as a young scholar foraged so often in one index after another, but quite in vain, for architects and artists whose work excited my interest and who I was sure were not insignificant, I had begun to wonder (for all my youthful confidence) if the fault could be mine after all and their work really unimportant. In his 1973 Leslie Stephen lecture at Cambridge, however, Quentin Bell said what only a major figure could get away with saying, and it became my battle cry. Writing of what he called the "grotesque travesty of history" that so riddled art history in those days, he boldly declared:

> It is not right and proper when we allow our value judgments to lead us into a falsification of history, that is to say when the historian allows his own personal predilections to determine which facts should and which facts should not be recorded. . . . The student [for example] who relies upon Professor Janson's large and handsome history of art, published in 1962, or an Upjohn, Wingert and Mahler's *History of World Art* (1957) . . . will not discover that the Pre-Raphaelites ever existed. There is . . . a kind of semi-mythology masquerading as history which is confidently imparted to students . . . and then, as any examiner knows to his cost, is regurgitated in the form of almost pure misinformation.

At first I went at the problem of trying to arouse interest in the art and architecture I liked — which I learned was rather patronizingly put down as "historicist" by the then still triumphant "modernist" establishment — by writing what I'm afraid were really my own polemics. In my two earliest books, *The Second Settlement* and *Church Building in Boston*, each privately printed for limited circulation and more enthusiastic than critical, I had begun to argue the case for historicist architects, and in two later (and better) books, *All Saints' Ashmont: A Centennial History* and *Ralph Adams Cram: American Medievalist*, to focus on the work of Cram and Bertram Grosvenor Goodhue, whose historicism (or eclecticism, or whatever one cares to call it) yielded one brilliant synthesis after another. The Cram book in particular cheered me because it was published by the Boston Public Library to mark the first retrospective exhibition anywhere of Cram and Goodhue's work. This exhibition began in Boston in December of 1975 and then went on to open in New York the following May. As the opening speakers included Ada

Louise Huxtable, John Coolidge, Kenneth Conant, Walter Whitehill and Henry-Russell Hitchcock, I think it fair to say that though it was a small show and necessarily limited in scope, the Cram exhibition helped to do for the study of the Gothic Revival in this country what was done for the study of the Classical Revival, also in 1975–1976, through the marvelous Beaux-Arts exhibition mounted by the Museum of Modern Art in New York. Indeed, its sponsorship of such a show in the first place constituted a historic revolution. Suddenly, my enthusiasms were not just respectable; they were becoming fashionable.

Notwithstanding this, I no more desired to go on writing historicist polemics than I wanted to continue reading modernist polemics; I wished instead to avoid the critical limbo that sort of thing thrives in and to write not polemics but history — the sort of history that would restore the balance the modernist zealots had disrupted and that would put architectural history back together again by placing modernism *and* historicism *in context*. This interested me all the more because I had begun to conclude that the late nineteenth- and early twentieth-century historicists who had taken so different a road from Louis Sullivan's and Frank Lloyd Wright's had nevertheless begun at the same place — with that fecund progenitor (as it turns out) of both schools, Henry Hobson Richardson. Moreover, at about the same time my own scholarly enthusiasms were usefully broadened by a visit to Chicago, where I had been invited by the Illinois chapter of the Society of Architectural Historians to lecture on Cram at the Art Institute of Chicago. I went really to see the work of the Boston historicists Cram and Shepley, Rutan and Coolidge in Chicago. What struck me, however, were Louis Sullivan's magnificent Stock Exchange Trading Floor and a long evening's talk with Leland Roth, who helped me see that McKim, Mead and White and Cram, Goodhue and Ferguson were two sides of the same architectural coin.

The result was the thesis, central to *Built in Boston* and rather revolutionary in 1978 — illustrated here by Plates 6 and 7 — that the work of McKim and Cram particularly, characterized alike by a cool, severe restraint that still was richly detailed and gravely beautiful, constituted the superb climax to date of the Classical and Medieval traditions in the New World. And that, in turn, nicely fitted with my increasing certitude that the overall cultural history of the 1880–1930 era, particularly in Boston, had been misjudged and undervalued. Unlike such writers as Van Wyck Brooks, I thought New England's Indian Summer had been itself a very great flowering — and that its architecture reflected that fact. Thus the chance offered me by Little, Brown/New York Graphic Society Books to do a full-fledged architectural history of Boston was very welcome. Boston, after all, was sufficiently old and important that its cultural and architectural history often led the nation and thus offered an author the opportunity for more than local attention to his causes. Furthermore, I had a far longer agenda in those days than just righting the modernist-historicist balance.

The other causes I sought to push forward were more local but as keenly held, perhaps because they were more personal. Though I spent my winters as a child at boarding school and my vacations at my parents' summer home, our family house is in Dorchester, on Jones Hill, where my maternal grandparents had settled, after their marriage, in 1908. A great-aunt lived nearby in Roxbury; our doctor lived in Brookline; the awning man was from South Boston; my godparents' home was in West Roxbury; a good friend lived in Jamaica Plain, another in Newton; I had gone to boarding school in Wellesley — and I had not noticed that these areas were notably duller than other places. Yet in book after book that claimed to be about Boston, these neighborhoods and suburbs of the city were as conspicuously absent as the historicist architects were from the art histories, and it seemed to me distorting and impoverishing to ignore those areas at the expense of endless repetitions of the glories of the Downtown–Beacon Hill–Back Bay–Cambridge axis.

I did not then, nor would I now, dispute that this axis is the heart and center of Boston, and as such I naturally had many affectionate associations there. Take one street: my maternal grandfather lived as a graduate student on Mount Vernon Street in 1905–1907; my grandmother's best friend, Grace Turkington, lived on the street in the 1930s — not far from another house on Mount Vernon Street where I spent much of my own college years in the late 1960s sitting at the feet of Professor George R. Ursul, one of my first mentors. I loved Beacon Hill. Similarly, I was at home in the Back Bay; as a youth I spent much time in the old Pierce mansion on the water side of Beacon Street, where my mother managed the practice of a Boston psychiatrist. As for Cambridge, my father was a graduate of Harvard College and had grown up in one of those large and splendid houses in the neighborhood of Brattle Street. Thus I had no quarrel with the axis; rather, I did with so many authors who insisted that it was all there was of Boston worth writing about. Again, what was needed was context — the forgotten and ignored architecture of such places as Roxbury and Newton had to be integrated into the overall Boston scene and find its proper niche and measure.

Another cause was equally dear to me: it seemed dubious that so many *kinds* of Boston's buildings were slighted in books about the city. The splendid theaters of my youth — the Majestic, the Metropolitan, the Oriental, the Colonial — were often not even mentioned; nor were the superb parish churches of the western suburbs, or those endless ranges of three-deckers I used to peer at out of the car window on our trips to and from Dorchester. Well, I was very ambitious! Still, it seemed clear that by integrating historicism and modernism and by dealing with all the various, long-ignored neighborhoods and suburbs of Boston and the equally neglected building types, an architectural history of Boston could be written that would both surprise and stimulate.

That *Built in Boston* continues to do so a decade later and now appears in its third printing and first paperback edition, published, moreover, by a distinguished university press, is very gratifying. But though I am glad to say the book as a whole needs no revision to continue to reflect my view of Boston's architectural history, there are a number of repairs necessary, of which I hope the reader will take careful note.

Two of these repairs embarrass me. First, the Fenway Studios must now take its place in *Built in Boston* as a building of citywide importance. Designed by Parker, Thomas and Rice in 1905, it is the most important Boston landmark in the modernistic Arts and Crafts style. My friends, who know I am an avid collector of Dard Hunter, a leading Arts and Crafts designer, never tire of twitting me for this omission. *Mea culpa.* Even more inexplicable is the fact that I should have ended *Built in Boston* with the Gropius House in Lincoln, totally disregarding Eero Saarinen's M.I.T. Chapel of 1955. This chapel has long been the only "modern" building hereabouts I've really liked (until in 1970 at the Massachusetts Health, Welfare and Education Service Center Paul

Boston's foremost Arts and Crafts landmark, the Fenway Studios on Ipswich Street. The street facade is shown above, the entrance portal and front doors below. Courtesy of Fenway Studios.

The interior of the M.I.T. Chapel. The bronze-toned altar screen is by Harry Bertoia. Photograph by Calvin Campbell, courtesy of Massachusetts Institute of Technology.

Rudolph endowed Boston with a glorious "Baroque" exterior staircase)! I have always been deeply moved at the chapel by the way light enters the interior; filtered through the surrounding trees and softened by the gently moving water of the moat, the light is reflected by the water through the arcades of the moat into the interior, where it reflects and scintillates against the undulating brick walls inside the chapel. No building is at once more dynamic and more dreamlike — striking in contrast with a campus that otherwise seems to consist mostly of unimaginably long linoleum-clad corridors that lead from one parking lot to another.

While on the subject of modernism, I should also like to note that although I tried very hard to do full justice to its history in Boston, ten years ago I did not know (as I do now from reading Elizabeth Sussman's "Taking a Risk" in *Dissent: The Issue of Modern Art in Boston*, the catalogue of three 1985–1986 exhibitions at the Institute of Contemporary Art) that "what appears to have been," in Sussman's words, "the first exhibition to introduce the new [Bauhaus] architecture of Europe to the United States" took place in Harvard Square in 1930. Sponsored by the Harvard Society for Contemporary Art and organized by Philip Johnson, this Bauhaus show, which then traveled to Chicago, preceded by two years the more famous exhibition Johnson and Henry-Russell Hitchcock organized on the same subject at the Museum of Modern Art in New

The interior capitals of the Buick Building are worth a second glance: those are automobile mechanics rather than medieval figures. Photograph by Richard Cheek from *Buildings and Builders* by Nancy Lurie Salzman, Boston University, 1985. Used by permission.

York. Nor did I know until exploring Doris Cole's *Eleanor Raymond, Architect* (Boston, 1981) that Raymond, among the first important women architects, had designed for her sister in Belmont in 1931 a house featured in 1933 in *Architectural Forum* as the first International style house erected in New England.

There are also a number of buildings in the more traditional styles that I neglected in 1978 but wish to note now. Significantly, nearly all are commercial or industrial landmarks, a type of architecture I have never been very interested in, and that would never dominate my work, but one that nonetheless is too important a part of Boston's architectural history for me to continue to neglect. The marvelous enameled terra-cotta Berkeley Building of 1905 by Codman and Despredelle, on the corner of Boylston and Berkeley streets, is one such. Another is the mercantile Gothic Gilchrist Building of 1912 on Washington Street, designed by Bigelow and Wadsworth. Furthermore, I'm afraid I did not in my youth venture into the leather district and did not until recently as a historian see any need to repair the error; thus it came as a complete surprise to me to experience the tremendous sweep and presence of the Melcher Street warehouses and, indeed, to be introduced to the whole Boston Wharf Company area around Summer Street, so much of it the work, ca. 1887–1920, of the company architect Morton D. Safford. In like vein, though I remember my childhood delight whenever I passed the windows of "Fuller's Folly," as the Fuller Cadillac automobile showroom on Commonwealth Avenue was called, I slighted that whole building type as well as the Kenmore Square area where most of Boston's early twentieth-century automobile dealerships were erected. Two buildings particularly need to be noted: the Fuller Building itself, at 808 Commonwealth Avenue, the work in 1928 of no less than Albert Kahn; and the Buick Building at 855 Commonwealth Avenue, yet another work by Arthur Bowditch, designed in 1919 and now the Boston University School for the Arts. The auto mechanics who appear in the Gothic capitals of the Buick Building's interior columns are particularly charming examples of the modernism of historicism.

To some extent, these omissions may be explained by the fact that only recently has much been published in this area by those who know something of such work, and this brings up the whole question of those books which have appeared since 1978 that I wish to add to the bibliography of *Built in Boston*. I learned about the Boston Wharf area from *Boston Landmarks of Industrial and Engineering History: Four Tours* (Boston,

1984); the automobile dealerships are discussed in Nancy Salzman's *Buildings and Builders: An Architectural History of Boston University* (Boston, 1985). Such publications are vital building blocks of urban history. They cause no sensation, but in their plodding, patient documentation of this and that apparently only very ordinary building they add much to our overall knowledge of the city. In Salzman's book alone, to cite some examples: the Dorchester architect of the streetcar suburbs, A. H. Vinal, emerges as "a major architect of the west Back Bay"; the documented interior work of Little and Brown is augmented by new buildings of theirs, including the virtually unknown and amazingly vivid green marble opulence of the Harriet Richards House at 101 Bay State Road, which can now be compared with the Somerset Club's well-known and very refined Directoire drawing rooms; and Shepley, Rutan and Coolidge turn out to have designed at the corner of Bay State Road and Deerfield Street a house for Peter Brooks, he of the Monadnock Building in Chicago, whose severe tastes so influenced the Chicago style. It is appropriately austere. Furthermore, the fact that not only Arthur Little but also Edmund Wheelwright lived in houses of their own design on Bay State Road (increasingly, so it seems, rather an "arty" area at the turn of the twentieth century, comparable to Huntington Avenue around Symphony Hall) enlarges our overall knowledge of Boston's social geography at the time. Salzman's book adds many such pieces to the still far from finished Boston jigsaw puzzle.

No less important is the city's architectural ornament. To the bibliography under Section G, Metalwork, one may add an excellent book: Michael and Susan Southworth's *Ornamental Ironwork: An Illustrated Guide* (Boston, 1978), which has much documentation of the work of Samuel Yellin of Philadelphia, though not enough of Frank Koralewski of the Krasser Company of Boston, who was distinctly in the same class. Also of interest is my own "Johannes Kirchmayer: A Carver of Saints," commissioned by the Goethe Society of Boston, which appeared in *Germans in Boston* (Boston, 1981).

A number of popular books should also be noted, such as *Lost Boston* by Jane Holtz Kay (Boston, 1980); her work, as well as that of Robert Campbell, the *Boston Globe* critic, is always interesting. Then there are two widely available architectural guides to the city, Donlyn Lyndon's *The City Observed: Boston,* published in 1982, and Michael and Susan Southworth's *A.I.A. Guide to Boston,* published five years later. Though each book deals importantly with eighteenth-, nineteenth-, and early twentieth-century buildings and not just with "modern" landmarks, both betray the fact that they were written not by architectural historians but by architects trained in an era when architectural schools preferred to teach urban design rather than architectural history. Nevertheless, both are worth buying. I remember, for example, how startled I was at the Southworths' insight about the Jordan Marsh building of 1948, a building I would not ever have thought anyone could convince me was worth much; "distinct Post-Modernist tendencies" was their surprising and quite inspired conclusion, and this historian was taught thereby yet another lesson about how all of us tend to undervalue the just-past styles of our own lifetimes, to which we are too close. I called Jordan's "an absurd 'Modernistic' Federal Revival" building when I wrote this book ten years ago. I was wrong. Another example, this time from Lyndon's book: he points out (though we cannot know if any distinction should be made between the firm and its senior partner) that the Henry Bigelow of Bigelow and Wadsworth, who designed the marvelous

79 Milk Street, one of two long-overlooked intown office buildings in the modernistic Arts and Crafts mode. Courtesy of the Macomber Company.

fifth floor of the Athenaeum in 1913, one of the finest interiors in Boston, designed the amazingly different Gilchrist Building on Washington Street the year before. That's the kind of weaving together of apparently unconnected threads that advances our overall historical knowledge of the city. Lyndon is surely right, moreover, in noting that the wonderful grotesques of the Gilchrist Building, being the work of the Athenaeum's architect, must be seen as "intentionally droll."

Henry Forbes Bigelow reminds me that amid this discussion of books written I should, perhaps, touch also on books not written that *should* be — soon. Bigelow is such a case. He is one of a number of important architects of regional and even national reputation about whom not nearly enough is known. Were I writing *Built in Boston* today, I would want to study such people more closely, rather as I was able in 1978 to study C. H. Blackhall, then not widely known. There are so many of these architects. Even such firms as the Shepley/Coolidge office and Perry, Shaw and Hepburn fall into this category. One thinks of Bigelow particularly because to his superb Classicism at the Athenaeum must be added not only the stylish commercial Gothic of Gilchrist's but also the most unusual modernistic Arts and Crafts office building of 1904 at 79 Milk Street. This has lately intrigued me because I had not previously noticed the elegantly chamfered corner detail — an oblique void that as it widens toward the top seems to make the building tip backward — and the topmost cornice, which takes the form of a trumpet-shaped cove inset with triangular and pendant green and white terra-cotta plaques. (The raw data for 79 Milk Street, though without any discussion of its unusual stylistic aspect, are found in the *Central Business District Preservation Study* by the Boston Landmarks Commission, an invaluable compendium published in 1980.) Interestingly, when I told my old friend the Boston architect William Buckingham, of Basnight, Buckingham and Partners, about my interest in this building, he remarked that he thought it was the first building erected by the well-known old Boston builders, the Macomber Company. Upon inquiry, they sent me their firm's history, in which 79 Milk Street is in fact described as their "first contract . . . one of the first structural steel buildings in the United States . . . revolutionary in design. . . ." It must indeed have looked revolutionary as it rose at the turn of the century in Post Office Square, then dominated by the old Sub-Treasury and its neighbors, illustrated here on page 42. It is, in Buckingham's words, "second cousin to the Monadnock Building in Chicago." And only thirteen years later. (Another modernistic Arts and Crafts building, pointed out to me by Daniel Coolidge, is 262 Washington Street, the work of Arthur Everett of Everett and Mead in 1901.)

To return to books actually written: three recognized scholars who have given us significant work relating to Boston are Cynthia Zaitzevsky, whose *Frederick Law Olmsted and the Boston Park System* came out in 1982; James F. O'Gorman, whose *H. H. Richardson: Architectural Forms for an American Society* was published in 1987; and William Morgan, who wrote, in 1983, the first full-length study of a famous Boston architect, Henry Vaughan, *The Almighty Wall: The Architecture of Henry Vaughan*. But far and away the landmark books of the last ten years are Abbott Lowell Cummings's definitive *The Framed Houses of Massachusetts Bay 1625–1725*, published in 1979; and *Harvard: An Architectural History* by Bainbridge Bunting and Margaret Henderson Floyd, who edited and much enlarged Bunting's original manuscript. An outstanding scholarly book, the Harvard history was particularly welcomed by this writer because my own principal scholarly work over the last decade (most of it for *Harvard Magazine*) has arisen out of my admiration for the Georgian Revival masterworks at Harvard of Coolidge, Shepley, Bulfinch and Abbott. In this connection, I should also like to note *The Colonial Revival in America* (New York, 1985). Also of very great interest because it touches on so many Boston architects and artists is *"The Art That Is Life": The Arts and Crafts Movement in America 1875–1920* (Boston, 1987). For me this book was a particular pleasure (to round the circle, as it were, of this introduction), for prominently featured in the Arts and Crafts exhibition at the Museum of Fine Arts, Boston, for which the book is a catalogue, was All Saints' Church, Ashmont, Cram and Goodhue's first church and the building, then long forgotten, that first fired up my interest in architectural history fifteen years ago as a young man in Harvard College.

NEW acknowledgments are few but notable. I am glad for the help of both Archie Epps and William Strong in guiding me toward the University of Massachusetts Press and its director, Bruce Wilcox, who has been throughout a pleasure to work with; and of Betsy Pitha, my old friend and now head of the Trade Copyediting Department at Little, Brown and Company, for copyediting this introduction, thus ensuring a necessary stylistic consistency. Tom Parker of the Bostonian Society found for me the illustration I have long coveted for the front cover, and I am grateful to Robert Douglas Hunter and Elizabeth Ives Hunter for directing me to David Loury, who provided the photographs of the Fenway Studios.

I must add that as I now spend more time with the Building Committee for the restoration of the McKim Building of the Boston Public Library than I do writing books, I have good reason to thank Kevin Moloney, Arthur Curley, Victor Hagan, and our architect, Daniel J. Coolidge, for keeping my architectural wits in good order. The cover illustration of this new edition of *Built in Boston*, which shows the McKim Building, is intended to mark the 100th anniversary of its erection, which will be celebrated in 1995, as well as the restoration of this landmark, one of the chief architectural glories of the New World.

Finally, I must enlarge on the last of my acknowledgments of ten years ago, for since my mother's death it is necessary to record a debt to her far greater than I then indicated. The daughter of a learned and dedicated but not very worldly clergyman, Lucien Stanley Groves, and of a brilliant businesswoman, Margaret Shand Groves, who (to put it tactfully) kept the family solvent, my mother in persevering through four years of the Great Depression to her bachelor's degree was herself among a small number of college-educated women in the America of the 1930s. Thus by my arrival it was a family tradition that such things as one's scholarship mattered far more than one's income. The knowledge of so unusual a standard in this materialistic age, and the way my mother believed in me against all odds and helped me in my career as she had my father before me (even to giving up her own opportunity for a graduate degree) is surely the most important acknowledgment of this book. So much was this the case that when Professor Margaret Henderson Floyd used to marvel in the 1970s at my productivity, as one book followed another, culminating in *Built in Boston*, she would say: "Ah, yes, but your mother is your secret weapon." So she was: fundamentally, everything I ever write will always be dedicated to Geraldine Groves Tucci.

D. S.-T.

Shandleigh House,
Jones Hill, Dorchester

26 February 1988

FOREWORD

WALTER MUIR WHITEHILL

THE TWO DAYS before Christmas 1977 will stick in my memory because of the pleasure that I had in reading the manuscript of Douglass Shand Tucci's *Built in Boston: City and Suburb*. The book moves so skillfully from one thing to another that it is difficult to put down. One wants to find what is coming next. Moreover, several chapters, based on the author's research in previously unexplored areas, offer new material and ideas of great interest.

Last year I contributed an introduction to *Architecture Boston*, an excellent book produced by the Boston Society of Architects with text by Joseph L. Eldredge, F.A.I.A., which carries the reader around central Boston, Charlestown, Roxbury, and Cambridge of the present day, explaining skillfully what is to be seen there. As it is a publication of the Boston Society of Architects, it rightly gives considerable space to the work of the years since World War II. *Built in Boston* proceeds on chronological rather than geographical lines, undertaking to show what happened architecturally in Boston at different periods from the late eighteenth century, and why. Thus Mr. Tucci often discusses buildings that have disappeared or fallen out of general esteem or even good repair, like some of the twentieth-century theaters.

Writing in 1945 in *Boston after Bulfinch: An Account of its Architecture, 1800–1900*, the late Walter H. Kilham, F.A.I.A., observed: "Writers on architecture have usually avoided saying very much about the work of the nineteenth century, especially in the United States, but as a matter of fact this era of rapid expansion provides in its architecture a highly instructive picture of the developing culture of the nation."

At the beginning of the nineteenth century the practice of architecture was considered to be within the grasp of any literate gentleman who had a mind to try his hand at it. When Charles Bulfinch returned from a "Grand Tour" in 1787, he settled in Boston, "pursuing no business but giving gratuitous advice in architecture," derived from his travels, as an accommodation to his friends. When financial reverses made employment necessary, Bulfinch turned to the serious practice of architecture, and within a few years transformed the face of his native town. Another Bostonian, fifty-five years younger than Bulfinch, Edward Clarke Cabot, who had raised sheep in Illinois and Vermont, stumbled into architecture by winning in 1846 the competition for a new building of the Boston Athenaeum. In his late twenties at the time, he had not been in Europe. However, he had looked at books owned by the Athenaeum to some purpose. Although Cabot's brown sandstone facade was obviously of Italian Renaissance inspiration, it only dawned on me last year, when I was writing the catalogue for the American showing of the Palladio exhibition, that it was derived from Palladio's Palazzo da

Porta Festa in Vicenza. When I found among the early nineteenth-century holdings of the Athenaeum a copy of Ottavio Bertotti Scamozzi's great folio *Le Fabbriche e i Disegni di Andrea Palladio* (Vicenza, 1776), in which the facade of that palace figures as plate seven in volume one, then the source of Cabot's inspiration became clear.

During the third quarter of the nineteenth century, architecture in Boston began to assume the air of a profession, as those who wished to practice it sought formal training, rather than relying on travel, books, or apprenticeship in an existing office. The sixteen-year-old Richard Morris Hunt, having been taken to Paris by his family soon after his graduation from the Boston Latin School in 1843, studied at the Ecole des Beaux Arts and worked under Hector Martin Lefuel, who was engaged upon additions to the Louvre and the Tuileries. Returning to the United States after nine years, Hunt opened in New York in 1858 a studio in which he trained younger men in the principles of architecture he had been taught in Paris. William Robert Ware, graduated from Harvard College in 1852, and Henry Van Brunt of the Harvard class of 1854 studied architecture in New York with Hunt, while Henry Hobson Richardson of the Harvard class of 1859 went to Paris to the Ecole des Beaux Arts to get French training at first hand. Ware and Van Brunt, who established a partnership in Boston in 1863, created an atelier in their new office for students on the order of Hunt's. This was so successful that in 1865 Ware was charged with the establishment of an architectural school in the recently founded Massachusetts Institute of Technology. This outstanding new school, which for the first time in the United States offered training in design according to the method of the Ecole des Beaux Arts, caused Ware in 1881 to be invited to found a similar school of architecture at Columbia University.

The American Institute of Architects was established in New York in 1857. A decade later the Boston Society of Architects was organized to seek "the union in fellowship of all responsible and honorable architects and the combination of their efforts for the purpose of promoting the artistic, scientific, and practical efficiency of the profession." Edward Clarke Cabot, who, after his success in the Boston Athenaeum competition, continued to practice architecture, was president of the society from 1867 to 1896, and thereafter honorary president until his death in 1901.

At the beginning of the nineteenth century Boston was a seaport, whose 24,397 inhabitants were almost entirely of English origin. At the end of the century, it was a polyglot industrial city of 560,892. Half of the 1900 population was Irish. A fifth hailed from the Maritime Provinces. Because of the considerable number of immigrants from Russia, Italy, Germany, and other countries, less than 11 percent were what might be considered traditional New Englanders. Even the landscape was changed during the nineteenth century by means of great landfilling operations, undertaken to make room for the burgeoning population. These changes, combined with those in the practice of architecture, make the nineteenth-century buildings of Boston "a highly instructive picture of the developing culture of the nation," as Walter Kilham noted.

In the third of a century since the publication of his book, a generation of younger architectural historians discovered the joys of nineteenth-century buildings, admiring things that their parents either ignored or ridiculed as eyesores. Ware and Van Brunt's Memorial Hall at Harvard is a case in point, although the Harvard Corporation has not yet been persuaded to restore its tower to its original splendor. The neighborhood of

Quincy Market, in jeopardy not so many years ago, has been rescued by the Boston Redevelopment Authority, and is alive with people. The publication of Bainbridge Bunting's *Houses of Boston's Back Bay* in 1967 caused many Bostonians to realize that these buildings were not only the places where their relatives had lived but remarkable examples of nineteenth-century architecture. Mr. Tucci carries his exploration through the first four decades of the twentieth century to the point where the migration of Walter Gropius to Harvard caused an abrupt change in Boston architecture. Now that there is increasing boredom with the austerities of the "International Style," which has moved from *avant garde* to "old hat," it is worth reexamining the traditional architecture that it replaced.

Built in Boston naturally discusses many familiar buildings that have been studied by others, but a good half of the book is based upon its author's personal research and observations. Mr. Tucci has an incurable habit of looking at his surroundings and then trying to discover who built what, and why. As a senior in Harvard College half a dozen years ago, he studied the history of the Harvard Houses. He has written about his own Jones Hill neighborhood in Dorchester. His work in organizing the papers of Ralph Adams Cram and other architects and craftsmen in the Boston Public Library led first to the publication in 1974 of his *Church Building in Boston, 1720–1970* and the next year to a great Cram exhibition at the library, for which he wrote *Ralph Adams Cram, American Medievalist*. A centennial history of All Saints' Church, Ashmont — Cram's early masterpiece in the region — also appeared in 1975. In a secular mood, Mr. Tucci prepared in 1977 a walking tour of Boston theaters, concert halls, and movie palaces for the City Conservation League. In all of these studies he spread so wide and deep a net as to bring up a rich haul of unfamiliar material, which he skillfully presents in this book.

Since the period described is one in which Boston was overflowing its boundaries, Mr. Tucci rightly considers the architecture of neighboring towns, whether or not they were formally annexed to the city. Once public transportation brought places within easy reach of downtown Boston, houses proliferated in the same way in Dorchester, which became part of the city in 1870, and in Cambridge and Brookline, which are independent municipalities. In Chapter 4, "Streetcar City, Garden Suburbs," he gives an enlightening account of this process, using Jones Hill in Dorchester, which he knows intimately, as a point of departure. He indicates that large houses on small lots there were deliberately planned that way from the beginning, and that their proximity to each other and to the sidewalk was not the result of subsequent intrusions. He suggests that this sprang from a memory of the first decade of the nineteenth century on Beacon Hill when Bulfinch was designing for Harrison Gray Otis and others freestanding houses that, due to shortage of land, were later incorporated in solid blocks.

He may well be right, for I have never been able to fathom why, around Brattle Street in Cambridge, on, let us say, Fayerweather Street, people built in the late nineteenth century large, often expensive, and sometimes well-designed free-standing houses on diminutive lots. To me there is more privacy in a Back Bay block, or in one in London, Paris, Rome, or most European cities. But the hankering to have a freestanding house, even if your land is so small that you can look into your neighbor's side windows, is not exclusively a Bostonian or an American folly. In Barcelona, where the Gothic city and the huge nineteenth-century *ensanche* that enfolds it consist of solid blocks of apartments and houses, there is at the head of the Paseo de Gracia a region of luxurious free-standing villas, built on as exiguous pocket-handkerchiefs of land as anything in the Boston suburbs.

Chapter 5 on apartment houses and Chapter 9 on theaters and movie palaces present useful ideas about ubiquitous structures that most Bostonians have simply thoughtlessly taken for granted. The pioneering Hotel Pelham of 1857 and its 1870 neighbor, the Boylston, at the corner of Tremont and Boylston streets, have long since vanished, as have the apartment houses in Copley Square. The first apartment house on Commonwealth Avenue, Ware and Van Brunt's Hotel Hamilton of 1869, was demolished in the last decade by developers who hankered to put a taller structure on the site. As they were foiled by legal action, the lot once occupied by the hotel at the northwest corner of Clarendon Street is still vacant, save as a children's playground. Two blocks up at Exeter Street, the Hotel Agassiz (191 Commonwealth Avenue) of 1872 is still considered a delightful place to live, although it has passed the century mark. Mr. Tucci follows the evolution of the apartment house through Boston and the suburbs, calling attention to significant examples that many of us have passed for years without thinking about.

His account of the theaters particularly intrigues me, for as a child I was taken to see *Ben Hur* in Edward Clarke Cabot's Boston Theatre (of the 1850s) in Washington Street. Then too I delighted in the "crystal waterfall staircase," electrically lighted, with which B. F. Keith had adorned his adjacent Bijou Theatre. When I was in Boston Latin School sixty years ago, my idea of a Saturday morning's diversion was to see a film in the Modern Theatre in Washington Street — then correctly named, for it was built in 1914 — before going on to look for books at Goodspeed's, Smith and McCance, De Wolfe-Fiske's, Lauriat's, and in Cornhill. As the theater district has fallen upon evil days, we tend to forget how many, and how splendid, playhouses were built in the period covered by this book. Unlike the Boston Opera House, most of them are still there, although often in a state of sorry dilapidation.

Interesting as these novelties are, the true point of *Built in Boston* is that it follows local architectural taste from Bulfinch through the Greek Revival, the Italianate, the French Second Empire, and Victorian Gothic to H. H. Richardson; on to the Colonial Revival, the Classicism of Charles F. McKim, and the Gothic vision of Ralph Adams Cram, and makes these transitions seem plausible in relation to the pluralistic culture that emerged during the phenomenal nineteenth-century growth of Boston.

In regard to the eclecticism that prevailed from 1890 to the 1930s, Mr. Tucci observes that "well-traveled and well-educated architects, with well-stocked libraries of measured drawings and photographs of seemingly everything ever built and an endless supply of excellent immigrant craftsmen, coincided with clients equally well-traveled and well-educated and (until 1930) with more money than they often knew what to do with." The Boston Public Library owes much to the mutual understanding and shared enthusiasms of architect and client, for during its construction the president of the trustees was Samuel A. B. Abbott, who later became the first director of the American Academy in Rome. Abbott and McKim egged each other on, enjoyed the process, and obtained superior results. The architect Herbert Browne, who knew Italy intimately and loved to find there marble columns, busts, and bas-reliefs, had a similarly close relation with some of his clients. The design of the music room at Faulkner Farm in Brookline emerged from the combination of four colossal marble columns and a painted octagonal room that he found in Mantua, and a set of tapestries that his client, Mrs. Brandegee, already owned. While the columns determined the height of the room, its length was established by the size of the tapestries, and the Mantua room became a slightly elevated stage where musicians could perform.

Mr. Tucci obviously sympathizes with the belief of the eclectics "that the historical associations of a style were crucial to a building's functional expression, provided all the modern conveniences were worked into it." Mr. Tucci is young enough to be able to do so. The fear of being thought old-fashioned, ill-informed obscurantists led too many of my generation to ignore or deprecate such a masterpiece of traditional eclecticism as Lowell House at Harvard, which still pleases the eye while usefully serving the purpose for which it was designed nearly fifty years ago. Mr. Tucci is free from such prejudices. I greatly like his book. I wish Walter Kilham were still around to enjoy it.

Walter Muir Whitehill died on March 5, 1978, as this book was going to press. I first met him at the Club of Odd Volumes in 1972 when I was a senior in Harvard College, and I will always recall how he welcomed me to those distinguished precincts as if I had just written a brilliant first book. Later that year, when I did send my first book to him — timidly, for it was not brilliant — back from Mr. Whitehill came the first of many warmly encouraging letters. Though we were often associated publicly, it is for these more private kindnesses that I will chiefly remember him. Once I had to be in North Andover; nothing would do but that Mr. and Mrs. Whitehill should meet me at the bus stop, drive me to and from my appointment, give me a most handsome lunch, and deliver me back to the bus stop at the end of the day. Recently, Mr. Whitehill did me another kindness; as it turned out, the last: on Christmas Day of 1977 he called me at home to tell me how much he had enjoyed Built in Boston. *He talked long and eloquently of Boston buildings and Boston friends, nicely relating everything to my manuscript — in part, no doubt, because he must have guessed that there was no one whose opinion of my work mattered more to me. It is for that reason, when I learned of his death, that I asked Dennis Crowley and Stuart Myers, for whom this book was written, if I might dedicate it instead to Mr. Whitehill's memory. I am grateful to them for encouraging me to do so.*

Introduction

HIS BOOK is the result of a course in the history of architecture in Boston that I was invited to give by Harvard University in 1977 at the Center for Continuing Education under the Faculty of Arts and Sciences. That course, in turn, derived from a series of public lectures that John Corcoran persuaded me to undertake in the spring of the same year at the Women's City Club of Boston, where I first felt the sense of outrage and helplessness any instructor must feel when he realizes that there is just no book at all to give to students about a subject worthy of a great many books. Thus when Robin Bledsoe of the New York Graphic Society asked me if I would care to revise my lectures for publication, I agreed at once.

Although I was born in the city of Boston, I did not really grow up in the city, which as a boy I saw only briefly when home from school. Summers too were spent elsewhere. But I was fortunate in having older friends who knew Boston well: Harrison Hale Schaff, David Landau, Francis Moloney, George Ursul, and Jim Hart. It was through them — particularly Dr. Landau, who bought and restored a Back Bay town house, and Professor Ursul, who undertook a similar restoration of a South End house — that with neither design nor fervor on my part I finally discovered Boston as a young man. For me, such was my taste and ultimately my vocation, this meant Boston's buildings. Nor was I surprised in 1976 when forty-six architects, critics, and historians throughout the country were asked by editors of *The Journal of The American Institute of Architects* to name "the proudest achievements of American architecture over the past 200 years" that only New York City gathered as many nominations (twenty-nine) as Greater Boston. The city of Boston alone, which is a much smaller part of its metropolis than are most other central cities in the United States, accumulated more nominations than all but two cities, New York and Chicago. Architecture in Boston, though this is the first full-length history of the subject, is obviously a large part of architecture in America.

There are any number of ways one might set about such a book. What I have done is to integrate my own research with that of other scholars into a general survey that is strongly rooted in Boston's overall cultural history and emphasizes the influence of six great architects — Bulfinch, Richardson, McKim, Cram, Sullivan, and Gropius — though Bulfinch and Gropius are, respectively, prologue and epilogue. Two themes are interwoven throughout: I have sketched the architectural contours of Boston, what could be called the architectural topography, as it has expanded and differentiated itself into recognizable "built environments," while at the same time following the thread of style and fashion through its many shifts and vagaries. The treatment is not

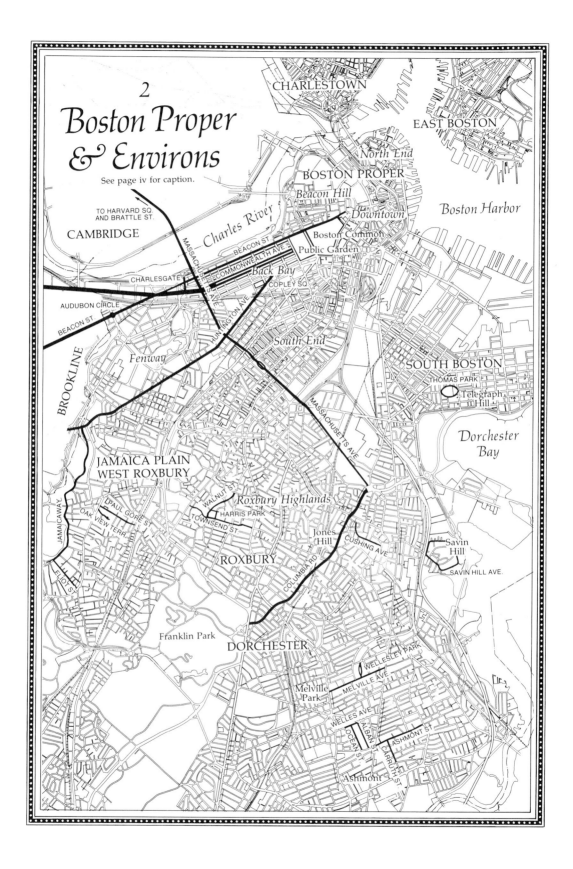

2
Boston Proper
& Environs

See page iv for caption.

TO HARVARD SQ.
AND BRATTLE ST.

CAMBRIDGE

CHARLESTOWN

EAST BOSTON

North End

BOSTON PROPER

Beacon Hill

Downtown

Boston Harbor

Charles River

BEACON ST.

COMMONWEALTH AVE.

Boston Common

Public Garden

CHARLESGATE

Back Bay

COPLEY SQ.

AUDUBON CIRCLE

BEACON ST.

BROOKLINE

Fenway

HUNTINGTON AVE.

South End

SOUTH BOSTON

THOMAS PARK

Telegraph
Hill

MASSACHUSETTS AVE.

Dorchester
Bay

JAMAICA PLAIN
WEST ROXBURY

JAMAICAWAY

OAK VIEW TERR.

PAUL GORE ST.

WALNUT ST.

Roxbury Highlands

HARRIS PARK

TOWNSEND ST.

ELIOT ST.

ROXBURY

Jones
Hill

CUSHING AVE.

Savin
Hill

SAVIN HILL AVE.

COLUMBIA RD.

Franklin Park

DORCHESTER

WELLESLEY PARK

Melville
Park

MELVILLE AVE.

WELLES AVE.

OCEAN ST.

ALBAN ST.

ASHMONT ST.

CARRUTH ST.

Ashmont

exhaustive; this is not the mammoth study that the history of Boston's architecture will surely yield one day. What I have tried to do is to show what David McCord has called "the swing of the pendulum rather than the bowels of the clockworks; to let a handful of leaves in their venation suggest the tree itself; to bid the story of but three or four individuals acknowledge the story of literally hundreds." I have, on the other hand, sought to build this book as I do my course from fairly simple foundations to what is, finally, a more complex profile. The book thus develops as it progresses so as to introduce the reader through fairly detailed discussions of a few pivotal architects and buildings to increasingly complex factors in both the philosophy of architecture and in design itself — ranging from the Gothic church to the apartment house and the movie palace; three building types in the development of which in this country Boston has played a conspicuous and too long overlooked part.

About half the book is drawn from my own research. The section on the Harvard Houses derives largely from an unpublished history of them I coauthored with David McI. Parsons as the result of a grant for that purpose from the Harvard Faculty of Arts and Sciences in my senior year at Harvard College in 1972, though the conclusions here are entirely my own. The streetcar suburbs chapter proceeds from much subsequent research since my book of 1974 on that subject, *The Second Settlement,* but it still owes a great deal to the generous funding of my work by St. Margaret's Hospital for Women. Any kind of history of a great city must depend to some extent on building blocks of neighborhood history (Bunting's architectural history of the Back Bay, for instance) and if a dozen or so other Boston institutions would do for their neighborhoods what St. Margaret's did for Jones Hill in Dorchester, we should know much more about Boston. The Cram chapter is rooted in my study of Cram and his work, an effort made possible by his successor firm, Hoyle, Doran and Berry, and by the Boston Public Library and the First American Bank for Savings. The chapter, "French Flats and Three-Deckers," is the result of entirely unpublished research I have undertaken on my own, as is also the section on Louis Sullivan and Boston, an interest stimulated by my trip to Chicago in 1976 to lecture at the Art Institute for the local chapter of the Society of Architectural Historians. Through "Bunny" Selig's generosity, I was allowed to see Sullivan's superb Stock Exchange Trading Floor being restored and rebuilt into the Art Institute. I had just previously attended the unveiling of the Sullivan plaque in Boston, and a train of thought was stimulated, the results of which are published here. Finally, the chapter on the Boston rialto derives from my monograph of that title, published in 1977 by the City Conservation League.

Throughout, I have indicated my principal sources in the text. Complete checklists of source material consulted for selected Boston building areas, building types, and architects are also included. Otherwise, each of the chapters documents itself. (A list of abbreviations used in the captions and bibliography is given on page 235.) When the designer or date of a specific building is not general knowledge, the address of the building has always been given, and this will always yield the relevant sources at either the building department of the city or town in which the building is located or in the Boston architecture card index maintained at the Fine Arts Department of the Boston Public Library. That card index, itself the source or verification for many attributions here, includes also the results of data I have unearthed elsewhere. If I have thus

FIGURE 1. Tremont Street at Beacon Street, ca. 1860. King's Chapel is visible in the left foreground. To the right are the spire of the Park Street Church, the Old Granary Burying Ground (hidden), and Isaiah Rogers's Greek Revival hotel, the Tremont House.

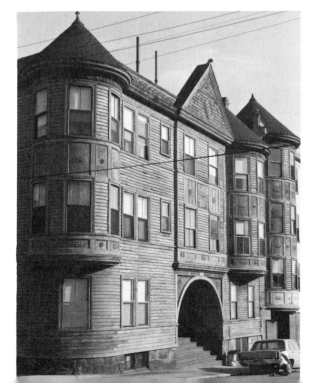

FIGURE 2. Tremont Street, opposite the Old Granary Burying Ground, 1895. Gridley J. Fox Bryant's Horticultural Hall (1865) appears at the far left.

FIGURE 3. The Other Boston: an unattributed and now deteriorating three-decker on Paul Gore Street in the Jamaica Plain section. Of a building type that since World War II has been spurned increasingly by anybody who can afford better and that (until very recently) was also completely overlooked by architectural historians, this anonymous tenement illustrates vividly how striking late nineteenth-century vernacular design could be — and how fragile is much of Boston's architectural heritage today, when such buildings are virtually unnoticed.

been able to avoid what Sir John Betjeman has called a "rash of foot and note disease," I have consequently had to ignore Henry Adams's admonition: "to overload the memory with dates is the vice of every schoolmaster and the passion of every second rate scholar." The date of every building touched on is given in the text or in the captions. Otherwise to traverse so long a period would ensure that many would lose their way.

Dates of buildings, of course, are always problematical: Symphony Hall, for example, and the first Museum of Fine Arts were designed many years before they were built. Even in the case of buildings where design and construction were continuous, one can choose the date of the drawings, or of their publication, or of the groundbreaking, or of the dedication. And sometimes, in the case of quite large buildings, different parts were designed, begun, and opened in different years and often are the work of different architects. In general, I have dealt with these problems by settling on the date the building was sufficiently completed to be opened for use. Otherwise I have usually indicated that the date given is that of its design or completion or whatever. In the case of (mostly) major works, the inclusive dates given are the date the plans were begun and the date the building opened. In the case of minor works, dates derive largely from Building Department records; otherwise I have used what might be called the most authoritative sources for whatever area or building type or oeuvre is involved. For example, for Bulfinch, Kirker's *The Architecture of Charles Bulfinch;* for McKim, Leland Roth's appendices to the new edition of the monograph on the firm's work; for Back Bay houses, Bainbridge Bunting's *Houses of Boston's Back Bay;* and in many instances, Walter Muir Whitehill's always reliable works.

I have relied here upon the more or less standard words and terms used by architectural historians, though even when they do not fall into the category of jargon, these are almost never luminous. For years scholars sought and failed to find something better for even so basic a word as Gothic — and most of the terms now universally used are invariably misleading or confusing. Nor is there any way out of this — historians as in so many things are trapped by the history they study: by no means are all shingled houses "Shingle Style"; the streetcar suburbs are to my mind full of town houses; the Queen Anne style has very little to do with Queen Anne; and one might fill a sizable book and also waste a great deal of time ruminating about the innumerable refractions of words like "eclectic," "modern," "picturesque," "romantic," and so on. As every attempt I am aware of to reform this vocabulary has only added to the confusion, I have resisted the temptation to attempt my own reform. Yet throughout the book I have used two words — "Medieval" and "Classical" — in a way that I hope will be helpful. The idea derives from Harmon Goldstone and Martha Dalrymple's *History Preserved: A Guide to New York City Landmarks and Historic Districts* (New York, 1974), where all these terms were organized into two overall categories: the Classical tradition and the Romantic tradition. For a variety of reasons I would dispute the value of one term and the authors' definitions of both. But the *idea* of thus organizing stylistic terms in this way seems to me a good one, for throughout the period covered by this book, two great traditions in Western architecture have animated Boston: the Classical tradition, work characterized by orders of columns, capitals, and entablatures that show a descent from Greece and Rome, either directly or through the Renaissance, and which are characteristically symmetrical in massing and detail; and the

Medieval tradition, work that shows an affinity for the Middle Ages and is characteristically organic, asymmetrical, broken, or rambling in mass. Both traditions have been continually submerging and reappearing throughout American architectural history, and both have often shaded into each other. A building may be Classical in detail and asymmetrical or Medieval in overall massing. In that case one can only call it "picturesque," a word architectural historians use too much, but necessarily; some would capitalize it and virtually erect it into a style of its own.

Another word, the use of which may at first confuse, is Boston, for the definition in these pages parallels, as it should, that of each historical period dealt with — in the sense that Boston expands in each chapter as it expanded historically, from town and city to metropolis (see Maps 1 and 2). Thus in 1800 Newton is not treated as part of Boston, for it was then isolated and quite unrelated to the early nineteenth-century town of Boston. By the 1850s, however, it was an emerging suburb whose architecture is briefly considered because it was related to the city's, and after the 1870s it was culturally, socially, and architecturally a part of Boston (so much so that Boston College is in Newton, not in the city of Boston) and is treated as such. Except for occasional forays to discuss Bostonians' country houses and for one or two types of buildings no longer extant in Boston in a given period, it is in this manner that Boston's meaning expands in this book from one period to the next. It is also for this reason that this book ignores such notable seventeenth-century suburban Boston architecture as the Old Ship Church in Hingham and the Saugus Iron Works. Neither place could be called a suburb until the late nineteenth century. The bibliography, however, includes sources for all the "pre-suburban" architecture of every city and town now in the Boston Metropolitan District. Some areas naturally possess much more significant architecture than do others. A corollary problem is that places like the Back Bay, Dorchester, and Cambridge have been extensively studied and documented; other places like Everett, Newton, East Boston, or Hyde Park have scarcely been noticed.

Finally, I hope that *Built in Boston* reflects generally the great sense of pride I take in the accomplishments of a number of my colleagues in the Boston/New England Chapter of the Society of Architectural Historians — particularly Robert Bell Rettig, Margaret Henderson Floyd, Wheaton Holden, Bainbridge Bunting, Theresa Cederholm, and Cynthia Zaitzevsky. Each has in one way or another labored very hard to document Boston's architectural history. Others, like Ada Louise Huxtable of *The New York Times*, Leslie Larson, the founder of the City Conservation League, Gerald Bernstein of Brandeis, Eduard Sekler of Harvard, and A. McVoy McIntyre, of the Beacon Hill Civic Association, are due perhaps as much credit for bringing the subject so forcefully to the attention of students and the public. Indeed, I sometimes think that these dedicated men and women deserve better of Boston, which is too important a place to be left entirely in the hands of bureaucrats and city planners.

D.S.T.

Boston
March 1978

BUILT IN BOSTON

I have always loved building, holding it to be not
only the highest achievement of man but one in
which, at the moment of consummation, things
were most clearly taken out of his hands and per-
fected, without his intention, by other means, and I
regarded men as something much less than the
buildings they made and inhabited, as mere lodgers
and short-term sub-lessees . . .

— Evelyn Waugh
Brideshead Revisited

1

BEFORE AND AFTER BULFINCH

IN THE IMAGINATION of the world Boston holds a secure place. Yet what part in this architecture plays, or what kind of architecture, it is hard to say. Samuel Eliot Morison, perhaps the preeminent American historian of this century, likened at least one Boston architect "to a cathedral builder of the thirteenth century [to whom] came visions transcending human experience, with the power to transmute them into reality." But it was not Bulfinch or Richardson that Morison likened to the Master of Chartres; it was Donald McKay, the naval architect. And that "Boston should have carried the clipper ship to its ultimate perfection" was for Morison Boston's, and America's, incomparable architectural achievement. "The *Flying Cloud*," wrote Morison, "was our Rheims, the *Sovereign of the Seas* our Parthenon, the *Lightning* our Amiens . . ." and as the images of these famous ships arise in our minds, his eloquence is irresistible:

A summer day with a sea-turn in the wind. The Grand Banks fog, rolling in wave after wave, is dissolved by the perfumed breath of New England hayfields into a gentle haze, that turns the State House dome to old gold, films brick walls with a soft patina, and sifts blue shadows among the foliage of the Common elms. Out of the mist in Massachusetts Bay comes riding a clipper ship, with the effortless speed of an albatross.

Though Morison naturally pointed in this famous passage from the city itself to its thronging harbor, elsewhere in *The Maritime History of Massachusetts* he admitted that he had such respect for Bulfinch that he was "tempted to ascribe his pure taste and perfect proportion to an ocean origin; but," he went on, "curiously enough, land architecture grew steadily worse in Massachusetts as naval architecture reached perfection in the clipper ships." Here, at least, we can disagree.

Consider the relative importance of architecture in Boston when young Charles Bulfinch sailed from its harbor (Figure 4) for his European tour in 1786 and when Henry Hobson Richardson embarked for his trip to Europe not quite a hundred years later, in 1882. Bulfinch left a town by no means rude. Boston's mid-seventeenth-century wooden folk Gothic — of which only the steep gabled Paul Revere House of about 1680 (Figure 5) survives today — had begun to give way to the Renaissance tradition. Christ Church (Figure 6), a kind of "folk Wren," had been followed by the Old South Meeting House in 1729; and at every level from the ca. 1711 Town House (now the Old State House; Figures 206–207) down to simple dwellings like the Crease and Capen houses of about the same time (later, respectively, the Old Corner Book Store and the Old Union Oyster House), the more horizontal Renaissance tradition, increasingly in brick, had made its presence felt more and more. In 1737 Boston was endowed as well with its first stone building, the granite Hancock House on Beacon Hill. And in the mid-

FIGURE 4. Boston from the South Boston Bridge.
Lithograph by Deroy after a drawing by J. Milbert.

eighteenth century, when Boston was both the vice-regal seat and the largest English-speaking community in North America, the town had overcome its Puritanism sufficiently to accept what is called the High Georgian mode. Boston accumulated a number of splendid buildings in this manner, a provincial interpretation of English Palladianism, but strongly influenced by James Gibbs and thus a continuation of the Wren tradition. Perhaps the most famous are Faneuil Hall (see Figure 17), later enlarged but in its original style, and Peter Harrison's King's Chapel (Figure 7), which, involving as it did the introduction into Boston of Anglican liturgical elegance, exercised a wider than merely architectural influence on Puritan Boston.

Boston's Georgian spires nonetheless bravely punctuated the skyline of what was still a basically Medieval town when Bulfinch sailed for Europe in 1786. In fact, Boston's architecture then amounted by any but the standards of the New World to very little. Yet what a different place it was from which Richardson began his European tour almost a hundred years later. One need not share Henry-Russell Hitchcock's enthusiasm to understand the importance of his assertion that Richardson, Boston's leading architect in 1882, was by then "the greatest architect in the world." Bulfinch and Richardson bracket an extraordinary century in the history of architecture in Boston.

Much as one might like to say something new about Bulfinch here, the old and venerable idea that he virtually created Boston architecturally is more or less true. Previously, architecture in Bos-

5

6

Seventeenth- and eighteenth-century architecture.

FIGURE 5. Paul Revere House, 19 North Square, North End. Exterior surfaces and interior treatment date from a 1908 restoration by Joseph Chandler, but the structural skeleton is original, ca. 1680. Except for the Medieval street plan still evident in parts of downtown and the North End, this folk Gothic house is all that remains of the appearance of the seventeenth-century settlement.

FIGURE 6. Christ Church, North End, 1723. The steeple of what is commonly called the "Old North Church," the work of William Price, dates from 1740 and has been several times rebuilt. The church was restored in 1912 by R. Clipston Sturgis and Henry C. Ross.

FIGURE 7. Peter Harrison. King's Chapel, 1749. Some of the ornament derives from the first church, including the altarpiece, the gift of King William and Queen Mary in 1696.

7

ton had been a series of episodes. Bulfinch changed all that dramatically. Stylistically, he continued the English Renaissance tradition, for though it led the political revolution of the colonies, Boston sought no cultural declaration of independence. One sees a reflection of this in Bulfinch's work, which in turn reflected his own admiration of the English Neoclassicists Sir William Chambers and especially Robert Adam. In fact, Bulfinch's style has been called not only "Federal" but "American Adam." But Bulfinch made that manner his own, as is evident in the Massachusetts State House (Figure 8) he designed upon his return from Europe and which was begun some years later, in 1795.

In the State House, frankly derivative of the central riverfront pavilion of Chambers's Somerset House in London, begun in 1778, one can see at a glance how Bulfinch lightened and refined his sources, achieving a more delicate building, the attenuated proportions of which are characteristic of his work. The simplicity of the brick piers and arches of the first floor has been particularly admired: they form, William Pierson has written, "one of the most expressive and lovely passages in American architecture." Inside, Bulfinch marshaled a most distinguished sequence of state rooms. The old Senate, now the Senate Reception Room, is perhaps the handsomest room in Boston: barrel-vaulted and graced by two rows of free-standing Ionic columns, its high-arched windows open generously to Beacon Street and Boston Common. The old House of Representatives, now the Senate, is the grandest apartment, notable for its great sunburst of a dome, whose radiant flat ribs lift gracefully to a lofty apex of delicate fluting (Plate 2). One sees here as throughout Bulfinch's work the elegant spiderwebs of pliant and crisp detail for which he has been so much admired (Figure 14). Its effect is

even more striking in his first Harrison Gray Otis House (1796), where the recent painstaking restoration by the Society for the Preservation of New England Antiquities has yielded unsuspected Federal color combinations — light bluish green with detail picked out in white, for example — that reveal a fine use of color to differentiate and highlight detail.

Bulfinch's chief legacy to Boston was his introduction of Neoclassical town planning. His Tontine Crescent of 1793–1794 was remarkably advanced for its time and not only in Boston (Figure 9). Harold Kirker has observed that although the famous crescent at Bath and perhaps the plan for another in London were Bulfinch's inspiration, not even London had a crescent at this time. The Tontine Crescent must have been a magnificent sight: sixteen brick houses, painted gray and with white pilasters, ranged on either side of a central archway, swept graciously for almost five hundred feet around a tree-shaded park. At the end of the crescent, the shape of which has survived in Franklin Street today, Bulfinch built Boston's first theater in 1794 and in 1800–1803 what became shortly thereafter Boston's first cathedral, Holy Cross Church, erected for the Roman Catholic bishop of Boston, Jean-Louis A. M. LeFebvre de Cheverus. What a whole new world it must have seemed — for in crescent, theater, and cathedral, as in the Massachusetts capitol, Boston was straining for the first time toward an architecture of European finish. Alas, the whole brave parade lasted little more than fifty years, so relentless was the later push of business in this quarter: the theater was destroyed in 1852; the crescent about 1858, and, finally, the cathedral about 1862. But the *idea* of the Tontine Crescent, as we shall see, proved more durable.

Bulfinch's concept of residential design has nonetheless been widely misunderstood. His blocks of row houses

Public buildings by Charles Bulfinch.
FIGURE 8. Massachusetts State House, Beacon Hill, 1795–1798. See also
Plate 2.
FIGURE 9. Tontine Crescent (left) and Boston Theatre, 1793–1794, showing
the theater as originally designed. Demolished.

10

11

12

Residential architecture by Charle
Bulfinch on Beacon Hill.
FIGURE 10. The third Harrison Gra
Otis House, 45 Beacon Street,
1805–1808, as it originally appeare
showing also (right) Alexander
Parris's Sears House at 42.
FIGURE 11. The same two houses a
they appear today, connected by
third house.
FIGURE 12. The second Otis House
Mount Vernon Street, 1800–1802.

always possessed architectural unity; none resembled in any way the massed shoulder-to-shoulder irregularities, for instance, of present-day Beacon Street. As Frank Chouteau Brown pointed out many years ago, Bulfinch essayed connected row house blocks in conjunction with parks — either his own or a public park in the case of Colonnade and Park rows, two splendid ranges of brick town houses, now destroyed, with which he framed Boston Common along Park and Tremont streets between 1803 and 1812. Otherwise he continued to prefer, as did his whole generation, the traditional detached or free-standing town house, set close by the street and the neighboring houses but in its own garden lot. Thus, when the new State House precipitated the development of the adjacent area, Bulfinch's plan was very different in this new quarter. The area was gained by leveling one of the three hills that then rose behind the State House and dumping it into the water where Charles Street now is, the "first instance," in Walter Muir Whitehill's words, "of dumping the tops of hills into coves," and an expedient way of enlarging the small peninsula upon which Boston had been founded that was to become a habit in the nineteenth century. Since this more extensive development called for more than a narrow range of houses facing the Common, Bulfinch imagined here great free-standing town houses. Several survive, but they are easily overlooked because they have usually been subsequently connected to each other (Figures 10, 11). This fate befell the Otis House on Beacon Street, for example, the original appearance of which is clear in Figure 10. That Bulfinch did not foresee its later connection by another house to the nearby Sears House is evident when one notes the ample bay of the Otis House's oval salon, which, in fact, had to be embedded into the connecting house when that

was built. The bay is still there today to document Whitehill's observation that "as we admire the red brick houses around Beacon Hill today, it is well to remember that to Bulfinch, and those of his contemporaries who survived into the 1840's and '50's, these same houses connoted horrid crowding. . . . This was, alas, the penalty of a growing population."

What happened is easily understood. As land became scarcer on the small peninsula, land values increased so alarmingly that no sensible homeowner could for long justify the financial loss involved in keeping his garden. The result has proved charming to our eyes for some time. But it is only on Mount Vernon Street, above Louisburg Square, that Bulfinch's design concept survives — in the splendid house at 85 Mount Vernon, the second that Bulfinch erected for Harrison Gray Otis (Figure 12). Built close by the sidewalk, the carriageway on its eastern flank, its haughty facade of brick and pilaster is felt all the more keenly for its garden setting. And the design concept one sees here, though short-lived on Beacon Hill in the increasingly crowded early nineteenth-century city, was to prove as enduring a memory for Bostonians as that of the Tontine Crescent.

The reader may have been puzzled to observe that Bulfinch built two houses in Boston for Otis. Actually, he built three, for this famous Federalist merchant and sometime congressman and mayor of Boston sought so insistently for more amplitude and greater state that he sold his first Bulfinch house on Cambridge Street, only to sell after a while his second on Mount Vernon Street in favor of the third house, which Bulfinch built for him in 1805–1808 facing Boston Common. (A fourth house, Oakley, also by Bulfinch, was built by Otis as a country seat in Watertown.) Nor was Otis's elegance untypical of the Federalist era. It may well be thought to symbolize as much as crescent, theater, and cathedral the new character of Bulfinch's Boston.

This last Otis house is a culmination in more than one sense of Bulfinch's work, for despite the splendid new Neoclassical vistas he introduced into Boston, some scholars have felt that Bulfinch's designs were really rather unimaginative. Yet Pierson's analysis of the third Otis House is eloquent:

In this superb building all ornamental pretense is stripped away. . . . In actual measurement the façade forms a simple rectangle only slightly wider than it is high. As seen from the street, however, it gives the appearance of being tall in proportion. Bulfinch has created this impression through subtle and expressive means. By spacing the windows more closely vertically than horizontally he has drawn them into five rising tiers. Then he has accelerated this vertical movement by varying the shapes of the windows at the different floor levels. Those in the basement are conventional classical rectangles. On the second — in this case, the principal — floor, however, they are full-length and triple-hung so that in proportion they are very tall and narrow. Those on the third floor are shorter by one sash but still tall; at the top they are conventional rectangles again, identical to those in the basement. The result is a swelling graded sequence from small to large to medium to small which tapers off toward the top. This is the primary rhythm of the façade. But a second rhythm is also found in the vertical spacing of the windows. The closest together are those in the basement and on the second floor, those farthest apart are on the second and third floors. The medium spacing is between the third and fourth floors. Together these two changing sequences form an interlocking gradation both in size and interval which not only increases the sense of verticality but does so with the same qualities of rhythmic grace that are experienced in the controlled curvatures of an oval.

"The shape and location of the windows *are* the design," declares Pierson, who saw in the subtlety and buoyancy of this facade a mature masterpiece: "one of the first creative outbursts by a native architect in American history."

FIGURE 13. Peter Banner. Park Street Church, 1809. The steeple is a splendid example of how Classicists reinterpreted an essentially Gothic form. Solomon Willard's Egyptian Revival gateway to the Old Granary Burying Ground is in the foreground.

Bulfinch inspired a good deal of work in his characteristic style by others. Chief among these was Asher Benjamin, an architect who practiced in Boston after 1803 and is perhaps most noted for his pattern book of 1797, *The Country Builder's Assistant,* the first architectural book both written and published in this country. Among his best-known Boston buildings are the Charles Street Meeting House of 1807 and the Old West Church of 1806. Two other architects of this period who cannot be overlooked are Peter Banner, whose Park Street Church (Figure 13) possesses undeniably the most beautiful spire of its type in Boston, and Samuel McIntire, the famous Salem designer, who so far as is known got no closer to Boston than Waltham, where he designed in 1793 the Lyman House, but whose work is so distinguished that no Bostonian could omit mention of it in any survey, however brief, of this period. Also in Waltham, an environ of Boston then popular for country residences, is Gore Place. Built by an unknown architect in 1805, it is among the finest New England houses of its period. Finally, one cannot forget the housewrights who built in Bulfinch's style so much, for example, of Chestnut Street on Beacon Hill between 1800 and 1830; this street possesses an outstanding parade of fanlights.

Yet nothing can rob Bulfinch of his dominance during this period. Boston was surely his singular achievement. It is impossible not to compare Bulfinch with Wren: what the master did for London in the late seventeenth century, Bulfinch in the early nineteenth century did for Boston. In Joseph Hudnut's words, Bulfinch found Boston "a bewilderment of narrow vistas and left it with a window upon the world."

A SEVERE granite grandeur had by 1815 begun here and there to vary the urbane red-brick Federal streetscapes Bulfinch had created — in much the same way that the wooden Medieval town of the seventeenth century had been in the eighteenth century interrupted by increasing numbers of Georgian spires. But one easily forgets that the bricks of the Tontine Crescent were painted gray — as for that matter those of the State House may have been. Bulfinch probably used stone as little as he did because it was not easily available and consequently very costly; when the Middlesex Canal of 1803 made Chelmsford granite accessible, Bulfinch began at once to use it in his monumental work.

His Suffolk County Court House of 1810–1812 was of ashlar construction. The first of its kind in Boston, it pointed toward the work of Bulfinch's disciples. This was true as well of Bulfinch's last Boston work, the magnificent Chelmsford granite building of 1818–1821 that bears his name at the Massachusetts General Hospital. But it was Alexander Parris, Bulfinch's superintendent on the hospital job, who was to impress upon Boston the latter phase of Neoclassicism to which the Federal genre gave way in the 1820s — the Greek Revival.

The transition from the Federal to the Greek Revival is perhaps best seen in two houses almost certainly by Parris on Beacon Street, now the Women's City Club (Figure 16). Talbot Hamlin has pointed out that at the City Club the Adamesque delicacy of Federal detail has almost completely disappeared in favor of stolid Greek forms. "Of actual Greek detail," he noted, "there is but little . . . but of prophetic hints of its spirit — of its concentrated richness contrasted with broad simplicity, of its feeling for large scale . . . there is a great deal." These houses, Hamlin observed, "can scarcely yet be called Greek Revival, but they show the style in gestation."

A natural enough repercussion of such widely read books as James Stuart and Nicholas Revett's *The Antiquities of Athens,* which brought more and more forcefully to the attention of Europeans and then Americans in the early nineteenth century the grandeur of the Greek architecture that lay behind the Roman Classical achievement, the Greek Revival was also acceptable to Bostonians for other reasons. Their sympathy (though, significantly, in Lord Byron's wake) for the Greeks in their war of independence was only to be expected. Though the War of 1812 had not been at all popular in Boston, the way Americans generally identified with the Greek war of independence may also be seen as

14

15

16

Federal and Greek Revival Design.
FIGURE 14. Charles Bulfinch. 9 Park
Street, Beacon Hill, 1803–1804. Detail
of doorway. The house is extant but
altered.
FIGURE 15. Edward Shaw. 59 Mount
Vernon Street, Beacon Hill, 1837. De-
tail of doorway.
FIGURE 16. Attributed to Alexander
Parris. 39–40 Beacon Street, Beacon
Hill, 1818, now the Women's City
Club. The sumptuous early
nineteenth-century interiors of both
houses are intact but a fourth floor
was added in 1888 by Hartwell and
Richardson.

something of an attempt at the long delayed cultural declaration of independence: the Greek fashion was an architecture, as Professor Pierson has suggested, that attempted to reflect the sense of national identity for which Emerson argued in 1837 in his "American Scholar." On the other hand, one wit has opined that the Greek Revival really succeeded because it was egalitarian enough for the Jacksonians and elegant enough for the Federalists, which is probably very close to the truth of the matter in Boston. Walter Kilham's suggestion was even more to the point: "all building committees," he observed, "like columns."

This last remark strikes me particularly because in 1822 Boston had actually become a city, abandoning the town meeting form of government that was scarcely able any longer to bear the burden of shaping its growth. Slowed before the revolution, that growth had begun again in the 1800s, and evidences of it were everywhere. Quite aside from the extensive filling of this period, it was at this time that Boston first availed itself of another device that in the end would increase its size vastly more than land-fill operations; in 1804 Boston annexed the part of the neighboring mainland town of Dorchester that is today South Boston. Meanwhile, bridges flung out more and more routes into neighboring areas (including South Boston, Cambridge, and Charlestown) that it took no prophet to predict would one day also be annexed in one way or another to the capital city. By the 1830s railroads too had begun to open new transportation corridors in and out of the city. Boston was booming; and short of a fire nothing so stimulates architecture.

How revolutionary the new Greek fashion could be can still be keenly felt by anyone who has ever noticed amid the reticent brick facades of Beacon Street the stark white swell-front of the Sears House at 42, designed by Parris in 1819 (Figures 10, 11). One need also only compare Bulfinch's lovely Federal doorway at the nearby Amory House of 1803–1804, with its wealth of serpentine elegance (Figure 14), with the massive Greek Revival post and lintel doorway of 59 Mount Vernon Street (Figure 15) to see the difference between the two modes. The popularity of the Greek style derived as well, however, from the fact that it was more often easily assimilated into the Federal red-brick residential streetscape. The Greek forms, more massive and substantial and more rectangular than curvilinear in detail, were organized in much the same way as the lighter Federal elements had been, as is evident all over Beacon Hill, where Federal and Greek houses keep very sympathetic company.

But the radical new quality heralded by the sheer granite of the Sears House found its opportunity easily enough in monumental architecture. In 1819, Parris introduced into Boston at St. Paul's Church the most distinctive characteristic of the monumental Greek mode, the full-scale temple front. Five years after St. Paul's, Parris designed the new Quincy Market development, the focus of which is the central market building (Figure 17). The great Greek Revival landmark at the height of that style in Boston, nothing like it had ever been seen in the city before. There had been larger and longer buildings, but the gleaming white granite grandeur of the central market building, which stretches for 535 feet from one great columned portico to the other, was unprecedented in Boston. The project involved the destruction of many older buildings, the filling in of several docks, and the creation of virtually a whole new quarter where long rows of uniform granite buildings yielded a market area of unusual distinction. And within a decade even the market was to be somewhat eclipsed by the

great Boston Custom House (Figure 18), designed by Ammi B. Young.

But if the Greek Revival was thus able to shape both the grandeur appropriate to the city's growing commerce and to assimilate itself more often than not unobtrusively with the red-brick residential streetscape, it also spawned in Boston a radically new kind of architecture that is perhaps best called "architectural construction." This is characterized by the use of granite monoliths in a trabeated or post and lintel fashion; in other words, instead of blocks of granite laid up for perhaps five or more courses on either side of a window, for example, one great monolithic granite post on each side of the window supports a monolithic lintel; thus this use of granite has been called skeleton stone construction (Figure 19). The finest surviving examples today are the two market buildings (1824–1826) by Parris that flank the central market, but the most recent scholarship suggests that monolithic

granite was used in 1810 in Uriah Cotting's Boston Custom House and six years later in his Cornhill business blocks, neither of which are extant. In fact, the first such use of this technique may have been by Bulfinch himself — in 1814–1815 at his Massachusetts Fire and Marine Insurance Building and his Manufacturers and Mechanics Bank, both of which have also been destroyed.

This monolithic granite architecture is also characteristic of the work of the two other architects who importantly influenced Boston at this time — Isaiah Rogers and Solomon Willard. Rogers trained in Willard's office, and once on his own he designed a number of notable Greek Revival buildings in Boston, including in 1842 the Merchant Exchange, the Tremont Theatre (1827), and the Brazer's Building (see Figure 206), where his granite construction was sufficiently innovative for us to discuss it more fully in Chapter 8, under late nineteenth- and early twentieth-century

18

Greek Revival Boston.
FIGURE 17. Alexander Parris. Quincy Market Development, 1824–1826. Faneuil Hall (1740–1742), as enlarged by Bulfinch in 1805–1806, can be seen behind the central market.
FIGURE 18. Ammi B. Young. Boston Custom House, 1837.
FIGURE 19. Post and lintel granite construction at Parris's South Market.

"Modernism." Willard, who like Parris was largely self-taught, worked on several of Parris's buildings: he carved the decorative panels of the Sears House, for example, and the capitals of St. Paul's Church. And it was Willard who more than perhaps any other Boston architect at this time founded his design on monolithic granite by developing explicitly the fondness for Egyptian forms that seems to us today so inexplicable a part of what is supposed to have been, after all, a Greek revival.

Actually, these Egyptian forms are readily explainable. They reflect a persistent stylistic undercurrent throughout the nineteenth century; so much so that there is even a mid-nineteenth-century Second Empire house at 57 Hancock Street on Beacon Hill that rejoices in an Egyptian mansard roof unique in Boston and possibly in America. The fascination with things Egyptian, inspired by the widely publicized archaeological publications that resulted from Napoleon's otherwise rather fruitless adventures in Egypt in 1798, was sustained by the instinctive response of so many to the peculiar quality that things Egyptian seem to invoke in relation to the dead. Thus the great gate of Mount Auburn Cemetery of 1842 by Jacob Bigelow (a replica in stone of an 1832 gate) and Willard's own gate at the Old Granary Burying Ground both exhibit the flaring cavetto cornice on flanking pylons that is perhaps the most characteristic form of American Egyptian Revival architecture (see Figure 13). Willard also executed a notable series of obelisks in Boston during this period: the Franklin monument in the Old Granary Burying Ground of 1827; the Harvard Memorial of 1838, and the immense Bunker Hill Monument of 1825–1843, both in Charlestown. This last, in particular, illustrates the almost superhuman scale and relentless paucity of ornament that is even more pronounced in the Egyptian fashion than in the Greek style.

It is this factor that explains why both seem so similar for all their stylistic differences: in each mode the inherent character of monolithic granite dominated, and this became more and more characteristic of Boston architecture after 1820. In the Bunker Hill Monument the granite courses are two feet seven inches high; at Mount Auburn Cemetery the cornice of the gateway is a twenty-two-foot-long granite monolith; in the retaining wall of the Old Granary Burying Ground there is one piece of granite thirty-three feet long; while the twenty-two columns of the Boston Custom House weigh forty-two tons each, and had consequently to be dragged to the site by no fewer than twelve teams of horses and sixty-five yokes of oxen. Willard, in fact, was so concerned with what might be called construction rather than design that it seems clear he made little distinction: he purchased a quarry in Quincy and he himself supplied the granite used in Young's Custom House. "He was," Kilham notes, "exhilarated by the difficulties of the current fashion which decreed the use of enormous monolithic columns, and spent much thought in devising improved machinery for their handling and transportation." Such was Boston's passion for monolithic granite that it led to what has been called the first American railroad, when Gridley Bryant, the builder of the Bunker Hill Monument, built a kind of tramway to enable him to move huge slabs of granite from his Quincy quarry.

This disinclination to separate design and construction, this insistence on the unity of the two (which appears to have been widespread throughout the east at this time), is reflected as well in the slight differentiation then made between the architect and the engineer. A number of important contemporary works were as much engineering as architecture, including such extant landmarks as the

16

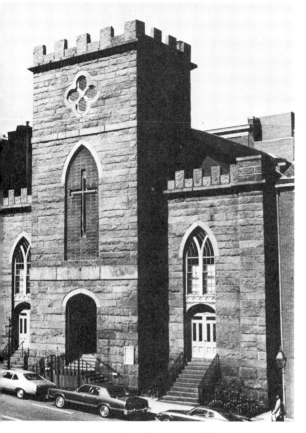

FIGURE 20. Attributed to Solomon Willard. Bowdoin Street Congregational Church, now the Mission Church of St. John the Evangelist, ca. 1831–1833.

great five-sided granite fortress with its massive projecting bastions that was built on Castle Island in South Boston in 1833 by the engineer Sylvanus Thayer, who also was responsible for Fort Warren (1834–1863) on George's Island. Loammi Baldwin's Charlestown Navy Yard dry dock (1827–1833) is another case in point. It is thus often difficult to label people during this period. Baldwin was primarily an engineer; he is often called, in fact, "the father of civil engineering in America." But though at the Charlestown Navy Yard Baldwin worked on the dry dock with Parris, Baldwin himself designed, apparently on his own, Holworthy Hall at Harvard in 1811. Even Parris was listed in the 1818 Boston di-

rectory as both "architect and engineer"; and after having served as Baldwin's assistant he became chief civil engineer of the Navy Yard at Charlestown, where he was responsible for a number of buildings, including the famous Ropewalk (1834–1836), a two-story granite building over one-quarter mile long, which began operation in 1838 and was closed only in 1970. So persuasive a factor was granite construction at this time that during the 1830s the inherent character of this material dominated the new vogue that was beginning to challenge the dominance of the Greek Revival — Gothic.

It is certainly true that if one had chosen to tour Greek Revival Boston in 1840, walking, for example, from the Custom House to the Quincy Market and up past the Merchant Exchange to the Tremont Theatre and down Tremont Street past the Tremont Hotel to St. Paul's Church, one would have seen a government building, a market, a merchant exchange, a theater, a hotel, and a church where the diverse functions of each had been expressed by columned Greek porticos. At its height the Greek Revival was a kind of universal style. And if it seems boring, that is perhaps why the Greek fashion was waning by the 1830s. In its place there developed a taste for Gothic, essayed by Solomon Willard, for example, at his Bowdoin Street Congregational Church (now the Mission Church of St. John the Evangelist; Figure 20).

That style was not new to Boston; the Gothic mode, when not fashionable, seems merely to go underground. Even Bulfinch had attempted a Gothic church, the no longer extant Federal Street Church of 1809, and it is also possible that St. Augustine's Chapel (1819), still extant in South Boston, is by Bulfinch. But early nineteenth-century American Gothic, in its way as literary a taste in its allegiance to Horace Walpole and Sir Walter Scott as was the Greek Revival in its admiration for Lord Byron, did not seek its inspiration in Boston's own seventeenth-century folk Gothic, but in the full-fledged civic and ecclesiastical Gothic of the Middle Ages. And as Gothic principles were scarcely understood at all, these early and distinctly naive Gothic buildings took on the coloration of the Greek Revival as they had of the Federal mode in Bulfinch's day. Thus the Federal Street Church and St. Augustine's seem more Federal than Gothic in feeling; in the same way Willard's Bowdoin Street Church, particularly, seems for all its battlements to possess a peculiarly stolid and massy feeling more akin to the Greek Revival than to Gothic. This was also true of the most exuberant of the Gothic structures that became so fashionable when the public had tired of temple fronts: George M. Dexter's Fitchburg Railway Station of 1847 (near where North Station now stands); Gridley J. Fox Bryant's SS Peter and Paul in South Boston (1845–1853); and even Jacob Bigelow's fantastic chapel at Mount Auburn Cemetery — an 1858 replica of an 1843 building — seem to possess fundamental characteristics that proceed, if not from the Greek Revival, not from Gothic either. Rather, these characteristics proceed from the one thing all these buildings, Greek, Egyptian, and Gothic, have in common: granite itself, whether it built pediments, pylons, or battlements, had really become Boston's dominant style by the 1840s.

The results, insofar as Gothic was concerned, were not happy. Granite Gothic, stolid and ponderous, is not comparable with its English parish church models in the way that Bulfinch's work, for instance, is comparable with Adam's. But that simply reflects the fact that no Neogothicist emerged in Boston in the 1830s or forties whose skill equaled Bulfinch's as a Neoclassicist. In the 1850s such a man would appear — Richard Upjohn. But it is significant that just as Bulfinch's work has often been called "American Adam," scholars have also increasingly concluded that Boston's granite architecture — in whatever "style" — is, in fact, one style — the Boston Granite Style. Sometimes happily, sometimes not, whether through genius, accident, or naiveté, Boston architects had shown by the 1840s that they would shape the common, inherited tradition of Western architecture to their own purposes. This adaptive tradition (evident, for instance, in the way in which Wren reinterpreted the Gothic spire classically) had long characterized Western architecture and it was the background for the architecture of the next hundred years in Boston.

2

The Great Traditions

THE "AMERICAN ATHENS," the epithet that has frequently been applied to Boston as her culture began to mature in the mid-nineteenth century, is not, as one might think, closely related to the Greek style. It is true that Louisburg Square, the famous Greek Revival enclave on Beacon Hill, was built up finally in the 1840s and that in 1850 the square's proprietors erected there a statue (by whom nobody knows) of Aristides the Just, the Athenian statesman and general (Figure 21). But it was for the most part only in residential design that the Greek vogue lingered into the forties. Moreover, the American Athens has seemed to most scholars much more literary and philosophical in essence than architectural or even artistic. Yet whether one looks as did Morison toward the clipper ships being built in East Boston or as would a medical historian to the epochal demonstration of anesthesia at the Massachusetts General Hospital in 1846 or as did Charles Dickens toward such pioneering institutions as the Perkins Institution for the Blind, which began operating in 1832, it is increasingly evident that Emerson, Thoreau, and Hawthorne were but the standard-bearers of a community whose cultural horizons were beginning to broaden in every respect at the beginning of its third century of existence. And architecture in Boston in the 1840s and early fifties — on the eve of the Back Bay — only *seems* less vital. In reality this transitional period heralded the ar-

chitecture of the late nineteenth century that is now so much admired.

Since Boston's settlement, architectural design had more or less amounted to keeping up with the unfolding Renaissance. Seventeenth-century buildings, whether one looks at the steep gables of town houses like the Paul Revere House (Figure 5) or at rambling "lean-to" country houses like the Fairbanks House in Dedham (Figure 76), were fundamentally a rude, wilderness reflection of English vernacular Gothic forms: "Folk Gothic," in John Coolidge's words, "survived into the age of Bernini." We often misunderstand this because the Puritans naturally avoided *the* Gothic building type — the church — and built, instead, meetinghouses. (In Anglican Virginia, on the other hand, a recognizably Gothic parish church, begun ca. 1632, survives to this day.) Somewhat belatedly, because Gothic lingered longer in England than anywhere else in Europe, Boston in the eighteenth century gradually abandoned the Medieval tradition: early Georgian design, the High Georgian mode of the mid- and late eighteenth century, and the Neoclassicism of the Federal and Greek periods had in each case reflected the step-by-step evolution from Gothic through the various stages of the Renaissance attempt to repossess the glories of ancient Roman and then of ancient Greek architecture. There was, certainly, a distinct time lag as the Renaissance filtered through in each stage to England and then to America.

FIGURE 21. Louisburg Square, Beacon Hill, 1826–1844.

But by the 1840s, Boston's built environment, an accumulation by then of two hundred and more years, reflected clearly the nature and term of the city's history; it possessed a little folk Gothic and a great deal of English Renaissance architecture, provincial, to be sure, but increasingly distinctive. In the 1840s, however, Boston would begin the process of amassing a great number of architectural forms — early Renaissance palazzos, for instance, and a huge Gothic cathedral — that the New World was too new to have ever possessed.

One might explain this phenomenon by asserting that the Renaissance had by the middle of the nineteenth century exhausted its ancient sources. One need

not hazard that controversial assertion, however; it is only necessary to understand that European and American architects began to seek their inspiration at this time not in antiquity, but in the Renaissance itself, and even in the Gothic architecture it had banished. Thus though the emerging Italianate vogue of the forties in America came to this country by way of England, Italianate design was fundamentally a revival in the mid-nineteenth century of the Italian Renaissance forms that had in the fifteenth century attempted to revive ancient Roman forms. At first glance this seems scarcely very sensible. But the key to understanding all of this is to be found in observations long overlooked in this connection, such as Fiske Kimball's, that Renaissance forms "were no more literal imitations of [ancient Roman forms] than the Roman forms themselves had been imitations of Greek forms." As Kimball pointed out: "partly because of medieval survivals, partly because of inadequate knowledge of antiquity, partly even in criticism of the antique, the architects of the Renaissance modified the [ancient Classical] forms so that they are unmistakably theirs." This adaptive tradition, which as we have seen also naturally marked Boston's architecture in the seventeenth and eighteenth centuries, explains why nineteenth-century architects who had come to admire the earliest Renaissance architecture for its own unique architectural character attempted to revive those early Renaissance forms in the Italianate style. Bostonians, conscious that they were no less the heirs of Western culture because they lived on its periphery, claimed all these forms of *their* ancestors as logically as they claimed the common law, for example, or the Christian religion; thus they reached back at mid-century to add to Boston's built environment architectural forms its late settlement had denied it.

However confusing, chronologically, Italianate design may appear, its success was immediate and its influence pervasive. This is not, however, reflected in present-day Boston because a great number of important Italianate buildings have been destroyed. A particular loss was the Boston Museum (Figure 22). One of several new playhouses of the 1840s (called a museum to allay "Puritan" sensibilities), it was designed by Hammatt and Joseph Billings in 1846. Its facade, 164 feet long with rows of gas globes glowing above its iron balconies, must have been the most felicitous sight in Boston. Another Italianate building of importance that has not survived was the Boston Public Library (Figure 23). Designed by C. F. Kirby in 1858, it stood on

Boylston Street where the Colonial Theatre now is, and of all these buildings it possessed perhaps the most characteristic Italianate features: not only a heavy console-supported balcony and balustrade, a projecting and deeply overhanging cornice, corner quoining, and an overall heavy sculptural and arcaded feeling, but also the round arched windows with "Medieval survival" tracery so typical of the early Renaissance. Fortunately, one of the city's earliest and handsomest Italian palazzos has survived — the brownstone Boston Athenaeum (Figure 24), designed by Edward Clarke Cabot, who secured this important commission in rather an interesting way. As Walter Kilham pointed out, the plot to be used was sharply indented at the southeast corner by a triangular projection of the Granary Burying Ground, containing some graves that could not be disturbed. "The other competitors followed the angular indentation, which caused awkward projections into the interior all the way up through the building. [But] Cabot . . . simply carried the rear wall straight across making a segmental arched niche in the basement to accommodate the graves."

Cabot seems also to have been the principal designer in 1854 of the Boston Theatre on Washington Street (Figure 25). A huge and palatial 3000-seat opera house, it was more impressive than the splendid new 2000-seat Music Hall built from the designs of Snell and Gregerson near the corner of Tremont and Winter streets two years earlier. The importance of both halls is evident in Mark A. DeWolfe Howe's remark that it would not thereafter be necessary "to ask a visiting Jenny Lind to sing in the Fitchburg Railroad Station," for both these and the other buildings of the Italianate mid-century we have been discussing expressed architecturally an overall and increasingly cosmopolitan cultural growth at this time — in the performing and vi-

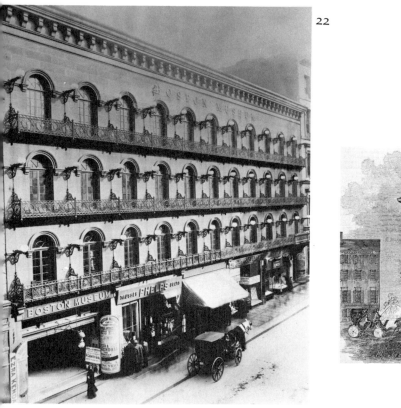

22

23

Three mid-nineteenth-century Italianate landmarks.
FIGURE 22. Hammatt and Joseph Billings. Boston Museum, a
playhouse completed in 1846 and now demolished.
FIGURE 23. C. F. Kirby. Boston Public Library, 1858. Demolished.
FIGURE 24. Edward Clarke Cabot. Architect's elevation of the
principal facade of the Boston Athenaeum, completed in 1849. It
is derived from Palladio's Palazzo da Porta Festa in Vicenza.

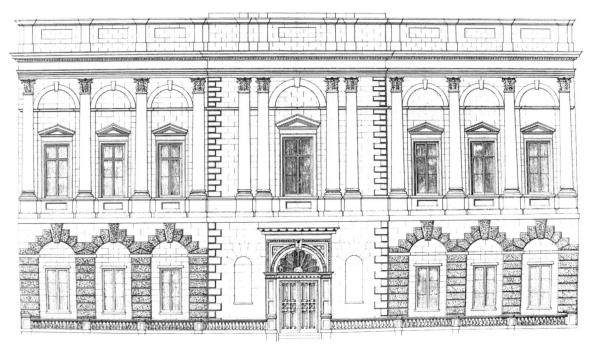

FIGURE 25. Edward and James Cabot and Jonathan Preston, from
preliminary plans by André Noury. Boston Theatre, 1854, one of
the three great American opera houses of the mid-nineteenth century.
Demolished, although the Keith Memorial Theatre (now the Savoy)
stands in part upon the Boston Theatre's foundations and is almost
identical in overall plan.

sual arts as well as in literature and thought generally. It was at the Boston Theatre, for instance, in 1854, that Boston first heard Beethoven's *Fidelio*, three years before the founding of *The Atlantic Monthly*, the more often cited symbol of this lively age. The new Athenaeum also possessed a sculpture gallery as well as a painting gallery; the first such extensive facilities in Boston, they were the seeds for the Museum of Fine Arts of some years later. The Boston Public Library was the first free municipal public library in the world. Like Bulfinch's en-

semble of crescent, theater, and cathedral of 1794–1803, Boston's palatial new mid-nineteenth-century parade of libraries, playhouses, galleries and, perhaps most of all, the immense new opera house shows how broadly based was her cultural growth. Nor were the architectural settings worthy only in size: the nineteenth-century playwright Dion Boucicault, for example, thought the Boston Theatre "beyond question the finest theatre in the world."

Another reflection of this widespread growth in all the arts and of its increas-

26

27

Re-creation in the Classical tradition.
FIGURE 26. Patrick Keeley and/or Arthur Gilman.
Church of the Immaculate Conception, South
End, 1858. The interior is probably Gilman's
work; the exterior is usually attributed to Keeley,
perhaps in collaboration with Gilman.
FIGURE 27. Possibly by Daniel Badger. McLauthlin Elevator Building, 120 Fulton Street, ca.
1863–1869.

ingly cosmopolitan character was lavish ceremonial and musical splendor, from the beginning a notable feature of the Roman Catholic Church of the Immaculate Conception built in the South End in 1858 (Figure 26). This church is also a splendid example of how the best mid-century American architects translated the Classical tradition into the idiom of their own time just as surely as had the Renaissance architects. The building's design has been attributed to Patrick C. Keeley, a New York designer, and the leading architect in the Roman Catholic tradition in this country in the last half of the nineteenth century. Better known as a Gothicist (one of his earliest churches in the Boston area, St. Rose of Lima in Chelsea, built in 1860–1866, is Gothic), Keeley also designed several notable churches in the Classical tradition, but it is likely that he collaborated on the design of the Immaculate Conception with a well-known Boston architect of the time, Arthur Gilman, to whom the church has also been solely attributed. It is a remarkable building. One sees the "Medieval survival" typical of Italianate design in the tall windows to either side of the central pavilion of the facade and also in the Palladian window of the central pavilion. Similarly, the pavilion is quoined, though the facade itself is adorned at its corners with pilasters. The architect also used both dressed and rough-cut granite on the exterior of this distinguished ensemble of so many historical forms that nonetheless cohere beautifully in one of the handsomest buildings in Boston.

How contemporary this seemingly rather antique Classicism could be in the mid-nineteenth century is particularly evident in the fact that the Italianate vogue lent itself with uncanny distinction to a quite new structural development: the cast-iron facade. These facades were hung in prefabricated sections on the fronts of commercial buildings whose principal source of light (as in the Venetian palaces) was the street (in Venice, the canal). Stylistically appropriate in that this style provided for as many and as large windows as possible, the arcaded Italianate front also suited exactly the requirements of the new structural technique: prefabrication of a number of identical units. This technique was pioneered in New York City but Boston possesses several fine examples: the McLauthlin Building (Figure 27) at 120 Fulton Street is perhaps the handsomest, though the Richards Building of 1867 at 110–116 State Street is more representative of Italianate cast-iron work, even though it has been somewhat altered.

This mid-century "antique" Classicism also took on new life in Boston's environs, and to take the full measure of both the Italianate and Gothic modes one must have recourse to what were by 1850 "bedroom suburbs." It will thus serve more than one purpose to follow the example of Bostonians in the 1850s and enlarge our purview.

W OOD WAS THEN as now the usual residential building material in Boston's suburbs. Although in the Greek Revival period the full-scale temple front was not beyond the carpenter-builder's ability (a quite splendid house of this type, built about 1840, survives today at 2 Dane Street in Jamaica Plain), the suburban carpenter-builder usually simply applied Greek rather than Federal detail after about 1820 to the symmetrical, clapboarded, and detached-house type that had remained virtually unchanged since the early Georgian period. But the Yankee carpenter, in rather an inspired way, was quick to see that by raising somewhat the pitch of the roof and by turning the narrower gable end of such a house to the street he could achieve a kind of temple front that, proceeding directly

Mid-century Italianate and Gothic forms in suburban Boston ca. 1850.
FIGURE 28. 9 Myrtle Street, Jamaica Plain.
FIGURE 29. 9 Brewer Street, Jamaica Plain.

29

from the conventional gable and corner-boards (rendered as pediments and pilasters), would seem the most natural thing in the world. Such ingenuity, born of trying to reflect in wood a by then essentially masonry style, carried over as well into the carpenter-builder's Italianate work, and was in turn stimulated by the fact that in the suburbs, where free-standing houses and ample lots were still possible and consequently allowed more freedom of maneuver, the transition from the Greek Revival to the Italianate vogue led to a "breaking up" of the traditional symmetrical house.

One can see the effect of this "breaking up" into a more picturesque and broken silhouette at 8 and 9 Myrtle Street in Jamaica Plain where stand Boston's most dramatic Italianate villas (Figure 28). Here, in wood, are many of the conventional Italianate characteristics we saw in brownstone at the Boston Public Library on Boylston Street — paired roundhead windows, heavy, protruding balconies, and a deep, overhanging cornice, significantly not carried across the gable to at-

tempt any form of pediment. This towered, picturesque, suburban Italianate is quite different, however, from that of the rigidly symmetrical boxlike library, and the difference derives not only from the way these asymmetrical houses are massed. It proceeds as well from the character of the fanciful jigsawed wooden brackets that support the cornice and are so keenly felt as a part of the overall design that such houses are often called "Italianate-Bracketed." The Myrtle Street houses show how the carpenter ingeniously applied his jigsaw to the problem of approximating in wood the early Renaissance cut-stone detail of buildings like the old Public Library. Near 8 and 9 Myrtle Street, at 9 Brewer Street (Figure 29), is another asymmetrical house where the picturesqueness of the massing is also equaled by lively wooden detail, but where the jigsaw yielded, not Italianate brackets, but bargeboards and drip moldings; for 9 Brewer Street, built at about the same time as the Myrtle Street Italianate houses, is Gothic. Or, rather, *Gothick*. In this case the "k" added to the word Gothic is the equivalent of adding "Bracketed" to Italianate: both acknowledge the originality as well as the folk quality of the Yankee builder.

Mid-century Gothick cottages closely paralleled the development of the Italianate villa. The Gothick Frederick Sears House of the 1840s or fifties at 24 Cottage Farm Road in Brookline resembles as much as the Myrtle Street Italianate houses those perspectives that appeared in the widely read books of the 1840s and fifties by Alexander J. Downing, the landscape designer and architect who was the great champion of the picturesque at mid-century. In fact, both the Italianate and Gothick modes reflect the beginning of the Victorian search for the picturesque as well as illustrating how ingeniously the Yankee builder endowed both modes (as surely as he had the Greek Revival style) with a new and distinctive character.

The chief Gothic vehicle for the picturesque in the 1850s and sixties was, however, a more sophisticated mid-century American adaption of European forms where both picturesqueness of mass and the use of local material yielded a far more important building type — the Gothic village church — that was becoming increasingly at this time the centerpiece (along with the railroad station!) of the picturesque suburbs. Longwood, in Brookline, was one of the most famous such suburban areas, because it was socially exclusive and laid out and built up according to an overall plan developed by a prominent Bostonian; the same David Sears, in fact, whose Boston town house by Parris we have already discussed. Typically, the railroad station came first. But in 1860–1862, Sears built Christ Church, Brookline, and it is significant that it was modeled by Arthur Gilman after St. Peter's Church, Colchester, England, the Searses' ancestral home — evidence of the way in which Bostonians justified reviving styles that,

while never known in their fullness in the New World, were nonetheless perceived as a part of a cultural heritage common to both Americans and Europeans.

One of the earliest and perhaps the most important of the first generation of picturesque village churches in the Boston area is also in Brookline — St. Paul's Church (Figure 30). It was designed by Richard Upjohn, an English Gothicist who settled in Boston in 1834 and studied for the next five years in Alexander Parris's office. When his close friend the rector of Trinity Church in Boston became rector of Trinity Church in New York City, Upjohn moved there in 1839 to design for that parish perhaps his masterpiece. Yet St. Paul's has, I think, rightly been called by the architect's biographer the "most attractive country church" by Upjohn, who was by 1850 the preeminent Gothicist in America and a leading figure in the High Church Anglican ecclesiological movement that stimulated the Gothic Revival in Augustus Pugin's wake. Like the L-shaped Italianate-Bracketed villa and its companion, the Gothick cottage, St. Paul's was decisively asymmetrical; rather than continuing the axis of the nave, Upjohn's tower stands off center.

One also sees at St. Paul's a distinctive quality that arises from the fact that in the same way that the carpenter-builder used wood in lieu of cut-stone detail on his Italianate villas and Gothick cottages, Upjohn used what was at hand, and probably for the first time in a church — pudding stone. An unusually warm and richly variegated conglomerate that began to be quarried at mid-century in and around Boston, the character of this stone is as distinctive to the Boston area as Quincy granite and for that reason alone St. Paul's seems to belong in Victorian Boston as much as in Medieval England. And because of Upjohn's sensitivity to this material and

FIGURE 30. Richard Upjohn. St. Paul's Church, Brookline, 1848–1851. Boston's great landmark of the mid-nineteenth-century Gothic Revival in pudding stone. Only the exterior survives today.

FIGURE 31. Gridley J. Fox Bryant's Mercantile Wharf Building, 75–117 Commercial Street, 1857. Mostly of large-scaled and rough-hammered granite ashlar with monolithic granite piers, this has been called the masterpiece of what is known as the Boston Granite Style.

because of his strong, quiet massing and fine proportions, St. Paul's also illustrates vividly that local materials imaginatively used by an architect rather than a carpenter might yield not only a strikingly indigenous but also a distinguished and sophisticated architecture. As Gothic, in fact, St. Paul's is in this sense comparable to the best Italianate work in the city itself — Boston's waterfront warehouses — where in this case local granite in the hands of another skillful architect was shaped in the same decade into an even more indigenous and splendid accomplishment.

It was in 1856–1857 that Gridley J. Fox Bryant, the son of the builder of the Bunker Hill Monument and the most prominent commercial architect in Boston, designed the famous State Street Block opposite the Custom House and the equally splendid Mercantile Wharf Building nearby (Figure 31). Each is characterized by a severe granite grandeur. The State Street Block, alas, survives only in part. But as long ago as 1946 Walter Kilham declared that "if a vote were taken for the best piece of architecture in the city, the State Street Block would get mine." Kilham went on to assert — and not just of the waterfront work, but of most of Boston's mid-century Italianate, including the old Boston Public Library and the Boston Museum — that "it was indigenous, not copied from foreign models, and has more right than any other to be considered as a true American style. It was absolutely functional, and if architects had continued with it a style might have developed which would have been as American as a Red Indian." What striking evidence it is of how well Americans adapted the Italianate style that this "seemingly antique classicism," which with its companion Gothic style heralded a century of revivalism in America, was discussed in a chapter Kilham entitled "Plain American." He ad-

mitted that this vogue was "closely related to the 'Italian Villa' style which set the pace for numerous country and suburban houses." But for Kilham that made no difference. Nor is this the last time we shall hear such a lament for this or that manner which, had it only been continued, might have yielded a vital American style. Such a style, increasingly a preoccupation in the nineteenth century, has proved always illusive. In the face of St. Paul's, the State Street Block, and the Mercantile Wharf Building, however, what is clear is that a vital *American* architecture — in the sense of an American adaption and reinterpretation of *any* style common to the Western tradition — was entirely possible.

The next fifty years more than bore this out. The history of architecture in Boston would yield not only a distinguished school of Gothicists led by Ralph Adams Cram, whose work would be acclaimed as an important continuation of Gothic design, but the granite Italianate work is increasingly seen today as an important hinge in American architectural history. The State Street Block, particularly, is notable for its monolithic granite construction, and this construction derived, as we saw in the last chapter, from Bulfinch's work. And as we will see later (Figure 186), it was an important source for Richardson and through Richardson, for Louis Sullivan. When one realizes how picturesque design would flower in the late nineteenth century in Queen Anne work and that the cast-iron facade to which Italianate design lent itself so well was an important precursor of the curtain-wall skyscraper, one can see how seminal mid-century architecture was. It was also in itself a considerable achievement, not unworthy of the American Athens. Confronted with the grandeur of mass and strength of design of Boston's harborfront granite architecture, Henry-Russell Hitchcock has pronounced these ranges of warehouses "hardly equaled anywhere in the world." They were the first of Boston's buildings of which that could have been said.

THE Italianate Classicism that emerged in the city in the 1850s and the picturesque Gothic church type of the same decade in the suburbs not only evolved simultaneously, but in the 1860s were increasingly if incongruously seen next door to each other in the city proper, where the effect of the Upjohn church type — informal masses of pudding stone or fieldstone about an off-center broach-spired tower — seems to have banished the stolid and symmetrical Gothick church almost at once. This development was universal. At St. Paul's in Dedham, for example, where Arthur Gilman had designed a symmetrically massed, center-tower church in 1845, the same architect, after the first church burned down, designed in 1857 an equally asymmetrical church similar to St. Paul's in Brookline. Perhaps the widest use made of the Upjohn church type in the Boston area was by Alexander R. Estey, a native of suburban Framingham and the architect in 1864 of St. John's Church in that town, who became a leading church architect in the 1850s and sixties. His earlier churches, like the Prospect Congregational Church in Cambridge (1851), continued the old symmetrical, center-tower church type. But by 1867, when he designed two important churches, the Old Cambridge Baptist Church and the Church of Our Saviour in Brookline, both were variations on the Upjohn church type, which was by then the norm throughout Greater Boston. Notable examples are Ware and Van Brunt's First Church of 1865 in Boston (Figure 48) and their St. John's Chapel at the Episcopal Divinity School in Cambridge (1868); the First Congregational Church, Cambridge, de-

signed as late as 1870 by Abel C. Martin; and the Harvard Congregational Church in Brookline (1873–1875), the work of Edward T. Potter, which illustrates how this mode survived into the High Victorian period in more colorful guise.

The result in the city proper was a startling rupture in the architectural unity that had characterized Boston's streetscapes for well over a century. On the one hand, the Classical tradition remained normative for secular architecture generally. Though Italianate could be either sparse or florid in feeling, Classical work generally remained invariably formal and symmetrical in the city, where the academic tradition proved tenacious; the picturesque massing of the Italianate villa and the Gothick cottage were clearly perceived as essentially suburban; the large double house at 70–72 Mount Vernon Street (1847) attributed to Upjohn possesses as severe, symmetrical, and academic a facade as was imaginable. But the more severe and Classical such secular work, the stronger was the contrast with the picturesque Upjohn church. In the Georgian and Federal periods, the church had simply essayed the universal style on a larger scale; its only distinctive feature, the Medieval spire, had been "classicized" after the manner of Wren. And in the Greek Revival period it would have been hard to differentiate several churches from nearby city halls. Even during the 1830s and forties, when Gothick churches in the heart of the city were common, so also were Classical churches. Moreover, the Gothick of this period was almost invariably stolid and symmetrical (Figure 20). But in the 1850s and sixties (and we simply do not notice the incongruity because we are so used to it) Boston built increasingly Classical and symmetrical blocks of secular buildings invariably interrupted at every other street corner by asymmetrically massed Medieval churches of the village type in pudding

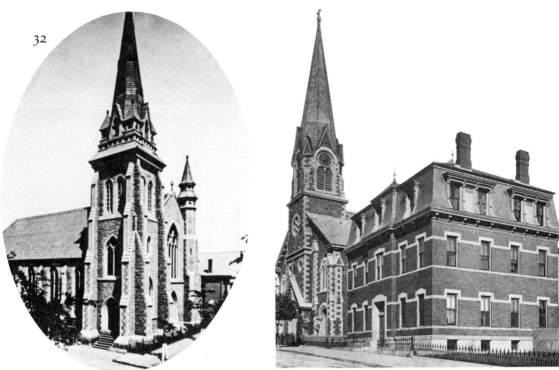

32

33

Mid-nineteenth-century development in Charlestown, East Boston, and South Boston.

FIGURE 32. Patrick Keeley. Church of The Most Holy Redeemer, East Boston, 1851.

FIGURE 33. Patrick Keeley. St. Francis de Sales Church, Charlestown, 1859. In the foreground is the parochial residence.

FIGURE 34. The Loring House, 787 East Broadway, South Boston, 1864, and, across the street in the background at 788, the Dana House, 1868.

34

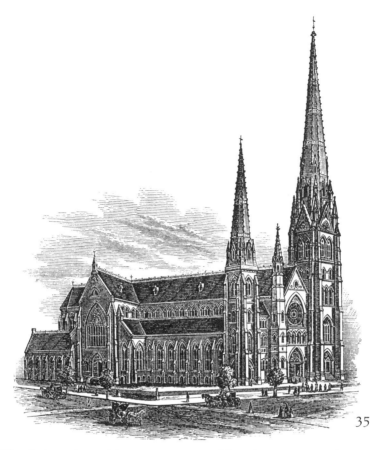

35

Classical secular architecture punctuated by picturesque Medieval
churches was characteristic of the new South End.

FIGURE 35. Patrick Keeley. Cathedral of the Holy Cross, 1865–1875,
one of the largest Gothic cathedrals in the world.

FIGURE 36. Columbus Avenue, ca. 1870.

FIGURE 37. Jean Lemoulnier, possibly in association with Gridley J.
Fox Bryant. Deacon House, 1846–1848. Demolished. Some interior
detail is in the Museum of Fine Arts, Boston.

stone and fieldstone that in such a Classical context were wildly picturesque indeed. Once one thinks of it, this architectural duality emerges as a chief characteristic of the new residential districts that evolved in the city in the 1850s.

The settlement of these areas was undertaken in large measure to counter the movement of so many to the suburbs, which by mid-century was becoming alarming. At first none of the new residential quarters seemed very successful in offsetting this exodus. By the 1850s, Charlestown and South Boston were both connected to Boston by one or more bridges and East Boston by ferry lines, and all three areas (particularly South Boston) offered splendid harbor views from historic old hills that only awaited development. Kilham remarked long ago that why fashionable Boston did not flock at once to "the breezy hills of South Boston with their splendid marine views is one of the unsolved questions in Boston's history. . . . The only answer I can give, is that the Lord in His wisdom saved for His poorer and less fashionable children the beautiful area which their wealthier cousins disdained." Actually, at the summit of these hills, where lovely residential squares with parks were laid out — on Belmont Hill and particularly on Webster Street in East Boston, around Monument Square in Charlestown, and at Thomas Park on Telegraph Hill in South Boston — handsome town houses were built in the 1850s and sixties and many survive today (Figures 34, 231). All three areas were endowed as well in the 1850s and sixties with imposing and picturesque churches. Patrick Keeley designed for the Church of the Most Holy Redeemer in East Boston a Gothic church whose spire is almost 200 feet high (Figure 32). In Charlestown, he designed a similarly lofty stone-towered Gothic church for St. Francis de Sales parish (Figure 33). Still another was erected

from his designs for St. Augustine's parish in South Boston.

The great towered churches, like the hilltop town houses, were quickly surrounded, however, by the extensive manufacturing and harbor-front industries that were naturally attracted to such coastal communities. These had made a sufficient impact by the time all three areas became easily accessible that fashionable residences seemed far less feasible than working-class housing. Thus only such persons of means as had business interests nearby to which they wished to keep close were attracted even to the hilltop enclaves. In South Boston, for example, a still handsome mansion at 788 East Broadway (Figure 34) was owned by Otis Dana, who was certainly a Boston merchant of old family and ample means. But he made his own fortune building up a good deal of South Boston's working-class housing.

37

Nearby, at 787 East Broadway, Harrison Loring built in 1864 another fine mansion that is still there today. But Loring clearly desired not only a view of the harbor but of his shipyard at City Point. Otherwise, fashionable Boston disdained South Boston, despite the fact that all the older upper-class residential areas developed in the eighteenth and early nineteenth centuries were rapidly deteriorating either because of the expansion of the commercial quarter or because of the need for shelter of the huge numbers of immigrants that were increasingly drawn to Boston in this period. Thus the city had really no choice at mid-century but to widen the still narrow Neck that connected Boston to the mainland and to create on filled land a much-needed fashionable new quarter.

No doubt realizing that this would also make access to the suburbs that much easier, the city fathers made efforts in 1851 to annex the nearest one, Roxbury. These efforts were not successful. But in the meantime the Neck was widened and what is now known as the South End built up steadily in the 1850s and sixties. A brief circuit of this area will disclose that, as in the rest of the city, red-brick Classical residential streets were regularly punctuated with asymmetrical Gothic churches. One of the finest is the Tremont Street Methodist Church (now the Good Hope Baptist Church) designed by Hammatt Billings in 1860–1862, which possesses no fewer than two lofty towers at opposite ends of the building. The most important, however, is the second Holy Cross Cathedral (Figure 35), the plans for which were drawn by Keeley. It was begun in 1867 and the fact that it was not finished until 1875 points up the immensity of the task, for Holy Cross can hold 7000 people, 3500 seated. One hundred seventy feet wide at the transepts, 120 feet high, and 364 feet long, its vast interior encompasses considerably more than an acre and it was with great civic pride that *King's Handbook of Boston* repeated in every edition that Boston's new cathedral was larger than those of Strasbourg, Pisa, Venice, and Salisbury. One is naturally suspicious of Victorian enthusiasms, but Holy Cross is in fact as large as Westminster Abbey. And

though its design is not necessarily superior to the Medieval cathedrals and abbeys it surpasses in size, the fact that Keeley's massive pudding stone exterior remains impressive today even without the planned 200- and 300-foot spires testifies to the basic strength of his design.

When one turns from the cathedral and from the dozen or more smaller churches of its type to the surrounding residential and public architecture of the South End, however, the effect is quite different. The huge Chickering Building (1853) is relentlessly Classical and symmetrical. So too are the houses of the South End (Figure 36). In Chester Square, for example, built up in the 1860s and seventies around a park once much more elegantly garnished, these houses are also substantial and handsome and sometimes even lavishly detailed. But though typical of the mid-century in the Classical context they provided for dozens of Medieval village churches, the houses were not in themselves stylistically progressive for their time; they continued even into the 1860s the by then increasingly old-fashioned Greek Revival swell-front. In overall plan the South End was also conservative. Its best feature was the series of residential squares, modeled after the Tontine Crescent. Worcester Square, in particular, with its gently rounded edges and regular cornice line, is worthy of the comparison. So also is the great sweep of Chester Square, though it lacks the architectural unity of Bulfinch's crescent. But even this feature of the South End plan soon appeared uninspiring in the face of the new architectural fashion that overwhelmed Boston in the early 1860s, the first intimation of which was the outstanding exception to the stylistic conservatism of the South End — the Deacon House (Figure 37).

The work of a French designer, Jean Lemoulnier, probably under Bryant's auspices, this house was built in 1848 quite close to the corner of Washington Street and Massachusetts Avenue. It was not only endowed with remarkably sumptuous interiors — with paintings on walls and ceilings by both Boucher and Fragonard and fittings by Sèvres as well as carved gilt panels from Claude-Nicolas Ledoux's Hôtel Montmorency in Paris, destroyed in 1848 — but it possessed as well the first mansard roof in Boston. (That kind of two-sloped roof, with an almost flat upper slope and a lower one steep enough for windows and often flaring out with a concave curve at the eaves, is named for the two seventeenth-century French architects who popularized it, J. H. and François Mansart.) Yet the pomp of the Deacon House, as of the South End generally, did not long survive. Twenty-three years after its erection the house and its furnishings (some of which may be seen in the Museum of Fine Arts in Boston today) were sold at auction. Indeed, as early as 1863, William Dean Howells's *The Rise of Silas Lapham* portrayed Lapham as having been able to buy "very cheap of a terrified gentleman of good extraction who had discovered too late that the South End was not the thing, and who in the eagerness of his flight to the Back Bay threw in his carpets and shades for almost nothing." Neither fashion nor the mansard style — which by the early 1860s was pretty much the same thing — would flourish in the South End. By then, Boston was flocking instead to the Back Bay.

VERY slowly in the 1850s and then with a rush after 1860, after more than two hundred years on the periphery of British architectural circles, Boston suddenly surrendered to a passion for things French. The brilliance of the court of Napoleon III exercised, of course, a worldwide influence, as many memoirs

of traveling Bostonians in these years testify. And it must be said that the luster of this regime was reflected not only in dress and decor and manners, but more than is perhaps usual in architecture. Paris became under the third Napoleon a kind of universal architectural idol. And of its new buildings none, perhaps, was more admired than the new Louvre of 1852–1857. It directly inspired the Boston City Hall of 1861–1865, with its paired and superimposed columns, rich, sculptural details, and massive, lofty mansard (Figure 38). One of the earliest major Second Empire buildings in America (over which this style swept in the next decade), the City Hall was designed by Gridley J. Fox Bryant, who also designed the now destroyed first Horticultural Hall on Tremont Street in 1865 (Figure 2), and by Arthur Gilman. It was, moreover, followed almost at once by Bryant's handsome plan, now obscured by the destruction of several buildings and the haphazard introduction of others, for the Boston City Hospital in the South End (Figure 39). One senses, in Bryant's explanation of his design to the hospital authorities in 1861, a good deal of the reason Boston surrendered so quickly to things French during this period: "the particular style chosen," wrote Bryant, "is the modern style of Renaissance architecture, a style which stands confessedly at the head of all the forms of modern secular architecture *in the chief capitals of the world*." The emphasis is mine, and it surely discloses the root of this new style's popularity. Boston celebrated its growth into one of the largest Catholic centers in the world by erecting a vast Gothic cathedral. Similarly, in the secular sphere, the city's overall ambition to take its place among the "chief capitals of the world" could only be realized by taking as its secular model the splendors of Second Empire Paris. That was the model which shaped the Back Bay.

35

38

The debut of the Second Empire in Boston.
FIGURE 38. Gridley J. Fox Bryant and Arthur Gilman. Boston City Hall,
1861–1865. The building has been recycled into an office building.
FIGURE 39. Gridley J. Fox Bryant. Boston City Hospital, South End, 1861.
Only portions of the flanking buildings have survived and these are now
surrounded and obscured by later construction.

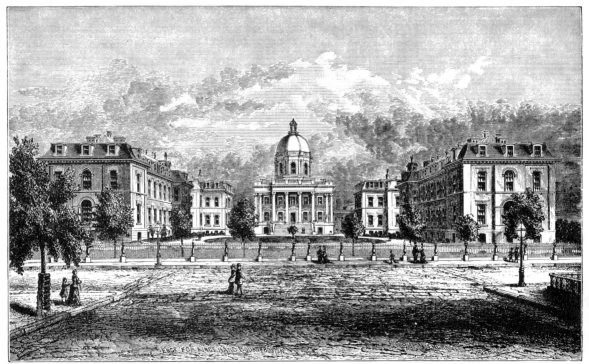

The Back Bay plan ranks with that of Washington, D.C., as the outstanding example of city planning in America in the nineteenth century.
FIGURE 40. Commonwealth Avenue, looking east from Exeter Street, ca. 1885, the centerpiece of the area's spacious and ornamental grid.
FIGURE 41. Charles River Embankment, two blocks to the north of Commonwealth Avenue, as it appeared ca. 1915. Both the Commonwealth Avenue Mall and the embankment emerged as connections between the Public Garden and the Fenway, thus forming the first stages of Frederick Law Olmsted's famous "emerald necklace," the Boston Park System. See also Plate 1.

Since 1814, this area had been a great mill dam, the earthenwork dike and stone seawall of which are in fact still in place under Beacon Street today, and sewers continued to discharge into the area though it had been cut off from the flow of tide. There was thus more than one reason for its filling. A tremendous undertaking, one of the largest such projects in history, it was a dramatic demonstration of Boston's vitality at this time. Filling began in September of 1857 and as the fill worked its way down the avenues, the houses followed, a block or two behind. So, too, did Boston society. It was to this splendid new quarter that John Lowell Gardner and his new wife, Isabella Stewart Gardner, moved in 1860–1862 to the house at 152 Beacon Street where she began her art collection. Four years later a fine new house at 10 Commonwealth Avenue (Figure 45) was built by Thomas Gold Appleton, a leading figure in Boston society who Oliver Wendell Holmes once remarked "spilled more good things on the wasteful air in conversation than would carry a 'diner-out' through half a dozen London seasons." By 1870 Holmes himself had committed what he called "justifiable domicide" and moved to the Back Bay. Nor is it difficult to understand why.

The contrast to the South End's incoherent plan could not have been greater. As Bainbridge Bunting has pointed out, the Back Bay's great axial scheme constituted "a sharp break from the English cell-like, additive scheme of private residential squares which had previously guided Boston's building. Commonwealth Avenue is probably the handsomest boulevard created in nineteenth-century United States" (Figure 40). Eight splendid blocks long, from Arlington Street to Massachusetts Avenue, 240 feet wide from block to block, with a central mall planted with four parallel rows of trees, Commonwealth Avenue, in Bunting's words, "expressed

[Boston's] will to assume a place among the great cities of the world." So too did the whole Back Bay plan, which Lewis Mumford has asserted ranks with L'Enfant's plan for Washington as "the outstanding achievement in American city planning of the nineteenth century." Five parallel axes, formed by the major streets, clearly emulated the Second Empire boulevard system of Paris and attempted to create in Boston an urban environment of truly grand scale (Plate 1). The plan was carried to a kind of extreme in the alphabetical sequence of names of the cross streets — Arlington, Berkeley, Clarendon, Dartmouth, Exeter, Fairfield, Gloucester, Hereford. Furthermore, three-syllable names alternate with those of two syllables.

The new area was also characterized by an extraordinary amplitude and spaciousness: 43 percent of the land directly owned by the Commonwealth was dedicated to streets and parks, a generosity probably unparalleled in mid-century urban planning in the United States. Commonwealth Avenue itself opened off the magnificent new Public Garden, designed by George F. Meacham in 1860. Along with this amenity, over the years a gradually expanding riverfront park was built, beginning with a 100-foot-wide promenade in 1893 (Figure 41) and culminating in this century with the Storrow Embankment. Another important aspect of the Back Bay was its ornamental character; as opposed to the South End, where very few statues or monuments were ever attempted, both the Public Garden and Commonwealth Avenue were embellished with a great number of them. Among the earliest were Thomas Ball's equestrian statue of Washington (1869), widely regarded as one of the finest such works in America (visible in Figure 43), and William Rimmer's statue of Alexander Hamilton (1864) on Commonwealth Avenue. Many more would follow: the Back Bay was to become a

FIGURE 42. The crest of the Classical and Gothic traditions in Boston in the mid-1860s: the corner of Berkeley and Newbury streets in the Back Bay, ca. 1865. Left, William G. Preston's Museum of Natural History, 1863, now Bonwit Teller; right, R. M. Upjohn's Central Congregational Church, 1866, now the Church of the Covenant. These two buildings make an interesting comparison with the two earlier landmarks, St. Paul's Church in Brookline and the Mercantile Wharf Building on the waterfront, shown in Figures 30–31.

French Academic domestic design in the Back Bay in the 1860s.
FIGURE 43. Looking across the Boston Public Garden toward the massed, symmetrical blocks of Arlington Street to either side of Commonwealth Avenue.
FIGURE 44. Attributed to Gridley J. Fox Bryant. 1, 2, and 3 Arlington Street, 1861.
FIGURE 45. 8–10 Commonwealth Avenue, 1864.

44

45

symbol of the city as a work of art in its integration of parks, fountains, and statues with both residential and public buildings.

These last added immeasurably to the distinction of the new quarter. Three buildings set a sufficient standard of excellence. William G. Preston's superb Museum of Natural History (Figure 42), now Bonwit Teller, and its long-destroyed companion, the first building of the Massachusetts Institute of Technology (1864), introduced into the Back Bay a restrained French Classicism reminiscent of the Place de la Concorde, while Arthur Gilman's Arlington Street Church (1860) was scarcely less distinguished. Moreover, the houses of the Back Bay were as different in character from those of virtually the same period in the South End as was the Back Bay's monumental axial plan. Approaching the Back Bay along Beacon Street, one can see houses similar to their South End cousins that illustrate this point. Eighty-nine Beacon (1852) is Greek Revival; 96 Beacon, one of two houses remaining of a block of several designed by George M. Dexter in 1849–1850, is a handsome example of the fashionable Italian manner. But once one gains Arlington Street, the change is stunning.

One ought first to look at Arlington Street from the Public Garden (Figure 43), ''whose gaudily brilliant flower-beds,'' Whitehill has written, ''like its swan boats, irresistibly recall a French park of the Second Empire.'' The same spirit animates the streetscape beyond: though ruptured now by one or two later buildings, the majestic, harmonious, mansard blocks of Arlington Street constitute still a splendid frontispiece to the Back Bay, disclosing not only the monumental axial plan of this spacious, ornamental district, but the role these Second Empire blocks were intended to play in this plan. The unity of overall design is striking and beautiful. Every house,

and all of them as a streetscape, is as symmetrical as the spacious grids of the street plan they rise from. Facades are typically axial and flat, from the sheer, uniform planes of which a rigorously chaste, correct, and logical architectonic detail projects crisply to emphasize the crucial structural points of doors and windows. For example, 1, 2, and 3 Arlington Street, attributed to Gridley J. Fox Bryant, are each flat, symmetrical, and architectonic (Figure 44). But these three houses are also conceived clearly as a part of the larger symmetry of the block; which is massed a-b-a — that is, two flanking pavilions projecting so as to frame symmetrically the center house, the whole block tied together by the crowning mansard roof.

Similar compositions occur at 401–407 Beacon Street (1867), designed by Snell and Gregerson, and at 110–130 Marlborough Street (1868) where in a group of eleven houses massed in five parts, not only the two houses at each end project but also the three central houses. A variant scheme, where unity of design is achieved by the regular repetition of the same facade in the same plane used many times over, occurs at Bryant and Gilman's 20–36 Commonwealth Avenue (1860). The smaller the number of houses encompassed, of course, the harder it was to achieve symmetry in the narrow town house lot. Yet 154 Beacon Street, built in 1861, and 17 Marlborough Street, built in 1865, show how ingeniously even one narrow house could achieve an impressive symmetry, though a common device was to design matching houses — as at 8–10 Commonwealth (Figure 45), which are in themselves and as a pair fine examples of the flat, axial facade with correct and sober architectonic detail. This pervasive symmetry also extends to interiors. Insofar as was possible the same axial composition that governs the overall plan of the Back Bay, the blocks of houses, and the individual

FIGURE 46. Peabody and Stearns's New York Mutual Life Insurance Company Building (1874–1875) and, attached on the right, Nathaniel J. Bradlee's New England Mutual Life Insurance Company Building (1873). Both demolished. Notice the vertical aesthetic of the New York Mutual Building; it was completed in the same year as Mutual's similar and only slightly taller New York City building, which has been called one of the first skyscrapers in the world.
FIGURE 47. A. B. Mullet. Boston Sub-Treasury, begun in 1869. Demolished.

47

house, governs as well the interiors of the 1860s where mantelpieces, windows, and doors also are apt to be axially arranged.

All of this, so reminiscent of its model, Baron Haussmann's Parisian boulevards, was not only more coherent and for its time more progressive than the design concept of the South End, it was also more disciplined and more theoretical, based as it was on abstract, formal rules of composition. The South End was instinctive and intuitive, a continuation of the Boston tradition; the Second Empire architecture of the Back Bay was academic, and as it was not intuitive to Boston architects, the question at once arises: how did these architects, suddenly, in the late 1850s and 1860s, learn it and ultimately master it?

This problem still intrigues scholars, but the attributions of many of the houses on or near Arlington Street of the late 1850s and sixties, which set the area's tone, are significant: 1–3 Arlington Street is attributed by Bunting to Bryant; three houses of 1859, which stood where the Ritz-Carlton Hotel now is on Arlington Street, are known to have been designed by Richard Morris Hunt; 16 and 17 Arlington were designed by William Preston; and 20–36 Commonwealth Avenue, quite near Arlington Street, was the work of Bryant and Gilman. Of these four architects, who appear to have been the leading exponents of the French style in Boston, three studied in Europe — Gilman, who almost certainly designed the Back Bay street plan itself, Hunt, and Preston. The last two are also known to have studied in France: in fact, Hunt was the first American student at the Ecole des Beaux Arts in Paris (where he worked under H.-M. Lefuel on the new

Louvre), while Preston's elevation for the first Massachusetts Institute of Technology building in the Back Bay is actually signed "Paris, 1863." Preston also points up the fact that the traffic between Boston and Paris was apparently not all one way, for Preston's father, Jonathan, assisted Edward Cabot in 1854 in the final design of the Boston Theatre (Figure 25), and Cabot's design is known to have been based on the work of an otherwise unknown French architect, André Noury, whose presence in Boston at the time Lemoulnier was working on the Deacon House is suggestive. In fact, though little is known about Boston's early French connections, they appear to have been numerous and important.

An especially tantalizing connection, for example, is the painter William Morris Hunt, who settled in Boston in 1862. Many strands met in the career of this artist, of whom it was said that after chatting with him one felt the rest of the world was dead. Very much at his ease among the literati (he was a member of the famous Saturday Club where he forgathered with Emerson and Agassiz and most of Boston's leading lights of the time), Hunt was responsible for the wide patronage by Bostonians of the Barbizon School. The brother of the architect Richard Morris Hunt, whose early French work in Boston has already been touched upon, Hunt's studio was in the same building as the office of two other important architects, Snell and Gregerson, whose French Academic work was frequently distinguished. Hunt's friend Elihu Vedder implied in his memoirs that Hunt knew these architects, and they were certainly the architects of Hunt's Back Bay town house, designed in the French manner for R. M. Pratt in 1867 at 405 Beacon Street.

As scholars have probed more deeply into French influence in Boston in the mid-nineteenth century, it has also become evident that its effect, though episodic, was widespread in Greater Boston as early as in the late forties and fifties. At about the same time he was at work on the Deacon House, Lemoulnier designed at least two other no longer extant French houses in suburban Brookline and Jamaica Plain, while Henry Greenough, the architect brother of the sculptor Horatio, is now known to have designed several mansard-roofed houses in Cambridge in the early and mid-1850s. Nor was the Back Bay the only part of the city proper where the new style dominated. Because the Back Bay has survived, one tends to forget that it was in Post Office Square (where nothing of this period has survived) that in the 1860s and early seventies the French vogue erupted into its gargantuan civic climax. On one side of the square two magnificent insurance buildings stretched for 100 or more feet (Figure 46) — Nathaniel Bradlee's New England Mutual Life Insurance Building and Peabody and Stearns's Mutual Life Insurance Building, both built, like Arthur Gilman's Equitable Building in the adjoining block, just after the Great Fire of 1872. The Mutual Life Insurance Building (1874–1875) was particularly impressive — a sumptuous marble extravaganza; its tower achieved a height of 234 feet and gilded balconies and crests garnished its gleaming white marble. On the other side of the square stood A. B. Mullet's much maligned but undeniably impressive Boston Post Office and Sub-Treasury (Figure 47). Begun in 1869, it was 200 feet long, 100 to 126 feet high, a grandiose ensemble of pavilions and orders and heavily loaded mansards with enormous sculptural groups by Daniel Chester French. Many thought this stupendous ensemble somewhat degenerate. Many more were fiercely proud of it.

In retrospect, the exuberance of this monumental civic array (particularly the tower of the Mutual Life Insurance Building) also illustrates the gradual

FIGURE 48. At first the Back Bay streetscape reflected the same division into Classical residential and institutional architecture and Gothic ecclesiastical architecture that had obtained in Charlestown, East Boston, South Boston, and the South End. Looking down Berkeley Street, ca. 1875: the spire of Ware and Van Brunt's First Church of Boston (1865) appears to the right; in the background is the tower of R. M. Upjohn's Central Congregational Church (1866).

breaking down of the chaste and disciplined Academic style of the 1860s. A few Back Bay houses (Snell and Gregerson's 163 Marlborough Street of 1871, for example) continued the tradition with distinction. But by the early seventies the architectural unity so prized in 1860 was waning. In Boston the strict symmetry and clarity of French Academic design did not survive the decade of the 1860s in which it had reached its zenith. Even the Second Empire style could not for long check the Victorian infatuation with the picturesque.

Actually, it is often forgotten that in one respect the Back Bay was picturesque from its beginning. Like the Immaculate Conception in the South End, Gilman's Classical Arlington Street Church was an outstanding exception in the Back Bay, where the fact that both public and residential Classical design was more academic than in the South End only made the Back Bay's Upjohn-type churches of the 1860s seem all the more wildly picturesque (Figure 48). Significantly, among the first of these churches to be built were two designed by firms whose work in the suburbs has already been discussed — Emmanuel Church (1862) on Newbury Street, still another pudding stone village church by Alexander R. Estey (though extensively enlarged by Frederick R. Allen in 1899); and the Central Congregational Church on the corner of Berkeley and Newbury streets (1866), designed by Upjohn's son, R. M. Upjohn, who increasingly took the lead in his father's office during this period. Admittedly, the Central Church, with its magnificent 236-foot-high spire, is a more formal, urban type of Gothic. But it is still assymetrical, picturesque — and of pudding stone — and the contrast with the Museum of Natural History (Figure 42) of only three years earlier is striking.

But just as Boston was by no means wholly French in the 1860s (for all the logic of the Back Bay street names, the names themselves are aggressively Anglophile), so also even though the strict French mode broke down in the 1870s, Boston's French connections remained a vital cultural undercurrent. These connections, though not yet by any means thoroughly documented, had been deeply rooted and had yielded much more than mansard roofs. As we will see in Chapter 5, for example, the unknown architect (possibly Gilman, perhaps Snell) who designed the famous Hotel Pelham in 1857 is most interesting not because he endowed it with the first mansard in the city proper but because the Pelham was the first "French flat" hotel (that is, apartment house) in America, an innovation the effect of which is still with us today. Similarly, when in 1865 the school of architecture at Massachusetts Institute of Technology was started (two years before the Boston Society of Architects was started), William Ware, who headed the school, not only introduced Beaux Arts methods of instruction into Boston, but thereby founded the first architectural school in the United States. Less obvious but scarcely less significant is the fact that just as Boston had been led by Hunt to patronize the Barbizon School before many Frenchmen did, so also in the last quarter of the nineteenth century Boston pioneered in collecting the pictures of the French Impressionists. Indeed, Boston's expanding culture yielded a school of "Boston Impressionists." Their work is increasingly admired today and is still another example of what curious alchemies resulted from America's close study of French art and architecture in the nineteenth century. In Childe Hassam, for example, who was born in the Boston suburb of Dorchester in 1859, Boston found a painter whose Impressionist images of the city are as evocative as any of Paris. In his *Boston Common at Twilight* and particularly in *Rainy Day, Boston,* Hassam endowed Boston's Parisian aspirations with a distinction that was at once convincing and indigenous.

The fact that the city Hassam evoked throughout the 1880s and nineties was, as we shall see, considerably more complicated, architecturally and otherwise, than the Second Empire Back Bay of the 1860s only underlies the fact that from her Parisian aspirations of the 1860s Boston steadily evolved toward a more complex and highly original architectural accomplishment and one that would be of world importance. The decade of the 1860s was the eve of Richardson, who from 1859 to 1865, while the Back Bay was beginning to build up, had been quietly at work in Paris, where in 1860 he entered the Ecole des Beaux Arts. Five years later, he returned to the United States and in 1874 settled in Boston, where he had won in 1870 the commission to design yet another Back Bay pudding stone church. By then, however, the metamorphosis of Boston had begun: the French Academic vogue was yielding to the vividly picturesque architecture of the 1870s.

3

H. H. Richardson's Boston

IGH VICTORIAN BOSTON, richly
textured and dramatically
massed about picturesque
towers, is nowhere better seen or more
keenly felt than along Dartmouth Street,
between Commonwealth Avenue and
Copley Square. Only a few blocks from
the regular masses of symmetrical Second Empire houses of the 1860s on Arlington street, this Dartmouth Street
vista of the late 1870s and early eighties
marks a fascinating shift in taste. It is
best seen, perhaps, at the intersection of
Commonwealth Avenue, for the two notable picturesque buildings there of
about 1880 are actually drastically altered
Second Empire buildings of about 1870.
At the northwest corner is the Ames-
Webster House, which still shows
enough of the original mansard house
Peabody and Stearns built there in 1872
to set off all the more strikingly the majestic tower, porte cochere, and conservatory that John H. Sturgis and Charles
Brigham added to this house in 1882
(Figure 50). Much the same thing happened across the street on the southwest
corner a year earlier at the Hotel Vendome, where one can see the nature of
this shift in taste even more clearly because there the 1871 building has survived as part of the larger building
of 1881 one now sees. Designed by William Preston, this 1871 Second Empire
building on Dartmouth Street had a
rigorously symmetrical principal facade.
But one can see at a glance how, when
J. F. Ober enlarged the Vendome in 1881,

without altering the earlier building he
massed the new Commonwealth Avenue
facade so as to use Preston's building as
a part of a much larger and asymmetrical
ensemble (Figure 49) which reflects
dramatically the Victorian passion for
the picturesque.

Subdued for a decade and more (with
the exception of the Upjohn church type)
by the formal Classical tradition of the
city proper and by the French Academic vogue, this passion thereafter
erupted again with such force that by
1875 clusters of buildings like Merrill G.
Wheelock's Masonic Temple (1867),
Cummings and Sears's Hotel Boylston
(1870), and Nathaniel J. Bradlee's Young
Men's Christian Union (1875) at Tremont
and Boylston streets (Figure 51) had endowed Boston in places with not just a
picturesque but a startlingly Medieval appearance. Even the Back Bay
was transformed. One need only walk
up Dartmouth Street toward Copley
Square from Commonwealth Avenue to
see this. At the northeast corner of Newbury Street is an explicitly Medieval
house, built for himself by the architect
J. Pickering Putnam in 1878. Opposite
stands J. L. Faxon's brilliant red terra-
cotta Hotel Victoria of 1886; startlingly
Moorish in its detail, it was not the only
building in that style in Boston by the
1880s. On the southwest corner is William Ralph Emerson's Boston Art Club
(1881), where the elaborate surface detail
does employ Classical motifs, but with
an asymmetry as deliberate as that of the

46

building's massing. And behind the Art Club's towered and gabled silhouette rise majestically the lofty polychromatic Gothic tower and greenish copper lantern of Cummings and Sears's New Old South Church of 1874, shaping with the Art Club the most distinguished picturesque ensemble in the city (Figure 52).

This is even more true today than it would have been in the 1870s or eighties, because as one looks across Copley Square toward Trinity Church (Figure 61), that landmark is now only a magnificent episode in a square robbed of its once vivid picturesque architecture. The great symbol of the immense and pathfinding genius of Richardson, whose presence pervades this period, Trinity was mirrored in the eighties by the old S. S. Pierce Building (Figure 60), designed by Edwin Tobey (1887). Behind the church, on the corner of Boylston and Clarendon, stood another Medieval building, Peabody and Stearns's redbrick Hotel Brunswick (1874), and where the Copley Plaza now stands was John H. Sturgis's vivid Gothic Museum of Fine Arts; the building Walter Kilham observed "caused a sensation" when it was completed because it introduced the large-scale use of exterior terra-cotta ornament into America (Figure 53).

Splendid enough without, perhaps the most remarkable aspect of this quarter is within. The decoration of Trinity Church is scarcely less notable than the church's overall design; in Richardson's own words: "a rich effect of color in the interior was an essential element in the design." Moreover, Trinity's decoration has been characterized by James O'Gorman as "a cultural event of the first importance in American history," and by Van Wyck Brooks as marking "the break of the Boston mind with its Puritan past." Certainly, it heralded that break. The work of John La Farge, Trinity's frescoes were the first such work of importance by an American artist, and La

Farge's glass, particularly the great lancets over the west door, are incomparable. They achieve, in the words of Charles Connick, who was *not* a disciple of La Farge, a "luscious quality of glassiness," while the overall effect of La Farge's glass and murals, and of the glass of Burne-Jones and William Morris amid rich, Byzantine stenciling in red, gold, and green, moved Henry-Russell Hitchcock to compare the interior of Trinity with that of St. Mark's in Venice; Richardson's decoration seemed to Hitchcock to fill the church "with a sort of coloured mist." (Plate 5.)

The decoration of John H. Sturgis's interior at the Ames-Webster House is on a domestic scale almost as remarkable: surmounting the great four-story stairwell is a mural-cycle by the French painter Benjamin Constant, which was also originally enhanced by La Farge glass (Figure 54). Nearby, in the Central Church and the Arlington Street Church, there is also a distinguished parade of stained glass by various of the designers for Louis Tiffany, whose wistful, naturalistic forms and hand-blown iridescent Favrile glass were so characteristic of this period. (Of particular interest is the early and innovative lantern in the Central Church, originally a part of the Tiffany Chapel at the 1893 Chicago world's fair.) This new concern with architectural decoration extended as well to sculpture, and the work of John Evans and his associates is comparable to La Farge's in glass and fresco in that it marked virtually the beginning of architectural sculpture of distinction in this country. Evans, who is of particular interest because his studio was in Boston, executed the carved detail at Trinity as well as at Richardson's Brattle Square Church (Figure 64), where Frédéric Auguste Bartholdi (he of the Statue of Liberty) modeled for Evans the tower frieze whose trumpeting angels have earned the church the affectionate sobriquet

49

50

Commonwealth Avenue at Dartmouth Street, Back Bay, in the late nineteenth century.

FIGURE 49. Hotel Vendome, on the southwest corner. The original hotel (now altered since a recent fire), designed by William G. Preston in 1871, stands on the corner; J. F. Ober's enormous addition of 1881 is on the right.

FIGURE 50. Ames-Webster House, 306 Dartmouth Street, across the street, an 1872 house by Peabody and Stearns, seen here as remodeled in 1882 by Sturgis and Brigham. See also Figure 54.

FIGURE 51. High Victorian Boston: Tremont and Boylston streets, ca. 1878. On the left is Merrill G. Wheelock's Masonic Temple of 1867 (demolished); to the right is Cummings and Sears's Hotel Boylston of 1870 (demolished); in between is Nathaniel J. Bradlee's Young Men's Christian Union of 1875, extant but now shorn of its tower.

FIGURE 52. Dartmouth Street, looking toward Copley Square, ca. 1885, perhaps Boston's most picturesque vista of the period. In the foreground is William Ralph Emerson's Queen Anne masterpiece, the Boston Art Club of 1881. Behind it rise the richly detailed tower and lantern of Cummings and Sears's New Old South Church of 1874.

FIGURE 53. Sturgis and Brigham. The first building of the Museum of Fine Arts, Copley Square, as originally envisaged by the architects; designed in 1870. The Copley Square facade (left) was completed in two parts in 1876 and 1879; the principal facade (right) was never built. Demolished.

54

Back Bay interiors of the 1880s were often as spacious and ornamental as the Back Bay itself, another manifestation of the city as a work of art.

FIGURE 54. Looking up the stairwell of John H. Sturgis's Ames-Webster House, 306 Dartmouth Street, toward *The Justinian Cycle,* the only known murals in the United States by the French Academician Benjamin Constant. The stained glass by John La Farge has unfortunately been removed, but this sumptuous house, which has been called "a Back Bay Queen Anne palace," has otherwise been sensitively recycled into suites of offices.

FIGURE 55. The drawing room of Carl Fehmer's Oliver Ames House at 355 Commonwealth Avenue, on the corner of Massachusetts Avenue, 1882.

55

"The Church of The Holy Bean Blowers." Also notable in this period was the work of the A. H. Davenport Company of Cambridge (Plate 4), whose wood carving and joinery adorned not only Trinity Church but in later years St. Patrick's Cathedral in New York City and the White House in Washington. Among Back Bay houses, Davenport's finest joinery is probably to be found at the Mason House (1882) at 211 Commonwealth Avenue.

La Farge's and Davenport's domestic work (and also Evans's, for he worked on many Back Bay houses) is doubly significant, for the sense of the Back Bay as itself a work of art, which we saw developing in the 1860s, was reflected as well in the decor and furnishing of the Back Bay house. By the 1880s such houses were more and more likely to be the abodes of men and women, leaders in thought and action, whose drawing rooms, centers of an elegant and ceremonious life-style, were as consciously "artistic" as the statues on Commonwealth Avenue. In 1876, when Charles Wyllys Eliot published his *Book of American Interiors*, fifteen of the twenty-two rooms described were in Massachusetts and of these fifteen, nearly half (seven) were in the Back Bay. One of the most sumptuous was that of the Oliver Ames House of 1882 on the corner of Commonwealth and Massachusetts avenues, the drawing room of which (Figure 55) was described by William Seale as very much in the spirit of the 1870s and eighties in that "every inch of [it] showed the conscious touch of artistic effort." Nor did all this represent merely ostentation. Thomas Gold Appleton, whose house at 10 Commonwealth Avenue (Figure 45) was touched upon in the last chapter, was one of the largest subscribers to the building fund of the new Museum of Fine Arts in Copley Square, and the owner of 99 Beacon Street, John Spaulding, left an extraordinary collection to the museum, including paintings by Manet, Matisse, Van Gogh, Renoir, Cézanne, and Degas — all of which had adorned his Back Bay home.

One may also see in and around the residential Back Bay the stylistic background of the great picturesque landmarks of this period built in Copley Square. Forty-one Brimmer Street, built in 1869 (probably by Ware and Van Brunt), is an excellent example of what Bainbridge Bunting has called the "Panel Brick" style (Figure 56), characterized by ornament that arises from the bricks themselves, which project or recede from the facade (in a stepped corbel table at the cornice, for example) and yield a variety of planes often in the form of recessed panels. Such detail, being worked in the facade itself and tending thus to spread over its surface, creates discreetly the animated and dynamic facade so characteristic of the picturesque manner. The next step, the use of not one or two but of several differing and contrasting materials in the same facade, can be seen at Sturgis and Brigham's Hollis Hunnewell House of 1869 at 315 Dartmouth Street. One of the first examples of exterior ceramic decoration on any Boston building, this work heralded the same firm's use of ornamental terra-cotta the next year in the Museum of Fine Arts. The background of Trinity Church itself may be seen at Richardson's Brattle Square Church of 1870. And in the same block as the church is another herald: the house that Charles Cummings built for himself in 1871, on the corner of Clarendon and Newbury streets, the year before he earned the commission to design the third great picturesque landmark of Copley Square, the New Old South Church. There is perhaps no more striking indication in Boston of the force of picturesque design at this time than that Cummings's house is more aggressively Medieval than the Brattle Square Church itself. In fact, it was the first full-blooded Medieval house in the Back Bay. Red brick, black brick, salmon-colored brick,

The architecture of the late 1860s and 1870s was increasingly marked by facades of contrasting materials and lively detail.
FIGURE 56. A Panel Brick house at 41 Brimmer Street at the foot of Beacon Hill (1869), possibly by Ware and Van Brunt.
FIGURE 57. Architect's perspective of the same firm's Memorial Hall, Harvard University, Cambridge. One of the great Ruskinian Gothic landmarks in America today, Memorial Hall was designed between 1865 and 1871 and completed in 1878.
FIGURE 58. Victorian Gothic in its suburban incarnation could be as vivid: the Haskell House, 83 Vista Street, Newton, ca. 1870.

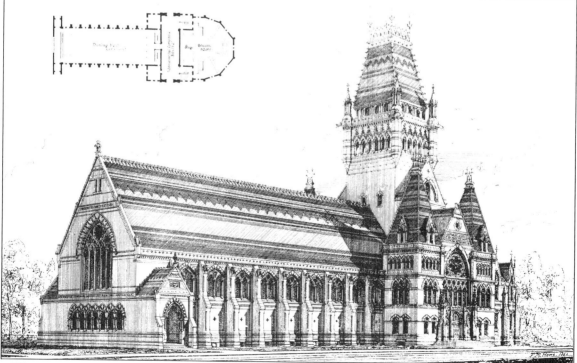

and cream-colored sandstone with polychromatic slate are disposed freely and vividly in the service of huge, cylindrical donjons whose conical roofs compete with a roof structure so elaborate as to defy description.

Not all the background of Copley Square is to be found in the Back Bay. Just as during the Second Empire period the mansard roof appeared first in residential design outside the city proper, the Copley Square Museum of Fine Arts was foreshadowed by Sturgis's Pinebank of 1869–1870 in Jamaica Plain, built for Edward N. Perkins, the chairman of the Fine Arts Committee of the Boston Athenaeum, which first recommended the establishment of the museum. In fact, Boston's earliest and perhaps greatest landmark of the new mode is not in the city proper at all, but in Cambridge — Harvard's Memorial Hall (Figure 57). That extraordinary building was designed by two Boston architects, William Ware and Henry Van Brunt, both Harvard men who had studied with Richard M. Hunt. Along with Sturgis and Brigham and Cummings and Sears, they were leading exponents in Boston of the new picturesque vogue.

LIKE Commonwealth Avenue and Holy Cross Cathedral, each of which in its different way signaled Boston's ambition to rise to the great world and take her place in it, Memorial Hall was Harvard's first attempt to express her rise from a small New England college to a great university. Designed between 1865 and 1871 and finished in 1878, Memorial Hall is 310 feet long and up to 115 feet wide; it rivals in size as much as Holy Cross such great Medieval cathedrals as Lichfield. Stylistically, however, Memorial Hall is quite different from Holy Cross. Walter Kilham tells the story of how in 1911 Abbott Lawrence Lowell took a new professor of architecture just arrived from Paris (it was Eugène J. A. Duquesne) on a tour of the Yard; Lowell

proudly pointing out the cherished square brick boxes, Hollis, Stoughton, and the rest, Duquesne bowing and saying, "Ah, oui," "très chic," "c'est charmant," etc., and Lowell dreading the moment when they should come to Memorial Hall. Finally they turned a corner and Memorial [Hall] appeared, all its pinnacles shining in the sun, and the gilt clock striking like a band coming up the street. Duquesne stopped short, gesticulated, and exclaimed, "Ah, voilà, quelque chose!" — "Ah, there at last you have something."

How to account for it? The extent to which this vivid new polychromatic vogue swept over Boston reflects the fact that its advent coincided with the Great Fire of 1872, which forced a virtual rebuilding of the business district. Coincidental, too, was the fact that Copley Square began to be built up at this time, as did the streetcar suburbs we will discuss in the next chapter, where some of the most vividly picturesque buildings are found (Figure 58). But what of the new architecture itself? Fundamentally, these buildings of the late sixties and seventies, vividly coloristic, sometimes rambunctious in feeling, yet as often undeniably magnificent, reveal the deep new need of the time in an increasingly industrial and ugly age to dream romantically of a picturesque past. Such was the energy of the post–Civil War period, the dream was necessarily somewhat strident; Memorial Hall *itself* was rather like a brass band stepping up the street. On the other hand, these buildings also revealed how tired Boston architects had become of paraphrasing what had become an academic formula, long mastered. After about 1870, architecture in Boston became increasingly experimental, individualistic, as asymmetrical as it had lately been symmetrical; broken and picturesque in massing and more and more inventive in detail.

Medieval survival and Medieval revival.
FIGURE 59. Triangular Warehouse, built
near Dock Square in Boston, ca. 1680.
Demolished.
FIGURE 60. Edwin Tobey. S. S. Pierce
Building, Copley Square, Back Bay, 1887.
Demolished.

59

60

And at its best it would also attempt a more sensitive handling of materials and a greater emphasis on good craftsmanship. Because, stylistically, the new picturesqueness of the seventies and eighties was couched overwhelmingly in Medieval terms, which spread from churches to virtually every building type, it can seem to us an even more improbable appropriation on the part of the New World than the Italianate palazzos of the mid-nineteenth century. Yet if one compares the S. S. Pierce Store of 1887 in Copley Square with Boston's Triangular Warehouse of about 1680, one can see that at least one variety of picturesque design would refer in a very real sense to Boston's earliest architectural tradition (Figures 59–60). The Triangular Warehouse was Medieval *survival;* the S. S. Pierce Store was Medieval revival. Notwithstanding the connection of late nineteenth-century picturesque design with Boston's late seventeenth-century architecture, had one inquired in the 1860s or seventies about sources — especially for the polychromatic Gothic of

Memorial Hall — most architects would have pointed to England, whether they liked Memorial Hall or not.

Its detractors, who would seize upon Memorial Hall's contrasting banding and christen it the "streaky bacon" style, united around critics like Clarence Cook, who wrote in the *North American Review* in 1882 that both the new Museum of Fine Arts and Memorial Hall were the products of architects whose heads were "crammed full of remembered bits of Old World architecture and [whose] portfolios [were] stuffed with photographs of more and more bits." They preferred buildings like the University Museum at Harvard, near Memorial Hall. Designed by Henry Greenough and George Snell (two architects of strong academic tendencies) only eight years before Ware's first design (1865) for Memorial Hall and added to by Greenough and Snell in 1871, while Memorial Hall was under construction, the museum is plain and clean-cut, factorylike in its design. Added to repeatedly until as late as 1913 in the same sparse style, it was not,

54

however, a popular alternative. Admired by persons of Cook's persuasion because of its simple functionalism, it was bitterly attacked by others, including Charles Eliot Norton. The first professor of the history of art at Harvard (1874–1899), Norton was, in Martin Green's words, "the Arbiter Elegantiarum of American high culture" during this period, standing "between America and England (and to a slighter extent between America and Europe, and between New England and the rest of America) explaining and evaluating each to each." His evaluation of the University Museum was devastating: "Its bare, shadowless walls, unadorned by carven columns or memorial statues, will stand incapable of affording support for those associations which endear every human work of worth." And though he later came to dislike Memorial Hall (largely because as an economy brick was substituted for masonry), it was Norton who almost certainly played the key role in determining the building's style — which by its admirers was called Ruskinian Gothic, in honor of Norton's close friend John Ruskin, the English architectural critic who in one scholar's words had "bewitched America" by 1870. Ruskin's predilection for Italian Gothic is, in fact, the stylistic background not only for Memorial Hall, but for the Copley Square Museum of Fine Arts and the New Old South Church.

Although Ruskin's preferences were felt with particular force in Boston because of Norton's prestige, Norton was not the only channel of communication between England and America. Margaret Henderson Floyd has pointed out in her discussion of the background of the architect of the Copley Square Museum of Fine Arts that John H. Sturgis's

standards and his architectural education were totally English, and he had fortuitously been acquiring these during one of the most dynamic periods of artistic and architectural thought in England — the 1850's, decade of the Great Exhibition, the Crystal Palace, John Ruskin's *Stones of Venice* and *Seven Lamps of Architecture,* the maturity of the Gothic Revival and the Pre-Raphaelite influences of Rossetti.

Unlike the foreign-born architect, Sturgis as a Bostonian had permanent contacts in both England and America through his father, senior partner of Baring Brothers Banking House, who was living in London, and through his own and his wife's families in Boston. Constant travel kept him in current touch with matters architectural in England on an annual basis, and his talented young partner [Charles Brigham] with a good hand for business proved more than able to manage the firm during his long absences.

In 1876 still another channel was opened — *American Architect and Building News.* Increasingly lavishly illustrated, this journal was the first periodical published in America for the professional architect. Another innovation, in 1883, was the Rotch Traveling Fellowship. Founded through the Boston Society of Architects, it was the first such fellowship endowed in America and greatly facilitated European travel for many who might not otherwise have been able to afford it. The nation's first architectural school; the first American architectural periodical; the first traveling fellowship in the country; all these started in Boston between 1865 and 1885 and testify to how vital an architectural center the city was becoming.

By the mid-1870s, though American architecture was increasingly picturesque and Medieval, it was no longer Ruskinian but Richardsonian. Such was the personal nature of the architectural achievement of the man held by most scholars to have been Boston's — America's — greatest architect.

BORN near New Orleans in 1838, Henry Hobson Richardson came

55

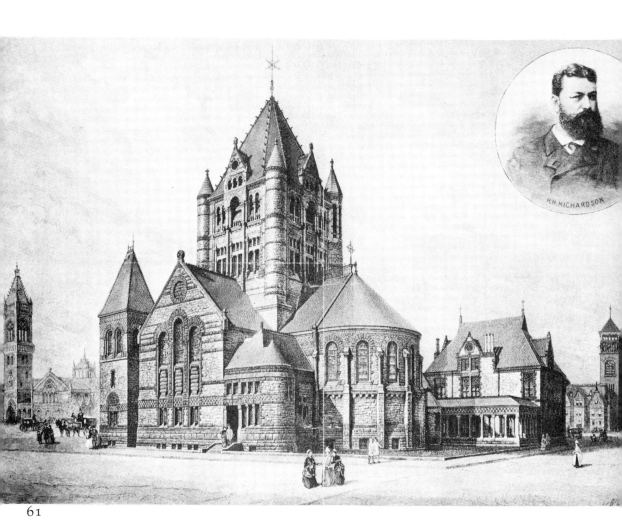

61

first to Boston with the Harvard class of 1859. Thereafter, as has been noted, he studied at the Ecole des Beaux Arts in Paris, working for a time for the architect Theodore Labrouste, and upon his return to this country he began his practice in New York in the mid-1860s. He moved to Boston in 1874. The massive, robust authority of his Trinity Church (Figures 61–62), reverberated so quickly and so intensely in the imagination of both architects and the public generally that it overwhelmed almost at once every other mode insofar as monumental civic and ecclesiastical architecture was concerned. A free adaption of the eleventh-century Romanesque of Auvergne in Aquitaine and crowned with a tower masterfully adapted from the Old

Cathedral at Salamanca, Trinity was deeply rooted in the Middle Ages; yet in the force of its design it was not only demonstrably Richardson's own, it was comparable in its own way with any Medieval model one might cite for it. Here was, not an American style, but an American architecture that was the master, not the servant, of its sources; a building couched in the terms of a venerable style, but a style suffused with a new vitality and power.

Richardson's architecture was by no means unrelated in this early period to the fashions of his time. Grace Church in Medford (1867), one of his earliest churches, and now the oldest extant church of his design, is demonstrably an outgrowth of the Upjohn church type.

56

H. H. Richardson. Trinity Church, Copley Square, Back Bay, 1872–1877.
FIGURE 61. The church and the parish house with intervening cloister and garth, from Clarendon Street.
FIGURE 62. The garth from the cloister, showing Richardson's masterful stonework. The interior of Trinity is shown in Plate 5.

One can see as well in his Winn Memorial Library in Woburn, finished in 1877, a banded entrance arch of the sort common to Ruskinian Gothic buildings. But Richardson's Sever Hall (Figure 63) of the next year at Harvard, built in sight of Memorial Hall, illustrates of what a different order was Richardson's work at its best. Sever is more than a masterpiece. Like Trinity, it is both old and new, but in Sever's case Richardson's inspiration was not only Medieval but closely related to the old Georgian buildings of the Yard, with which Sever is, in fact, very sympathetic: Sever's distinction lies chiefly in the fact that its almost Classical serenity of mass catches perfectly the spirit of the dormitories of the old Yard even as its discreet cut-brick detail and low towers and broad-arched entrance establishes its modernity in its own time. Of all Richardson's Boston buildings, however, it is the Brattle Square Church (Figure 64) in the Back Bay and the Crane Memorial Library in Quincy (Figure 65) where one can perhaps most easily identify the fundamental quality that characterizes his work: his remarkable ability to discipline and yet not emasculate the picturesque. One may discern this quality as well in the suburban stations Richardson designed for the Boston and Albany Railroad in Framingham, Auburndale, Brighton, and Waban. Particularly notable is the Chestnut Hill Station (Figure 66). Wrote Hitchcock in 1936: "By a strict expression of function and material Richardson made asymmetrical design formally monumental instead of merely picturesque." It was, Hitchcock asserted, a "very rare achievement in the long history of architecture."

Richardson was not a theorist. He did not, as Cram would, pour out his ideals and concepts in book after book. One has accordingly to discover Richardson's techniques through the eyes of scholars who have studied his work, and perhaps the best description of how Richardson could discipline the picturesque is Bainbridge Bunting's analysis of the Trinity Church Rectory on Clarendon Street as originally built, before the third story (which does not improve but on the other hand does not destroy the design) was added in 1893 (Figure 67):

The coherence of the Clarendon street elevation results from the complex equilibrium which the architect maintains between a sequence of interrelated though diverse elements. The crux of the design is the placement of the seven second-story windows. Identical in shape but spaced at slightly vary-

63

64

65

67

H. H. Richardson's Boston.
FIGURE 63. Sever Hall, Harvard University, Cambridge, 1878.
FIGURE 64. Brattle Square (now First Baptist) Church, Back Bay, 1870–1872.
FIGURE 65. Crane Memorial Library, Quincy, 1880–1884.
FIGURE 66. Boston and Albany Railroad Station, Chestnut Hill, 1883–1884.
FIGURE 67. Trinity Church Rectory, 233 Clarendon Street, Back Bay, 1879.
Another story was added by Richardson's successor architects in 1893.

ing intervals, these windows are separated by three panels of cut brick decoration. At each end of the house, two windows enframing a brick decorative panel form a unit of design which aligns with the banks of the windows in the first story and with simple gables on the third level. As the brick panel between the right pair of windows is wider than on the left, there is space for four mullioned first-floor windows on the right side but only three on the left. The larger right-hand gable further reflects this irregular spacing of second-story openings. Two second-floor windows, also separated by a decorative panel, are set symmetrically over the wide arch of the entrance porch. The seventh window of the series establishes the position of the single transomed window of the first story and the smaller dormer in the roof. Thus the unsymmetrical but orderly spacing of these seven second-story windows is echoed in all parts of the facade.

One is reminded here of Pierson's discussion of Bulfinch's third Harrison Gray Otis House, where, as we saw, the placement of windows and their shapes and sequences control utterly that masterpiece. But there is obviously present in the Trinity Rectory another dimension and the key to it is in the words "unsymmetrical but orderly spacing." It is Richardson's inspired adjustment of the features of the facade so as to achieve asymmetrically a genuine reciprocity of parts that establishes something comparable to symmetry and balance but at once more pleasing and more profound — equilibrium. Bunting goes on to explain how this is achieved.

Although the opposing gabled units use identical elements, that on the right is considerably larger than the left, with a wide bank of mullioned windows, larger panel of brick decoration, and bigger gable with round-arched window. This greater size and the way that the right section is isolated from the rest of the facade by the downspout give to it a weight that its counterpart on the left does not have. Counterbalancing this emphasis on the right section, however, is the deep-shadowed arch of the entrance porch and the larger dormer window above it which are located left of center. This equalization of

weights is facilitated by a repetition of identical window shapes in both halves of the composition, a repetition which allows the eye to move freely across the facade in a horizontal direction. Furthermore, the varied window shapes on all floors are unified by the use of window panes of almost equal size. The composition is also held together by four bands of smooth stone which carry across the facade, three related to the first-story windows and one at the height of the main cornice.

Though such subtleties in Richardson's work were naturally lost on most architects, the effect of these buildings, as Kilham remembered, was such that the "arrival of the Romanesque was nothing short of a blitz." Van Brunt and Howe's Cambridge Public Library of 1888, built two years after Richardson's death at only forty-eight, was distinctly Romanesque, *Richardsonian* Romanesque, as the style came to be known, so personal was it to its creator. It is a handsome building. So, too, is the Cambridge City Hall of the same year, by Longfellow, Alden, and Harlow. But these are the exceptional work of outstanding architects. More typical were the increasingly gloomy and soporific Richardsonian Romanesque buildings that succeeded the Ruskinian mode more and more in Boston as elsewhere. It used to be said of Bismarck's successors that they attributed Bismarck's extraordinary success to his habitual dictatorial, bullying manner, which was easily copied, but that they forgot the genius behind the bully, which could not be copied. So it was with Richardson; as he had loved great masonry arches it was easy to conclude that such things were the root of his genius and easier still to go on reproducing them forever. But as we shall see shortly, those who learned most from Richardson — McKim, Cram, Sullivan — almost never couched their work in Richardsonian Romanesque. Nor did that vogue completely dominate even at the height of Richardson's influence.

IN the mid-1870s the evolution of style and fashion in Boston accelerated incredibly. The Cathedral of the Holy Cross (Figure 35) and Memorial Hall (Figure 57) were both designed initially between 1865 and 1867; both were erected in the early seventies and substantially completed in 1874–1875; Trinity Church was built between 1872 and 1877. Any Bostonians who attended the respective opening ceremonies of these three buildings (all of which occurred between 1874 and 1877) could thus scarcely be blamed if they were confused by the wildly different architecture each event celebrated. Upjohn Gothic, Ruskinian Gothic, Richardsonian Romanesque — all reached their zenith in Boston in the mid-1870s — and although the first was to be heard of no more, the second to shine very brightly but only for a moment, and the last to dominate the next decade or more in monumental design, aspects of each lingered on for many years and shaded into one another. Even more confusingly, if the Bostonian who attended these opening ceremonies chanced to be building a house by the late seventies or early eighties, he was probably building in none of these styles. For undergirding the picturesque movement by then and throughout the 1880s was an even more kaleidoscopic vogue, Queen Anne — a term that derives from the work of contemporary British architects (chiefly R. Norman Shaw), whose announced purpose was to recover the English tradition of beautifully crafted buildings that they felt had survived as late as Queen Anne's reign (1702–1714). The effect of their attempts to do so, naturally couched at first in terms of Elizabethan manors and Flemish guildhalls, coincided with the picturesque mood of this country and was apparently felt in Boston as early as 1870 in Weld Hall at Harvard, which Ware and Van Brunt designed midway in their work on Memorial Hall. By the late 1870s, this influence was pervasive.

Less a style than a family of styles, Queen Anne ought really to be thought of as disclosing a state of mind, an *attitude* toward architecture, the innumerable refractions of which defy description. Many scholars, for example, treat both the discreet Panel Brick manner and the Ruskinian mode as a kind of introductory Queen Anne, and these and other picturesque vogues shaded so quickly into each other in the 1880s that it is easy to lose oneself in stylistic confusion. Nor is it enough to say, as did Osbert Lancaster, that the essence of Queen Anne is that its admirers were chiefly driven by "a real loathing for symmetry." It is true that Queen Anne work was usually both asymmetrical in design and Medieval in feeling. But if one searches for its positive rather than for only its negative qualities, it is, I think, true to say that it was most strongly characterized by inventiveness and whimsy. In some way or other it was usually both animated and individualistic — and when such individuality in composition was sought in every dimension, the results were naturally striking (Figures 68–75).

On the exterior, for example, broken, plastic masses, richly textured in surface, often yielded dramatic volumes of space inside — where complex stair compositions, broken into many runs of different direction, typically sought to create a sense of spatial and decorative virtuosity. The use of many varying, richly textured materials on the facade usually reflected a similar disposition of materials within. At 211 Commonwealth Avenue, for example, the reception hall is finished in lustrous mahogany, the library in exuberantly carved quartered oak, the parlor in delicately detailed enameled trim, while the dining room is enhanced by rich, variegated marble. Within and without, design also sought effects we scarcely suspect today. On any one fa-

68

69

70

71

72

73

Back Bay and suburban Queen Anne work by Cabot and Chandler.
FIGURE 68. 12 Fairfield Street, Back Bay, 1879.
FIGURE 69. 1 Melville Avenue, Dorchester, 1880. Demolished.

74

75

The many faces of American Queen Anne.
FIGURES 70, 71. 1 Fairfax Street, Ashmont, ca. 1890, west facade and east facade.
FIGURE 72. Clarence H. Luce. 130 Mount Vernon Street, corner of River Street at the foot of Beacon Hill, 1878 remodeling of a ca. 1840 house.
FIGURE 73. William Ralph Emerson. House at 24 Pinckney Street, Beacon Hill, ca. 1885 remodeling of an 1802 stable.
FIGURE 74. 27 Carruth Street, Ashmont, ca. 1885.
FIGURE 75. Cabot and Chandler. 257 Marlborough Street, Back Bay, 1883.

cade, for instance, both materials and planes were frequently distributed so as to annex the sun itself to their purpose through the play of light and shade. This could be all the more vibrant if the sunlight was suffused through trees so as to dapple the textures of the facade with a constantly changing, rippling light. Similarly, quartered oak was particularly popular for interior woodwork because its light blond highlights, running against the darker and more dense grain of the wood, catch sunlight as vividly as the dense grain rejects it. And if this light is suffused not only through trees but through stained glass, a quartered oak staircase dappled in effervescent vermilions and greens on a sunny afternoon is a vibrant and wonderful thing.

Queen Anne design could also be very simple. It was, in fact, enormously diverse — as is sometimes evident in any one building. At 1 Fairfax Street in Dorchester, there is a splendid unattributed house whose principle facade is nothing if not adventuresome: typically pierced by an unexpected and whimsical window, the chimney disappears into a large second-story bay or oriel, only to emerge finally to divide and surmount a dormer window in the roof (Figure 70). On another facade of the same house, however, one sees a similar eccentricity of design expressed in strikingly simple terms through a variation in window size and placement (Figure 71). If one then looks diagonally across Carruth Street to another unattributed Queen Anne house, one can see how both elaboration in mass and variation in window shapes and sizes may be combined in so distinguished a manner that though 27 Carruth Street is asymmetrical and fanciful, its features are so nicely adjusted in every dimension that the architect has achieved a quality of repose (Figure 74).

To attain such an effect was not easy, as so many bizarre Queen Anne houses testify. It was also more difficult to ac-

complish in the connected streetscape of the city proper, where one had usually only one or at best (on a street corner) two facades to work with. Thus perhaps the best Back Bay Queen Anne design is a corner building — Emerson's Boston Art Club (Figure 52). In overall design it is beautifully poised and coherent, but the building is not only asymmetrically massed: it is shaped on Newbury Street into a robust and elaborate design while on Dartmouth Street the effect is much simpler and is chiefly dependent on an ingenious distribution of windows of various shapes and sizes. These Dartmouth Street windows, once one studies them as an ensemble, clearly evoke the Palladian motif; an excellent example of how inventively and subtly the Queen Anne architect often handled historical forms. To best study in the city proper the two approaches we have isolated at 1 Fairfax Street and at the Art Club — the one approach seemingly elaborate, the other apparently very simple — one ought, however, to go to Beacon Hill, where stand perhaps the finest Queen Anne houses in Boston.

The best-known, though it is usually described as a kind of eccentric Bavarian dollhouse, is the conspicuously yellow and red tiled residence that challenges so charmingly the red-brick quarter at the corner of River and Mount Vernon streets (Figure 72). The first floor is built of cement, plastered; the second story is of tiles made in Akron, Ohio, which according to a contemporary report in *American Architect and Building News* were "the first of [their] kind ever manufactured in this country, after an English pattern." It was aptly christened the "Sunflower Castle" by Oliver Wendell Holmes, who thereby caught hold at once of the characteristically optimistic Queen Anne motif, visible here on the second story. Originally built in 1840, the house in its present form was designed by Clarence Luce in 1878 and is

64

somewhat similar to a house by Luce at 76 High Street in Brookline, built two years later. In fact, the "Sunflower Castle" is simply an excellent example in an unexpected place of Queen Anne design. So also is another Beacon Hill curiosity that is strikingly simpler in effect: the so-called House of Odd Windows at 24 Pinckney Street (Figure 73), another remodeling (ca. 1885), in this case by William Ralph Emerson. The fact that no two of its windows are alike intrigues people too much and obscures the superb design of this facade, where one sees how simple Queen Anne could be, and how distinguished in the hands of the architect of the Boston Art Club. Notice the "eyebrow" window that swells up from the roof.

That one of the finest Queen Anne facades in the city should possess utterly no ornament at all is particularly significant because it is often the simplest Queen Anne that has in retrospect been most admired. Indeed, the calibre of design at 24 Pinckney Street (though not this specific house, which was beyond his purview) is precisely that to which Bunting pointed when he remarked that "Boston architectural firms produced some exceptionally good work in the Queen Anne vein. For vigor of design and calibre of craftsmanship, a number of Back Bay residences are comparable to contemporary British work." The Back Bay houses he calls particular attention to — which include 357–359 Beacon (1885) and 505 Beacon (1888) by Carl Fehmer, and 283–285 Beacon (1885) and 257 Marlborough (1883) by Cabot and Chandler (Figure 75) — are singled out not for their exuberance, but because of their sensitivity to proportion and to materials, simply but finely used in compositions of distinction. In both qualities, moreover, Bunting perceived a possible foundation from which "a modern architectural expression" might have been evolved. He observed:

Undoubtedly the Back Bay's most original work was done in connection with a simple use of materials, and, in a sense, this movement symbolizes Boston's artistic maturity. Here her architects produced something of their own. . . . Boston designers stood on the threshold of an indigenous architecture, even as Chicagoans of the same decade were pioneering in the field of architectural engineering.

Bunting's assertion about the best of Back Bay Queen Anne is strikingly similar to Kilham's lament that the best Italianate design in Boston might have developed into a "truly American style." Thus one sees again the way the nineteenth-century revivals, imported perhaps somewhat improbably to this country, proved finally so susceptible to adaptation in the hands of American architects that at their best they seem always to subsequent generations to have been too quickly abandoned with no thought for their potential. This has also seemed true in the case of the Shingle Style, which paralleled Queen Anne work in Boston's suburbs.

ALTHOUGH seventeenth-century Boston Medieval survival had been too primitive to yield ready models for picturesque urban architecture — except, perhaps, for the Triangular Warehouse! — there was in the suburbs a very attractive and indigenous folk medievalism (an example is the seventeenth-century Fairbanks House in Dedham; Figure 76) that triggered in Queen Anne architects a creative response of unusual distinction widely known as the Shingle Style. The Boston architect who most scholars would agree was chiefly responsible for at least the initial development of this style was William Ralph Emerson. He designed a number of large and important houses in suburban Boston — in Canton, Jamaica Plain (Figure 82), Magnolia, and

76

77

78

Medieval survival and revival in the Victorian suburbs.
FIGURE 76. Fairbanks House, Dedham, ca. 1636.
Late nineteenth-century work by William Ralph Emerson in the suburb of Milton.
FIGURE 77. Misses Forbes House, 7 Fairfax Street, 1876.
FIGURE 78. Glover House, 320 Adams Street, 1879.
FIGURE 79. Emerson's own house, 201 Randolph Avenue, 1886.

79

throughout the North Shore — but perhaps the best way to gain a feeling for his evolution of the Shingle Style is to focus on three houses that he designed in 1876–1886 in the suburb of Milton.

An early Emerson house, the Misses Forbes House (Figure 77), shows the way in which the wooden house generally could achieve qualities of design and finish equivalent to the brick house (Figure 56). The chief characteristic of such "Stick Style" houses, somewhat (though remotely) influenced by Swiss chalet and Medieval half-timbered work, is the network of wooden framing members that subdivide the facade, a skeletal system suggesting structure though really bearing no relation to it, and yielding, as did Panel Brick work, a series of panels; in the case of the Forbes House this includes diagonal bracing. At the Glover House (Figure 78), one sees emerging the personal idiom of the architect; Vincent Scully's analysis focuses on

the mountainous sweep of the shingled roof, adjusting itself from gable to gable and then gliding down like a deeply sheltering wing over the piazza. . . . Through its continuous adjustment, all the subsidiary masses are pulled together into one plastic and richly surfaced mass, various but coherent, indicative of plastic volumes within, and expressive of shelter.

Finally, if one studies Emerson's own house, one can see by focusing again on the roof the essence of his mature work (Figure 79). Cynthia Zaitzevsky has pointed out that in his own house Emerson achieved "a continuity of roof and wall toward which he had been working for at least a decade, a continuity emphasized by the shingles, which, plain and not fancily cut, stained and weathered a dark brown, uniformly clothe all surfaces of the building." Significantly, the Emerson house is as interesting a comparison with the seventeenth-century Fairbanks House as the S. S. Pierce Building is with the Triangular Warehouse. Yet Emer-

son's house is by no means a reproduction. Rather, he caught the spirit of the seventeenth-century work and breathed new life into it nearly two centuries later.

The Shingle Style did not always recall seventeenth-century work so explicitly. Kragsyde, erected in 1882–1884 by Peabody and Stearns at Manchester-by-the-Sea, was decidedly a late nineteenth-century building (Figure 80), and an undoubted masterpiece. It is hard to believe that the overall coherence and refinement of this dramatic and mountainous shingled house, astride its majestic crag, could ever have been surpassed. So much so that Scully could not restrain himself from reflecting that the shingled surface of Kragsyde must have seemed "like a thin membrane over echoing volumes, as the boom of the surf below reverberates low and deep through the house." Kragsyde, demolished some years ago, was a kind of apotheosis of the Shingle Style. But Shingle Style houses of importance in Greater Boston survive: for example, the Bryant House in Cohasset (1880) and the Stoughton House in Cambridge (Figure 81), both designed by Richardson, whose work in the view of some scholars decisively influenced the mature Shingle Style. Though Hitchcock points out that the Bryant House proceeds in large part from Richardson's admiration of seventeenth-century work like the Fairbanks House, one can easily see in both Richardson houses — as at the Emerson House and at Kragsyde — characteristics unique to the Shingle Style itself.

The most important of these is the sense of a continuous shingled skin, which is stretched tautly around the structural frame on the exterior and seems to swell out (like the eyebrow window; see Figure 74) or hollow into the house in response to interior volumes, which thus seem to shape the exterior. These volumes, open and informal, are

Two Shingle Style masterpieces.
FIGURE 80. Peabody and Stearns. Kragsyde, Manchester-by-the-Sea, 1882–1884. Demolished.
FIGURE 81. H. H. Richardson. Stoughton House, 90 Brattle Street, Cambridge, 1883.

FIGURE 82. William Ralph Emerson worked also in the streetcar suburbs: 101 Forest Hill Street, Jamaica Plain, ca. 1880.

often said to constitute a free adjustment of space to function; and the theory does, indeed, proceed from the Medieval design concept that a building grows organically from within to whatever exterior shape, no matter how odd, the interior needs. But it could not be too odd: unlike the seventeenth-century Fairbanks House, the Emerson House's felicitous exterior shape was not accidental. It was contrived. Informality, as people so often forget today, can be as much work as formality. In fact, architecturally, it is much more work; no architect could lose track of his exterior composition while designing his interior spaces without running great risks, and the Shingle Style was all the more demanding of the architect because of its "free" aesthetic. The interior, for example, ideally developed around a great manorial "living hall," where the main entrance to the house was usually an integral part of an ensemble of entrance, fireplace, and inglenook (a cozy conversational alcove) that was also a common feature of Queen Anne houses generally. This required of a busy architect, who could scarcely repeat himself blatantly too often, a prodigious imagination, and it is not surprising that Richardson's dramatic living hall at the Paine House in Waltham (1884) is perhaps the most famous of its kind in the Boston area. Who does not relish Hitchcock's description of the stairs, which, he wrote, "pour down into the room like a mountain cataract"? At a much more ordinary level, the effect of such an interior could still be dramatic (Figure 104).

The Shingle Style, which was developed by architects who were at the same time shaping Queen Anne design generally in the 1880s, may thus be said to disclose yet again how strong a stimulant to original and indigenous design the various nineteenth-century revivals could be: Vincent Scully has called the Shingle Style "a unique American

achievement, one which has since been acclaimed by the whole world." In this case, however, New England's own seventeenth-century Medieval architecture played a crucial part. This led for the first time to the conscious revival and adaptation of an *American* historical style.

I T WAS Robert Swain Peabody who appears to have first pointed out that the seventeenth-century Fairbanks House in Dedham "would delight Mr. Norman Shaw," the chief luminary of the English Queen Anne movement so closely studied by American architects of similar bent. This interest in early American folk design significantly coincided with the 1876 United States Centennial, which naturally turned many minds toward America's Colonial past generally. The year after the Centennial a group of New York architects, including Charles Follen McKim, of whom more later, undertook a sketching trip along Boston's Colonial North Shore. Peabody himself went on a similar trip with Arthur Little to study Colonial houses in Portsmouth, New Hampshire, and in 1877 Peabody explicitly linked Queen Anne and Colonial in a paper to the Boston Society of Architects and in *American Architecture and Building News*. In the same year Little published the first architectural book on Colonial design: *Early New England Interiors*. Thus in the late 1870s and early 1880s, having discovered that there was in seventeenth-century American folk Gothic an American equivalent of sorts to the Medieval work the Queen Anne movement in England was trying to revive and develop forward, American architects increasingly transferred their attention for the first time to their own architectural history. The result was that as the British Queen Anne movement began to reenact and interpret English architectural history from late Medievalism to eighteenth-century Classicism, American architects tended increasingly toward a parallel reenactment, not of British architectural currents in the eighteenth century, but of the American Colonial architecture that from folk Gothic to High Georgian and Federal had reflected those English currents in a provincial way. The result was a "Colonial" Revival; that is, a revival of the eighteenth-century Georgian architecture that had succeeded folk Gothic.

Boston architects, naturally enough in view of their close touch with the Queen Anne movement, but also because of Boston's important Colonial architecture (which after the 1870s was increasingly admired and restored), were particularly susceptible to such tendencies. Two are of special interest: Robert Peabody and Arthur Little. Peabody was born in New Bedford in 1845, but moved early to Boston, after his father, a Unitarian clergyman, accepted a call to King's Chapel. After Boston Latin School and Harvard College and a brief period in Gridley J. Fox Bryant's office, Peabody studied first with Van Brunt and then in the late 1860s became associated with the Atelier Daumet at the Ecole des Beaux Arts, forming the famous partnership with John Goddard Stearns in 1870 that yielded Peabody and Stearns, a firm that in many ways would be to Boston what McKim, Mead and White were to New York and Burnham and Root to Chicago. Little, who designed a number of striking houses along Boston's North Shore (in Manchester, Swampscott, and Marblehead), was born in Boston in 1852, grew up at 2 Commonwealth Avenue, and after Chauncey Hall School studied at M.I.T. and apprenticed in Peabody's office before opening his own office in 1879. Both men in the late seventies designed early and important Colonial Revival houses. In Peabody's case, his Denny House on Brush Hill Road in Milton (Figure 83) has been called by

Wheaton Holden "a pivotal house in the emergence of the American Colonial Revival," while Little's Cliffs of 1878 in Swampscott has been characterized by Walter Knight Sturges as "the prototypal Colonial Revival House." Cliffs was the more remarkable of the two, for the hip roof and simple rectangular and horizontal shape of its main mass foreshadowed the future of the Colonial Revival. But Cliffs was an episode, however prophetic, and the Denny House (on which Little may have worked) is much more typical of the first stage of the Colonial Revival in the late 1870s and 1880s, when architects began more and more frequently to introduce blatantly Georgian details into houses such as the Denny that remained basically Queen Anne in their complex and asymmetrical massing.

This was not founded in ignorance. Rather, it derived from the fact that architects who had forsaken the French Academic formula for the more "creative" Queen Anne felt themselves quite capable of "improving" the Colonial work they increasingly admired. The frontispiece of the Carey House (Figure 84) at 28 Fayerweather Street in Cambridge, for example, designed by Sturgis and Brigham in 1882, resembles that of the Hancock House in Boston, of which Sturgis had prepared measured drawings; but at the Carey House this frontispiece is off center, and one cannot doubt that Sturgis's asymmetry is deliberate. Nor were such early attempts to revive Georgian forms, generally classified by scholars as "the Picturesque Colonial Revival," restricted to wooden suburban houses. At Rotch and Tilden's 211 Commonwealth Avenue (1882), a house whose lavish and varied Queen Anne interiors have already been touched on, the detail throughout this house is conspicuously Georgian, but is often imaginatively conceived. The front doorway, for example, is thought to have been modeled on a design by Asher Ben-

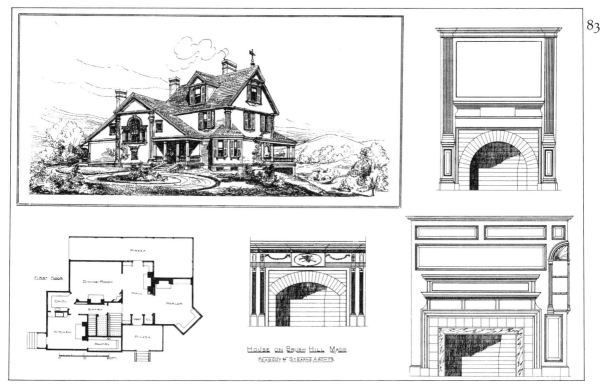

The early Colonial Revival was heavily influenced by Queen Anne asymmetry.
FIGURE 83. Peabody and Stearns. Denny House, Brush Hill Road, Milton, 1877.
FIGURE 84. Sturgis and Brigham. Carey House, 28 Fayerweather Street, Cambridge, 1882.

jamin, but Rotch persuaded Benjamin's composition into a kind of elliptical niche, which makes this doorway very much Rotch's own; so much so that a Colonial purist of the time pronounced the doorway a very bad copy. But that was to miss Rotch's point. He could easily have essayed a better copy. That he did not do so reflects Rotch's taste, not his ignorance of Benjamin's. And today there are not lacking scholars who admire both Sturgis's and Rotch's imagination, or at least respect the ingenious way in which they freely adapted Georgian forms in their own ways.

In such ways did the Queen Anne movement resolve itself finally into a full-fledged Colonial Revival that by the 1890s had shed its Queen Anne auspices altogether and yielded buildings that today are frequently mistaken for Bulfinch's own work. What an endless cycle of shifting tastes is the history of architecture and its telling! The architect who had become bored with French Academic Classicism and yielded to Queen Anne inventiveness so willingly that even when he discovered the charms of American Georgian he could not help "improving" upon it, was led finally by the Colonial Revival back to another kind of academic Classicism, so carefully modeled after Bulfinch's work that no Colonial purist had much to complain of after 1890. But if the purists were happy then, scholars have not been since. Many have argued that architecture in Boston crested in the mid-1880s. At the height of Richardson's career and at the point when Boston architects had achieved a mature local Queen Anne architecture and at the same time pioneered in developing in the city's environs a Shingle Style of unique distinction, Boston was perhaps the most vital architectural center in the country. Accordingly, many have deplored the abandonment of the

highly inventive modes of the seventies and eighties in favor of a Colonial and ultimately an overall Classical Revival that seemed by comparison academic and even archaeological. Like Bunting, who concluded that the best Queen Anne work in the Back Bay of the mid-1880s stood on the threshold of an indigenous architecture, Vincent Scully, the scholar who first formally delineated the Shingle Style, has asserted that in the mid-1880s "it is possible that a decisive opportunity for American culture was lost because confidence in invention failed those to whom the opportunity was presented." Instead of developing the Shingle Style, Scully lamented, Boston architects, and Eastern architects generally, abandoned that task — and the future of American architecture — to Frank Lloyd Wright, whose early work is widely thought to have proceeded from the Shingle Style just as much as did the Colonial Revival.

The reader will recall similar reactions as style has succeeded style in these pages. Very often when a shift in fashion leads architecture in a new direction that leaves behind a particularly distinguished accomplishment, such a regret has been voiced by those who see in what was abandoned the potential for that illusive "Americanism" for which American architecture has ever striven. But as we shall see shortly, that same "American" quality, and a profound originality as well, would later on be discovered by other scholars in the Classical and other "academic" revivals that succeeded the Queen Anne and Shingle vogues. Neither taste nor the history of taste stands still.

Before discussing that Classical Revival, however, we must turn to other innovations in Boston's architecture during this period, innovations more fundamental than style.

4

STREETCAR CITY, GARDEN SUBURBS

To walk the length of Beacon Street from Joy Street to Charlesgate and then walk back from Charlesgate along Commonwealth Avenue to the Public Garden is to trace the history of architecture in Boston in the nineteenth century — from Bulfinch's own work to the most exuberant Queen Anne of the seventies and eighties and the ensuing picturesque Colonial Revival — the development of which we will take up in Chapter 6. But even if one were to extend one's purview to include the few more blocks of houses on Beacon Hill and in the Back Bay that lie behind Beacon Street and Commonwealth Avenue, one can still traverse in an afternoon what was the only first-class residential quarter in the city proper in the late nineteenth and early twentieth centuries. Accordingly, many members of the rapidly growing professional and merchant class who by the 1880s presided over Boston lived elsewhere. Henry L. Pierce, for example, whose bequest in 1896 of over a quarter of a million dollars to the new Museum of Fine Arts was the largest such gift to that institution in the nineteenth century, lived in Dorchester, one of several such suburbs that by the 1870s were no longer independent cities and towns. Pierce did not have to move in 1872 to be elected mayor of Boston, for by then the town of Dorchester had been annexed to the city of Boston. In the later nineteenth century, suburbs were easier to annex than were coves to fill, and this fact transformed Boston at this time and precipitated a revolution in residential design.

The nature and extent of this development is clear in an 1888 publication, E. O. Stanley's *Boston and Its Suburbs*. The first section, "Walks about Boston," includes the business district, Beacon Hill, the North End, and the Back Bay and the nearby factory and working-class areas of Charlestown, South Boston, and East Boston. The title of the second section, "Drives about Boston," which includes Brookline, Brighton, Newton, Jamaica Plain, West Roxbury, Cambridge, Roxbury and Dorchester, Quincy and Arlington, illustrates clearly, however, how completely the old inner suburbs had by then been merged into one enlarged city in contemporary thinking. The distinction made between "Walks" and "Drives" also reflects nicely the nature of this newly enlarged Boston; it was commuter railroad lines (there were ten railroad stations in the city proper in 1888) and ultimately the increasing network of trolley lines and subways that made Boston's expansion possible. By trolley, a Dorchester resident could reach his office in the city proper as easily as could a Back Bay resident. Accordingly, Sam B. Warner, Jr., in his pioneering study of three of these new residential quarters — Dorchester, Roxbury, and Jamaica Plain — christened them "streetcar suburbs."

Another contemporary publication, *Bacon's Dictionary of Boston*, issued in 1883, conveys some sense of the enthusiasm the new suburban residential quarters aroused and notes those that were generally thought to be the most fashionable:

The suburbs of Boston are famed as the most beautiful in the world . . . nature has been assisted by art in a way that has entirely girdled the city with a succession of delightful communities. . . . The most famous and fashionable of all the suburbs lie to the southward and westward, with beautiful rural estates of Boston's merchant princes. Milton, Brookline and Newton, in particular, stand in the front rank in this respect, although but little in advance of Dorchester and West Roxbury. The northern suburbs also contain many delightful estates. . . .

It seemed at first as if the city of Boston would absorb those cities and towns Bostonians began to spill into in the 1850s and then inundated after the 1870s. Ultimately, however, only six voted to join the city: Roxbury (1868), West Roxbury (including Jamaica Plain and Roslindale), Charlestown, and Brighton (1874), Dorchester (1870), and Hyde Park (1912). Newton and Brookline were among many communities that declined annexation. Illogically, stubbornly, they and most of the rest of the suburbs clung tenaciously to their "independence," thus divorcing their political life from their cultural and economic life. As Warner noted in *Streetcar Suburbs:*

No period in Boston's history was more dynamic than the prosperous years of the second half of the nineteenth century. . . . In fifty years it changed from a merchant city of 200,000 inhabitants to an industrial metropolis of over a million. In 1850 Boston was a tightly packed seaport; by 1900 it sprawled over a ten-mile radius and contained thirty-one cities and towns.

Although they could avoid annexation, none of the suburbs could avoid the effects of growth. Few realize that many — including Belmont, Holbrook, Melrose, Norwood, Somerville, West-

wood, Maynard, Winchester, Norwell, Everett, Rockland, and Whitman, for example — were incorporated as separate municipalities only in the 1840–1900 period. Another result of metropolitan growth is the number of suburban towns that became cities in this period: Cambridge and Roxbury did so in 1846, and by 1900 Charlestown, Lynn, Chelsea, Somerville, Newton, Gloucester, Brockton, Malden, Waltham, Woburn, Quincy, Everett, Medford, Beverly, and Melrose had followed suit.

85

All these communities possessed their own architecture. The seventeenth-century Stetson House in Dover; the so-called Old Castle in Rockport, dating in part from 1678; the eighteenth-century Derby House in Danvers (moved from its original location in Peabody); and the Fisher-Richardson House of the same century in Mansfield may be said to stand for their fellows in almost every town-become-suburb, many of which (the Lee House in Marblehead, for example, built in 1768) are of singular architectural interest. So also are many nineteenth-century buildings. Often, of course, these were designed by local architects: Wesley Lyng Minor, for example, who settled in Brockton in 1882, designed the Brockton City Hall (1890–1891) and a number of fine houses,

In the 1870s and 1880s suburban institutional architecture increasingly rivaled that of the inner city.

FIGURE 85. Hammatt Billings. College Hall, Wellesley College, Wellesley, from Lake Waban, ca. 1885. Demolished.

FIGURE 86. J. H. Besarick. St. John's Seminary, Brighton, 1881–1889.

FIGURE 87. Schickel and Ditmars. The Basilica of Our Lady of Perpetual Help, better known as the Mission Church, Roxbury, 1876. The towers of the basilica were added by Franz Joseph Untersee in 1905.

FIGURE 88. An example of suburban commercial architecture of some distinction: Whitney Hall, the former S. S. Pierce Building, 1324–1334 Beacon Street, Coolidge Corner, Brookline. Designed by Winslow and Wetherell in 1898–1899, it was the suburban counterpart of the S. S. Pierce Building in Copley Square (Figure 60).

including the remarkably preserved Kingman House at 309 Main Street (1886), which possesses extensive mural decoration by Alexander Pindikowsky. Sometimes, too, New York architects worked in Boston's suburbs: P. C. Keeley designed the Church of the Nativity in Scituate (1872; demolished). Nonetheless, most suburban work was done by Boston architects.

The image of picturesque towers lifting from wooded hills by lakes, rivers, or coastline — as well as the crowding in what was increasingly "intown" —lured many institutions to the suburbs, and as many architects. Wellesley College (Figure 85), for example, begun in the suburb of that name in 1875, was largely the work of Hammatt Billings, Ware and Van Brunt, and Heins and La Farge. Most of this development was closer to the city proper. In particular, Brighton and nearby Newton, its hills reminiscent of Rome's, began in the 1880s to take on the character of what has been called a "Little Rome," so extensive was the Roman Catholic institutional development there. St. John's Seminary, its early buildings designed by J. H. Besarick and built in the 1880s of Brighton pudding stone quarried on the site (Figure 86), still crowns the hills above Chandler's Pond, and was surrounded in this century by Archbishop's House and the Chancery; by Boston College, of which more later; and by St. Elizabeth's Hospital, the last two of which moved there from the South End. In Medford the Tufts College Chapel of 1882 by J. Philip Rinn stands at the crest of another hill. As the suburbs grew, many new public buildings were also naturally required. Of town halls, perhaps the most remarkable was the vividly picturesque Wellesley Town Hall and Library by Shaw and Hunnewell (1881) and the dramatically sited Belmont Town Hall, designed in the same year by Hartwell and Richardson. The Arlington Public Library was

designed by Cabot, Everett and Mead (1892); Dedham's Public Library by Ware and Van Brunt (1888); and the nearby railway station (1883) by John Sturgis. Four years later Charles Brigham designed the Stoughton railroad station as well as (with John Spofford) the first of several extant buildings at the Foxboro State Hospital. Other important suburban work by Boston architects includes the Lynn City Hall (1867; demolished) and the Gloucester City Hall of 1869–1871, both designed by G. J. F. Bryant's office.

An enormous number of churches were also naturally built by Boston architects in these new residential areas, for the weekday commuter was much less likely to commute on Sunday morning. Particularly fine examples are the Assumption in Brookline (1878–1886) and Christ Church in Waltham (1897–1898), both by Peabody and Stearns, who did an enormous amount of suburban work, including the Chelsea Town Hall of 1909 and dozens of schools throughout Brookline, Newton, and West Roxbury. Many of these churches were as large and lavishly decorated as any in the city proper. Peter Paul Pugin designed an enormous and elaborate high altar reredos for Sacred Heart Church in East Cambridge (1883); and the Church of the Most Precious Blood in Hyde Park, designed by Charles Bateman in 1885, was endowed with a rich interior of variegated marble and lustrous woodwork. The most ambitious was the Mission Church in Roxbury (Figure 87). Boston's basilica (in fact as well as name: its official name is the Basilica of Our Lady of Perpetual Help) is an enormous and impressive church, begun in 1876 and completed in 1910. Designed by Schickel and Ditmars with towers by Franz Joseph Untersee, it holds 4000 people and seats 2000. Much smaller, but as important because it is an outstanding example of High Victorian picturesque design, is Ware and Van

Brunt's St. Stephen's Church (1880) in Lynn.

So extensive was Victorian suburban development that one could go on in this vein indefinitely. The commercial architecture of the new areas is also worthy of attention. At Quincy Square and at Coolidge Corner in Brookline (Figure 88), there are splendid late nineteenth-century half-timbered retail and business blocks that ought to be carefully preserved and restored. In Dorchester, the Walter Baker Chocolate complex, designed for the most part by Winslow and Wetherell in 1888–1892, is an impressive red-brick complex that extends for nearly a block on each side of a large intersection. A great deal of excellent sculpture also adorns the suburbs: one thinks of Henry Hutson Kitson's figure of Sir Richard Saltonstall in Watertown, Bela Pratt's Soldiers and Sailors Monument in Malden, and Cyrus Dallin's *The Hunter* in Arlington. Sometimes the only work in Boston of important sculptors is in the suburbs. This is true of Albert Atkins, whose best-known local work is his War Memorial in Roslindale, and of Lee Lawrie, the sculptor of the famous *Atlas* at Rockefeller Center in New York, whose only Boston commissions will be found in Forest Hills Cemetery in West Roxbury and at Richmond Court in Brookline. The most important suburban landmarks, however, have either been touched on already or will be later in this book. The streetcar suburbs are interesting chiefly for their houses.

Most of these were built in by far the largest of Boston's suburbs, Dorchester. A quiet rural town when it was annexed to Boston, by the First World War it was challenging Providence and Worcester in population. In fact, Dorchester became the largest community in New England except for Boston itself, of which it remains the largest part; its population within fifty years of annexation jumped from scarcely 12,000 to nearly 200,000. It was an unprecedented expansion, which like the filling of Back Bay shows the city's extraordinary vitality in the late nineteenth century. So huge and so diverse is Dorchester that it is a kind of microcosm of all the streetcar suburbs, and is thus perhaps the best introduction to their design concept.

How little we understand the architectural history of Boston is evident in the assumptions that will usually arise in any comparison of an early nineteenth-century streetscape (Beacon Street across from Boston Common, for example, the evolution of which we discussed in Chapter 1) with a late nineteenth-century streetscape, such as lower Cushing Avenue on the western slope of Jones Hill at Upham's Corner in Dorchester, one of the few areas in the streetcar suburbs that has been sufficiently researched to serve as a case study. Stylistically, the two streetscapes reflect the different fashions of the early and the late nineteenth century. But insofar as the streetscape — the relation of one house to the other — is concerned, just as most people assume because of our present-day definition of "town house" (connected to a similar house and built nearly on top of the sidewalk) that Beacon Street was meant to look the way it does today, so also because of our present-day definition of the suburban ideal (amply set back and widely separated houses obscured by trees and grounds and hidden along curvilinear streets) we assume that on Cushing Avenue later houses must have been inserted between the original houses, resulting in the densely packed housing characteristic of the streetcar suburbs. But these assumptions are both untrue. As we have seen, Beacon Street's character today derives from later houses that connected what

89

Lower Cushing Avenue, Jones Hill, Dorchester.

FIGURE 89. Looking eastward; from right to left are the Southworth House (designed by Sylvester Parshley, 1899); the Chamberlain House (attributed to David Chamberlain, 1875); the Hoadley House (Henry J. Preston, 1886); the Sylvester Parshley House (Sylvester Parshley, 1893; see also Figure 117); the Chadwick House (William G. Preston, 1895; see also Figure 91); and the Gallier House (W. H. Besarick, 1894). To the far left is St. Mary's Church (Henry Vaughan, 1888; chancel and transepts by Hartwell and Richardson, 1893).

FIGURE 90. Subdivision plan of lower Cushing Avenue after it had been largely built up, including the houses that appear in Figure 89. Because houses were often owned by wives and because of changes in ownership, the Southworth House (directly behind the Dyer House) appears on the map as owned by Sarah F. Parshley and the Chamberlain House as owned by S. Parshley.

90

had been free-standing town houses into the present-day blocks (Figures 10, 11). It is the Cushing Avenue streetscape (Figure 89), however at odds with our present-day definition of suburban these densely massed houses may be, that appears today exactly as its designers and first residents intended. This becomes clear when one studies its development.

The first person to comment upon it was David Clapp, head of one of the old Yankee families that had dominated the town of Dorchester between its founding in 1630 and its annexation to Boston in 1870 in much the same way that a number of Boston families had wielded great influence in the capital city. Clapp's family had lived on Jones Hill since the early 1700s. Yet when he noted in a history of the hill he wrote in 1883 that on the nearby Dyer estate "instead of three or four scattered farmhouses, one may now see scores of beautiful dwelling houses," this venerable Dorchesterite was delighted, remarking how fortunate it was that the hill had attracted homeowners with "the means and capacity to improve and adorn a naturally fine location." Clapp, to be sure, profited from it; in 1889 he broke up his own estate into house lots and made a great deal of money. But he not only proudly named the new street he laid out after the Devon estate (Salcombe) from which the Clapps had come to Dorchester in 1630; he also built a house on one of his new lots for himself and three nearby for his children. And Clapp's enthusiasm reflected Micah Dyer's, whose subdivision of his estate Clapp approved of so heartily.

"The venerable Micah Dyer," as Justin Winsor called him in *Memorial History of Boston,* was a graduate of Tilton Seminary and Harvard Law School and a descendant of a seventeenth-century Massachusetts settler. Though his wife belonged, like Clapp, to an old Dorchester family (Mrs. Dyer's grandfather had

helped fortify Dorchester Heights during the Revolution), Micah Dyer was from a leading Boston family. Contemporary biographical directories noted particularly Dyer's role as a pioneer in women's professional education in this country: he was the first president of the Female Medical College of Boston, which merged with the Boston University School of Medicine to become the first medical school in the United States to grant a full medical degree to women. Mrs. Dyer, a leader in Boston social and club circles, was herself a founder of the Women's Charity Club, under the auspices of which began the New England Hospital for Women and Children and the first school of nursing in the country. The Dyers were thus "old money" insofar as both the city of Boston and the town of Dorchester were concerned and when Dorchester was annexed they were ideally suited to subdivide their estate — where their continued presence as houses rose all around them between 1875 and 1900 not only lent great prestige to the new residential area but illustrated that, like Clapp, they regarded such development as an improvement. (So also did their son, who lived in the Dyer House until his retirement in 1918.) Moreover, the fact that Micah Dyer sold his Union Park town house in the South End in 1865, and moved to Jones Hill and the Dorchester house that thereafter was his only Boston residence, indicates that Dyer intended all along not to create a country estate but a new residential quarter of the enlarging city.

He seems at first to have envisaged connected row houses. When he first subdivided his estate in 1874, retaining what had been the estate house for himself (on a much smaller lot), the subdivision plan he filed showed narrow, 2000-square-foot lots, usable only for row houses. But although a long, curvilinear street, Cushing Avenue, was laid out through Dyer's land in 1881 to provide access to St. Mary's Infant Asylum, which had located at the hill's summit, in twelve years Dyer attracted only one buyer, and that buyer had bought *two* lots and erected in the center of them one clapboarded, free-standing house very similar to Dyer's own. Accordingly, in 1886, a new subdivision plan was filed that abandoned the narrow lots and provided for large 5000- and 6000-square-foot parcels that could serve only the large, free-standing houses now standing on them (Figure 90). However small the Cushing Avenue lots now seem, they are thus more than twice the size Dyer had originally intended and as they all sold at a regular rate throughout the 1880s and nineties it is clear such lots were what was wanted. But, one wonders, by whom?

A hundred years later one cannot exactly reconstruct the population of any neighborhood. But the unusually intensive research undertaken in this area has yielded a good deal of data about Dyer's new neighbors. On or facing these two short blocks of fifteen houses on lower Cushing Avenue between Wilbur Street and Upham Avenue, developed by Dyer, the original homebuilders of 1875–1900 included eight persons of whom something is known. James Humphreys Upham, who built 40 Cushing Avenue (Figure 116) in 1895 and lived there until his death, was the last chairman of the Board of Selectmen of the Town of Dorchester, a trustee of the Boston City Hospital, and treasurer of the Grand Commandery of the Knights Templars of Massachusetts and Rhode Island. One of the leaders of Yankee Dorchester (he was a descendant of the merchant after whom Upham's Corner had been named around 1800), Upham illustrates as did Clapp and Mrs. Dyer that old money as well as new would put down roots in the new subdivision. Upham was also the chairman of the Dorchester Committee of Robert Treat Paine's prestigious As-

FIGURE 91. William G. Preston. Chadwick House, 20 Cushing Avenue, 1895.

sociated Charities, and Paine's youngest son, George Lyman Paine, the rector of St. Mary's Episcopal Church, was Upham's neighbor at 21 Cushing Avenue, across the street.

Paine and his wife rented from Sylvester Parshley, who built 21 Cushing in 1900 next to his own home, which he had built at 17–19 Cushing Avenue in 1893 (Figure 117). Parshley was among the foremost builders in New England. One of three partners in the firm of McNeil Brothers, one of Boston's major builders in the late nineteenth century, Parshley superintended the building of many of the great houses of the Back Bay, Fifth Avenue, and Newport, where the firm built the Vanderbilt estate, Rough Point, for Peabody and Stearns. They rebuilt 46 Beacon Street into Eben Jordan's palatial residence, built 199 Commonwealth Avenue for McKim, Mead and White, and were also responsible for a whole range of public buildings: including the R. H. White department store on downtown Washington Street, several buildings at Harvard, and the great Sub-Treasury and Post Office building in Post Office Square (Figure 47). Parshley's own chief work was the

Senate Reading Room in the Library of Congress in Washington.

Behind his own house, Parshley built a third house in 1897–1898 for his son, Wilbur, after whom the adjoining street was named. Eventually, from about 1900 to 1921, Parshley rented this house to James Edgar Southworth, for whom Parshley built the adjoining "automobile house" in 1910. A prominent Boston merchant of old family (listed in the Social Register), Southworth was general manager of the Wheat Export Company and of the United States Grain Exchange and, according to his *Transcript* obituary, "handled all the grain shipped from the port of Boston during the First World War." Another house, 35 Cushing, was built for himself by the Reverend John Ballantine, the pastor of the nearby Pilgrim Congregational Church; the house next door was built in 1896 by Amanda Loguee, treasurer of the Clifton Manufacturing Company of Boston, New York, and Chicago. And across the street, 20 Cushing was built in 1895 by Joseph Houghton Chadwick (Figure 91). The president of the Chadwick Lead Company and a founding trustee of Boston University, Chadwick was described in a contemporary report in the Boston *Traveler* as the "Lead King of Boston." Finally, 36 Cushing Avenue was built by Robert Bampton, Chadwick's partner.

These eight residents of both sides of the curving streetscape erected on Dyer's land — Upham, Paine, Parshley, Southworth, Ballantine, Loguee, Chadwick, and Bampton — having all been (like Dyer) persons of some consequence in Boston, are easier to "reconstruct," biographically, a hundred or so years later, than their neighbors. But, since Warner has documented the fact that the "one basic pattern" organizing these suburbs was "segregation by income," we can assume the neighbors were Bostonians of a similar type. All but one were Bostonians, as opposed to pre-annexation Dorchesterites; every resident but one of these fifteen houses maintained his principal business address in the city proper. All were Yankee, Protestant, and relatively wealthy. As had been true on Beacon Hill at the beginning of the century, when the patriot Federalists had succeeded to the state of the exiled Loyalist gentry, most of the residents of newly built up Cushing Avenue at the end of the century also represented new money, which tended here as in the Back Bay to build more pretentious houses than did the scions of the patriot families that by the 1890s represented old money. The older families, though fewer, were, however, more important: it was the old money on Jones Hill, the Clapps', the Dyers', the Uphams', the Paines', and also St. Mary's Episcopal Church's, that naturally attracted the new money. And it is also clear that throughout the area, a web of personal connections among homeowners, developers, and architects (who were sometimes the same people) determined the shape it finally took.

The Dyers, for example, were among the most prominent Methodist families in the city: and this cannot be unconnected with the fact that at the foot of Cushing Avenue, next to the Dyer House, a large, towered stone Methodist church was built in 1890. Boston University was the centerpiece of Methodism in Boston, and Chadwick, who built 20 Cushing five years after the church was built, was, as we have noted, a founding trustee of the university. Chadwick, like Parshley, bought all the lots around his house and started to develop his land, inviting his partner, Robert Bampton, to build 36 Cushing in 1897. Bampton, however, was Episcopalian, doubtless the more easily drawn to Cushing Avenue by the erection there in 1888 of a new St. Mary's Church for the famous parish where Bishop Phillips Brooks had been confirmed and where Governor

Henry J. Gardner had been a parishioner. And it was St. Mary's that evidently prompted Parshley to build 21 Cushing, which, immediately it was built, was rented successively by the two rectors of St. Mary's of this period. A third church in Upham's Corner, Pilgrim Congregational, yielded, as we have seen, another of these houses, built by its pastor.

As Irish Catholic families began to appear in these blocks after the turn of the century, St. Margaret's Hospital, which evolved out of St. Mary's Infant Asylum, was increasingly a part of this web. Patrick McDonald, who lived at the corner of Cushing and Jerome, a state representative and close friend of Mayor John Fitzgerald, was treasurer of the hospital; Edward J. O'Neil, senior partner of O'Neil and Parker of Boston and sometime president of the Massachusetts Casualty Underwriters Association, who bought Chadwick's mansion in 1914, was McDonald's successor as the hospital's treasurer. Similarly, John Arthur Foley, who bought 2 Wilbur Street in 1918, was clerk of the corporation and president of the medical staff at St. Margaret's. A graduate of Harvard College and Harvard Medical School, Foley was also president of the New England College of Pharmacy and professor of clinical medicine at the Boston University School of Medicine. When one recalls that throughout the whole twenty-five-year development of these blocks virtually all the lots for sale were owned, successively or simultaneously, by Dyer, Upham, Parshley, and Chadwick, and sold with deed covenants requiring houses of similar character to those alrady built ("not detrimental to a first-class residential area"), one begins to suspect how carefully the development of these two blocks was controlled by a group of people whose mutual connections and interests are so evident. This is reflected, too, in the architecture of Cushing Avenue.

Chadwick's house (Figure 91) was designed by William G. Preston, whose important Back Bay work we have already noted. Preston, who probably also designed Bampton's house next door, had designed many buildings for Boston University, as well as the Chadwick Lead Building itself, still extant in downtown Boston on High Street. Four Cushing Avenue houses were designed by W. H. Besarick, the city architect of Boston. They stand, significantly, to either side of St. Mary's Church, of which Besarick was a parishioner. In fact, Besarick, Preston, and Parshley (who was his own designer) designed nine of the fifteen houses on these two blocks. That and the fact that other architects working in the area were well-known designers and that these were expensive houses (averaging about $10,500 each) account in large part for the area's architectural quality.

Another factor was St. Mary's Church. A Gothic church of national importance (William Morgan has noted that it possesses "probably the finest timber roof of its kind in the United States"), St. Mary's was the first and only parish church in the city designed by Henry Vaughan, one of the original architects of Washington Cathedral. Half-timbered and very domestic in feeling, St. Mary's established a superb anchor for Cushing Avenue, which sweeps down gently to the church from the corner of Upham Avenue, where stands a Medieval house of 1894 (Figure 116) by another British architect, Herbert Moseley. Across the street from St. Mary's is a fine Medieval house, designed by Henry J. Preston in 1886 (Figure 92). Next door, Parshley's own home at 17–19 Cushing (Figure 117) is a Queen Anne house of great distinction and coherence of design whose Georgian detail effects a superb transition to Chadwick's house, which like all the rest of these houses is decisively Georgian. In fact, the houses of William and Henry Preston, Parshley, and

Besarick, clustering about Vaughan's church, form one of the finest architectural ensembles in the streetcar suburbs. And every house stands exactly today as far from its neighbors as its first home-builders and architects desired! Clearly, wealthy and prominent citizens insisted upon such densely massed houses. Chadwick and Parshley, for example, bought up most of Dyer's remaining lots and built upon them (next door to themselves) other large houses on equally small lots — though both owned enough land to indulge, had they wished to, in "estates." It was a design concept created by the homeowners themselves.

The best way to discover why this apparently curious design concept was preferred on Dyer's land to either estatelike spaciousness or connected town houses is to inquire briefly into what may have lured these homeowners to Dyer's lots in the first place. This is not as difficult to determine as one might think. First, these houses were all built after the 1876 Centennial in an area whose important Colonial landmarks received much attention in Boston's guidebooks of the time. An 1885 guide to the city, for example, noted that the burying ground at Upham's Corner, on the other side of St. Mary's Church, dated from 1634, that Richard Mather was buried there, and that a few blocks away stood the Blake House (ca. 1650). The same guide, noting of Upham's Corner that "nowhere else can be seen the blending of old and new than here," went on to point out that the prestigious quality of the area was being maintained and that "a great number of beautiful mansions have been erected in recent years." Nor were more practical things overlooked in this guide; no prospective homeowner could have failed to notice that fifteen of the eighteen stores listed in the Dorchester section of the guide were in Upham's Corner, or that it was also a crossroads of several rail and trolley lines. If this sounds more like building a city than a suburban refuge, that fact is significant. The crest of Upham's Corner commercial development came quickly, in the early 1920s, and it was very urban indeed: it was there, within two blocks of Parshley's home, that John and Paul Cifrino developed a store that was "unique in the history of food stores" and one that Professor William Marnell describes at length in his fascinating *Once Upon a Store: A Biography of the World's First Supermarket*. He admits it is a perilous claim but points out that no one has challenged it.

Another sign of the area's growth was the new Columbia Road parkway. This road, the principal access to Dyer's side of the hill (its parklike character was destroyed in the 1950s in favor of more traffic lanes), connected Franklin Park and the Dorchester Bay waterfront: the first, the largest park in New England, the second, a yachting center of importance. And its effect seems to have preceded it. Dyer, who had gladly yielded land for Cushing Avenue, similarly encouraged the construction of the new parkway: in his *American Series* biography, in noting that Dyer's progressive tendencies were frequently the incentive to active measures for the public good, Dyer's biographer cited as the best example of this that "anticipating the ultimate construction of Columbia Road some years prior to the commencement of work upon that splendid thoroughfare, Dyer, at considerable personal expense, set back the ancient trees upon the street line of his fine estate at Upham's Corner in order to facilitate the improvement." Dyer's lots also possessed splendid views of not only the parkway but the Dorchester waterfront it extended to: *King's Handbook of Boston* throughout the 1870s described the Jones Hill view as "overlooking Boston and its thronging suburbs and the island-strewn harbor and the open sea beyond, as in a bird's-eye view."

Unfortunately, no real estate advertisements have been discovered in further support of all this, but on April 27, 1870, an advertisement did appear in the *Transcript* for one of the adjoining Jones Hill subdivisions that stressed that the estate house would remain, to set the tone of the area; that the ocean views were "unsurpassed"; and most important of all, that these Jones Hill lots were "the finest property *within three miles of State Street* now on the market" (my italics). Thus it is not surprising that, when one turns to the houses themselves, their design reflects most of these factors.

In some respects, this is obvious: most houses, for example, have lookout towers, glass-enclosed "sky parlors," or third-floor porches to take advantage of the view. As the area built up, twelve of the houses were increasingly Colonial Revival, not only recalling the general fashion of the day but, of course, reviving the historical Colonial image of the area. All the houses are free-standing in garden settings, thus reflecting the same concern with preserving and enhancing the landscape evident in the adjoining Columbia Road parkway, itself the result of Bostonians' determination to halt the progressive obliteration of the landscape that had been under way in Boston since the early nineteenth century, when even the small gardens around Beacon Hill houses had fallen victim to the scarcity of land. And if one notices not only their garden settings but also the regular alignment to each other and to the street of all these densely massed and similarly scaled houses, it will be evident that their design reflects more than anything else their proximity (by trolley) to State Street — indeed, to the business district of the city proper. In fact, this proximity explains the whole curious design concept of large mansions on seemingly tiny lots. Today, what distinguishes these densely massed houses in our perception is their lack of land: what distinguished

them in the minds of those who built them was that they possessed any kind of grounds in the first place, for these houses — built by men who were not Dorchesterites so much as Bostonians — were not in our sense of the term suburban houses at all. Cushing Avenue's increasingly Colonial Revival houses were a more profound and fundamental "Colonial Revival" than we suspect. They were an attempt to revive in the vast new lands of the city the ideal town house — detached, and on its garden lot — that had been so characteristic of Boston until the scarcity of land had begun to obliterate that ideal in the 1820s (Figures 10, 11). In fact, several homeowners on Cushing Avenue possessed country homes — but not on Cushing Avenue.

T HAT parks and parkways, as well as trolleys, knit the streetcar suburbs into the city is very important. These areas were called "garden suburbs" long before they were christened "streetcar suburbs" because Boston's park system was closely related to them. The work of Frederick Law Olmsted, who was by the 1870s the foremost landscape designer in this country and perhaps in the world, the development of the park system, like the Back Bay itself an outstanding example of nineteenth-century urban planning, has been described by Cynthia Zaitzevsky:

From 1878 until his retirement in 1895, Olmsted helped the Park Commissioners refine their 1876 master plan for a park system, as well as designing the individual parks. The core of the park system was its continuous portion or the "emerald necklace," consisting of five major parks (Back Bay Fens, Muddy River Improvement, Jamaica Park, Arnold Arboretum and Franklin Park) and their connecting parkways. Commonwealth Avenue connected the new park system with the existing Common and Public Garden. In 1897 Columbia Road was widened and joined to

The design concept of the streetcar-suburb detached townhouse: the Hoadley House, 15 Cushing Avenue (1886), a representative upper middle-class single-family house.
FIGURE 92. The house is shown flanked by other large detached houses, massed closely and regularly to each other and to the street, and is seen past the block-long retaining wall that frames the "block park" — a terraced garden setting common to all the houses, whose lots are significantly unbroken by fencing or planting on lot lines.
FIGURE 93. Detail of Hoadley House tower, showing the proximity of the house to the civic and commercial towers of nearby Upham's Corner (see Figure 90), already a busy retail center by the 1880s.

92

the Dorchesterway and the Strandway, linking Franklin Park with Marine Park in South Boston. Individually, the five major parks are among the most important and innovative of Olmsted's designs. Together, they form a five-mile corridor of continuous parkland that has long been recognized as a landmark of urban planning [Plate 1].

A major factor in the development of the parks was the fact that however well designed new "garden" suburban subdivisions might be, their effect in the long run would be to dramatically cut down open spaces if these new subdivisions were not connected by parkways and adjoining parklands, generously dispersed. As Edwin Bacon pointed out:

When the desirability of parks in the sense of New York's Central Park, Brooklyn's Prospect Park and Philadelphia's Fairmount Park, was suggested here, it was common to say: "But

Boston does not need parks; look at our suburbs! They are parks in themselves." Early in the 'seventies of the nineteenth century the rapid changes in the suburbs caused by the expansion of the city . . . made increasingly evident the importance of doing something.

Today, when the park system itself has barely survived in some places and when the small gardens of a street like Cushing Avenue seem a very pale reflection of that system, it is hard to see their connection. One can do so easily, however, by studying Figure 101 (the Jamaicaway) and then Figures 92 and 93 (Cushing Avenue). Notice that shrubbery along Cushing Avenue more often hugs the house than marks the lot lines, where fences seldom occur and were, in fact, sometimes prohibited by deed restriction. Notice, too, that the effect of this landscape design is to create a kind of large "block park," visually a *common* setting for *all* the houses of the block. The effect was often greatly heightened (as on Cushing Avenue) by retaining walls running uniformly around all the houses of the block and yielding a block-long grassy terrace from which the houses rise. The point is that it was a garden setting — with its corollary: light and air on all four sides of a house — that the detached town house wanted; not yards or gardens of any size for any purpose such as recreation or food growing; this would have been absurd one block from a major commercial center, Upham's Corner (Figure 93). Actually, the houses on Cushing Avenue and other such streets have just about as much land on all four sides as houses on Commonwealth Avenue have on one side (Figure 158).

A problem here is that we have lost track of a continuing factor in residential design in Boston that can be traced back to Boston's first important row houses. When Bulfinch was forced by his financial failure to abandon the second crescent he had planned to build facing the Tontine Crescent and built instead a series of free-standing double houses, it was the free-standing houses that became the most fashionable, according to Frank Chouteau Brown, "even though the side yards were *very narrow*." The italics are my own and point to how deep-seated in Boston was the preference for even the narrow yards of semi-detached houses as opposed to the block of connected houses, two walls in each of which had to be windowless. Admittedly, the Tontine Crescent inspired Bostonians to emulate it for generations. But this was at least partly due to scarcity of land and not because the detached house had ceased to be the ideal. Thus, in 1838, E. C. Wines noted that on what is now downtown Summer Street the gardens of the houses were such that "Town and Country seem here married to each other." And a half-century or more later

this ideal was still very much alive. How vibrantly is clear from Edward Everett Hale's observation in 1893 that

As late as in 1817, in a description of Boston which accompanied a show which a Frenchman had made by carving and painting the separate houses, it was said, with some triumph, that there were nine blocks of buildings in the town. This means that all the other buildings stood with windows or doors on each of the four sides, and in most instances with trees, or perhaps little lanes, between; as all people will live when the Kingdom of Heaven comes.

For Hale, for countless thousands more, the Kingdom *had* come, so to speak, in the streetcar suburbs. And just as the Tontine doubles, when compared with the Tontine Crescent, looked more desirable, despite their small yards, so also did Cushing Avenue when compared with a street of connected town houses (Figures 110, 111). Significantly, Edward Everett Hale lived, not in the Back Bay, but in Roxbury Highlands.

In 1878 this area was described in *King's Handbook of Boston* as a quarter "sought by those 'well-to-do' citizens who desire to establish their homes not too far from 'down-town' and where the advantanges of both city and country can be agreeably combined" — echoing, however unconsciously, in an 1878 description of the Highlands E. C. Wines's comment in his 1838 description of Summer Street, which by the 1880s was a bustling shopping area. Another contemporary source, Edward Stanwood's *Boston Illustrated* of 1872, described the Highlands in these terms and at the height of the Back Bay's prestige:

. . . on Elm Hill Avenue, and between it and Walnut Avenue, some of the best houses are located. Many of these are veritable palaces, representing all styles of architecture and varying in cost from $12,000 to $60,000. Many of them are surrounded with trees, shrubbery, flower gardens, or grassy lawns, adding to the beauty and attraction of the streets and

94

Both attached and detached town houses were characteristic of the streetcar suburbs.

FIGURE 94. J. Williams Beal. Harris Wood Crescent, Fountain Square, Roxbury Highlands, 1890.

FIGURE 95. One of the houses finally built on Townsend Street, at 140–142, one house removed from the Harris Wood Crescent, ca. 1890.

FIGURE 96. Another connected residential block in the streetcar suburbs, again facing a park. Murdoch Boyle. 1791–1821 Beacon Street, Brookline, 1907.

95

96

avenues as excellent driveways. Walnut Avenue, Humboldt Avenue, and Elm Hill Avenue all lead up to Franklin Park, and the two latter end at Seaver Street, which skirts its northern side.

A particularly elegant area, two blocks from Walnut Avenue, grew up around Fountain Square, where on the Harold Street side, J. Williams Beal, a well-known Boston architect of the period, designed a block of houses that must rank among the most lovely ensembles of picturesque connected town houses in Greater Boston (Figure 94). They still survive in fair condition. Built at a cost of about $160,000, this block constitutes a kind of Queen Anne Tontine Crescent of fifteen attached brick and half-timbered town houses, the architectural unity of which is not equaled by any Queen Anne group anywhere in the city. Still another example of the way the Tontine Crescent persisted in Bostonians' imagination, this splendid block is not, strictly, a crescent; significantly, however, it was originally called Harris Wood Crescent. The houses of the next few years on Townsend Street alongside this block were often equally picturesque, particularly 140–142 and 148 Townsend (Figure 95); this last, like the Harris Wood Crescent houses, is brick on the first floor with full half-timbering above. These houses were also fashionable; the 1897 street directory shows the president of the Odorless Excavating Company living at 148; the treasurer of the E. T. Cowdrey Company at 136; the treasurer of R. J. Todd Company at 146; and the president of the Bay State and Boston Gas Illuminating Company at 140, all with business addresses in downtown Boston. But these Townsend Street houses were also as radically different from the Back Bay as the crescent was similar, for all of them, like those on Cushing Avenue, were free-standing and in garden lots. And if this design concept of large free-standing houses set in garden lots *not* facing a park, together with town houses that *were* connected facing the park, sounds familiar, it should — it was Bulfinch's design concept of one hundred years earlier.

Nor are Harris Wood Crescent and Townsend Street unique in this respect. At 1791–1821 Beacon Street in Brookline, from Dean Road to Clinton Path, a block of fifteen red-brick connected houses (Figure 96) was built in 1907 by Murdock Boyle, a Dorchester designer who worked also in the Back Bay. But these connected houses facing the Beacon Street parkway give way to detached houses if one follows either Dean Road or Clinton Path (both of which, like Cushing Avenue, have no parks) away from Beacon Street. In fact, when we have at last integrated the history of the streetcar suburbs into the larger history of the expanding Victorian city, it will surely emerge that where the city grew by annexation, the significance of streets like Townsend Street and Cushing Avenue lies in the fact that developers were able in the much enlarged late nineteenth-century city to reverse the trend established in the small, early nineteenth-century city when large, densely massed but detached town houses on ample lots were abandoned in favor of narrow lots and attached houses.

Two streets, of course, make a small case study. But it seems clear that neither Cushing Avenue nor Townsend Street was eccentric in its design concept. The same principle is evident along all upper middle-class Dorchester streets. The lavishly detailed Queen Anne house with its unusual stained-glass arched window at 35 Melville (Figure 97) on the corner of Allston was designed in 1882 by the then city architect of Boston, Arthur H. Vinal, as his own home. As grand a house as Upham's or Chadwick's on Cushing Avenue, it is similarly sited, a few feet from the sidewalk. So too are the neighboring houses that Vinal also built, ap-

98

97

Representative upper middle-class streetcar-suburb town houses.
FIGURE 97. Arthur H. Vinal. Vinal House, 35 Melville Avenue,
Dorchester, 1882.
FIGURE 98. Samuel J. Brown. Mitchell House, Walnut Street
between Highland Avenue and Austin Street, Newton, ca. 1885.
FIGURE 99. Wright House, Pearl Street, East Somerville, ca.
1890.
FIGURE 100. 369 Harvard Street, Cambridge, 1877.

99

100

parently to stimulate development and control it carefully by establishing the street's character. These houses, 29, 35, 37, and 39 (this last an attribution) together with 33, designed by L. Underwood in 1886, constitute one of the most sumptuous ensembles in the city of late nineteenth-century streetcar-suburb architecture. Diagonally across the street from Vinal's house, at 96 Lyndhurst Street, is another large house (designed in 1896 by A. B. Pinkham), the interiors of which are among the most lavish and unusual in the city.

The same design concept is also evident along Carruth, Alban, and Ocean streets at Ashmont. The most famous house in this area, a great mansarded mansion on Welles Avenue, purchased by Mayor John F. Fitzgerald after his rise to prosperity, has been torn down. But for our purposes 61 Alban Street is more significant, for here again one finds the house of another well-known architect, Harrison Atwood, who was at one time city architect of Boston. Atwood's house, which he built for himself in 1881, possesses a splendid interior and is also sited close to the sidewalk and to neighboring houses, some of which Atwood also built himself. On nearby Beaumont and Carruth streets (Figure 74), two of the grandest residential streets in the city, the same design concept is again evident in the parade of fine mansions by such architects as W. Whitney Lewis, Longfellow, Alden and Harlow, Willard M. Bacon, and Edwin J. Lewis, Jr.

Study the streetscapes illustrated in Figures 89, 90, 92, 95, 97, 99, or 106. Notice the regular alignment of these houses, each to each other and to the street; notice their similarity of size, scale, and finish; observe that their garden setting — for reasons we have already touched on — yields no quality of cottage or lane. Instead there is a public, formal aspect. These are front-facing, densely massed, regularly aligned,

similarly designed and scaled town houses — built by a generation determined to breathe again, in a more livable residential city where they would be delivered from the tyranny of the windowless wall and the narrow row house. And no doubt because clapboards and shingles can be painted varying colors, thus offering whatever scope for individuality was wanted, one sees on such streets not only a generally uniform setback but a relentless uniformity of cornice line maintained through all the stylistic changes of the period far more rigorously than in the Back Bay.

This design concept spread rapidly, as any circuit of Boston's suburbs will show. Not only Newton (Figure 98) but Melrose and Watertown possess many areas of this sort that have yet to be documented. Cambridge abounds in such streets, notably Harvard Street (Figure 100). Two eighty-four is a splendid detached town house designed in 1887 by Hartwell and Richardson; so also are 280, designed in 1886 by C. J. Williams, and 298, designed in 1888 by John Hasty. Farther up the street is a large Colonial Revival house at 340 that was designed in 1897 by Arthur Vinal. Like Vinal, Hasty worked also in Dorchester, where he designed 30 Pleasant Street in 1897, though perhaps his best house of this type that is known is 20 Highland Avenue in Cambridge. Other fine examples of this house type may be noted on Pearl Street in Somerville (Figure 99), and in Jamaica Plain (Figures 82, 101).

So persuasive did this design concept become that even where houses faced parks in the streetcar suburbs such houses were increasingly not attached (as at Harris Wood Crescent) but freestanding. Notable examples are Emerson Garden in Brookline, and Wellesley Park (Figure 102), Mount Bowdoin, and Sunset Circle in Dorchester, but whole streets were sometimes also laid out on this principle. One of these is on Avon

Boston's streetcar suburbs were as often called "garden suburbs."
FIGURE 101. Jamaica Pond neighborhood of Jamaica Plain, typical of
upper middle-class suburban subdivisions of the late nineteenth and
early twentieth centuries. Notice the relationship between the garden
lots of such detached town-house streets and the nearby park, one of
many of Olmsted's Boston Park System, which by 1900 extended from the
Back Bay through Jamaica Plain, West Roxbury, Roxbury, and Dorchester
to Dorchester Bay.
FIGURE 102. An even stronger relationship between the park system and
streetcar-suburb subdivisions is evident in such enclaves as Wellesley
Park in Dorchester, 1885–1900, one of a number of ensembles of detached
houses built around small private parks of the sort favored by Bulfinch
and found in the 1840s and 1850s on Beacon Hill (Figure 21) and in the
South End. So great was the extent of land in the streetcar suburbs
that while attached housing was often built facing such parks (see
Figures 94, 96), detached housing was increasingly preferred whether
or not the houses were massed around a park. Another residential park
is shown in Figure 105.

FIGURE 103. Samuel J. Brown. Fottler House, 389 Washington Street, Dorchester, 1900. A splendid example of the upper middle-class streetcar-suburb detached town house. For other work by Brown, see Figures 98 and 104.

Hill in Cambridge, where on Walnut Street, despite the fact that there is an ample fifty-foot setback on a parkway seventy feet wide, the houses are not attached but free-standing.

The extent to which the design concept of huge town houses, massed closely to one another and to the street, was carried is evident in the Fottler House of 1900 in Dorchester (Figure 103), located on the crest of Washington Street, overlooking the city and the harbor. It would be absurd in the face of its pretentiousness to believe its owner could not have afforded more land. Nor, in view of its proximity to the sidewalk, can one conclude this mansion was a country house. In fact, like most Bostonians of this class — including Mayor John Fitzgerald, who summered in Hull — Fottler possessed a summer residence, in Harwich Port. In both its design and siting, his Dorchester residence is unmistakably a detached town house.

Throughout this discussion of the streetcar suburbs I have stressed upper middle-class houses for a number of reasons. Warner pointed out that of "the richest 1 percent of the population" of Boston,

the richest among them sometimes purchased an expensive town house in the Back Bay, sometimes built estates in the country, sometimes even owned both. Many, however, took advantage of their greater control over hours of work and the fashion for suburban life to build big houses on the best streets and finest prospects of suburban Boston. Such houses appeared both at great distance from Boston where railroad transportation had to be relied upon, and closer to town in the old high-priced pockets of land where former estates had been cut up into large and expensive parcels. Sections of Jamaica Plain and Roxbury highlands throughout the last third of the nineteenth century enjoyed a steady building up of such enclaves. Dorchester and most suburban communities came to contain at least a few streets and houses of Boston's wealthy.

He also noted that "in the 1840's and 1850's when relatively small numbers of middle class families had moved to the suburbs they had done so out of a clear preference for a rural setting," but after 1870 "the new commuter's choice of the rural ideal was a less clear one . . . he desired an architecture which would provide some of the effect of the row house facade — the public presentation of an impression of wealth and social standing." Warner cited Townsend Street as an example. But in an overall, general, nonarchitectural study such as his, streets like this naturally were touched on very briefly. In an architectural history, their importance is obviously much greater.

In the first place, it was naturally the upper middle class who could afford to build the most interesting houses in every style during this period. Many such houses are cited throughout this book. The craftsmanship of Parshley's house at 17–19 Cushing Avenue (Figure 117) for example, was not uncommon; nor was that of 102 Ocean Street at Ashmont (Figure 104), designed by Samuel J. Brown. Such examples might be multiplied all over the streetcar suburbs. Particularly interesting are the lavish interiors of 16 Sacramento Street in Cambridge (1883), probably the work of Ware and Van Brunt, and of 70 Salem Street in Malden (Plate 4). The fact that the Cambridge house was the residence of the president of the Shaw Furniture Company and the Malden house the home of the owner of A. H. Davenport Company and that the ornament of both houses was done by those famous woodworking firms (just as Parshley's firm detailed his house) is significant: because many of Boston's leading designers and craftsmen lived in the streetcar suburbs, one

FIGURE 104. Samuel J. Brown. 102 Ocean Street, Ashmont, 1899. Detail of the stairwell, an example of the lavish interior detail typical of the better streetcar-suburb house.

105

Central middle-class streetscapes in the streetcar suburbs reflected the fashions set by upper middle-class streetscapes.
FIGURE 105. Oakview Terrace, Jamaica Plain.
FIGURE 106. Hampshire Street, Everett.

106

finds there a great deal of their best work. But I have stressed upper middle-class houses chiefly because the wealthy were free to do what they wished in terms of housing as the middle and lower classes were not. When one discovers that the "Lead King of Boston" built his 1895 mansion, not set back in the center of his several lots, but close by the sidewalk, on only one lot; that he then sold another lot to his partner for another and similar house; and that Parshley and Vinal and Atwood did the same thing; one wonders if the middle class in the streetcar suburbs and even to some extent the lower middle class were following a fashion established by the upper middle class in their densely massed houses, rather than only succumbing to a necessity.

Middle-class residential architecture was naturally less expensive and more apt to be designed by speculator builders. One block from Cushing Avenue, for example, William Wight built up a new street, Mount Cushing Terrace, in 1914, with a number of small two-family houses that cost about $4,000 each, or less than half the price of the big Cushing Avenue houses of fifteen to twenty years earlier. Nor does the slightly varying exterior decor of these two-families obscure the fact that each is the mate of the other. Close by a prestigious street like Cushing Avenue, a good class of buyers was to be expected, however; and throughout the streetcar suburbs, middle-class developers naturally sought proximity to upper middle-class areas. Just as the Back Bay speculator sought to emulate the design concept of the fashionable Back Bay connected town house, so the streetcar-suburb speculator sought to emulate the more fashionable houses of the streetcar suburbs. The houses of Mount Cushing Terrace, so poor in land and so densely massed as to seem a cruel joke played on the working class by a greedy speculator, seem actu-

ally to have been a reflection of streets like Cushing Avenue.

Perhaps the best example is Oakview Terrace in Jamaica Plain (Figure 105). The fact that the first house built there, 28 (1892), was designed by Longfellow, Alden and Harlow, may indicate an initial attempt at an upper middle-class street. But in the event, Oakview Terrace, as built up in the 1890s, was decisively middle class. As opposed to the houses of the 1890s on Cushing Avenue, which had cost an average of $10,500 each, the nineteen houses built in the same years on Oakview Terrace cost with one exception between $5500 and $6500. Yet Oakview Terrace, which not only emulates upper middle-class density but rises to a small, circular, parklike cul-de-sac, is utterly charming. A tree-shaded and altogether delightful street, it illustrates superbly how at half the cost the middle class could enjoy the amenities of the detached town house. This meant much more for the middle class, whose only alternative to streets like Oakview Terrace was South Boston or East Boston or Charlestown (and not on their lovely hilltops) or marginally respectable and declining lodging-house areas like the South End. And behind those areas there were only the close-packed tenements of the slum districts. (Some idea of what these were like is evident in Mayor Andrew Peters's report in 1918 that while the density of population in Jamaica Plain and West Roxbury was 2500 per square mile, in the North End the figure was 125,000.)

How fundamentally we have misunderstood the streetcar suburbs is clear if one studies for a moment Beals Street in Brookline, where the house at 83 may not at first impress. But this was the first home of Joseph and Rose Kennedy after their marriage, where President John F. Kennedy was born. It is, of course, a modest house, suitable for a young couple starting out, and not at all the equal of Mayor Fitzgerald's Ashmont mansion. But Joseph Kennedy was a rising banker, his wife the daughter of Boston's mayor, and their choice indicates the regard in which such small, middle-class, streetcar-suburb houses were held.

THE design concept of the streetcar suburbs could contract (usually on the middle-class level; Figure 106) but it could also expand, especially at the upper and upper middle-class level. On Melville Avenue in Dorchester, while Arthur H. Vinal was establishing the densely massed streetscapes we have been discussing, several other architects at the other end of the street were developing a more spacious variant with more generous setbacks and circular drives leading under porte cocheres to large barns. Established in 1879 by E. A. Poe Newcomb in his design of 6 Melville, this more ample design concept was firmly established in 1880 by Cabot and Chandler in their design for 1 Melville Avenue (Figure 69). The same firm built another house of this type at 3 Melville in 1881; George Meacham had designed 10 Melville across the street along similar lines in 1880; and Cummings and Sears followed suit at 5 Melville in 1884. As the class level was demonstrably the same at both ends of the avenue, it is not at all clear what to make of this more generous concept. Stables, a sure sign of wealth in one sense, were also odorous and it was no doubt for that reason that they were sometimes prohibited on upper middle-class streets. It was only about 1910, when automobiles came into use among the upper classes, that, where there was room, the successor to the carriage house, the "automobile house" (with chauffeur's quarters), appeared on Cushing Avenue and Townsend Street. Previously, horses and carriages were kept at nearby commercial stables, as on Bea-

con Hill and in the Back Bay. It is thus unclear whether stables on Melville Avenue necessitated the larger lots or were simply a repercussion of them. And it is also unclear what either the larger lots or the stables may mean otherwise.

This more spacious concept is naturally only found in upper-class and upper middle-class areas, but even in those areas it is usually the exception rather than the rule. Two houses designed by Julius Schweinfurth illustrate the lack of any correlation, for example, between the size of a house and its setback. A very large house of his design for James Hathaway in Brighton, built in 1898, is set back in spacious grounds. Yet his Frederick Coffin House of years later in Brookline, though as large as the Brighton house, is set close by the street, on the sort of terrace we saw on Cushing Avenue and on Melville Avenue. And just as really large houses of "estate quality" were sited right on the sidewalk, small houses might have enormous setbacks. The key, perhaps, is to be found in this evocation of Newton from an 1888 Boston guidebook, which also illustrates the enthusiasm the newly emerging suburbs aroused.

Newton, the most favored and delightful among the many attractive suburbs of Boston, is distinctly a city of beautiful homes. It has been appropriately designated the "City of Villas." . . . Newton is noted for its magnificent country seats and luxurious dwellings, its superb drives, exquisite scenery and elegant surroundings, its beautiful lawns, gardens and conservatories, and is the home of many of the foremost and wealthiest of Boston's merchants, manufacturers, scientists, artists, literary and professional men, who after the hours of active pursuits, retire hither to their palatial residences to enjoy the health imparting air amid the luxuriant surroundings of fruit, flowers and foilage. This is, in short, an ideal American community, and represents the highest development of New England civilization — the very apex of our social structure, so-to-speak.

"City of Villas," of course, refers to the

Two Newton houses, ca. 1890–1900,
showing the variety in design concept
and particularly in setback of upper
middle-class streetcar-suburb housing.
FIGURE 107. Haskell House, 888 Beacon
Street, ca. 1890.
FIGURE 108. Julius Schweinfurth. Dennison House, Newtonville, 1900.

108

FIGURE 109. Alexander W. Longfellow,
Jr. 115 Brattle Street, 1887. Designed by
Henry Wadsworth Longfellow's
nephew for the poet's daughter, this
house is but one house removed from
its famous progenitor, the Vassall-
Longfellow House of 1759, and the
newer house represents a much more
profound Colonial Revival than many
suspect. Few realize that more of Brattle Street is Colonial Revival than Colonial.

densely massed house type: "villas" was also the term used by the *Rand McNally Guide to Boston* to describe the houses of Jones Hill, though like so many favored terms of those days it is not very appropriate. We are also told that Newton possessed "magnificent country seats" — to which, however, commuters returned every night — which means they were not in the usual sense of the terms country houses as opposed to town houses. What it may mean is that these quite large houses on many acres were fall and spring houses. Many wealthy Bostonians of this period maintained three houses: Colonel Oliver Peabody, for example, possessed a town house on Commonwealth Avenue, a country estate in Maine, and a third house on Adams Street in Milton that was used in the spring and fall but was regularly described in Bacon's *Boston: A Guide Book* as "the fine country seat of the late Oliver W. Peabody." Many of the more generously sited houses of this period in the inner suburbs may have been of this type. On the other hand, others may represent an attempt to combine in one house both a winter town house and a country summer house, an option the suburbs allowed.

Several Newton and Brookline houses are of interest in this connection. One was built by Edward H. Haskell, the president of the Haskell-Dawes Machine Company in Boston. Haskell, who was president of the New England Baptist Hospital, a director of the First National Bank of Boston, and the donor of a number of buildings to several colleges, appears to have been close to being a millionaire. Like Chadwick, however, he built his house at 888 Beacon Street in Newton (Figure 107) scarcely a few yards from the sidewalk. Charles S. Dennison, on the other hand, who owned the Dennison Manufacturing Company of Boston (with offices all over the country and in England), chose a more spacious de-sign concept for his Newton house, designed by Julius Schweinfurth in 1900 (Figure 108). Robert Peabody, the architect, essayed a similar spaciousness when he built his house of 1876 at 50 Edgehill Road on "Pill Hill" in Brookline. Set in nearly two acres, it scarcely sounds like a town house. Yet that was its function. When Peabody moved to another house of his design in the Back Bay in 1901, he sold the Brookline house but he did not sell his summer home at Peach's Point in Marblehead. Clearly, all one can conclude is that tastes differed, so much so that palatial estate mansions continued also to be built in this period in the inner suburbs. For instance, the Brandegee House at Faulkner Farm, on the Brookline–Jamaica Plain line, designed by Little and Browne in 1895–1899, contains seventy-two rooms and is set in a terraced Italian garden, one of the first works of Charles S. Platt.

This wide diversity of design concept in the inner suburbs is all the harder to define because, according to how subdivisions were landscaped and how the houses were sited, houses on one street can seem more estatelike or rural than houses on another street, even though the lot sizes are similar. Where the streets are curvilinear, the siting of houses informal and irregular, and the planting so disposed as to emphasize these features, there is naturally a more informal and even rural quality. Style is also important in this respect, as one can see on Brattle Street in Cambridge.

That Brattle Street should figure in this discussion of the Victorian detached town house will doubtless surprise many people. But just as we mistake the character of early nineteenth-century Beacon Street and late nineteenth-century Cushing Avenue, so also do we mistake the character of Brattle Street, which is actually more Victorian than Colonial. In fact, between Brattle Square and Elmwood Avenue there are only six pre-

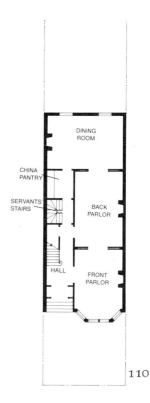

110

Representative attached and detached upper and upper middle-class town-house plans and lots, 1880–1920.

FIGURE 110. Plan of an attached house, 25 feet wide, in the Back Bay, where, Bunting notes, the great majority of houses were 25 or 26 feet wide. Note that in all but corner houses, light entered from only two sides and in the case of this typical plan, one reception room was without any windows whatsoever.

FIGURE 111. Plan of a detached house, 20 Cushing Avenue, Dorchester. In *Streetcar Suburbs*, Warner estimated that the ca. 1850 South End house covered 50 percent of a 2000–3000-square-foot lot; and that the expensive Back Bay house of the 1860s to 1890s used two-thirds of a 2300–2600-square-foot lot. By contrast, even a moderately priced middle-class streetcar-suburb single covered only 20 to 30 percent of a 4500–6000-square-foot lot. At the lower and lower middle-class levels, cheap intown row houses and tenements of the pre-streetcar era covered 80 to 90 percent of 600–1400-square-foot lots, while even cheap two-families and three-deckers in the streetcar suburbs used only 50 percent of 2400–2700-square-foot lots.

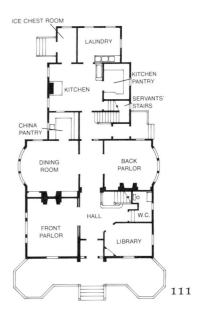

111

0 5 10 15 20 feet

Revolutionary houses; and only eleven more were built between the Revolution and 1854. Thirty-three houses along this magnificent street were built in the last quarter of the nineteenth century and the first years of the twentieth. The pre-Revolutionary houses, however, are in a sense as important to our discussion as the late nineteenth-century houses, for even before the Revolution Brattle Street was close enough to Boston to have emerged as perhaps the first example of the attempt to combine the pleasures of both town and country. Bainbridge Bunting and Robert H. Nylander have described Brattle Street in the late eighteenth and early nineteenth centuries:

One cannot write categorically, but for most of these families their Cambridge estate seems to have been a principal residence. Men like East Apthorp and David Phips appear to have lived here the year around. William Brattle, John Vassall, and Richard Lechmere owned houses in Boston, but the locations suggest that these were rental properties. Only John Vassall seems to have owned what might be called a proper town house (the former Faneuil House), but that was not acquired until 1772.

There is thus a very good reason to conclude this discussion of the streetcar suburbs on Brattle Street.

All the disparities in design concept we have discussed are evident on and just off this famous street: Longfellow Park was laid out (by Charles Eliot) rather formally in 1883 and its houses built up in a fairly regular alignment; Hubbard Park nearby, on the other hand, was laid out more informally (ca. 1886), achieving a much more picturesque and irregular quality. On Brattle Street itself, some large houses are informal in design and yet massed quite close to the sidewalk, including H. H. Richardson's Shingle Style masterpiece, the Stoughton House of 1883 at 90 (Figure 81), which Hitchcock has called "the best suburban wooden house in America." Other, more formal houses, such as the Colonial Revival house of 1887 at 115 (Figure 109), possess more ample setbacks and even circular driveways. And the fact that 115, designed by Alexander W. Longfellow, Jr., a nephew of Henry Wadsworth Longfellow, for the poet's daughter, derives stylistically from the poet's own house at 105 Brattle, built in 1759, is significant: as the Queen Anne and Shingle styles gave way throughout Boston in the late 1880s to the more formal and urban-looking Colonial Revival, the town house character of these "suburban" streets emerges more clearly to us, particularly on Brattle Street, where stand a number of the eighteenth- and early nineteenth-century prototypes of the Victorian detached town house.

Despite the disparities in design concept, one sees here as throughout the streetcar suburbs, when the trees are bare, that Brattle Street discloses the fundamental factor common to all the late nineteenth- and early twentieth-century suburbs: save for a few last-of-their-kind houses in the Back Bay, a hundred years after the Tontine Crescent it is evident that Bostonians at every class level rejected utterly the connected town house block and turned back instead to some version of the eighteenth- and early nineteenth-century ideal of the garden lot and the free-standing town house.

5

FRENCH FLATS AND THREE-DECKERS

N THE LATE NINETEENTH CENTURY Bostonians not only set their architects the task of reviving the free-standing town house; at the same time they required of them a violently contradictory achievement. Thus the architects who dutifully pulled the connected town house block apart into separate houses on garden lots in Newton and Dorchester were at the same time in the heart of the city more and more often expected not only to put the block back together again, but then to stand it up in the air, as it were; eight, nine, and ten stories high, and climbing every year a little higher, the apartment house was as far from the free-standing garden house as one could get. While there was for the latter a deep-seated, almost venerable precedent, there was scarcely any precedent at all in the United States for the apartment house when the first such building, the Hotel Pelham (Figure 112), appeared in Boston in 1857, on the corner of Boylston and Tremont streets. (It should be noted that most of the early apartment houses were called Hotel this or that, but such "apartment hotels" were quite distinct from commercial hotels catering primarily to transients. Though several commercial hotels encouraged permanent residents, apartment hotels did not seek transient guests, although they were popularly described as the habitats of the "newly wed and the nearly dead.")

Although Calvert Vaux had argued in an address in New York to the American Institute of Architects, in the year the Pelham opened, for the introduction of flats into this country, there seems no way at all to explain why Boston should have been endowed with America's first apartment house except by reference to the French influence we discussed in Chapter 2. That it *was* the first of its kind in any American city (except perhaps for New Orleans) seems clear, for the apartment house did not appear in New York City — where it would achieve its Victorian apotheosis in such buildings as the Dakota and the Ansonia — until 1869. Nor is it surprising, given the radical nature of the idea the Pelham heralded, multifamily occupancy, that it seems (with one possible but undocumented exception) to have been the only apartment house in Boston until the late 1860s; the first New York apartment house, R. M. Hunt's Stuyvesant Flats, was also unimitated for a decade. It is significant as well that one of the first four apartment houses built in Boston after the Pelham, Cummings and Sears's Hotel Boylston of 1870 (see Figure 51) was erected opposite the Pelham. The three that followed, however, were all in the Back Bay: Ware and Van Brunt's Hotel Hamilton at 260 Clarendon Street and the Hotel Kempton at 237 Berkeley, both built in 1869, and Weston and Rand's Hotel Agassiz of 1872 at 191 Commonwealth Avenue. Interestingly, the Hotel Vendome (Figure 49) on Commonwealth Avenue, a commercial, transient hotel that nonetheless catered to

FIGURE 112. Possibly by Arthur Gilman. Hotel Pelham, Boylston Street at the corner of Tremont Street, 1857. The Pelham, since demolished, was probably the first apartment house built in the United States.

FIGURE 113. Hotel Oxford, Huntington Avenue, Back Bay, ca. 1885.

113

permanent tenants, appeared about the same time, in 1871.

Thereafter, a great number of apartment houses appeared in Copley Square itself — notably J. Pickering Putnam's Hotel Cluny (1876), Levi Newcomb's Hotel Bristol (1879), the Copley (1882), and the Hotel Westminster, designed by Henry C. Cregier of Chicago in 1897. Throughout the 1890s the Copley Square concentration tended to spread toward Massachusetts Avenue up Huntington Avenue, where were built the Hotel Oxford (Figure 113) and the Hotel Ilkley (1890). All these have been torn down, but during the same period the residential Back Bay spawned twenty-three similar apartment houses, nearly all of which have survived, including the Aubry by William G. Preston at 149 Newbury in 1883, the Imperial at 308 Commonwealth Avenue in 1889, and the Royal, the first apartment house on Back Bay Beacon Street (at 295) in 1885, both designed by Samuel D. Kelly. The new fashion was also felt on Beacon Hill, where in 1885–1887 the Tudor, an immense apartment house designed by S. J. F. Thayer, was built on the corner of Beacon and Joy streets, and it was felt too

in the streetcar suburbs, where the earliest important apartment house of this period appears to have been the Warren, designed by Carl Fehmer (1884), in Roxbury Highlands. In the 1890s, these clusters of hotels throughout the city increased dramatically. But the supremacy of the Back Bay was reinforced by the erection of such deluxe apartment houses as the Marlborough by Willard T. Sears at 416 Marlborough Street in 1895; two apartment houses designed by McKay and Dunham, the Hotel Lafayette of 1895 at 333 Commonwealth Avenue, and the Tuileries of 1896 at 270 Commonwealth Avenue; and the huge Hotel Cambridge, designed by Willard Sears in 1898, at 483 Beacon Street on the corner of Massachusetts Avenue.

The evident movement toward Massachusetts Avenue flowered into another cluster at Charlesgate, in the mid-1890s — where the Hotel Charlesgate, designed by J. Pickering Putnam, opened in 1891, closely followed by the Colonial at 382 Commonwealth (1895) and the Torrington (1896–1899) at 384–388 Commonwealth (both designed by Arthur H. Vinal), and in 1897 by the large Hotel Somerset, a commercial and mainly transient hotel by Arthur Bowditch that catered to permanent residents. It was from Charlesgate that the apartment house spread into the Fenway and along Audubon Road through Audubon Circle to its principal suburban flowering on Beacon Street in Brookline. At the same time these fashionable clusters naturally precipitated a legion of middle-class apartment hotels. The *Boston Street Directory*, which first set off such hotels from the primarily transient type in 1878, listed 108 in that year. By 1890 more than five hundred were listed throughout the city, the chief middle-class hotels for the most part having been erected on Columbus Avenue in the part of the South End closest to the Back Bay. There one such, the Hotel Albemarle, designed in 1876, still stands in fairly good exterior condition on the corner of Columbus and Clarendon streets. It is not difficult, however, to differentiate the fashionable hotels, and a survey of the Boston Social Registers between 1890 and 1920 (in which years the number of apartment dwellers more than doubled) documents the important role Boston society played in the rise of the apartment house.

Although in the 1890s and later there grew up along the "Gold Coast" on Mount Auburn Street near Harvard Square a dozen or more fashionable apartment houses for young men of wealth at Harvard, most Social Register apartment dwellers in 1890 lived in or around Copley Square, particularly in the Victoria and the Brunswick, both commercial hotels, and in the Ludlow, the Cluny, and the Bristol, which were strictly apartment hotels. In the residential Back Bay the most fashionable place of residence was also a commercial hotel, the Vendome, though the Agassiz was very popular, as was the Oxford on Huntington Avenue. By 1919, however, much had changed. The Back Bay remained preeminent, but a perceptible

shift is evident: the Huntington Avenue apartment houses had declined by 1920 in social standing, and Charlesgate had emerged as the most prestigious address. Not only the Charlesgate itself, but the Colonial, the Torrington, and the Hotel Somerset possessed by far the most Back Bay Social Register tenants, while society generally was clearly following the march of the apartment house up Beacon Street into Brookline, where the most fashionable concentration was between Carleton and Powell streets (mostly at Richmond Court Apartments and the Wolloton) and between Summit Avenue and Lancaster Terrace (in the Stoneholm, the Colchester, and Brandon Hall). By 1920, the middle-class apartment house concentration had also shifted, from the South End to the Fenway.

The lead Boston society took with respect to the apartment house is even clearer when one notes that among the earliest tenants of the Hotel Hamilton, one of the first apartment houses erected, were Major and Mrs. Henry Lee Higginson. The head of Boston's leading banking house and the founder of the Boston Symphony Orchestra, Higginson lived there only four years. But when he moved in 1874 it was in order to occupy a suite in his own apartment hotel, the Hotel Agassiz, which he built on Commonwealth Avenue in 1872. Like so many Back Bay residents, Major Higginson moved at various times of the year: the summer found him at his home in Manchester-by-the-Sea, the fall at Rock Harbor on Lake Champlain, and the winter in his Back Bay apartment. Similarly, the new building type early attracted distinguished architects: not only Thayer, Preston, Fehmer, and Ware and Van Brunt, whose work has already been noted, but Clarence H. Blackall, who designed the Dana Chambers on Dunster Street and Oxford Court, both in Cambridge; McKim, Mead and White, the ar-

chitects of the fashionable block of bachelor flats at the corner of Charles and
Beacon streets; and both Cram and
Richardson, whose work of this kind we
shall discuss shortly. Architectural quality not unnaturally followed social quality. But I have stressed the high social
standing of the first apartment houses in
Boston for another reason. It is crucial to
understand that apartment living was
very much still another new *fashion* in
the late nineteenth century for the upper
classes, and as we have seen it is usually
a mistake to look at residential architecture generally without noting what effect
fashion as well as necessity may have
had. In this case, as with the streetcar-
suburb house type, the matter is crucial,
for the miles upon miles of new middle-
class apartment houses that marched out
of Boston in every direction after 1900,
up Commonwealth Avenue into Brighton, for example, dramatically changed
the city's scale and overall appearance.

S OMETHING of the design concept of
the city's first apartment houses as
understood during this period can be
gleaned from the 1885 edition of *King's
Handbook of Boston.*

The "French flat," or Continental system of
dwellings, sometimes called "family hotels," — a single tenement occupying the
whole or part of a floor, instead of several
floors in a house, — gained its foothold in
America by its introduction in Boston. Before
the annexation of the surrounding districts,
Boston is said to have been the most densely
populated city in America; and there was a
natural demand for economy in space. The
first building of the "French flats," or "family
hotel," class was the Hotel Pelham, at the
corner of Tremont and Boylston Streets, built
by Dr. John H. Dix about twenty years ago.
. . . This style of dwelling rapidly increased
in popularity, and now their number is so
great that it is hardly practicable to mention
them here. They range from the most palatial
and elegant structures, equally beautiful in
exterior and interior decorations, to plain and
comfortable houses adapted for people of
moderate means.

Rather unconvincing with respect to
origins — it was not until *after* the annexation of the surrounding districts that
the apartment house developed in Boston beyond just the one example of the
Pelham — this paragraph nonetheless
conveys much of the sense in which the
apartment house was early understood
in Boston, where the terms "French flat"
and "family hotel" were used throughout the late nineteenth century along
with "apartment hotel" to distinguish
apartment houses from commercial hotels. The crucial sentence, however, is
the first — "a single tenement occupying
the whole, or part of a floor, instead of
several floors in a house" — for the comparison of the individual "tenement" or
"apartment" or "suite" with the several
floors of the town house is the key to understanding this revolutionary new
building type. Unlike so many even
quite costly apartments today, the
upper-class apartment in this period attempted to *duplicate* the three- or four-
story single-family town house in most
respects and to *surpass* it in one respect:
the greater amplitude of the reception
area, which on one floor without a staircase could be contiguous and spacious
in a way impossible in the usual connected house of two or at most three or
four rooms on each floor. At the Cluny,
for example, the second floor suite (Figure 114) offered a reception area of five
contiguous rooms, four of them (reception room, parlor, library, and dining
room) off a central hall with coatroom
and water closet — and a fifth (a smoking room) off the dining room. There
were also seven bedrooms and two full
bathrooms with kitchen and service
areas. All this and fifteen closets on one
floor! Not all apartments were this large:
the Marlborough's suites were seven
rooms and bath; but five rooms and bath

Two Back Bay apartment houses by J. Pickering Putnam, one of the leading apartment house designers in late nineteenth-century Boston.
FIGURE 114. Hotel Cluny, Copley Square, 1876. Plan of second-floor suite. Demolished.
FIGURE 115. Haddon Hall, Commonwealth Avenue at Berkeley Street, 1894.

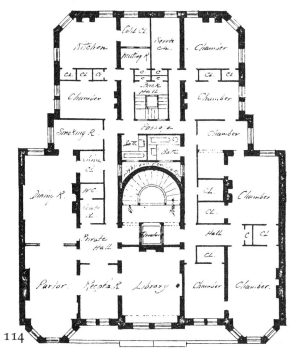

114

115

were the absolute minimum at the upper middle-class level. Indeed, how spacious such apartments typically were is evident in a 1923 request for a change of occupancy at the Hotel Gladstone in Dorchester (designed by J. H. Besarick in 1887): "put in new partitions in apartment on 6th floor so as to divide apartment into *three* small apartments" (my italics).

Such buildings also offered before they were common a host of luxuries: in 1895 the Marlborough, for example, advertised electricity in all rooms, twenty-four-hour telephone service, and all-night elevators. A great many possessed elegant dining rooms: *King's Handbook* noted, for example, that though the Oxford was mainly an apartment hotel it possessed a "first class restaurant." Others offered private kitchens, and *Ba-*

con's Dictionary of Boston noted that in many such buildings "the kitchens [of all suites] are clustered at the top of the [apartment] house," thus dealing with cooking odors. A report of 1917 at the Building Department documents the fact that at 187–189 Huntington Avenue, a small apartment hotel designed by A. H. Vinal in 1895, there were "janitor's and maid's rooms in basement," a practice followed at Richmond Court. Services also varied. In the bachelor flats at 66 Beacon, designed by McKim, breakfast was served in one's apartment, but lunch and dinner were presumed to be at one's club. Even middle-class apartment blocks in the South End, like the Hotel Albemarle (1876), at the corner of Columbus Avenue and Clarendon Street, possessed full bathrooms in each of their many suites, a luxury in the 1870s

105

even at the upper-class level. Such technological improvements, including central heating, were a key factor in the development of the apartment house. So also were elevators. Documentation is naturally spotty, but Bunting notes that there was an elevator at the Hotel Hamilton in 1869 and two at the Agassiz in 1872, and in 1886 *Bacon's Dictionary of Boston* noted that even "many of the less pretentious [apartment houses] have passenger elevators."

If one looks at Haddon Hall (Figure 115), a luxurious apartment building on the corner of Commonwealth Avenue and Berkeley Street designed in 1894 by J. Pickering Putnam, the need for an elevator is apparent. But the great height of most early apartment houses (which derived, of course, from the profit motive as well as from the increasing demand for suites) was a problem more easily solved on the inside than on the outside, where such buildings seriously marred the established scale of town house streetscapes (see Figure 158). Thus, although the individual apartment on any floor early achieved social parity with the town house, to which it was comparable and in some respects superior, the apartment building as a whole (in terms of its exterior appearance) was not widely welcomed. Ironically, if only the French flat fashion had caught on in Boston twenty years earlier, Commonwealth Avenue might have been a Parisian boulevard indeed; but by the time apartments were fashionable the low four-story town house had established a scale unsuitable to blocks of flats. On commercial thoroughfares there was no problem, which is no doubt why so many such apartment blocks were erected in Copley Square and on Huntington Avenue between Copley Square and the splendid new civic center — rivaling Copley Square in many ways — that emerged at the intersection of Huntington and Massachusetts avenues with the erection between 1900 and 1910 of Symphony Hall, Horticultural Hall, the St. James Theatre, the Mother Church, and the New England Conservatory of Music. In fact, apartment houses in Copley Square and on Huntington Avenue often had stores on the first floor, creating a distinctly cosmopolitan and even Parisian ambience compared with the rather staid appearance of Commonwealth Avenue. The same design concept (now being revived and sometimes thought to be quite radical) was often followed in nineteenth-century apartment blocks: the quite handsome apartment house John Hasty designed (1888) that still stands next to the Cambridge City Hall on Massachusetts Avenue provided one entrance to the first-floor shops and another to the apartments above. So had the Pelham, in 1857. But Commonwealth Avenue was not a commercial thoroughfare, and although Haddon Hall duplicated the side-hall-and-bay-window town house plan, it piled up this plan ten stories high. Nor were double-bayed apartment houses like the Imperial much more attractive, though they could be less high. They were scathingly called the "dumbbell" type.

An even more difficult problem confronted the apartment house designer in the streetcar suburbs, where on only a few main streets (Massachusetts Avenue in Cambridge, for instance, or Columbia Road in Dorchester) could the tall apartment block possibly be used. Yet so popular did this "horizontal" rather than "vertical" life-style become that by the 1890s there was a demand for it on the residential single-family streets of upper middle-class areas in the streetcar suburbs. Thus the ingenuity of the Victorian architect was taxed still further: obviously there were families of some means who preferred apartments to houses and renting to owning; but many of these families wished to enjoy these benefits not in huge intown apartment

117

116

French flats in the streetcar suburbs: two apartment houses on Jones Hill in Dorchester.
FIGURE 116. Herbert Moseley. 23 Upham Avenue / 41 Cushing Avenue, 1894. Across the street from this two-suite house is the single-family designed in 1895 by Edmund Freeman for James Humphreys Upham at 40 Cushing.
FIGURE 117. Sylvester Parshley. 17–19 Cushing Avenue, 1893, surely the most splendid two-suite house in the city.

blocks but in detached houses on garden lots in the streetcar suburbs. Could a suburban apartment house be contrived where each apartment would equal the streetcar suburb's detached town house in the way the Back Bay apartment house equaled the connected town house, which meant in the streetcar suburbs no windowless walls and on the exterior (so as not to disrupt the scale and overall appearance of the streetscape) the illusion of a single house? In fact, such a house type did evolve in the 1880s and nineties in the streetcar suburbs, and so well was the illusion of a single-family house preserved that we have in fact seen the result already without noticing anything amiss: on Townsend Street in the Highlands one of the four detached houses discussed in Chapter 4 was not a single-

family house — it was an apartment house of two suites: 140–142 Townsend, the home of the president of the Bay State and Boston Gas Illuminating Company (Figure 95). Similarly, in Micah Dyer's two-block development on Cushing Avenue in Dorchester only six of the twelve houses we discussed were actually single-family houses. The rest were apartment houses of two suites!

On these two blocks it is important to note the same social parity of single-family house and apartment house we saw in the Back Bay (see Figure 116). Though the first houses on these two blocks were singles, thereafter singles and two-apartment houses were built simultaneously. In fact, Joseph Houghton Chadwick, the Boston lead magnate, built his High Georgian mansion of 1895 (Figure 91) next door to one two-apartment house and across the street from another, for Sylvester Parshley's own house of 1893 was a two-suite house (Figure 117). Actually, of Parshley's three houses in these two blocks, two were apartment houses. Typically, both the single-family that he built next to his own house and the two-apartment house he built around the corner possessed Social Register tenants: the Paines (in the single) and the Southworths (in the two-suite house). What was important in the streetcar suburbs as in the Back Bay was not renting versus owning or single house versus apartment, but the overall quality of the neighborhood and of the living unit itself; its spaciousness, interior finish, and, in the case of the apartment house above all, privacy.

One of these Cushing Avenue houses, the Loguee House of 1896, may be cited as an example of the first and unsuccessful attempt to evolve an apartment house in the streetcar suburbs that would possess the general appearance of the detached single house (Figure 118). It is, in fact, a conventional double or semidetached house of the kind built since Bulfinch's day. But though each unit was open to light and air on three as opposed to only two sides as in all but corner houses in the Back Bay, there was still the one windowless wall between the two "houses," which in the streetcar suburbs was definitely second rate. Most important, the narrow, connected town house plan of each unit imposed the old two-room reception area off a narrow railroad track hall that the detached town house (and also the French flat) was specifically designed to avoid. Significantly, this is the only conventional double in these two blocks: all the other two-suite houses are designed on a quite different basis, the principle of which will be clear if we compare the Loguee House with the two-apartment house that Parshley rented to the Southworths and both with

a multifamily Brookline apartment block designed by Charles Newhall and all three apartment houses with the Chadwick House at 20 Cushing Avenue (Figures 118–120, 111).

Chadwick's single-family house may be taken as the upper middle-class streetcar-suburb norm: there is a spacious five-room reception area — a parlor, sitting room, dining room, and library off a large central reception hall. The back of the first floor is given over to the service area, the second floor contains bedrooms, and the third floor has a billiard room and servants' quarters. As in the Back Bay apartment house, fewer bedrooms and servants' rooms were necessary in an apartment, but absolute parity in reception areas was crucial: even elderly couples would expect to entertain according to the spacious fashion of the day. Thus by dividing the two-suite house *horizontally* instead of *vertically*, not only could one get light and air on four sides, one could also evolve exactly an equivalent of French flat spaciousness. Parshley's house (Figure 119) thus possesses a five-room reception area (off which also opened two private porches) with light coming from every side; a startlingly superior plan to that of the Loguee House, Parshley's plan is comparable to the apartment house plan (Figure 120) in Brookline in spaciousness and superior insofar as light and air are concerned. However, one or two bedrooms were insufficient even for the apartment dweller, who would also require at least one bedroom for a live-in servant; and there thus arose the supreme test for the apartment house architect in the streetcar suburbs. It was easy enough for Parshley to lay out two spacious reception areas on the first and second floors for two separate apartments, creating reception areas comparable with those in either a single house or the apartment block French flat, but no building in the streetcar suburbs that

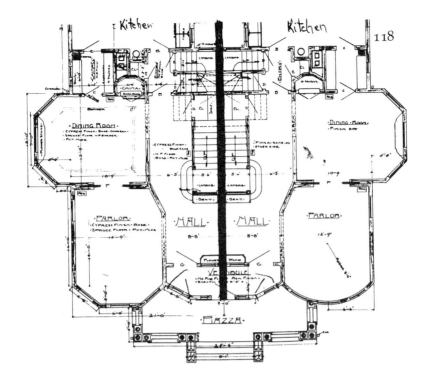

French flat apartment house plans in Boston, 1890–1910, compared with conventional detached double or duplex plans of the same period.

FIGURE 118. William Smith. First-floor plan of a conventional double house on Jones Hill, Dorchester, ca. 1895.

FIGURE 119. Sylvester Parshley. Second-floor plan of detached two-suite house on Jones Hill, Dorchester, ca. 1896.

FIGURE 120. Charles A. Newhall. Second-floor plan of part of an attached apartment house block on Beacon Street in Brookline, ca. 1910.

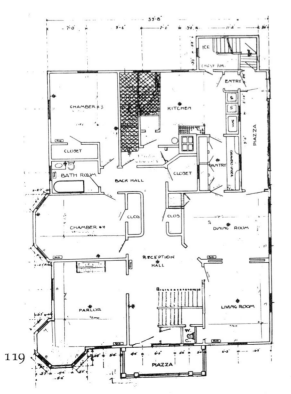

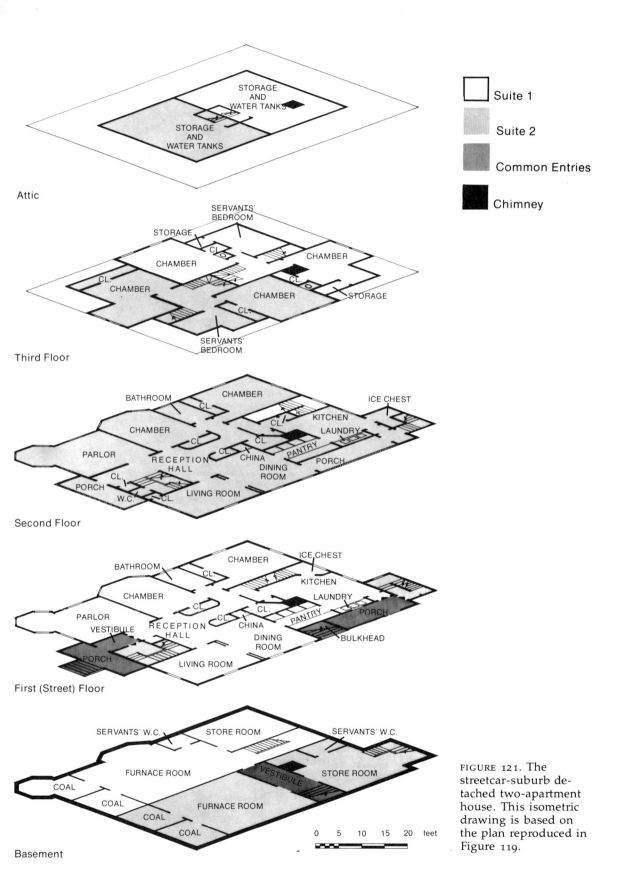

Attic

Third Floor

Second Floor

First (Street) Floor

Basement

Attic
STORAGE AND WATER TANKS
STORAGE AND WATER TANKS

Third Floor
SERVANTS' BEDROOM
STORAGE
CL.
CHAMBER
CHAMBER
CHAMBER
CL.
CL.
CHAMBER
CHAMBER
CL.
STORAGE
CL.
SERVANTS' BEDROOM

Second Floor
BATHROOM
CHAMBER
ICE CHEST
CL.
CHAMBER
CL.
KITCHEN
CL.
LAUNDRY
PARLOR
CL.
RECEPTION HALL
CL.
CHINA
PANTRY
PORCH
DINING ROOM
CL.
PORCH
W.C.
CL.
LIVING ROOM

First (Street) Floor
BATHROOM
CHAMBER
ICE CHEST
CL.
CHAMBER
KITCHEN
CL.
LAUNDRY
CL.
PORCH
PARLOR
VESTIBULE
RECEPTION HALL
CL.
CHINA
PANTRY
DINING ROOM
BULKHEAD
PORCH
LIVING ROOM

Basement
SERVANTS' W.C.
STORE ROOM
SERVANTS' W.C.
FURNACE ROOM
VESTIBULE
STORE ROOM
COAL
COAL
FURNACE ROOM
COAL
COAL

Suite 1
Suite 2
Common Entries
Chimney

0 5 10 15 20 feet

FIGURE 121. The streetcar-suburb detached two-apartment house. This isometric drawing is based on the plan reproduced in Figure 119.

preserved the appearance of a single house could manage, as did the Cluny, to accommodate four or five bedrooms as well on the reception area floor. Thus, the crucial problem: how in such a horizontally divided house could one contrive the access each apartment needed for additional bedrooms on the third floor and, indeed, for the necessary service, mechanical, and storage space each apartment required in both cellar and attic, while maintaining the absolute multifloored privacy of the conventional vertical double?

An ingenious solution was found: so ingenious it is difficult to illustrate in only two dimensions although there is no particular mystery about it (Figure 121). Each apartment had to be pierced vertically (in the way any house is pierced by chimneys, for instance, whose presence is not always obvious in plan) with several stairwells so arranged that staircases entirely private to the apartments they originated in led only to those portions of the cellar, the third floor, and the attic allotted to each apartment. But if the principle is not mysterious, its application was complex, called certainly for much ingenuity, and was also very expensive. The horizontal two-suite house required almost twice as many staircases — a costly part of construction — as the single-family, and two of everything from reception area mantlepieces to kitchens, bathrooms, and heating plants. In Parshley's house, as originally designed, one could go from the cellar to the attic in each apartment, but one could *not* go from one apartment to the other without leaving the house and ringing the front or back doorbell of the other apartment. It is also clear why the *second*-floor suite was the preferred suite in such houses, invariably the owner's if he lived on the premises. The second-floor *piano nobile* tradition enters in here; and as in any apartment house — at the Cluny, for instance — the space lost to a common hall or vestibule made the first floor somewhat less spacious. The second-floor unit was thus larger (particularly the reception hall, which gained not only a large adjoining stair hall at the expense of the first-floor unit's hall, but any space used downstairs for a common vestibule), while the first-floor entrance and service porches became on the second floor private living porches that extended the reception area significantly. The higher elevation gave also more light and air, and frequently magnificent water views in the case of hilltops. Lastly, the second-floor unit was one flight rather than two removed from each suite's "second floor" on the third floor.

Notice, however, that these advantages were unavoidable in the horizontal two-suite apartment house. And the first floor, being the first floor, possessed (traditionally) its own advantage. But if absolute parity between suites was not possible, an approximate parity *was* acceptable: an inevitable compromise that no expense could rectify. Where possible this parity was also expressed on the exterior: where two facades (in the case of a corner house) allowed separate entrance porches, outer doors, and vestibules for each apartment, such facilities were invariably provided on the front as well as at the back of the house. Indeed, two separate street numbers were used even when the same street turned the corner (as at 17–19 Cushing Avenue) to emphasize the double occupancy. Only in mid-block, where more than one entrance porch and outer door on one facade was obviously impossible if the scale of the streetscape and the appearance of a single-family were to be maintained, was one shared room permitted, as in any apartment house: a common entrance hall or vestibule. Even in mid-block, however, two numbers for one house, if it was a two-suite house, were frequently used, despite the common vestibule. That in itself was a minor compromise. It was in the matter of space of reception area and *multifloored privacy* that compromise was never possible if the horizontal two-suite house was to equal single-house living in a way the vertical double never could. By comparing the plans of another two-suite house, designed by J. Winslow Cobb in 1908 in Winthrop (though where in that town I cannot discover), with Parshley's house, and by extending the comparison to other apartment houses in both the Back Bay and in Brookline, some sense of the ingenuity required in the design of multifamily housing will be evident.

ALL the conventions and proprieties of single houses in a ceremonious and hierarchial age applied to any first-class apartment: separate bathrooms were required for servants, for example; dining rooms and kitchens had to be connected by china pantries; access to all rooms without having to go through other rooms was insisted upon. No relaxation in such standards was considered. Apartment house design was extremely complex, and many architects accordingly made it a specialty. In Boston it would seem that the chief apartment house architects between 1870 and 1900 were Samuel D. Kelly, McKay and Dunham, and J. Pickering Putnam. Putnam's practice was apparently the most extensive at the upper and upper middle-class level. Born in Boston in 1847, a graduate of Boston Latin and Harvard College, Putnam not only studied at the Royal Academy of Architecture in Berlin but was among the first Boston architects to study at the Ecole des Beaux Arts, in the late 1860s. His major Boston apartment houses include the Cluny, the Copley, Haddon Hall, and the Charlesgate, where his room layouts are brilliant, developing to

the maximum the inherent flexibility of "same floor houses" so as to allow contiguous reception areas and even whole apartments to expand or contract as required (Figure 123). One can see how flexibility of plan also appears in Parshley's plan (Figure 119): one of the four rooms opening off the central hall of the reception area opens also off the rear hall and depending upon which door is used this room can be either a fifth reception room or a bedroom. Moreover, Parshley connected four reception rooms with each other through three wide doorways, organizing spacious diagonal vistas the whole width of the house. Yet each of the four or five reception rooms is clearly differentiated, and they unfold in a highly logical and functional sequence: the stairs point one directly to the parlor, from which a long diagonal vista draws one to the dining room, from which there opens generously the "postprandial" living room or library, from which another door delivers one back to hall and staircase — without having to retrace one's steps, go through one room to gain another (except the hall, of course), or, indeed, to ask one's way at any stage. And it will be at once evident that the Putnam and Parshley apartment plans are in all these respects superior to the plan of Cobb's Winthrop house (Figure 122).

A particularly vexing problem in the apartment house plan was how to segregate decisively a contiguous reception area (adjoining a dining room and kitchen) with a contiguous bedroom area (adjoining a bathroom) without recourse to Cobb's long and narrow railroad track hall of door after door. Cram's discussion of the design of Richmond Court, an apartment house he designed in 1898 on Beacon Street in Brookline, touched on this problem at some length.

Each suite consists of nine rooms, not including halls or passageways, all with outside light and air, among which are a large reception hall, parlour, library, dining-room, and

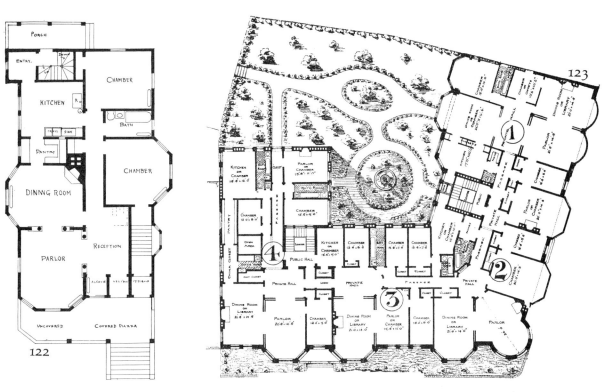

Examples of how reception, service, and sleeping areas might be segregated in apartment houses.

FIGURE 122. J. Winslow Cobb. First-floor plan by this well-known Shingle Style architect for a two-suite house in Winthrop Highlands, ca. 1908.

FIGURE 123. J. Pickering Putnam. Second-floor plan of the Charlesgate, 535 Beacon Street, Back Bay, 1891.

FIGURE 124. Cram, Wentworth and Goodhue. Plan of second floor (third and fourth floors are identical) of Richmond Court Apartments, 1213 Beacon Street, Brookline, 1898.

kitchen, this last being thoroughly isolated from the rest of the apartment, though communicating directly with the servants' staircases. . . . By means of an ingenious arrangement it has been possible to place the bed-rooms with their closets and bath, on a private passage separated by a door from the reception room and staircase hall; this device ensures the cessation of all those *contretemps* — often amusing indeed, but more often unpleasant — so familiar to the dweller in apartments; the entrance of a strange guest into one's bed-room under the impression that he is decorously making his way to the parlour; the tramp past a long range of mysteriously closed doors to the dining-room, or the apparently hopeless prominence given to the bath-room, being instances.

Cram's plans (Figure 124), however, though not guilty of the almost full-length railroad track of Cobb's design, still depend on admittedly short but still evident railroad tracks in each apartment. Parshley's, on the other hand, is much better. By *turning* the railroad track between the reception area and the bed-room area, he decisively separated the two areas (which cannot even be seen from each other) and at the same time by rounding the walls he used the reception area end of the railroad track to enhance the length of the reception hall, balancing, as it were, the other "wing" of the reception hall, which leads to the second-floor front porch. And by rounding both corners of the wall to the left of the railroad track, he introduced into the reception hall a kind of pavilion that adds enormously to its spatial excitement. It is a tour de force of planning.

Another important aspect of apartment design was that it should achieve parity with the single house in finish and detail as well as in privacy and spaciousness. In Parshley's houses, marble floors and lavish quartered-oak–paneled stairwells and reception rooms point up the fact that apartment houses, large and small, often offered reception areas as beautifully detailed as in any single-family house. At the Hotel Royal on Beacon Street, for example, there were parquet floors in the parlors, and at Richmond Court Cram noted that "the vestibules and staircase halls . . . are finished in oak, panelled for about two-thirds of the height of their walls, the stairs themselves . . . with elaborate newel posts and balustrades." In the individual apartments he pointed out that

The reception-rooms . . . have been wainscoted with oak to a height of five feet and six inches. The parlours are finished in enamel and the dining-rooms in oak, with a wainscot two-thirds the height of the walls. The bedrooms are finished in white, and the bathrooms in enamel-tiled wainscoting and floors, the plumbing appliances being the best of their several kinds, with porcelain tubs, nickel-plated trimmings, and fixtures of the most approved patterns. The kitchens and pantries are finished in hardwood.

It may be argued that though the streetcar suburb's two-suite apartment house was a more harmonious part of its streetscape than the Back Bay "dumbbell" apartment house, this effect was purchased through a dishonest facade, a factor that much exercised many people, then as now. Actually, as has been noted, where it was possible to express the two-suite horizontal house on a corner lot where each of the street facades could have its own entrance porch, this was nearly always done. Moreover, such "dishonesty" was frequent at all levels during this period. William H. Jordy points out that McKim, Mead and White's famous Villard Houses complex in New York of 1883, "concealed within its noncommittal palazzo elevations no less than six separate houses of varying sizes . . . one for [the owner], the rest for rent." Nor is every Back Bay town house what it seems. As Bunting notes, 326 Dartmouth Street is, so to speak, T-shaped, "with the wide bar toward the street and the stem at the rear, where the house narrows down to a single room fifteen feet wide" to allow the two neighboring houses to push into its sides. At 8 and 10 Commonwealth Avenue (Figure 45), to cite another example, the two apparently similar houses are really quite different: the library of 10 actually extends the whole width of the back of *both* houses on the second floor.

Just as the prestigious Back Bay apartment house spawned legions of middle-class apartment houses throughout the Fenway and on the main commercial streets of the expanding city, so also the characteristic upper middle-class two-suite apartment house of the streetcar suburbs must have influenced its ubiquitous middle-class variant — the two-family house, a type perhaps nowhere better seen than on Oakview Terrace in Jamaica Plain, which, as was noted before, constitutes generally a splendid middle-class streetcar-suburb comparison with upper middle-class streets. Again, on Oakview Terrace (Figure 105) only seven of the nineteen houses we discussed in Chapter 4 were singles: all the rest were two-families. And as was true of single-family houses, the two-family houses on Oakview built in the 1890s cost, with one exception, between $5500 and $6500 to build, or about half the cost of the Cushing Avenue two-suite houses of the same decade. The Oakview Terrace houses are, of course, much smaller. But their lesser cost also reflected the omission of several costly features of the two-suite house. Typically, for example, middle-class two-family houses had a common back staircase, thus compromising the principle of multifloor privacy. In the class-conscious 1890s this made a big difference. And it is significant that whereas on Cushing Avenue some of the grandest and costliest singles were built next door to already extant two-suite houses, on middle-class Oakview Terrace there was *not* the same parity between apartments

and single houses one sees at the upper middle-class level. The singles came first, then the two-families. Out of seventeen one- and two-family houses, between 1892 and 1895 all houses built (six) were singles; between 1897 and 1900, only one single was built, nine were two-families, and one was a three-family. Yet the two-families of Oakview Terrace, which provided garden lots massed about a circular park to persons who would otherwise probably have lived in one of the tenement districts described in the last chapter, are by no means intrusions architecturally in a singularly charming residential quarter.

N EITHER the Back Bay apartment house, nor the streetcar suburb's two-suite apartment house, nor their numerous middle-class progeny, were entirely satisfactory solutions, however, to the increasing need for multiple-family housing at all class levels in late nineteenth- and early twentieth-century Boston. The Back Bay apartment house was outlandishly big; significantly, it was a Haddon Hall type of apartment house, built about 1900 on Beacon Street, that caused the furor that led to the imposition of height restrictions for buildings in Boston. On the other hand, though the two-suite apartment house in the streetcar suburbs was harmonious enough in that setting, two-suite houses at any class level could not meet the increasing demand for apartments. Nor were they as profitable as three- or four- or even six-family houses.

The seemingly logical solution to the Back Bay problem — small three- or four-family houses only three or four stories high — was only occasionally attempted there. Two four-apartment houses at 187–189 Huntington Avenue have already been touched on; another was designed by Putnam in Copley Square in 1885, and two more were built

FIGURE 125. J. A. Halloren. Sutherland Appartments, a block of eight double three-deckers at 1714–1742 Commonwealth Avenue, Brighton, 1914, front and rear facades.

at 497 and 499 Beacon Street in 1888–1890. A few six-family houses were also built, notably the very fashionable trio at 384–386–388 Commonwealth Avenue in 1896–1899. But these stacked six apartments in six stories, rather than in only three in a wider house. Only at Audubon Circle are double three-deckers evident (Figure 126). It is in the same square, a too often overlooked and remarkably harmonious red-brick ensemble clustering about Cram's Second Church, one of the city's handsomest churches, that one may see Boston proper's most handsome three-decker, now the Eastman Funeral Parlor (Figure 127), designed by Kilham and Hopkins for Judge Henry S. Dewey. One could wish that such three-deckers and not "dumbbell" apartment houses had been built more often in the Back Bay. Widely published, this flat-roofed three-decker loaded three similar apartments one on top of each other, each with such amenities as eight fireplaces per suite. Each possessed a living room, sitting room, and dining room off its own hall, three bedrooms, kitchen, pantry, maid's room, and two baths, with a servants' common sitting room in the basement along with other service rooms. There

was a built-in "automobile room" accessible from the alley, and there was also a passenger elevator. But only three apartments, however harmonious in appearance in the Back Bay, were, in that heavily populated, highly taxed, and very fashionable area, rather a poor investment. Even double three-deckers were hard to justify in the Back Bay. Instead, the problems associated with the Back Bay apartment house found their resolution on Beacon Street in Brookline, where Olmsted's splendid tree-shaded parkway of 1886–1887 naturally attracted fashionable builders. Here, too, the tall dumbbell type was introduced (one of the most fashionable, the Wolloton, was of this type) but in Brookline there was sufficient space to encourage the development of a much more acceptable type — the courtyard apartment house.

Richardson appears to have had this type in mind for a Back Bay apartment house he began to design but never built. Henry-Russell Hitchcock, in *The Architecture of H. H. Richardson and His Times,* noted that the plan was "rather skillfully disposed about a central court. Thus there would have been more light than in the deep apartments of the new and disgraceful 'dumbbell' type actually

Three- and six-deckers at Audubon Circle on Beacon Street in the Fenway, a few blocks from the Brookline border.
FIGURE 126. Benjamin Fox. Double three-decker at 459–461 Park Drive, 1900.
FIGURE 127. Kilham and Hopkins. Three-decker apartment house, 896 Beacon Street, built as the residence of Judge Henry S. Dewey, ca. 1905. First-floor plan.

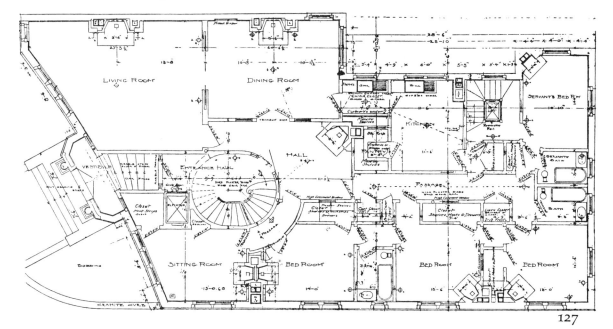

FIGURE 128. Cram, Wentworth and Goodhue. Perspective by Goodhue of Richmond Court Apartments, 1213 Beacon Street, Brookline, 1898. Probably the first apartment house in the northeastern United States massed and detailed like a great Tudor manor about a courtyard open to the street. The floor plan is reproduced in Figure 124.

erected in this decade on Commonwealth Avenue." In the event it was Ralph Adams Cram and Bertram Grosvenor Goodhue who appear to have introduced this building type into Boston — at Richmond Court on Beacon Street in Brookline (Figure 128). They explained themselves in the elegant brochure announcing the opening in 1898 of what is still, three-quarters of a century later, one of Boston's handsomest apartment houses. Cram wrote that a plan had

been chosen quite unusual in this country, though frequently found abroad. The apartments are grouped about three sides of a large open court, which is separated on the fourth side from the street by a light iron railing with tall brick and stone posts at intervals, and elaborately wrought ornament about the gateways, of which there are four, two larger ones for carriages, and two smaller for foot passengers. It has been the intention of the owner to render this court as beautiful as possible, and in befitting accordance with its situation on Beacon Street, perhaps the most beautiful as well as the most elegant of boulevards, and to this end it has been laid out and

adorned, like similar small private parks abroad, in the formal Italian fashion, with low box-hedges, clipped yews, flowers, and terraces. In the centre of the circular space formed by the driveway is set a fountain, from the cup of which rises the slight, graceful figure of a nymph in green bronze, modelled especially for its situation by [the distinguished American sculptor, Lee] Lawrie. From each suite a number of windows open on this court, and the view therefrom will be very different from the usual city prospect. Below lie the shrubbery, walks, and fountain, on the opposite side rises another wing of the building, while just without the enclosing *grilles* of wrought iron one sees all the life and motion of a brilliant thoroughfare.

Cram discussed particularly the problem of size.

Perhaps the chief objection brought heretofore against all apartment-houses, both city and suburban, has been their height — certain examples readily recalling themselves with horrible distinctness to the mind of every one, their monotonous stories being piled one above the other like veritable chimneys. The Richmond Court buildings are of quite another sort, however: but four stories in height, the effect of a large English Manor has been obtained, together with all its de-

sirable qualities of strength, dignity, and repose, while the court is not forced into fulfilling the ignominious function of a mere
light-well.

Thirty-six years later, when the relatively unknown architect of 1898 had become internationally distinguished,
Cram asserted in his memoirs that Richmond Court had been "the first attempt
to camouflage an apartment house
through the counterfeit presentment of a
great Tudor mansion" and if only because he lamented the fact, this is strong
evidence for Richmond Court's having
been the prototype. "From then on,"
continued Cram, "this sort of thing has
run riot in multifarious exaggeration all
over the Eastern seaboard, and I have
wondered many times since, if a measure of guilt does not attach itself to us
for what, unwittingly, we had done."
Yet, as in the case of the "dishonest"
two-suite house, there was good and in
this case even venerable precedent:
apartments for courtiers, after all, had
always been a standard feature of palaces.
And Boston is fortunate in many of
the local apartment houses that were
inspired by Richmond Court: the most
conspicuous and grandiose example,
begun in 1900, is Riverbank Court
Apartments (now Ashdown House), designed by Henry B. Ball and H. E. David-
son on the other side of the Harvard
Bridge, but perhaps the best is Burton
Halls in Cambridge, built at 10 Dana
Street in 1909 and designed by Newhall
and Blevins. Here the way the elements
of Richmond Court have been reorganized on an oddly shaped lot is imaginative. Certainly the grandest courtyard
apartment house, however, is the Stoneholm in Brookline (Figure 148).

If the low, courtyard apartment house
resolved the problem of the huge Back
Bay type of apartment building, it obviously was not a solution to the need for
larger than two-suite streetcar-suburb

apartment houses. On residential streets
of detached and usually wooden houses
there was overwhelming opposition to
any kind of sizable apartment house
and always the chance of losing one's investment if one altered the street's character too abruptly. Even in middle- and
lower middle-class areas, four-story
apartment hotels, whether of brick or
wood (around Central Square in Cambridge, for example, on Norfolk Street),
came so close for all their architectural
interest to being tenements that very
few were erected. Imaginations were
stretched, as a few surviving oddities
suggest: 382–392 Harvard Street in Cambridge, designed in 1889 by Richards
and Company, probably the apartment
house specialists who worked also in the
Back Bay, is a most interesting attempt to
organize a number of units with private
street doors into one wooden building
whose scale is not disruptive. Another
imaginative solution — building three
connected houses as one unit, a development of the old semidetached vertical
double — can be seen at 103–105 Raymond Street in Cambridge, designed
in 1898 by Blaikie and Blaikie, another
architectural firm that specialized
in multifamily housing and did work
in the Back Bay. This type of three-
family house, though undeniably impressive, was evidently thought too
wasteful of land and was only rarely attempted. Such houses also required at
least one windowless wall per unit.

The problem of the more than two-
family house in the suburbs seems to
have amounted to this: whether to bring
back the windowless wall in three or
more connected vertical units or to break
the two-story cornice line and pitch roof
streetscape with a full third story. Given
how strongly opposed to the windowless
wall the streetcar suburbs were, it is
scarcely surprising that the second
choice was almost universal and that the
three-decker emerged as the smallest

possible dwelling of more than two apartments where the essence of streetcar-suburb design — light and air on four sides of each dwelling unit — could be preserved. By 1878 photographs of the Mission Church in Roxbury disclose great ranges of these three-deckers on every side. In the city of Boston it is estimated that between 1870 and 1920 over 16,000 were built — over 20 percent of all the city's dwelling units today. "Boston's weed," someone has called them; but that is far from true. The much maligned three-decker for which Boston is so notorious is a fascinating building type, too long overlooked and unsung.

A NYONE who knows Tennyson's stirring line — "the rushing battle-bolt sang from the three-decker out of the foam" — will know that the pre-architectural usage of the term "three-decker" was chiefly naval, like "skyscraper," which meant originally the topmost sheet of sailing vessels. Much nonsense has been written to explain the extension of the term to three-story houses, but the logic of the extension is surely clear: a "three-decker" was in the first place "a line-of-battle ship carrying guns on *three decks*" (my italics), to quote from the *Oxford English Dictionary*, and there have thus been by extension "three-decker novels" (novels in three volumes); even a "three-decker brain" (in Holmes's *The Professor at the Breakfast-Table*); and as devoted followers of the *Forsyte Saga* may recall, Jolyon Forsyte, on the occasion of his third marriage, to Irene, was christened a "three-decker" by an unkind relation. The term also has had other architectural uses: New England, for example, is full of "three-decker pulpits."

The actual origin of the house type itself has mystified scholars. In its characteristic form, the three-decker is a three-story house with one apartment of six or seven rooms on each floor, opening off common front and rear stairwells. It appears in varying forms throughout the country, but seems to have originated in New England. In *Housing Problems in America*, Prescott Hall recounts the tale of a Worcester architect who, having badly underestimated the cost of a mansard house of his design, persuaded his builder to recover their profits by omitting the mansard and carrying up the walls of the house on each side to a flat roof. Like Mrs. O'Leary's cow, the story is on the one hand of a kind too easily spread and on the other hand is just possibly true. Certainly, the mansard roof (first used in downtown Boston, significantly, on an apartment house: the Pelham; Figure 112) provided virtually a full third floor, and there are three-deckers here and there throughout Boston that seem to disclose a relationship between the mansard house and the three-decker. In East Boston, many of the earliest three-deckers are mansard-roofed on the front, while the side and rear walls are carried up the full three stories: at Edward Everett Square in Dorchester there is a house still with its side and rear mansards whose front facade (presumably later) was carried up the full three floors. Nearby, at Everett Avenue, is also a most interesting block of three-story connected mansard houses (ca. 1875) that look very much like prototypal three-deckers because the mansarded third floor is not continuous and gives way in places to the sheer three-story facade. Yet the 1885–1886 *Dorchester Blue Book* discloses that these were connected, single-family houses.

The problem of the origin of the three-decker has been compounded, moreover, by scholars who have concentrated on lower-class three-decker construction and having isolated these from their wider architectural context seek the origin of the three-decker house type *only* in the tenement reform legislation of the 1870s that made lower-class three-decker construction more profitable for speculators than tenements, and in the expanding trolley network that allowed the lower classes increasing access to the suburbs. What has been widely overlooked, however, is that the three-decker *as a building type,* at all class levels, is the streetcar-suburb version, on the detached town house streetscape, of the French flat apartment house.

One of the few scholars who have noticed this is Robert Bell Rettig, who, on the basis of his own research into this subject for a projected but unfortunately never completed study, pointed out in his *Guide to Cambridge Architecture: Ten Walking Tours* that the Stanstead, a four-story 1887 apartment house on Ware Street in Cambridge, reflected "the emerging type of 'decker' apartment house." Later on, in the same work, he noted while touching on the Kensington, a huge 1902 apartment house of six stories on Magazine Street in Cambridge, that it was organized "on the 'decker' or 'French flats' principle," thus equating the two terms. Consider Haddon Hall in this light — and it requires very little imagination to perceive this apartment house (Figure 115) as virtually a "ten-decker" and then to imagine it, shorn of its upper seven stories, as a three-decker. Nor is this notion fanciful. As we have seen, Haddon Hall would thereby have been as harmonious a part of the streetscape as Judge Henry S. Dewey's three-decker at Audubon Circle (Figure 127) and have caused no furor, although in the Back Bay it would have yielded too few rents to be profitable.

The same close relationship is also evident if one compares a typical Back Bay "dumbbell" apartment house, such as the Imperial or the Belvoir, to the conventional double three-decker: each stacks two long flats running from flanking bays at the front to the rear on each floor off common halls. In fact, not surprisingly, the same architects often designed both types: just as Samuel Kelly's wooden decker at 20–24 Meacham Road (1894) in Cambridge is identical in design concept to his brick four-flat building (1889) at 423 Marlborough Street in the Back Bay, so also, on a larger scale, John Hasty's brick "apartment house," the Templeton (Figure 130) at 367 Harvard Street in Cambridge, is identical with his wooden double three-decker, the Lowell (Figure 131) at 33 Lexington Avenue in Cambridge, built five years later.

American Architect and Building News always reported the erection of wooden streetcar-suburb three-deckers as "3-story frame apartments." In an article in *The Brickbuilder* in 1905, entitled "Boston 'Flats,' " after discussing many of the latest and most fashionable French flat apartment houses in the Back Bay, the author observed that "the flats which are being constructed are nearly all in the line of small buildings, mostly of three stories, located in the outlying parts of the city. When not built of wood, these structures are commonly built of ordinary red brick." The article was surely referring to three-deckers. This is not surprising, for the use of "flat" and "decker" as equivalent appears to have been the norm at the turn of the century. In Russell Sturgis's *Dictionary of Architecture and Building,* published in 1901–1902, occurs this note: "The term 'flat' is entirely general and applies to any domicile on one story of a large building."

Judge Dewey's Back Bay three-decker, complete with elevator and working fireplaces, and the Lowell in Cambridge are also evidence for a related and too often overlooked fact: there was a social and therefore an architectural hierarchy of deckers as there was of every other residential type in this period. It is certainly true that most three-deckers were built (and not remarkably well) for the lower middle class and the lower class.

129

Three-, six- and eight-family apartment houses in the streetcar suburbs.

FIGURE 129. William H. Smith. Three-decker apartment house, 18 Church Street, Meeting House Hill, Dorchester, 1905.

FIGURE 130. John Hasty. The Templeton, double four-decker apartment house, 367 Harvard Street, Cambridge, 1895. Not surprisingly, Hasty also designed wooden deckers:

FIGURE 131. The Lowell, double three-decker apartment house at 33 Lexington Avenue, on the corner of Brattle Street, Cambridge, 1900.

130

131

Wooden three-deckers of unusual distinction exist throughout the streetcar suburbs, particularly in Jamaica Plain, Dorchester, Brookline, and Roxbury Highlands.

FIGURE 132. C. A. Russell. 801 Centre Street, Jamaica Plain, 1894.

FIGURE 133. Gardner Bartlett. 128 Davis Avenue, Brookline, 1904.

FIGURE 134. James T. Ball. Three-decker near Franklin Field, Dorchester, ca. 1908.

FIGURE 135. Charles E. Wood. 119 and 121 Dale Street, Roxbury Highlands, 1891.

So also were many apartment buildings — and many single-family houses
were mean and cheaply built singles
Judge Dewey or the residents of the Lowell would not have lived in for a moment. Just as there were elegant singles
and cheap singles, there were elegant
three-deckers and cheap three-deckers.
Fortunately, the cheap apartment houses
and two-families and singles did not dis-
credit those house types the way cheap
three-deckers have discredited that
house type; otherwise, we should be left
with scarcely any choice at all between a
castle and a hovel! The Lowell and Judge
Dewey's are outstanding examples.
But there are a great many more fine
three-deckers than most imagine.

Some of the finest reflect the picturesque vogue, such as 174 Elm Street (ca.
1891) in Cambridge and 801 Centre
Street (1894) in Jamaica Plain (Figure
132), where C. A. Russell, the designer,
attempted to mitigate somewhat the effect of the break in the streetcar-suburb
cornice line that resulted from the full
third story. Another most imaginative
Jamaica Plain three-decker is shown in
Figure 3. The classic and flat-roofed
three-decker could also be rendered with
distinction, as at 18 Church Street in
Dorchester (Figure 129). Perhaps the
most unusual three-decker thus far documented is at 128 Davis Avenue in Brookline (Figure 133). Designed by Gardner
Bartlett in 1904, this shingled house
has the expected porches only to the rear:
its facade is massed about a stuccoed entrance bay with half-timbering and dia-
mond-paned windows. When we look at
the very different but as handsome
three-deckers that adjoin it at 122 and
124 Davis (ca. 1900), it is not difficult to
see how mistaken are those who conclude that as a building type the three-
decker is worthy of little attention.

It is also a great mistake to assume that
three-deckers were never architect-
designed or were invariably designed by
inferior architects. The "Building Intelligence" column in *American Architect*
documents the fact that many well-
known architects designed as many
deckers as they did all kinds of apartment houses. And it is overlooked completely that several architects made a distinct specialty of three-decker design,
providing plans of excellent quality
for builders and developers and subsequently publishing them. One such
pattern book, published in 1908 by *Architects and Builders Magazine*, discloses
that one of the most influential was a
Dorchester architect, James T. Ball, who
submitted to the compiler of the book
the photograph reproduced here (Figure
134). Ball wrote:

Until the advent of this house in the vicinity of Boston, all three family houses had
been built on the narrow deep plan, say from
22 to 28 feet broad and 50 to 75 feet deep. A
builder, realizing how much easier it had
been for him to sell his broad two family
houses, made the request for this type in a
three-flat, and immediately it sprang into
favor and has been extensively copied
throughout this section. . . . In this design
we have a Colonial house both inside and
out. The rooms lead off from a useful large
square central hall, not from a long, narrow
dark corridor, as was the practice. There are
five rooms — bath and back piazza all enclosed under the one roof. All rooms are light
and sunny. . . . Finished plainly, this house
can be built for $6,000 complete, while $500
added would give the rich appearance presented by the accompanying illustration.
There are a dozen of these houses renting for
$25 to $30 per flat.

Each of the dozen houses of this design built (and in the event, no doubt,
many dozens more) would have been an
improvement on almost any street. But
Ball's three-deckers were not expensive.
In *Streetcar Suburbs,* Warner pictures a
most handsome pair of three-deckers in
Roxbury Highlands (Figure 135); subsequent research discloses that both
houses (at 119 and 121 Dale Street),
which Warner rightly observes are the

equal of much speculator building in the Back Bay, were designed in 1891 by Charles E. Wood and cost $7500. The disparity in prices of four Jamaica Plain three-deckers built in the ten years between 1892 and 1902 will document the wide range of the three-decker hierarchy: 40 Paul Gore Street, designed by Jacob Leopold in 1895, cost $3000; 38 Paul Gore, built by Joseph Bulley in 1892, cost $4500; at 46 Creighton, a particularly handsome pitched-roof three-decker was built by Robert A. Watson in 1902 for $5500; while C. A. Russell's decker at 801 Centre Street in 1894 cost $6500. Similarly, in Dorchester, at 8 Montello Street, T. Edward Sheehan, a local architect, designed a three-decker in 1892 that cost $7500 and another at 2 Montello (1897) that cost $12,000!

This hierarchy of three-deckers is reflected to some extent in what little is known of contemporary attitudes toward them. On Townsend Street in Roxbury Highlands, the rather elegant area (discussed in Chapter 4) just beside the Harris Wood Crescent, largely developed by Robert and Jessie Todd (who occupied 140 Townsend), also includes three-deckers built by the Todds themselves, who built single-family houses (at 144 Townsend); doubles (at 150–152 and at 166–168 Townsend); and a double three-decker at 170–172 Townsend in 1915. This last decker, however, was of brick; had a pitch rather than a flat roof; cost $20,000; and was given a setback of twenty feet. Nor is it clear that the introduction of three-deckers led invariably to a decline in the overall character of a street. In Brookline, for example, when a number of three-deckers were built about 1900 across the street from the Davis Avenue home of Charles Rutan, a partner in the prestigious firm of Shepley, Rutan and Coolidge (H. H. Richardson's successors), Rutan did not move; he was still there in 1913. On the other hand, at the same time the Todds

were building their three-deckers on Townsend Street, Cushing Avenue's residents made a point of insisting that the adjoining Mount Cushing Terrace of 1914 *not* be built up with three-deckers, and there is evidence that Chadwick's mansion was sold only on the understanding that the land behind it out of which Mount Cushing Terrace was created would be subdivided only for middle-class two-family houses. The data with respect to the acceptability of deckers are thus inconclusive. Nor do the often quoted protests of the time against three-deckers, which led by the 1920s to zoning changes in the city and suburbs that virtually prohibited them, at all clarify the matter.

A frequent charge — that three-deckers deteriorated rapidly, were fire hazards, and involved high maintenance — is substantially true of any wooden house; we know this now that so many streets of wooden mansions improperly cared for have become slums. The more serious charge — that they led to a decrease in land values — was never demonstrated; in fact, B. J. Newman followed that charge with the rather contradictory assertion that they also increased land values so that single houses were prohibitively costly in areas where much more money could be made by building apartment houses. This second charge also points up the fundamental and rather romantic predilection all the anti–three-decker forces shared for the single house: Newman's attack on deckers makes plain the fact that the prejudice against three-deckers was one part of an overall prejudice against *any* kind of apartment house. Newman thought, for instance, that "where many families use one entrance, the approach to the immoral home in a multiple building is less conspicuous than in a dwelling," and he indulged in the rather remarkable observation that "sex morality often is by subtle ways weakened through long established apartment house living." Such buildings, he concluded, were often "a shield to the lewd man and woman," and as marital discord was the more easily overheard and consequently the more embarrassing, he announced that "it is a short cut from the apartment house to the divorce court!" If none of this calls to mind the staid middle-class three-decker streets of the Highlands, neither does it seem to recall the Hotel Agassiz. Apartment dwellers, wrote Newman, were usually "nomads" characterized by a "lack of civic interest." Clearly, he did not know Major Higginson. He also pointed out that three-deckers were ugly because they were monotonous: by this standard, Louisburg Square would scarcely survive Mr. Newman's remarks.

Every charge leveled against three-deckers really fell of its own weight: if most were cheap, of what house type was this not also true? If most were speculator-built, so also were most houses, including many, for example, in the Back Bay; if they were expensive to maintain, so were all frame houses, however elegant; if deckers followed the streetcar, what didn't in the streetcar suburbs? If they were densely massed, so also were the houses of Melville and Cushing avenues. At a housing conference held in Boston in 1918, Charles Logue even went so far as to call the three-decker "an ideal type of house," and Marion Booth and Ordway Tead wrote in 1914 that even at the lower middle-class level,

the values which the tenant receives in this modern flat in the three-decker are so little short of luxurious that it is no wonder that they are in demand. A flat which rents for from $20 to $25 a month includes a parlor, dining room, kitchen with set tubs, cook stove with water heater attached, two bedrooms, front and back piazza, hot air furnace, electricity and hard wood floors.

That the data should be inconclusive with respect to the contemporary attitudes toward deckers surely points all the more directly to the effect of the three-decker hierarchy we have been discussing: how acceptable deckers were obviously bore some relation to what kinds of deckers were involved.

This decker hierarchy is, however, often misunderstood. The flats-over-the-corner-store variety, for example, was not necessarily the meanest type of flat housing. As we have seen, flats over shops were not unusual at the Social Register level in the Back Bay. What was important was what kind of flats over what kind of store and in what kind of neighborhood. Buildings of shops and flats on the corners of pleasant retail streets from which led upper middle-class residential streets offered far better accommodations than the barely detached rows of entirely residential three-deckers in South Boston. Nor is the space between three-deckers and their setback any guide at all to their quality; in fact, many three-deckers were built in connected blocks. Some of the most picturesque are in Brighton (Figure 125).

Such blocks are difficult to document because connected three-deckers look very much like connected single-family town houses. Indeed, just as many of the Cushing Avenue houses in Dorchester turn out to be two-suite houses, so also the row of handsome brick connected houses built in 1907 between Dean Road and Clifton Path on Beacon Street in Brookline, which we discussed in the last chapter, are, in fact, three-decker houses (Figure 96) and they are as elegant as their location would suggest. The residents of this block in 1914 included Mr. and Mrs. C. P. Seaverns (he was the president of Howe and French on Broad Street in Boston); Mr. and Mrs. Charles Lindsey (Mr. Lindsey was the manager of the Parker House, then perhaps Boston's leading hotel); several doctors and lawyers with business addresses on Beacon Street in Boston; and a number of what would today be called "junior executives." Each of these three-deckers reflects this class level. Every eight-room flat possesses four reception rooms opening through wide doorways into one another, and because the deckers are joined at their *narrow* rather than at their wide ends (a luxury unknown even in the most elegant single-family town houses) three reception rooms overlook Beacon Street and one scarcely notices the two short windowless walls. There are also two bedrooms, a kitchen, and maid's bedroom. A serving hatch between dining room and kitchen also documents the presence of servants. Each three-decker has marble staircases and elaborate tiled floors and each flat has a dining room paneled to a height of six feet in oak with a wood-burning fireplace. Brookline and Dorchester, particularly, abound in connected brick three-deckers, and one can always distinguish the class level at once according to whether they are connected at the narrow or wide sides.

Such buildings not only look like single-family row houses; as an ensemble they also look very much like one large apartment house. Yet this element of illusion may well be misleading. What is the difference between an apartment house and a block of connected three-flat houses? Having sought the origin and evolution of the three-decker in the French flat fashion, we may now find it instructive to work our way back from the three-decker to the clearly recognizable courtyard apartment house. One of the earliest of these is the Peabody in Ashmont (Figure 136). It bears one of the most august names in Boston, that of Colonel Oliver Peabody, a senior partner in Kidder, Peabody and Company, one of Boston's most important bankers, and a scion of a leading Boston family. It bears his name because he erected it to protect the church next door, All Saints, of which he was a parishioner. Situated

in one of Dorchester's upper middle-class areas, across the street from a railway station (later replaced by Ashmont Station on what is now the Red Line) and next door to a famous church, and the proud possessor of a celebrated name, the Peabody was designed as well by a distinguished architect, Edwin J. Lewis, Jr. Its multitude of picturesque chimneys are indicative of its amenities, which include working fireplaces in every apartment. Another amenity is that one gains access to the building principally through charming half-timbered porches that jut into the courtyard around which this brick ensemble is massed.

As we will see shortly, All Saints had been designed by Cram for the Peabodys, his first major patrons, and the Peabody apartment house, begun in 1896 while Cram was still working on the church, may well have been the inspiration for the full-fledged Tudor manor of Richmond Court, the courtyard apartment house Cram designed in Brookline two years later, the widely emulated design of which solved the problem of the ungainly Back Bay dumbbell type. Yet its four different building permits document conclusively that the Peabody is actually *four brick three-deckers*, connected to each other at their narrow ends just as are those on Beacon Street in Brookline, but massed in the case of the Peabody about a courtyard. The much maligned three-decker, whose origins we have sought in the French flat fashion of the 1870s and eighties, may thus in turn have inspired the eventual flowering of the French flat into its most plausible and distinguished form, the red-brick and "Tudor Manor" courtyard apartment house.

THE sense of illusion or pretension that has turned up again and again in this discussion of multifamily architecture — where all sorts of tricks were apparently played to make two-families look like one-families and three-deckers like apartment houses and apartment houses like Tudor manors — is, finally, a kind of clue that we have misunderstood the social conventions and therefore the architectural problem of Victorian multifamily housing.

How greatly we have misunderstood the social conventions can perhaps best be illustrated by comparing the Peabody to the Albemarle Chambers on Albemarle Street, in the South End, another red-brick courtyard ensemble of connected three-deckers (twelve in this case) built in 1899. The closeness of Huntington Avenue, then the dividing line between the fashionable French flat apartment house district and its middle-class and lower middle-class South End cousins, no doubt accounts for this complex, which is located off St. Botolph Street, which was respectable but certainly not fashionable. But the Albemarle Chambers, designed by Israel Nesson, was not only built two important blocks away from fashion but also directly next to very busy railroad tracks, and its social standing was naturally vastly inferior to that of the Peabody. Such indices of the time as *Clark's Boston Blue Book*, which included a directory of members of Boston's clubs and a visiting list of the residents of the better streets, listed every resident of the Peabody. The Albemarle Chambers (indeed, Albemarle *Street*) was scrupulously avoided; as was St. Botolph Street. Aside from location and such amenities as room layout and working fireplaces, the Peabody and the Albemarle Chambers are virtually identical. But it was precisely such amenities, and privacy and spaciousness of living unit allied with the social calibre of the neighborhood (and not the relative proximity of one's fellow tenants or any question of ownership or renting), that counted. Thus by

the social conventions of the time, the Peabody was an apartment house and the Albemarle Chambers a tenement. And that was not an illusion.

Freed of the social misconception (that the gulf was between single and multioccupancy structures rather than between the costly and the cheap of each type), we are thus liberated from the architectural misconception — that multifamily architecture was increasingly misleading in appearance because it was perceived to be inferior to single occupancy. The multifamily architect was forced to misleading exteriors because while the demand for apartments rose dramatically at all class levels year after year, the scale of every type of residential streetscape in Boston was unfriendly to the apartment house. Haddon Hall, for example, was quite honestly an apartment house, but its type provoked a furor — not because it was an apartment house, but because it was not harmonious with the streetscape. Neither Richmond Court nor the Peabody provoked any furor at all. Each was misleading, as was the two-suite house, but each provided for the new horizontal life-style in a manner harmonious to already built-up single family streetscapes. Interestingly at the end of this thirty-year evolution of the horizontal flat or decker, the last few enclaves of connected single-family row houses built in the first years of the twentieth century in Boston — Charles River Square (Frank Bourne, 1909) and West Hill Place (Coolidge and Carlson, 1916) — can in each case be easily mistaken for an apartment house (Figure 137).

Each of these ensembles of connected red-brick town houses reflects Bulfinch's precept, discussed in Chapter 1, that connected dwellings should ideally face or enclose open space. But so also does Richmond Court. And that is the point. When the multifamily architect was able through the courtyard apartment house to build in the traditional scale of the

FIGURE 136. Edwin J. Lewis, Jr. The Peabody, 195 Ashmont Street, Dorchester, 1896–1897, an apartment house that consists of four connected brick three-deckers with servants' quarters under the roof. Two of the four entrance porches to each three-decker are visible in the courtyard. The ground-story apartments of the two three-deckers whose narrow ends face Ashmont Street were designed for doctors and incorporate waiting rooms and offices, features common to both intown and streetcar-suburb apartment houses. Patients entered through the private street-front entrances.

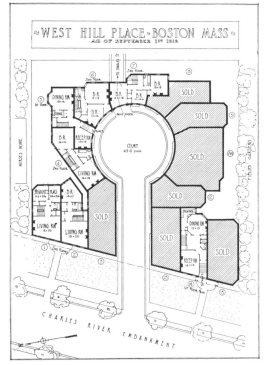

FIGURE 137. Coolidge and Carlson. West Hill Place, off Embankment Road at the foot of Beacon Hill, 1916. First-, second-, and third-story plans of single-family connected row houses on overall site plan.

FIGURE 138. De Vos and Company, et al. Longwood Towers, originally Alden Park Manor, Brookline, 1922.

single-family row house streetscape and to apply to the apartment house Bulfinch's precept about open space (that is, the courtyard), he achieved for those who preferred a horizontal rather than a vertical dwelling unit and to rent rather than to own an ensemble of horizontal dwellings as gracious in appearance as any row house square and as harmonious with Boston's traditional streetscapes. The misleading multifamily facades of Victorian Boston were not the problem: they were the solution to the problem of how to organize a great number of such horizontal dwelling units in streetscapes that were unfriendly in both the city proper and the streetcar suburbs. Moreover, once one thinks of it, the shift in fashion from the vertical dwelling unit to the horizontal dwelling unit had also importantly undergirded the revival of the detached streetcar-suburb town house: such houses, like French flats, which emerged during the same period in Boston, sought always for one-floor spaciousness in reception area and as much light and air as was possible. Significantly, at Longwood Towers (1922–1925) in Brookline, called originally Alden Park Manor and designed by K. M. De Vos and Company, with George R. Wiren and

Harold Field Kellogg as consulting architects, the development of the apartment house in Boston reached its climax in another red-brick Tudor design that went Richmond Court one better and broke up the courtyard apartment building into several detached buildings (Figure 138) ranged about a garden setting similar to that of the streetcar suburb's detached town house.

An apartment house luxurious enough that the president of Lever Brothers was counted among the tenants for many years, even its corridors are endowed with linenfold oak paneling. Like Richmond Court, which is divided into five halls — St. Albans Hall, for example, or Grafton Hall — Longwood Towers is divided into smaller sections with very British-sounding names — Arling Cross, Belden Cross, and Charing Cross — but at Longwood Towers these divisions are not entries off a courtyard but separate tower buildings of many apartments each, which rise from a huge three-story underground parking garage (no doubt the first such facility in Greater Boston) that is hidden from view by the garden setting. And in rather an uncanny way the design of Longwood Towers foreshadowed the future of Boston in the twentieth century.

6

CHARLES McKIM
AND THE CLASSICAL REVIVAL

BY THE 1890s, over a million people lived within a twelve-mile radius of the State House. And whether one lived in a huge apartment block, a conventional single-family house, or the most vernacular of three-deckers, if it was stylish in the nineties, it was relentlessly Classical. Nor was the fact that architectural style, after splintering into many modes in the Queen Anne period, had resolved itself through the picturesque Colonial Revival into a full-fledged academic Classicism unrelated to Boston's enormous growth. City and suburbs had become metropolis, and it was not unnatural (especially in the wake of the Colonial enthusiasms aroused by the 1876 Centennial) that once Boston's architects focused on their Colonial and Neoclassical heritage, they began to feel that a revived Classicism was what Boston no less than New York needed to order its growth in the late nineteenth century and to ennoble its aspirations. Aspirations? Most scholars have concluded that by the 1890s the "New England Renaissance" was dying. Yet New England's "Indian Summer" seems to have been rather more vigorous than we have been led to believe, and in order to understand this new Classicism we must accordingly reexamine the cultural background of late nineteenth- and early twentieth-century Boston, which was the context for the building that heralded the American Classical Revival — the Boston Public Library, built in 1888–1895 in Copley Square (Figure 139).

John Jay Chapman once asserted that he could "attach to almost every portrait in Venice an honored Puritan name." Similarly, Kenneth Clark's discussion of early fifteenth-century Florence is strikingly applicable to late nineteenth- and early twentieth-century Boston. For the puzzle we must now explore — why and how at the behest of hard-headed Yankee trustees the Boston Public Library arose in Copley Square in gleaming white Classical rebellion against its dark Ruskinian and Richardsonian Medieval environment — is akin to a paradox posed by Lord Clark. Given the character of the men who had made Florence so rich — "the bankers and wool merchants, the pious realists" — it seems at first glance baffling that suddenly out of the dark, narrow fifteenth-century streets arose those light, sunny Renaissance arcades that "totally contradict the dark Gothic Style that preceded and to some extent still surrounds them." Yet Lord Clark pointed out:

For thirty years the fortunes of [Florence], which in a material sense had declined, were directed by a group of the most intelligent individuals who have ever been elected to power by a democratic government . . . the Florentine chancellors were scholars, believers in the *studia humanitatis*, in which learning could be used to achieve a happy life, believers in the application of free intelligence to public affairs, and believers, above all, in Florence.

Commercially, nineteenth-century Boston also had been declining for some

FIGURE 139. McKim, Mead and White. Boston Public Library, Copley Square, Back Bay, 1888–1895. The principal facades.

decades. But that is not to say that Bostonians had forgotten Emerson's declaration: that Boston was "not an accident, not a windmill, or a railroad station, or cross-roads tavern, or an army barracks grown up by time and luck to a place of wealth; but a seat of humanity, of men of principle, obeying a sentiment and marching loyally whither that should lead them," and, as so many have observed in earnest and in jest, believing as they marched, above all, in Boston.

Admittedly, the comparison seems forced at first. Yet Whitehill has insisted that it has been the always renewable supply of "literate and responsible Trustees and treasurers [that] has done more than anything else to make Boston a center of civilization," and the comparison of late nineteenth-century Boston with fifteenth-century Florence is surely implicit in the way he dealt with the Bos-

ton volume in the University of Oklahoma Press's Centers of Civilization series, which was dedicated to cities that have "exercised a radiating influence upon the civilization in which they have existed." To the announced titles — *Athens in the Age of Pericles, Rome in the Augustan Age,* and *Florence in the Age of Dante* — Whitehill added, not Boston in the Age of Emerson, but *Boston in the Age of John Fitzgerald Kennedy.* When the book was published in 1966, he explained his choice by pointing to the fact that it was after 1870 that Boston had grown "far richer in the elements of civilization," citing the observation of Alfred North Whitehead in 1942 that "insofar as the world of learning today possesses a capital city, Boston with its various neighboring institutions approximates to the position that Paris occupied in the Middle Ages." In fact, it was precisely in the 1870–1900 period that Boston began to develop the galaxy of institutions for which it is now known the world over and to build in the New World, to which the balance of power was slowly shifting, the great center of Western learning and culture it remains today.

The list is astonishing. In the last half of the nineteenth and the beginning of the twentieth centuries there were founded in Boston a dozen or more universities, colleges, and schools of national importance: Tufts University, the Massachusetts Institute of Technology, Boston College, Boston University, Radcliffe College, Northeastern University, Simmons College, the New England Conservatory of Music, Wellesley College, and much of Harvard, including the schools of architecture and business administration, to name only perhaps the most distinguished. No less astonishing is the number of museums founded during this period; five at Harvard alone (including the Fogg and Busch-Reisinger museums), as well as the Gardner Museum and the Boston Museum of Fine Arts, this last (along with the Metropolitan Museum in New York, incorporated in the same year) the first true art museum in America in the modern sense of the term. Wherever one looks — at education, medicine, museums, music (the Boston Symphony Orchestra was started in 1881) — it is clear that no other period in Boston's history of three and a half centuries can equal for vitality this one.

All this has been greatly obscured by Van Wyck Brooks's conclusion, in *New England: Indian Summer, 1865–1915*, that by the 1890s "the Boston mind appeared to have lost its force." But in the very next sentence — "it was yielding, inch by inch, to the Catholic Irish" — one sees what Brooks meant. And when he cited as evidence of this decline the fact that by the early years of this century "the most prominent objects in Boston were the Catholic Cathedral, the dome of the synagogue [probably Temple Israel] and the dome of Mrs. Eddy's Mother Church," his point cannot be mistaken. The Boston that Brooks's study chronicles (especially the literary tradition upon which he focuses) *was* deteriorating. But a new Boston was evolving at the same time and it is a mistake to read into Brooks's record of decline the idea that because the new and evolving Boston was more pluralistic culturally it was inferior.

Late nineteenth-century Boston, which by no means lacked for Yankee building blocks (one thinks of Henry Lee Higginson's Boston Symphony Orchestra or of President Eliot's Harvard), was enriched immeasurably by the newer groups; Brooks himself instances Louis Sullivan, "a Boston boy born and bred — one of the first fine shoots of the Boston Irish." But Brooks could have said much more, relating not just the Catholic Cathedral to Louis Sullivan but the synagogue, for example, to a Lithuanian Jewish boy who had immigrated to Boston with his parents in 1875: the legendary scholar Bernard Berenson, who in 1952 at the age of eighty-seven wrote in his diary, "I still consider Boston my home." One wonders too, in connection with Christian Science, how much the fact that its founder, Mary Baker Eddy, was a woman enters in here. Certainly Mrs. Eddy was not the only woman whose achievements at this time were not taken very seriously. The same might be said for the pioneer women architects during this period, several of whom studied and practiced in Boston: Marion Mahoney Griffin, for example, who became Frank Lloyd Wright's chief draftsman, graduated from M.I.T. in 1894; Minerva Parker Nichols designed the Browne and Nichols School in Cambridge (1894); and Lois Lilley Howe, the first licensed woman architect in the country, was a lifelong resident of Cambridge. Whatever Brooks's motivations, however, in singling out so critically the Catholic cathedral, Temple Israel, and Mrs. Eddy's church, another person than Brooks might well have written quite another kind of book, as Whitehill ultimately did.

How ethnically diverse Boston was becoming is evident in Whitehill's estimate that by 1900 only 11 percent of the city of Boston's population were Bostonians of "traditional New England origin." Even in the suburbs one sees unmistakable evidence of this growing diversity: between the late 1850s and the early 1870s, for example, Protestant meeting houses in the suburbs of Stoneham, Danvers, and even in historic Lexington were remodeled into Roman Catholic churches: respectively, St. Patrick's, the Church of the Annunciation, and St. Brigid's.

Today, when this more pluralistic Boston, "the Boston of John Fitzgerald Kennedy," has become as much "Boston" in our minds as Mather's or Emerson's city, one can see, as have Howard Mumford Jones and Bessie Zaban Jones, that despite the city's late nineteenth-century literary and commercial decline, "to infer from this that the 'Boston mind' had weakened is mistaken."

The decaying "Indian Summer" image we have of the late nineteenth and early twentieth centuries in Boston persists because it is enshrined in our literature under august auspices. One thinks of T. S. Eliot and of Henry Adams — above all, one recalls Henry James, standing at the foot of Beacon Hill, gazing toward the Back Bay and the expanding metropolis beyond it. Wrote James:

It is from about that point southward that the new splendors of Boston spread, and will clearly continue to spread, but it opened out to me as a tract pompous and prosaic, with which the little interesting city, the city of character and genius, exempt as yet from the Irish yoke, had had absolutely nothing to do.

Even James, however, as we will see, found much that was impressive in the nineties in Boston. Nor is this surprising; the Joneses point out that Boston had become by the turn of the twentieth century "the cultural capital of the United States." And while one would not wish to carry the comparison to the Renaissance too far, or to extend its point carelessly to architecture, Vincent Scully has observed that the Queen Anne movement "recreated the whole process of the English Renaissance itself" in the direction that it took from "a late medievalism toward an eventual 18th century classicism." Furthermore, how one evaluates the increasingly Classical architecture of the 1890s will depend importantly on whether one sees it as shaped by the declining culture or by the aspiring and maturing culture, each of which paralleled the other in the same period.

Bainbridge Bunting's conclusion that the Georgian Revival he chronicles in the Back Bay illustrates a declining and complacent culture thus proceeds from a review of the overall cultural background of the 1870-1900 period in which he emphasizes three events: Cleveland Amory's "curfew" for entrance into Boston society in 1879; H. G. Wells's conclusion that by 1875 the "filling up" and closing of the Boston mind was complete; and the removal, also in 1875, of the executive offices of the Burlington Railroad from Boston to New York. Lewis Mumford, on the other hand, insists that "it is not by accident that Harvard's rejuvenation in science and scholarship under Charles Eliot coincided with the constructive enterprises of the Back Bay, in the generation between 1870 and 1900." Whereas Bunting cites the fact that in 1913 Boston could "overlook the Armory Show with genteel equanimity," Mumford notes that it was at the Museum of Fine Arts in the Back Bay that "the fresh world of color opened up by the French Impressionists was displayed long before either the Metropolitan Museum or the Chicago Art Institute were in a position to show similar work." And Mumford concludes that it was not only during this 1870–1900 period but "in the Back Bay that Boston first established itself as one of the centers of world culture in the arts and sciences."

In this light the increasingly Classical and Georgian Back Bay takes on a very different aspect that is surely applicable to the whole metropolis. Consider, for example, how George Santayana's boyhood memories of the Great Fire of 1872 document unconsciously at one and the same time Bostonians' growing pride in the 1870s and the increasing dissatisfaction of Santayana's generation (which matured in the eighties and nineties) with the picturesque seventies. He recalled in *Persons and Places:*

the contagious excitement and even pride felt by Bostonians at having had such a big fire. People would not speak of the London fire any more; they would say the Boston fire. Unluckily, for Boston, Chicago had had an even bigger fire; and more unluckily in my opinion Boston had no Wren to rebuild the town. That was the era of an architectural medley of styles imitated from picture-books by professional speculators and amateur artists.

Unconsciously, Santayana's boyhood thoughts echoed those of many of Boston's rising young architects. Four years after the Great Fire, Robert Peabody was already lamenting the effect of what he called the "bric-a-brac style"; by the 1880s this view was widespread. Considering Commonwealth Avenue in 1888, which as we have seen had grown into a very picturesque street during the Queen Anne period, C. H. Blackall found Boston's grand boulevard "about as disappointing as anything could be," its "once stately aspect" (that is, its French Academic buildings of the 1860s) having deteriorated into "a continual ka-

leidoscopic change of style and detail from house to house." What had seemed a charming and individualistic diversity at the height of the Queen Anne mode in the 1870s was increasingly perceived by the late eighties as fussy and strident, even degenerate.

This was the context of the Boston Public Library, which may also be taken as a sign of the underlying continuity between the old and exclusively Yankee culture and the new, more pluralistic culture then beginning to evolve. The old culture, Brooks admits, found no difficulty in the new library's Italian Renaissance architecture: Boston, he observes, "prayed over the Florentine library . . . and even made Florence and Venice Bostonian somehow because of its regard for Italian culture. . . . the Library seemed quite at home in a town where Italian studies, fostered by Norton and Longfellow, by Perkins and Lowell, were a part of the atmosphere all men breathed."

But it is perhaps more important, given the role of the public library movement, that the new Copley Square library marked a cultural achievement that was Boston's own; and one distinctly related to the city's increasing immigrant population. Today, opposite the library, in the center of Copley Square, is a memorial to one immigrant for whom the library was very important — Kahlil Gibran, the young Lebanese from Boston's South End who was so deeply influenced by the Boston Bohemia of the 1890s, discussed in Chapter 7, and who became one of the most widely read poets of the twentieth century. On the other side of the library is another monument — the new addition to the library, designed by Philip Johnson. Few realize that a significant part of its cost came from a million-dollar trust fund established by John DeFarrari. Probably he was not the barefoot newsboy reading in the old Boston Public Library whose presence there so impressed Matthew Arnold on his visit to Boston in 1883, but Defarrari was, indeed, in the 1880s a poor newsboy of immigrant stock, whose access to the library's books on economics enabled him to rise to great wealth and, in fact, prompted his generous gift to that institution.

These two penniless immigrant boys — the Lebanese poet-to-be and the Italian millionaire-to-be — are, as it were, the vital context of the Renaissance library. There was thus a function, and certainly a future, but there was no precedent for such an institution: the architects were asked to create for the first time in the world a huge metropolitan library for the general public as well as for the scholar. And the building itself, a commitment to this rather radical undertaking, seemed to many upon its completion a success "secured for civilization as well as for Boston." The new Public Library not only recalled architecturally the glories of the Renaissance; it marked one of several large nineteenth-century Boston achievements not unworthy of the association.

T HE first plans for the Public Library were, in fact, what a flaccid culture might well have been content with. Years later, Cram remembered that these plans (by the city architect) showed "a chaos of gables, oriels, arcades and towers, all worked out in brownstone" and that it had required "a growl of rage and indignation" before they were scrapped, a protest one of the library's trustees later pointed out was "started by [the city's] architects." A particular plea was made by Arthur Rotch, the architect to whom Cram was then apprenticed; there was "the keenest anxiety," insisted Rotch, "that this opportunity of making a building worthy of our far-famed public library should not be

lost." Freed of the city architect by the force of the public outcry, the library trustees chose the New York firm of McKim, Mead and White, largely, it would seem, because of the enthusiasm of one trustee, Samuel Abbott (who was a cousin of Mrs. McKim), for the Italian Renaissance Villard Houses in New York, then the most conspicuous evidence of that firm's commitment to what Joseph Wells called the "classical ideal." Wells, an influential designer in the New York firm, defined that ideal simply: "clearness, simplicity, grandeur, order and philosophical calm."

Actually, the trustees might have looked much closer to home for Italian Renaissance by McKim, the partner in charge, as it turned out, for nearly all the firm's Boston work, for the Andrew House of 1883–1884 at 32 Hereford Street (Figure 144) was among their earliest work in that mode, a reflection of the fact that though practicing in New York, McKim was closely connected with Boston. He had entered Harvard College in 1867 and remained there a year before going to Paris to study architecture and upon his return to this country he had been apprenticed to Richardson. Boston's architecture also strongly influenced McKim. He thought Bulfinch the greatest American architect and one of McKim's partners asserted years later that the leaning of the office toward the Classical dated from McKim's sketching trip to Boston's North Shore in 1877. McKim also married into a distinguished Boston family, the Appletons. Moreover, according to his biographer, "the plan and the general outline of the design [for the library] began to shape themselves in McKim's mind" at the Appleton House on Beacon Street, where he established a small, private office after he had received the library commission.

Not everyone liked McKim's plans. When the model of the new library went on exhibition in 1888 one newspaperman thought the design recalled a warehouse; the *Globe* compared it to the City Morgue. As the building rose, the *Herald,* in the spring of 1889, deplored the design: "What opportunities for splendidly broken skylines that western background affords the architect, but this flat-backed, flat-chested structure, promises to crush them to the earth." But the significance of McKim's design seems to have been felt at once and in ever-widening circles. As Leland Roth has pointed out, the promise of the Villard Houses was

fulfilled beyond expectation when the [library] was opened in 1895. Here all the resources of the architecture of the past were gathered together, fused with modern construction techniques and embellished with the finest works of art. Its interior was a virtual palace and the exterior drew together and gave final definition to the vast open space of Copley Square. . . . The Library also demonstrated the kind of public splendor that could be achieved when architects, painters and sculptors worked in concert. Here was a building which demonstrated that in America, as in Europe, the city would be a work of art.

Not only did the library exhibit, in the words of Cram, " a serene Classicism, reserved, scholarly, delicately conceived in all its parts, beautiful in that sense in which things have always been beautiful in periods of high human culture"; but its architectural art prompted Ernest Fenollosa to call the building "our first American Pantheon." In fact, a chief purpose of the building, wrote Charles Moore, was "to create a visible manifestation of the civic consciousness of Boston," and the result was an ensemble of decorative art that remains distinguished to this day.

McKim was a master of the dinner of persuasion, and he cajoled trustees, politicians, private donors, and artists into rising repeatedly to his costly enthusiasms. How difficult a process lay behind this splendor may be seen in his rela-

tions with Puvis de Chavannes. Moore notes that a witness to McKim's first meeting with Puvis in Paris in 1891 recalled: "the price was very generous indeed; the artist was evidently staggered. I noticed that he trembled and the silence became oppressive. Mr. McKim quietly urged the matter, praising the artist, who finally said: "the offer is princely, but the undertaking is great. Boston is distant, I am an old man; in fact, I am afraid. *Enfin, j'ai peur."* Puvis finally accepted but later declined under pressure of another offer in France. McKim tried again. He had a model made of the staircase, and sent it in 1892 to John Galen Howard, then studying architecture in Paris, pressing Howard to "call upon M. Chavannes and represent to him for the Trustees and this office our desire to have him undertake the work at his own price." Back in Boston, the library's growing cost called a halt to the negotiations, but McKim determined "to renew the attack upon Chavannes" while in Paris in the winter of 1893, and this time he succeeded. The result was the great sequence of murals on the main staircase, created by the artist with actual pieces of the marble before him, and with the graining of the marble painted as a guide on the bottom of each canvas, work William Jordy has recently pronounced as "among the outstanding examples of mural decoration in the country" (see Plate 6).

There were many failures. Projected work by both Whistler and La Farge was for one reason or another never realized; nor were Saint-Gaudens's sculptures for the facade. What was done was also unusually controversial. Many know that McKim's own gift, Frederick MacMonnies's *Bacchante,* proved too daring for Boston; but few remember that Sargent's *Synagogue* in his third-floor gallery cycle *Judaism and Christianity* so distressed many Jews that the legislature attempted to effect its removal. What was achieved

FIGURE 140. Boston Public Library, the Delivery Room. The doorways are of
blood-red marble, *rouge antique*, with variegated red and green Levanto
marble; the *rouge antique* mantelpiece they flank is 11 feet high, brilliantly
polished, and superbly carved. Above the entablature is one of a series of
murals by Edwin Austin Abbey entitled *The Quest of the Holy Grail*, which
endow the Delivery Room with a rich Pre-Raphaelite pageantry still much
admired today. The Delivery Room opens off the stair hall (Plate 6).

was, however memorable: Bela Pratt's much maligned but splendid figures of Art and Science at the main door (Figure 141); Daniel Chester French's bronze doors, ornament enough for a vestibule where also stands MacMonnies's figure of Sir Henry Vane; Augustus Saint-Gaudens's three facade panels and his superb medallion bust of Robert Billings (a Boston merchant and library benefactor) in the north arcade of the courtyard; Domingo Mora's facade colophons; Puvis de Chavannes's serene pastorale on the Grand Staircase; Edwin Austin Abbey's murals in the Delivery Room (Figure 140); the great mural cycle by Sargent (Figure 142) in the gallery that bears his name; even the work by lesser-known artists would be notable in any other building. The rich red Pompeian Lobby by Elmer Garnsey, the New York artist whose work can also be seen at the Library of Congress; the Venetian Lobby opposite, sea-green and bright with gold, the work of Joseph Lindon Smith, a Boston muralist; the *Triumph of Time* on the ceiling of the Elliott Room, which takes its name from the artist, John Elliott; all contribute to an ensemble of architectural art perhaps unequaled in nineteenth-century American architecture.

Yet at the heart of the library's splendor is what Royal Cortissoz called McKim's passion for "the pure structural character of a well-laid course of stone." To McKim, Cortissoz wrote, "building materials were what pigments are to the painter; he handled them with the same intensely personal feeling for their essential qualities that a great technician of the brush brings to the manipulation of his colors and he left upon his productions the same autographic stamp." Cortissoz remembered:

During the building of the Boston Library certain sheets of marble were to be put in the entrance hall — Numidian, I think they were — and their dimensions were determined by McKim with the utmost care. He regarded those dimensions as essential to the ensemble, but when the marble was delivered it was found that they had not been rigidly followed. Forthwith the sheets were rejected. The contractor argued at tremendous length and almost wept, but McKim was harder than the Numidian itself. He was dealing in marble as an artist deals in paint. . . .

The marble of the staircase was particularly hard to procure. Moore noted that McKim demanded "a certain, golden-yellow stone called *Monte Riete*, or Convent Sienna," which was available only "from a quarry owned by a religious order who only had a block or two taken out by primitive methods when the convent needed money." McKim not only needed some four hundred tons of this marble but also had to choose it carefully with respect to color, for the lightest marble in color is at the bottom of the staircase; the marble gets gradually darker and darker as one ascends; a superb example of the subtlety of his work here.

Insofar as the library as a whole is concerned one must discriminate. Who is not grateful today for its courtyard? Bates Hall is certainly one of the noble rooms of America. The scholars who point out that neither is a masterpiece are perhaps judging the building only by the lofty standards of facade and stair hall. Varying opinions of the different cycles of murals in the library will also probably continue to shift back and forth from good to excellent to awful so long as art historians draw breath. But the enduring merit of the Public Library is undoubted. It is not in some ways supremely functional. But the fact that there was no precedent for such a building must not be forgotten; nor Charles Moore's defense that a chief function of the building *was* to express civic pride: in 1888 the trustees had stated clearly that the library was to be "a palace for the people." It was also in some ways innovative. The tile vaults on the ground story by the Guastavino firm of New

FIGURE 141. Boston Public Library, detail of the principal facade, showing the figure of Art, one of two statues by Bela Pratt that grace the platform upon which the library stands.

FIGURE 142. Boston Public Library, south end of the Sargent Gallery, showing Sargent's lunette and frieze of *The Redemption*, mixed media on canvas, 1903. Although Sargent's great crucifix is not as vivid or blatant as Cram's similar Calvary at All Saints, Ashmont (Plate 7), Sargent's murals are more provocative than most realize, exhibiting in places what Martha Kingsbury has called a kind of "exalted delirium," evoking "sexuality, danger and perversity." But Sargent's work did not shock Boston: his points were made through innuendo, not anecdote. Beginning in 1893, Sargent worked for nearly thirty years on these murals, several of which were exhibited at the Royal Academy in London before their installation in the Boston library.

York and Boston (whose factory was in the Boston suburb of Woburn) constitute, according to Hitchcock, the first extensive use of such vaulting. But in the end each person will find his or her own reasons for liking (scarcely ever for disliking) the library and will find them in different places: in the dark splendor of the Sargent Gallery or in the sunlit courtyard, or, perhaps, in the pomp of the great doorways and mantlepiece of the Delivery Room. The last word, though, must be ceded to Henry James. Detained by the view from the windows of the staircase landing into the courtyard, which seemed to him, he wrote, like "one of the myriad gold-colored courts of the Vatican," he turned back readily enough to the great staircase, marveling at "its amplitude of wing and its splendor of tawny marble" and at what he characterized as its "high and luxurious beauty." At the library Boston found the grandeur it had mislaid on Commonwealth Avenue.

Until recently, that observation could only have been quoted with tongue carefully in cheek. Indeed, it used to be said of Richardson that he was building for the ages, and of McKim, Mead and White that they were building for the eighties! But our sense of the library's greatness as architecture has been growing now for almost a hundred years. Jordy's recent and brilliant analysis of the library's facade actually *adds* somewhat to McKim's presumed sources, but at the same time increases one's respect for McKim's handling of them. Calling it "thrice-sanctioned," Jordy concludes that the Roman Colosseum can have been only a starting point, that the other well-known source for the library's facade, Henri Labrouste's Bibliothèque Sainte-Geneviève in Paris, furnished only the most specific composition readily available, and that Leon Battista Alberti's San Francesco (Tempio Malatestiano) at Rimini certainly encouraged

McKim in his linear refinement of Labrouste's scheme and suggested as well motifs for detail. Jordy also agrees with Hitchcock that the general compositional scheme derives from a contemporary American source — Richardson's Marshall Field Warehouse of 1885–1887 in Chicago. These varied sources only hint at the complexity of the creative process by which such sources sifted through McKim's mind to their final resolution.

Writing generally of McKim, Mead and White's designs, Leland Roth has analyzed the extent to which the firm's designs differed from their models and drawn a startling conclusion.

The horizontal lines are strongly emphasized, multiplied or otherwise stressed, binding the whole design together. . . . The model is regularized, complex rhythms are simplified and variations made uniform, so that the design as a whole is more easily comprehended and given greater apparent unity. . . . The number of elements or components found in the model is reduced, simplifying the composition. Details become harder, sharper, crisper, and the entire building becomes tauter. The building's relationship to the ground is strengthened by the use of broad podiums, terraces, fans of stairs and similar devices. Ornament is most often confined to distinct areas where it approaches the point of saturation, setting up a sharp contrast between the blank wall surfaces and the enlivened zones of ornamentation.

Roth emphasizes in his discussion that "the underlying themes of strong horizontality, clear statement of component parts, tautness and strong relationships to the ground we can observe in the work of McKim, Mead and White are also characteristics of the architecture of Frank Lloyd Wright" and in every instance, he continues, "they are qualities that have been identified as uniquely American in feeling." Not unnaturally, Europeans may sometimes see this more clearly than we do: Roth quotes Le Corbusier's observation — "in New York . . . I learn to appreciate the Italian Ren-

143

144

Three Back Bay houses by McKim, Mead and White and a streetcar-suburb house by Julius Schweinfurth.

FIGURE 143. 303 Commonwealth Avenue, 1895.

FIGURE 144. Andrew House, 32 Hereford Street, corner of Commonwealth Avenue, 1883–1884.

FIGURE 145. 413–415 Commonwealth Avenue, 1890.

FIGURE 146. Julius Schweinfurth. Leighton House, Roxbury Highlands, 1894, a wooden detached house comparable with 32 Hereford Street.

146

145

aissance." In its American incarnation he thought it possessed "a strange new firmness which is not Italian but American." It is a refrain we have heard before, from the mid-century Italianate to the Shingle Style. And it is hard to mourn the rise of the Classical Revival in the face of the Boston Public Library, or to dispute the assertion of the plaque in McKim's memory there — that "in this building enduringly is revealed the splendid amplitude of his genius, an inspiration to all men."

I T was in the wake of the library that at the great World's Columbian Exposition held in Chicago in 1893, in part McKim's work, the gleaming white Classical court of honor, with its evocation of urban order and grandeur, dazzled America. In Jordy's words, the Boston Public Library "heralded the main impetus in American architecture from the nineties to the thirties." Boston's architects accordingly set out to shape the metropolis in the library's image.

Naturally, very few attempts were made to introduce this kind of monumental Classicism into residential Boston. McKim himself did so at the Algonquin Club at 219 Commonwealth Avenue in 1887 and at 303 Commonwealth Avenue (Figure 143) in 1895 with conspicuous success. Yet perhaps only one other Back Bay house, 297 Commonwealth Avenue (1899), designed by Peabody and Stearns, achieves a comparable distinction. Instead, the domestic reflection of the revived Classical tradition was usually Georgian Revival — the Weld House (1900) at 149 Bay State Road, by Peters and Rice, is by far the grandest — or, by the 1890s, explicitly Federal in feeling. Two of the handsomest houses in the Back Bay, Arthur Little's own house at 57 Bay State Road, designed by him in 1890, and the double

house at 413–415 Commonwealth Avenue (Figure 145) by McKim, fall into this category. Edwin J. Lewis's 240 Ashmont Street in Dorchester (1912) and Julius Schweinfurth's house for George Leighton in Roxbury (Figure 146) (so similar in feeling to the Andrew House; Figure 144) are excellent illustrations in the Georgian mode of the streetcar-suburb type in both brick and wood.

Such houses, which show the outcome of the picturesque Colonial Revival that we noted evolved out of the Shingle Style, not only constitute a kind of domestic mirror of the overall Classical Revival of the 1890s but also significantly reflect Boston's own early nineteenth-century Neoclassical work. Bunting has noted that the Andrew House is reminiscent of "Boston's old Greek Revival vernacular," and Roth has gone so far as to assert that the same house recalled Parris's double-bowed brick facade (1818) at what is now the Women's City Club (Figure 16). That house seems also to Bunting strikingly similar in its entrance composition to McKim's 199 Commonwealth Avenue, while Roth suggests that the McKim house at 303 Commonwealth Avenue (Figure 143) echoed the Sears House of 1819 (Figures 10, 11). The inspiration of West Hill Place and Charles River Square is also clear: each is yet another reincarnation of the red-brick residential square that had charmed Boston since the Tontine Crescent of 1794. In fact, in West Hill Place, Boston's architecture seems as circular, historically, as is this charming enclave in plan, and this reenactment in the early twentieth century of the architecture of the early nineteenth century can seem at first very perplexing. Yet Bunting remarks that not only are many Back Bay houses the "artistic peers" of their Beacon Hill prototypes, but also one might question whether Boston's late nineteenth- and early twentieth-century Georgian Revival is a case of "Georgian

The more flamboyant Renaissance-derived styles did not flourish in Boston, but there are two outstanding exceptions. FIGURE 147. Charles Brigham. Burrage House (now Boston Evening Clinic), 314 Commonwealth Avenue, Back Bay, 1899. FIGURE 148. Arthur Bowditch. The Stoneholm, one of Brookline's most fashionable apartment houses, 1514 Beacon Street, 1907.

147

148

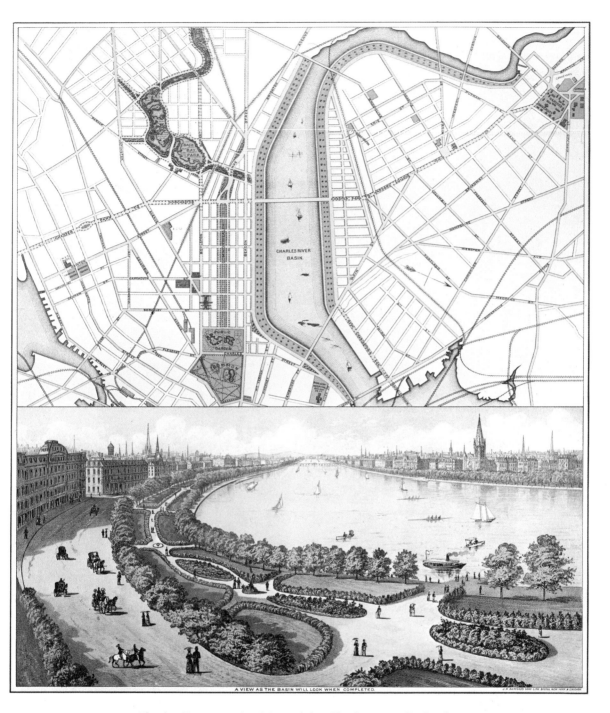

A VIEW AS THE BASIN WILL LOOK WHEN COMPLETED.

PLATE 1. Charles Davenport's vision of the Charles River Embankment, 1874. Although the Cambridge side (to the right) never quite lived up to these expectations, the grandeur of the Back Bay (to the left) as finally realized is evident in the plan, where its spacious axial grid stands out clearly. One can also see the Back Bay's relationship to Frederick Law Olmsted's Boston park system, the "emerald necklace" of parks that connects the Back Bay with downtown Boston at the Common and with the streetcar suburbs. Beyond the "Back Bay Park" at the top this system of parks was continued through Jamaica Plain and Roxbury to Dorchester Bay.

A century apart, Charles Bulfinch's interiors in the Massachusetts
State House (opened in 1798) and Clarence H. Blackall's Colonial
Theatre (completed in 1900) illustrate the range and diversity of
Boston's architecture. PLATE 2 shows Bulfinch's House of Representatives,
which has been the Senate Chamber since 1895. PLATE 3 shows the
principal lobby of the Colonial Theatre, one of the most admired of
Blackall's playhouses.

PLATE 4. The Back Bay was not the only new residential quarter of the expanding nineteenth-century metropolis to attract wealthy Bostonians. In 1891, A. H. Davenport, for example, built his home, designed by Chamberlin and Austin, at 70 Salem Street in Malden. The superb detailing of the quartered-oak stair hall and its furniture is typical of the work of Davenport's firm, which made most of the furniture designed by Charles McKim in 1902–1903 for the White House.

PLATES 5 through 8 show the principal interiors of the four great landmark buildings of late nineteenth- and early twentieth-century Boston. In themselves a fascinating comparative study (many of the same artists and craftsmen worked on two or more or all of them), the oldest is Trinity Church (PLATE 5). Built in 1872–1877, Trinity takes its acknowledged place among the great churches of the world. The frescoes were executed in 1876–1877 by John La Farge; the apse windows are by Clayton and Bell. Richardson's successor architects designed the chancel stalls (made by A. H. Davenport and Company), the chancel parapet (carved by John Evans) in 1902, and the pulpit (also by Evans) in 1916. The high altar and its ornaments (1938) were designed by Maginnis and Walsh, who also redecorated the entire chancel. Ernest Pellegrini of Irving and Casson modeled the bas-reliefs under the apse windows.

5

6

Charles McKim's work and Ralph Adams Cram's, both the issue in differing ways of Richardson's, constitute the crest of the Classical and Gothic traditions in American architecture. In the case of both men, Boston possesses the landmark building that became the national model in each tradition: McKim's Boston Public Library in Copley Square, begun in 1888; and Cram's Church of All Saints at Ashmont,

begun in 1891. PLATE 6 shows the great stair hall of the library, throughout which McKim achieved a marriage of art and architecture unique in this country in the nineteenth century. PLATE 7 shows the chancel of All Saints, where Cram and Goodhue and their artist-collaborators realized one of the most distinguished ensembles of Gothic Revival art in the world.

PLATE 8. Isabella Stewart Gardner's Fenway Court is perhaps best known
for its collection of old masters. Yet pictures were also painted *at* Fenway
Court (by John Singer Sargent, for example), and not only the personality of
the collection but above all its uniquely organic setting moved Henry
Adams to say to Mrs. Gardner: "You are a creator, and stand alone." "A
masterpiece of its kind," in Aline B. Saarinen's words, the ingenious design of Fenway Court was a revised and enlarged version by the architect
Willard T. Sears in 1899 of plans he had prepared for "Mrs. Jack" in 1896 for
a proposed home on Beacon Street, "the design [of which]," wrote Morris
Carter, "was entirely Mrs. Gardner's."

revival or *survival*" (my italics). He admits that one might reasonably argue that Georgian forms had never really utterly disappeared from Boston, citing 58–60 Commonwealth Avenue, a full-blown Georgian Revival house of 1866. Daniel Selig has made the same point, arguing that for this reason "it is not truly accurate to speak of such revivals in Boston" where Georgian and Federal forms had "appeared consistently and appreciably throughout the nineteenth century." And if one sees the domestic Georgian mirror of the Classical Revival as a continuation of an unbroken local tradition, one can see too why the overall Classical Revival was perceived in Boston in the 1890s not as a sign of backsliding, but as a revivification, even an enlargement, of an accumulated and indigenous local heritage of form and detail that was clearly susceptible to new and vital life in the hands of men like McKim. It is perhaps for these reasons that the Classical tradition in Boston only very rarely differentiated itself into the more exotic Renaissance-derived modes. Such buildings, however, being exceptional, are all the more valuable today.

Two Back Bay châteaux, for instance, are outstanding. The earliest, the design of Carl Fehmer for Oliver Ames in 1882, stands on the corner of Commonwealth and Massachusetts avenues, and its brownstone detail includes a series of panels that depict activities (reading, playing the violin, dining, for example) appropriate to the room over the windows of which they occur in the facade. At 314 Commonwealth Avenue (Figure 147) is deservedly the most famous of this type in Boston. The work of Charles Brigham, who designed this house after the manner of the châteaux of Chenonceaux, its extraordinary cut-stone detail, deeply undercut so as to hold shadow, is highly ostentatious by Boston's social standards, but one must be grateful for its superb craftsmanship. A number of French interiors are also notable: chiefly Little and Browne's double drawing room at the Somerset Club, sumptuously detailed with gilt daggers and eagles in the Directoire style, and Parker, Thomas and Rice's ballroom addition to the Baylies House at 5 Commonwealth Avenue. In the realm of public buildings there is also Winslow and Wetherell's French Renaissance Hotel Touraine (1899–1900) on the corner of Tremont and Boylston streets. Still handsome, though disfigured by first-floor alterations, it took its inspiration from the great royal château at Blois.

Not all the Renaissance-derived styles appeared under French auspices. In the Back Bay, for example, Bunting notes a Schweinfurth house (1895), characterized by sixteenth-century Spanish ornament, at 304 Commonwealth Avenue; a Jacobean-inspired house of 1903 by Chapman and Frazer at 240 Commonwealth Avenue; and a full-fledged Tudor manor house of two years later by the same architects at 225 Bay State Road, a type that naturally abounds in the suburbs. There are also a very few examples in Boston of the exuberant, lavishly sculptural, and dramatic Beaux Arts manner. As Daniel Selig has pointed out, "the Boston Beaux Arts often seems timid and meek, especially in comparison to the high fashion Beaux Arts of New York," but Schweinfurth's two houses at 426–428 Beacon Street, built in 1904, are distinguished and there are also two opulent Beaux Arts Baroque facades at 128–130 Commonwealth Avenue, built in 1905. One wonders if Arthur Bowditch could have been their architect? Certainly they are similar to his little-known Stoneholm apartment house at 1514 Beacon Street in Brookline (Figure 148). Built in 1907, the Stoneholm is the most magnificent building of its type in Greater Boston — a splendid Baroque extravaganza that holds the high ground above Beacon Street with great distinc-

Two comparisons with the first Museum of Fine Arts, shown in Figure 53.
FIGURE 149. Henry J. Hardenberg, Clarence H. Blackall, Associated. Copley Plaza Hotel, Copley Square, Back Bay, built in 1912 on the site of the first museum.
FIGURE 150. Guy Lowell. The second Museum of Fine Arts, the Fenway, 1909. Transverse section.

149

tion. Only the opulent, theatrical Baroque and rococo of the downtown theaters (see Chapter 9) is comparable.

How immediate and widespread was the Classical passion aroused by the library is perhaps most evident if one compares the old Museum of Fine Arts in Copley Square (Figure 53) with both the building that displaced it in 1912 — Henry J. Hardenberg and C. H. Blackall's superb Copley Plaza Hotel (Figure 149) — and with the new Museum of Fine Arts in the Fenway, designed by Guy Lowell, which opened in 1909 (Figure 150). Severely Classical (the second museum's great staircase and its Fenway facade rank in each case as the most monumental Classicism in Boston), the museum was but one of many vast, axial, and "imperial" structures erected by Boston institutions in the library's wake. Harvard's schools of law, medicine, and architecture, and its Widener Library and first Fogg art museum, the Boston Symphony Orchestra, the Massachusetts Institute of Technology, Chil-

dren's Hospital, the Boston Opera Company, Tufts University's Forsyth Dental Infirmary, the New England Conservatory of Music, the Christian Science Church, the Peter Bent Brigham Hospital — all sought, like the Museum of Fine Arts, to emulate in their buildings the library's pomp.

Very few architects attempted the overwhelming monumentality of Richard Morris Hunt's Fogg Museum of Art (1893; demolished) or of Edward T. P. Graham's Forsyth Dental Infirmary and Boston City Hall Annex (Figure 151). More typical is Kilham and Hopkins's Massachusetts College of Pharmacy (1920) or McKim's Symphony Hall (1892–1900), where the much richer ornament proposed was never carried out. Equally austere were the New England Conservatory (1901) and the Boston Opera House (Figure 152), both designed by Wheelwright and Haven; so chaste did the latter seem to one wit that he christened the new hall "the first Unitarian opera house." Even more severe are the original courtyard buildings of the Massachusetts Institute of Technology, designed by Welles Bosworth (Figure 153), though the site undeniably invites the effect. Seen from the Harvard Bridge, this great low-lying mass responds superbly to the spaciousness of the river's sweep. Siting, in fact, was a key factor in "imperial" architecture. It is not so much that great space was necessary as that it was a function of such architecture to organize and define its surrounding spaces. Thus South Station (1899), designed by Shepley, Rutan and Coolidge, may not be thought a finer building than the same firm's Langdell Hall (1906) at the Harvard Law School; but Langdell Hall can never really be seen because of its siting and landscaping. South Station, on the other hand, sweeps up the two streets it fronts upon to a majestic finale in Dewey Square that is felt by those who know it, so much motion is there, even when only part of the station comes into view down Summer Street. Similarly, Harvard Medical School (Figure 154), which is so magnificent that it annexes a 100-foot–wide boulevard with twenty-foot setbacks to its axial splendor, can be felt the minute one turns onto Avenue Louis Pasteur; one waits as one progresses up this tree-lined street for the flanking screens of trees to give way and disclose the square that spreads out in tribute to the massive white marble quadrangle. Designed by the Shepley office in 1906, it is as severe as Classicism usually was in Boston, but the glistening white marble and the high, balustraded terraces of the great court all lend an undeniable grandeur to the composition. Today, it still seems, as it did to Sylvester Baxter when it was first built, "like a fragment of the memorable White City at Chicago." All around the Fenway it is echoed in building after building — particularly in O'Connell and Shaw's Boston Fire Department Alarm Building (1925).

At the Massachusetts Institute of Technology, Boston was endowed with the dome of the Pantheon in Rome. At Harvard Stadium (1903–1910), designed by McKim, Mead and White, Boston gained a building reminiscent of the Roman Colosseum. At Union Station in 1894 (Figure 208) the Shepley office essayed a grandiose triumphal arch on the Roman model — now demolished but similar to the frontispiece of Commonwealth Pier. And in 1904–1906, Charles Brigham and Solon S. Beman erected for the First Church of Christ, Scientist, in the Back Bay a florid and grandiose basilica, the splendid dome of which lifted the Classical Revival up to dominate the city's skyline (Figure 155). It remained only for three architects — William Chapman, R. Clipston Sturgis, and Robert D. Andrews — to attach white marble Classical wings to the Bulfinch State House in 1914–1917. Its brick was painted white and thus yielded Boston a great axial capitol building, gleaming white (Figure 156). Such was the city's enthusiasm for the Classical ideal. In 1928, however, the powers that be happily had second thoughts and restored the original red brick. Even before the new white marble wings were added, however, the State House had grown in 1889–1895 by way of an enormous addition behind the Bulfinch building. Because the Bulfinch building had been painted yellow since 1855, this rear extension was of yellow brick. The dome had been covered with gold leaf in 1874, with the result that since 1928 the whole complex has become a kind of bird of paradise, with a red body, gold head, white wings, and yellow tail. Such are the dangers of an expanding sense of civic grandeur.

The State House extension, designed by Charles Brigham, is without question Boston's most maligned building. Cram could not tolerate it for a moment. In his memoirs he remembered that when he

Monumental Classicism in Boston.
FIGURE 151. Edward T. P. Graham.
Boston City Hall Annex, 1914. The
four colossal figures were modeled
by the sculptor Roger Noble Burnham.
They have been removed, but
Burnham's decorative panels on the
main doors of Graham's Forsyth
Dental Infirmary of the next year in
the Back Bay survive, as does his
architectural sculpture on the facade
of the Busch-Reisinger Museum at
Harvard.
FIGURE 152. Wheelwright and Haven.
Boston Opera House, Back Bay, 1909.
The decorative sculpture was the work
of Bela Pratt. Demolished.
FIGURE 153. Welles Bosworth.
Maclaurin Building in the Great Court
of the Massachusetts Institute of
Technology, Cambridge, 1913, looking
across Harvard Bridge from the Back
Bay.
FIGURE 154. Shepley, Rutan and
Coolidge. Harvard Medical School,
the Fenway, 1906.
FIGURE 155. Charles Brigham and
Solon S. Beman; completed by Brigham,
Coveney and Bisbee. Extension of
the First Church of Christ, Scientist,
Back Bay, 1904–1906.

151

152

153

FIGURE 156. The Boston State House as it appeared ca. 1920, after the red-brick Bulfinch building had been painted white to match the two white marble wings added in 1914–1917 by William Chapman, R. Clipston Sturgis, and Robert D. Andrews.

won the second prize in the competition he had been told that, for a consideration, the job could be his. In Cram's words, after the building was finished,

and what is sometimes known as the "fried egg" and sometimes as the "yaller dorg" extension had revealed itself before the gaze of an astonished public, I have sometimes wondered if I should not have been justified in waiving all ethical considerations and yielding to the plausible lobbyists, just on the chance that something a little less trying might have been attached to the admirable old Bulfinch front. In any case the actuality has served one minor purpose, for while I served my time as an instructor in architecture at Technology I could use it as the best existing example of a structure in which every

line, in which mass, detail, and material, together with the composition as a whole, was exactly and ingeniously wrong.

Today, this building's setting has been so barbarized by the turning of its balustraded park into a parking area that few would disagree with Cram. Yet of all the attempts to rival the spatial splendor and architectural art of the Public Library the Brigham extension is of particular interest because, like George Clough's Suffolk County Court House (1886–1895), it is contemporaneous with the library.

The Court House possesses an enormous lobby — nearly five stories high — that is endowed with an elaborate

FIGURE 157. Henry Forbes Bigelow. Addition to the Boston Athenaeum, 1913–1914. Fifth-floor reading room. The Athenaeum's interior is unique. Wrote David McCord: it "combines the best elements of the Bodleian, Monticello, the frigate *Constitution,* a greenhouse and an old New England sitting room."

parade of life-size allegorical figures by Domingo Mora. This great space is handled so ineptly, however, that it seems only wasteful and pompous, a startling reminder of what the Public Library might have looked like. But the State House extension is another matter entirely. The interior often recalls the library in its forms and detailing (the triple arches and balustrading of the Senate Staircase Hall) and in its materials (the Siena marble of the Hall of Flags), and though it does not in these respects achieve the distinction of the library, it is comparable both in plan and in its provision for architectural art. Brigham's well-thought-out ceremonial sequence of Sen-

ate Staircase Hall, Hall of Flags, and House Staircase Hall, this last rising spaciously to an enormous pillared lobby that leads into the House of Representatives, is unique in Boston, and the attempt to integrate mural decoration with figure sculpture is evident throughout the building. None of the murals has been widely admired, but the building's figure sculpture is frequently distinguished. Two figures are by Daniel Chester French: the statue adjoining the Senate Staircase Hall of the Civil War hero William F. Bartlett, and the heroic bronze figure of Governor Roger Wolcott that is backed by Richard Andrews's mural in the great hall outside the House

151

Shaping the "City Beautiful."
FIGURE 158. Charlesgate at Commonwealth Avenue, ca. 1900. Arthur Shurcliffe designed the balustrading (still extant, but overshadowed today by an access ramp to Storrow Drive); the statue of Leif Ericson is the work of Anne Whitney. Dedicated in 1886, the figure originally stood farther down the avenue.
FIGURE 159. McKim, Mead and White and Augustus Saint-Gaudens. The Robert Gould Shaw Memorial, Boston Common, 1897.

Chamber. The Senate Staircase Hall also possesses two sculptures by Bela Pratt, a large bronze relief of General Thomas G. Stevenson and the Army Nurses' Memorial, a powerful work unveiled in 1914.

Many more of Boston's Classical buildings sought to emulate the library's design concept with respect to architectural art. C. H. Blackall's Tremont Temple of 1896 possesses murals by Edmund C. Tarbell; Sargent himself executed murals for the staircase of the second Museum of Fine Arts and for Widener Library, as did N. C. Wyeth for R. Clipston Sturgis's Federal Reserve Bank of 1922. Another and very successful attempt of this sort was made by Henry Forbes Bigelow in his superb fifth-floor reading room (1913–1914) at the Boston Athenaeum, where he provided innumerable niches and broken pediments for the display of portrait busts (Figure 157). Nearby, at Congregational House, a series of facade reliefs by Mora show that the attempt to integrate art into architecture extended also to the exterior of buildings. This tendency had begun, as we saw, in the 1870s, and by the 1890s such work, though never common, became widespread. Not only the library but also the Opera House and the Museum of Fine Arts were endowed with exterior sculpture by Bela Pratt, and even business blocks were sometimes so adorned: William G. Preston's bank at 145 Milk Street, completed in 1906, rejoices in a number of allegorical figures by Max Bachman.

Many efforts were also made at this time to integrate sculptural embellishments into an architectural setting that in turn would integrate buildings into the landscape to produce a more formal and splendid cityscape. Perhaps the most extensive such effort was made at Charlesgate, where Commonwealth Avenue, as it crosses the bridge, was elegantly balustraded by Arthur Shurcliffe (Figure 158). Another was the Larz Anderson Bridge, designed in 1912 by Wheel-

wright, Haven and Hoyt, and built of brick surely in anticipation of the subsequent red-brick ranges of Harvard buildings it now links so beautifully, even though it has been ruthlessly shorn of its gilded lamps. Johannes Kirchmayer, the well-known architectural sculptor, modeled its sumptuous gilded mantlings, so sadly tarnished today. Most of these efforts were the results of collaborations of architects and sculptors. It is not generally known that Henry Bacon and Daniel Chester French, whose collaboration at the Lincoln Memorial in Washington in 1922 constituted perhaps the climax of the American Classical Revival, worked together on several important early twentieth-century monuments in Greater Boston, including the Longfellow Memorial off Longfellow Park in Cambridge (1914); the Parkman Memorial in Olmsted Park in Jamaica Plain (1906); and the White Memorial (1924) in the Boston Public Garden. Similarly, McKim, Mead and White and Saint-Gaudens collaborated on two Boston monuments: the Phillips Brooks Memorial (1910) in Copley Square, which has never (and for good reason) been much admired, and the Shaw Memorial opposite the State House (1897), which is on the other hand one of the most distinguished such ensembles in the country (Figure 159). The two trees that were planted within the Shaw Memorial between the Common and Beacon Street were actually a part of McKim's design and illustrate the way in which such ensembles sought to knit together into the streetscape not only architecture and sculpture but features of the natural landscape as well.

Nowhere else was the city balustraded so splendidly in the service of a great public building as at the Shaw Memorial. Looking up the steps to see the white marble wings of the State House rather than the Bulfinch portion, one would think one was in Washington —

but only for a moment — because although Boston possessed several architects at this time who instinctively thought in terms of monumental buildings and grand vistas and who longed to remake Boston in this pattern, they never succeeded in endowing even so conspicuous a place as Copley Square with the plaza and fountains it so desperately needed. The only such vista (except for Avenue Louis Pasteur) realized in Boston was the mall at Franklin Park, where a number of marble columns were salvaged from the interior of the 1837 Boston Custom House (when it was being rebuilt to support its tower in 1913) and erected into a lofty gateway. Only when French's sculptural groups from the Boston Post Office were placed at the other end of the mall in 1929 when that building was destroyed did Boston achieve a suitably grandiose Classical vista.

THE Classical Revival is easily ridiculed. But it was Vincent Scully, no disciple of McKim, who best expressed its value to us when he pronounced a valedictory on McKim's Pennsylvania Station in New York at the time it was brutally torn down. Now, one arrives in the new underground Pennsylvania Station and rides an escalator up to the street; in other words, wrote Scully, "one scuttles in today like a rat" — whereas through McKim's great vaulted concourse "one entered the City like a God." Boston has been more fortunate: the great Renaissance staircase of the Boston Public Library invites every man still to proud ascent, and that is not a bad definition of what the Renaissance was

all about in the first place. Nor can one forget that other remarkable building of this period, Fenway Court (Plate 8), completed eight years after the Public Library opened. Although it was too personal a creation to become an architectural prototype in any real sense, the setting Isabella Stewart Gardner and her architect, Willard T. Sears, created for the collection she bequeathed to the public moved one historian to exclaim that it seemed almost as if "the Venetian Renaissance had been reincarnated in Boston." Traditionally, of course, most art historians have been more impressed by Mrs. Gardner's paintings than by their setting; many would agree with Martin Green that it shows late nineteenth- and early twentieth-century Boston culture as more aquisitive and interpretive than creative. Yet that these are mutually exclusive values has not always been clear, especially when one remembers that Mrs. Gardner not only purchased Raphaels and Rembrandts; she also patronized Sargent, who surely caught the image of Boston in his time as definitively as did Stuart or Copley in theirs. Today one might well conclude, moreover, that Mrs. Gardner's unique ensemble of art and architecture, a Venetian palazzo "turned inside-out," is as much a work of art as any individual treasure in it. Even then, Henry James admitted as much: he called Fenway Court a "tour-de-force — no Evolution at all — but pure Special Creation in an adverse environment." Yet his last words are increasingly suspect as we begin to understand how much this "adverse environment" yielded Boston at the crest of her own renaissance.

7

RALPH ADAMS CRAM AND
BOSTON GOTHIC

THE RICHNESS AND VITALITY of Boston's cultural life in the 1890s was such that not even the force of the Boston Public Library and the Chicago world's fair of 1893 was able to narrow Boston's vision of herself or her architecture to only the Classical vista and colonnade. In 1891, even before the Public Library was completed, at an architectural exhibition held in the library, the plans of two totally unknown young architects for the small and then not very important Episcopal parish, All Saints in the Ashmont section of Boston, plans that were decisively Gothic, provoked for that reason a startled interest. One wonders how many people guessed then that by 1918, when Dean George H. Edgell of Harvard and Fiske Kimball published their history of world architecture, the church built from these plans (Figure 160) would be one of the four Boston buildings illustrated in that book and that like the other two late nineteenth-century buildings pictured, Trinity Church and the Boston Public Library, this Ashmont church would be seen by the authors as another national prototype — of a new Gothic Revival. One suspects that very few people, standing in the as yet unopened library, which at that very moment had eclipsed Trinity Church and Medievalism generally, could have seen this. Yet such was the force of the new vision and of the two Boston architects who launched it — Ralph Adams Cram and Bertram Grosvenor Goodhue — that right through to the 1930s this Gothic Revival would parallel the Classical Revival in extent and importance and its leader, Cram, would become the Boston architect of his generation who most importantly shaped architecture not just in Boston but throughout the country.

Two important churches may be thought of as significant bridges, as it were, between Trinity Church and All Saints, Ashmont. The first to be built was Sturgis and Brigham's Church of the Advent, designed in 1875 and finished by R. Clipston Sturgis, one of Cram's early mentors. The interior of the Advent (Figure 161) is not at first glance anything like that of Trinity. Yet actually, the two churches (built at almost the same time) are very alike in plan: both are more nearly Greek than Latin crosses, with short, stubby naves and enormous chancels and transepts to each side with balconies — in other words, both are in plan auditorium churches, designed about a central area, without the long, narrow Medieval nave. In detail, although the Advent possesses nothing like Trinity's frescoes, its original stained glass (by Kempe and by Clayton and Bell, two famous English makers) as well as its splendid later glass by Christopher Whall is of high quality and the figure sculpture in stone and wood throughout the interior has no parallel at Trinity. Most important, Sturgis's manipulation of interior space at the Advent is brilliant. The crucial factor is that he persuaded the conventional arches flanking the high chancel arch to very different disclosures: the arch to the right opens out grandly for its full height into a large Lady Chapel, while the arch to the left is filled in with the organ casework and opens out only below for one story through a heavy arcade into a much smaller chapel. The addition of low oak screens (executed some years later but obviously intended by Sturgis) between the arches into the Lady Chapel gave a wholly new dimension to the ingenious equilibrium. These densely carved screens hold to the planes of the walls below, while the arches above open out into a lofty secondary apse, thus foiling the left flank of the chancel, where the organ casework *above* holds to the planes of the walls. Volume and void are nowhere better handled in any Boston church.

rium. The effect of the two interiors as Cram and others (T. S. Eliot, for example) saw them on Sunday morning was even more striking, for the Advent was designed by Sturgis as a stage, not for preaching, but for the musical and ceremonial pomp of the Anglican Solemn High Mass. The Advent, not Trinity, was the cutting edge of the break with the Puritan past in Boston.

As was nearly always the case in late nineteenth-century Boston, the sources were English. The parish of the Advent was founded in 1844, eleven years after the start of the Oxford Movement in England, and its artistic ornament and liturgy caused a sensation in Boston. The boy choir of 1849 was among the first in the country and for some years the Epis-

160

Unlike Trinity, the Advent also possessed from the beginning a conspicuous high altar and reredos of Sturgis's design to which was added in 1892 the large openwork screen by Sir Ernest George and Harold Peto, in each case the gift of Isabella Stewart Gardner. The effect is not just more interesting than that of Trinity; in the way the Advent focuses finally on the high altar and at the same time spreads out at the church's flanks into a variety of perspective and light and shadow, its plan is transformed: the Advent is a temple; Trinity, an audito-

copal bishop of Massachusetts refused to make his annual visitation to the parish because, in Phoebe Stanton's words, the Advent had scandalized him "in using art." By the 1880s the Advent's rector was Charles Grafton (a founder of the Cowley Fathers, the first post-Reformation Anglican monastic order), who had been sent to Boston by the great Tractarian leader, Edward Pusey. Under Grafton the Advent's "Pugin-Medieval" pageantry and ornament became virtually a tourist attraction, "widely famous," in the words of *King's Handbook*

FIGURE 160. Cram, Wentworth and Goodhue. Perspective by Goodhue of All Saints' Church, Ashmont, 1891–1894. How could Cram and Goodhue in their first church achieve such a masterpiece? In fact, Thomas Tallmadge thought it an essential achievement for an architect like Cram, "who aspires to be a prophet." There must be, wrote Tallmadge, not only the element of surprise, but such an architect's first work must swiftly "swim into the ken of an astonished and needy world."

FIGURE 161. Sturgis and Brigham. Church of the Advent, Brimmer Street at Mount Vernon Street, at the foot of Beacon Hill, designed in 1875–1876. The church was completed after John Sturgis's death in 1888 by R. Clipston Sturgis in association with Henry Vaughan, who designed the pulpit and supervised the design of the west window; Ralph Adams Cram and Bertram Grosvenor Goodhue, who designed the interior of the Lady Chapel and much other interior ornament; and Sir Ernest George and Harold Peto, who designed the great openwork screen of 1891–1892 that surmounts Sturgis's high altar reredos.

161

FIGURE 162. Henry Vaughan. Chapel of St. Margaret's Convent, Louisburg Square, Beacon Hill, 1882. St. Mary's Church, Dorchester, Vaughan's only parish church in the city, is visible in Figure 89.

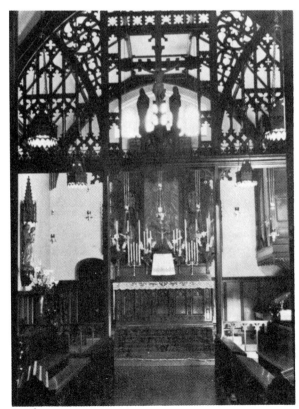

162

of Boston, "for its imposing ritual . . . large surpliced choirs and processionals [and] richly adorned and lighted altar." It is significant that the Advent's only rivals in the 1880s were the huge new Roman Catholic Cathedral of the Holy Cross and the Jesuit Church of the Immaculate Conception nearby.

The Advent's vivid Medievalism was echoed on a much smaller scale, by the other new High Church Anglican center of this period in Boston, St. Margaret's Convent in Louisburg Square. Its small but handsome chapel (Figure 162) is, so to speak, the second bridge between Trinity and All Saints, for it was designed by Henry Vaughan, a devout Anglo-Catholic who had been chief draftsman to George Frederick Bodley, the great English Gothicist. As Cram's chief mentor, Vaughan was thus able to introduce him at first hand to the English Gothic Revival, and in Vaughan's own work and in the English work Cram first saw during his trip to Europe in 1886, Cram perceived at once the same sort of creative spirit in the Gothic mode that had been evident to him in the Romanesque manner at Trinity. Converted to English Gothic, Cram converted also to Anglo-Catholicism in Rome in 1887 and upon his return to Boston was baptized and received into the Episcopal Church.

The effect the Oxford Movement had on Boston in the 1880s is suggested by the fact that Cram, the son of a Unitarian minister, was by no means the most prominent offspring of a Unitarian clergyman to become an Anglican. Two others were Colonel Oliver Peabody and Mary Lothrop Peabody, the daughter of the preeminent Unitarian divine in Boston at this time, Samuel Kirkland Lothrop. It was, in fact, a herald of sorts that it should have been Lothrop who commissioned Richardson to design a Medieval church for his congregation — the Brattle Square Church (Figure 64). That commission established Richardson

in Boston. And it was Oliver and Mary Lothrop Peabody who startled Back Bay Boston by leaving King's Chapel, perhaps the city's most prestigious Unitarian church, and converting to Anglicanism at All Saints, Ashmont, where they became Cram's first patrons and largely built for the parish Cram's first church in 1891–1894.

How Cram met them we do not know, although it may have been through R. Clipston Sturgis, who has been credited with designing the Peabody town house at 25 Commonwealth Avenue. But as it turned out the commission to Cram was as important as the one to Richardson, for All Saints signaled a new direction for the Gothic Revival in America and for American religious art generally: in Cram's wake that revival became not only more Medieval but explicitly Catholic. It was also an unmistakable sign of how the city was changing. Puritan Boston, by 1900 one of the largest Roman Catholic dioceses in the world and one of the seedbeds in America of the Oxford Movement, was by the early twentieth century also the center of a full-fledged revival of Medieval Catholic art — from churches to vestments — which by the 1930s had revolutionized the visual image of American Christianity. Culturally, the Puritan tradition was dying at its heart and would wither increasingly in the course of the twentieth century. So too, after the Second World War, would the Catholic artistic tradition, but in the meantime it stimulated Cram to an architectural achievement comparable with Richardson's and McKim's.

Cram insisted that All Saints constitute "a complete reversal" of American architectural design. He was determined, he wrote in 1899, that it "must have nothing of the artificial savagery of 'modern Romanesque'; nothing of the petty trivialities of those buildings that have been tortured into chaotic fantasies in the wild desire for an aggressive picturesqueness." But the fact that Cram led American church architecture at All Saints away from Richardsonian Romanesque as decisively as McKim did in the realm of secular design at the Public Library is less important than the fact that Cram insisted All Saints must not be "simply a study in archaeological experiment; it must be essentially a church of [the late nineteenth] century, built not in England, but in New England."

Cram asserted vigorously all his life that though architecture must naturally evolve out of the past, "if it remains in bondage to this older art, if it wanders in the twilight of the precedent or, in fear and trembling, chains itself to the rock of archaeology . . . it ceases to be art — ceases? no; it has never even begun; it is only a dreary mocking of a shattered idol, a futile picture puzzle to beguile a tedious day." Yet his illustration of this point of view was rather paradoxical — beginning with All Saints, he designed in the late nineteenth and early twentieth centuries a long parade of Gothic churches — thus posing starkly the underlying problems not only of his own work, but of revivalism as a whole and of both Richardson's and McKim's work particularly. As we will see in the next chapter, Louis Sullivan's early achievements in Chicago paralleled both McKim's Public Library and Cram's All Saints in Boston. From the perspective of today, Cram's insistence that All Saints was a building of its own rather than of some past time thus reads like a riddle. It is the riddle of explicit revivalism generally, which was the driving force in American architecture until the 1930s.

The underlying problem here is that we lose sight of two facts: first, that Cram was an avowed disciple of Richardson; second, that it was not Richardson's style that impressed Cram, but the way Richardson (and Vaughan and the English Gothicists) handled style. Like McKim, Cram repudiated Richardson's style but *not* Richardson himself, who Cram was correct in thinking would in future years be venerated not for the style but for the vitality he introduced into American architecture. We also overlook the fact that for Cram as for Richardson and McKim, modernity lay not in style but in how style was used. Thus Cram, at age twenty-two in 1885, in his diary, put his finger exactly on why he thought Richardson had so easily overwhelmed Victorian Gothic: American Gothicists "not only copy the deficiencies as well as the beauties [of Medieval Gothic] but they make modern necessities conform to Gothic forms. . . . It does not seem," wrote Cram to himself, "as though such servile copying is true art." Cram's definition of modernity emerges clearly: modern necessities ought not to conform to Gothic forms; it must be the other way around; the modern necessities must shape new Gothic forms. And this premise — that old styles cannot only be copied and adapted but can also be re-created — explains why Talbot Hamlin could call Cram's Gothic work "epochal" in the twentieth century and why Claude Bragdon (an ardent admirer of Sullivan) could in 1907 compare Cram with Sullivan: Cram, wrote Bragdon, could design Gothic churches "without dragging a train of absurd archaisms in their wake."

Though the distinctions between copying and adapting are clear enough, between adaptation of a style and its re-creation into new forms the topography is harder to chart. Montgomery Schuyler, a leading architectural critic at the turn of the century, put Cram's thesis this way: "the Gothic principle is the very principle of progress, and faithfully applied to modern conditions would result in an architecture as unlike in form [but] as kindred in spirit to the medieval building in which thus far it has found its most triumphant expression." Cram himself — so clear did all this seem to him — could not understand why Victorian Gothicists, instead of trying to take up the Medieval threads and logically develop them, chose to study to death the old Medieval forms, as if they were all the life Gothic could ever have. The question Cram posed had thus to do more than anything with *what was and what was not Gothic.* His primary contention was that it was organism, not form, that should be studied, "principles . . . not moldings." The American Gothic Revival, Cram thought, had exhibited invariably either a perverse scholarship in dead forms, un-Gothic because such a copybook Gothic had no artistic integrity; or a perverse spontaneity in new forms, un-Gothic because they did not arise from Gothic principles of design and construction. The former was a case, Cram thought, of careful reproduction: the latter of careless reminiscence.

It was not, significantly, Pugin's view, or the view of his disciples, like Upjohn. Pugin had held that Gothic "had gone its length" by the Reformation and that "it must necessarily have destroyed itself thereafter." Cram, on the other hand, in the little booklet describing the plans for All Saints that the parish issued in 1892, held that "beautiful as were the results of the religious builders of the 15th century, they themselves had almost infinite capacity for still nobler works," but that this capacity was never realized, for by the early sixteenth century "churches were no longer built, but destroyed instead"; and that modern Gothicists should emulate Richardson's capacity for original design and rather than building churches "that shall pretend to have been built in [the sixteenth] century [should] work steadily and seriously towards something more consistent with our temper and the times in which we live." Gothic was not dead, concluded Cram, only moribund — and misunderstood. The difference between Pugin and Cram is the difference between adapta-

tion (few talented architects *can* copy) and re-creation. Cram, wrote Charles Maginnis many years later, "pleaded without ceasing for an honest architecture of blood and muscle for the scenic mimicry of historic form."

All Saints was Cram's first attempt to achieve this ideal, and it is only his genius that misleads one at first into thinking that it is a careful "period piece" Perpendicular essay. In fact, Cram would have been bored to death with the picture-postcard replica of an English village church we imagine we see at Ashmont, as well as ashamed to have copied such a church. Not everyone liked everything about All Saints; Charles Eliot Norton wrote to Cram in 1892 that though the design seemed to him "well thought out," he wondered how Cram would "justify for our modern needs so heavy a tower?" Yet in 1916 one of Cram's partners told only the truth when he wrote that All Saints "formed the foundation of [the firm's] career and reputation." The famous view of the church — which probably appeared at one time or another in every American architectural journal of the period — is from the southeast (Figure 160), a point of view from which one can easily see why its grandeur of mass seemed to many to yield a kind of robust New World Perpendicular, all the more persuasive for "the skill with which," wrote Schuyler of the windows, "the depth of the wall is revealed." Though explicit in its reminiscence, All Saints is profoundly original. Inspired by English Perpendicular parish churches in its overall design and detailing, the Ashmont church also owes much to Trinity Church in its sense of disciplined picturesqueness. But the authority with which the great tower of All Saints leaves the ground, the dark grandeur of its tremendous volume, and the enormous, quiet majesty and striking simplicity of the whole church — all this was new in American architecture and

Cram, Wentworth and Goodhue. All Saints' Church, Ashmont.
FIGURE 163. The Great Tower, 1894.
FIGURE 164. The nave, 1892, looking toward the north aisle and the chancel.

very much at odds with the "gilded age" (Figures 163, 164). The sense of mass and masonry, utterly unadorned and robustly laid up, is by no means oppressive; John Coolidge has observed that the rough-textured and random-coursed walls of All Saints are ordered with such delicacy of feeling that they seem the work of an artist rather than of a mason, unconsciously echoing Cortissoz's analysis of McKim's use of marble in the stair hall of the Public Library.

Within, All Saints must have seemed even more astonishing: this great church is more simply conceived than many small wooden chapels of the time. "Serious and simple to excess! is it not?" Henry Adams's query might well have been applied to the All Saints nave. Though it was not immediately inspired by the Cloth Hall at Ypres, Cram's description of that hall is significantly the best description of his Ashmont nave: "a simpler composition could hardly be

imagined," he wrote, "or one more impressive in its grave restraint. . . . Its great quiet elements are left alone, not tortured into a nervous complexity. . . . The great hall [is] broken only by columns and arches and roofed with a mass of oak timbering like an ancient and enormous ship, turned bottom up." For a nave, of course, the simile is even more apt. All Saints was a remarkable achievement for a first church; so much so that of its type — the suburban as opposed to the city or cathedral church — it is almost universally regarded as his masterpiece. Some have gone further; John Coolidge once observed: "so much of what one admires at All Saints' survives dehydrated in Goodhue's solo performances; and so little in the later works of Cram."

How was it done? One needed to know Gothic so thoroughly and to think in it so naturally as to be able to use it as a kind of language, the vocabulary and grammar of which could then grow as it was stretched by the "modern necessities" Cram wrote of. He called this "creative scholarship." It might take many forms. Typical of his architectural programs, for example, was his conclusion that because fifteenth-century English design had "acquired its richness and fluency at the expense of certain [thirteenth-century] qualities of reserve, formalism and classical gravity," much might be evolved by applying "the lessons of suppleness and adaptability learned in the 15th century [so as to develop] through modern forms some of the qualities of composition, proportion, development and relation" that had characterized Gothic in the thirteenth century. One might argue that this was more scholarly than creative, but in other architectural programs of Cram's the scale seems to tip more clearly to creativity alone. The downtown church, for example, fascinated Cram. Because it had by his time to contend with soaring skyscrapers amid which the loftiest towers were futile, such conditions (he wrote in 1899), "being essentially modern and almost without precedent," offered the church architect his most exciting challenge in the twentieth century. Yet where adaptation ceases and re-creation begins is easier to define in theory than it is to explain in practice.

Cram's solution to Boston's apartment house problem, discussed in Chapter 5, is a case of adaptation; Richmond Court (Figure 128) was not, as we saw, without some stylistic justification and was both innovative and successful. Significantly, it does not possess battlements, Cram having concluded that these were scarcely necessary for an apartment house. (Lest this seem obvious, it should be stated that a later apartment house next door, Hampton Court, does possess battlements as did many twentieth-century apartment houses inspired by Richmond Court.) It is a small thing, but the lack of battlements discloses a crucial factor in Cram's work: whatever the architectural program, he insisted that worthwhile architecture, much less a creative scholarship, was impossible in any form unless it was rooted in a quality he early perceived in Medieval cottages: "Frank and simple and direct," he wrote, "built for use . . . they possess in the highest degree perfect adaptation to function, and therefore absolute beauty." Originality in design was only posturing for Cram, unless it arose from a structural need that in turn arose from function.

This principle did not result from a timid mind that sought refuge in the tried and true: yielding an innovative adaptation at Richmond Court, it is the root of Cram's re-creation at All Saints. There, the nave is not just simply conceived — it actually repudiates all the usual Gothic conventions of height to width to length. It is too wide for its length and too low for its width. Such originality is all the more striking upon discovery because though one feels a new quality at Ashmont, it is so quietly achieved that it is hard to identify. The reason, as Robert Brown observed, is that All Saints is original in design "not from any desire to be 'original,' but simply to honestly meet . . . present conditions." In this case the new condition was that the whole congregation expected to see both altar and pulpit. This compelled so wide a nave that Cram reduced the aisles to narrow ambulatories, a change in plan that suggested to him a change in elevation: he made the aisles very low, endowing instead the clerestory with the principal windows and consequently with an unusually lofty quality that discreetly reversed the usual Medieval proportions in both plan and elevation. The change in plan was adaptation. To have then expressed this plan so perfectly in elevation, thereby shaping a nave that was *finer* because of its unusual dimensions, the breadth and height of which imply and control the famous tower — that was re-creation. The result was a most "un-Gothic" nave by the standard of the copybook, but a nave of exceptional strength and amplitude that foretold many of Cram's later triumphs, including his masterpiece — the nave of St. John the Divine in New York (1916–1926), which startled A. D. F. Hamlin into admitting that it exhibited "such originality and boldness of invention as to form in reality a new and distinctly American chapter in [Gothic] development." It so moved Kingsley Porter, the Harvard medievalist, that he called Cram's nave "a tenth symphony."

It had happened before. Bates Lowry has written of the sixteenth-century attempt to revive the Classical architecture of antiquity — "Suddenly, in Bramante's work, buildings appear that seem to be *continuations* of the [ancient] Imperial Roman style rather than reinterpretations or copies of it." My emphasis illuminates the nature of the achievement of both McKim and Cram, whose work, like Richardson's, in whose vitality it was rooted, may be seen as two sides of the crest of nineteenth-century American architecture — when the adaptive tradition we have seen develop throughout that century flowered at last into an American architecture that was able to transcend adaptation.

McKim figures importantly in Boston architectural history because of the Public Library. But it is Cram's work — though only his Boston buildings can be discussed here — that is Boston's contribution to the climax of nineteenth-century American architecture.

Only recently have scholars begun to assess the impact of Cram on his time. Never popular among the architectural establishment because he did not admire the Ecole des Beaux Arts and decidedly unpopular in many circles because of his Socialist leanings and passionate Medievalism, Cram, scion of an old, distinguished, but not well-off Unitarian family, came to Boston in the 1880s as an architectural apprentice to Rotch and Tilden. A leading light of the Boston Bohemia of the 1890s, Cram, along with Bertram Goodhue, Alice Brown, Bliss Carman, Fred Holland Day, Herbert Small, Louise Imogen Guiney, and Richard Hovey (often in league with Ernest Fenollosa, Daniel B. Updike, and Bernard Berenson), was a vital part of this fin-de-siècle movement, which influenced so many currents of thought. During this period, Cram himself was art critic for the *Boston Evening Transcript*. His first appearance in that journal had been under the prophetic heading "Have We a Ruskin among Us?" and by the First World War Cram had indeed become not only the architect who represented Boston to the world, but a kind of "American Ruskin" whose earnest and controversial views surfaced everywhere in the 1920s, from the novels of F. Scott Fitzgerald to the Encyclopaedia Britannica. After he and Goodhue won the prestigious competition to design the United States Military Academy at West Point in 1903, Cram's reputation rose like a tidal wave and overflowed into a dozen vocations.

He and his designing partners (Goodhue from 1892 to 1914; Frank Cleveland and Alexander Hoyle from 1914 to 1942) designed well over fifty churches in over forty states and overseas for virtually every denomination and in nearly every imaginable style; a great many houses, libraries, and schools; and collegiate buildings at the University of Southern California, Rollins College, Notre Dame, Bryn Mawr, Wellesley, Princeton, Sweet Briar, West Point, and Rice University. In many cases they designed or supervised the design of whole campuses. The firm dominated American church archi-

FIGURE 165. Cram, Goodhue and Ferguson (Boston Office) with Okakura Kakuzo and Francis Gardner Curtis for Guy Lowell. Japanese Garden Court, Museum of Fine Arts, Boston, 1909, as originally furnished.

tecture between 1900 and 1940 and exercised an enormous influence upon American architecture generally and on the allied decorative arts particularly. In the meantime, though he had never gone to college, Cram became a distinguished Medievalist. He prefaced Henry Adams's *Mont-Saint-Michel and Chartres.* He was a founder of the Medieval Academy of America. As a Medievalist, he enjoyed a transatlantic reputation; no journal tackled his detractors more vigorously than did the *Times Literary Supplement* when it pointedly observed in 1916 that Cram "does not enjoy Gothic romantically or talk romantic nonsense about it; he hears its living music." He was also a scholar in Japanese art and a member of the visiting committee of the Japanese collection at the Museum of Fine Arts in Boston. His *Impressions of*

Japanese Architecture and the Allied Arts remains in print today and is a standard source in the field. For many years professor of the philosophy of architecture and head of the School of Architecture at the Massachusetts Institute of Technology, he was also a social theorist of some importance who strongly supported Franklin Roosevelt's New Deal; Albert Jay Nock once asserted that it was only Cram's reputation as an architect that had "overshadowed [his] claims as a philosopher." Finally, Cram was the foremost ecclesiologist of the Anglican Communion.

Cram established himself in all these fields through more than two dozen books and an avalanche of scholarly and polemical articles in upward of fifty journals in the United States and abroad, including five journals of which he was either a founder or editor, among them *Commonweal*. Indeed, Cram seems often to have created in his books the demand he and his partners then met at their drafting boards. But his writings are perhaps important today chiefly because neither Richardson nor McKim wrote very much, and it is only in Cram's books that one can discover the specific techniques of the "creative scholarship" he held was necessary to re-create rather than only adapt. It will thus serve more than one purpose to relate here these principles to his important Boston work, which constitutes the best case study imaginable in explicit revivalism and the many forms it could take. There is, for example, no more striking instance of how fundamental to Cram's work and how widely applicable was his theory of "creative scholarship" than the Japanese temple room and garden court (Figure 165) he designed in collaboration with the curatorial staff at the Museum of Fine Arts in Boston at the time of the opening of the present building in 1909. For generations his work there has been studied and admired: writing in 1910, Julia de Wolf' Addison marveled at the way in which Cram's rooms achieved "a wonderful harmony of great verisimilitude without being a servile copy of any existing building," while in 1928 G. H. Edgell pronounced these rooms "masterpieces . . . an achievement unsurpassed in American work or, for the matter of that, abroad." Here again, as at McKim's library, there lay behind Cram's work a timely and also an original purpose: timely in that these interiors were a setting for what was already the most distinguished collection of its kind in the world, and original in that, as Addison pointed out, "not until such a museum as this is seen, may a visitor fully understand the message of Japanese art as displayed in this way."

It is significant that the "inspiration" Addison thought the root of Cram's tour de force at the museum was exactly the aspect Whitehill emphasized in his own analysis of those rooms in 1970 in his *Museum of Fine Arts, Boston: A Centennial History*. In an attempt to explain how such strikingly appropriate interiors could have been created "without attempting to reproduce Chinese or Japanese interior decoration," Whitehill pointed to the use of "natural wood and plaster in a structural relation that has always pleased the *sensibilities* of the Japanese." The emphasis is my own. Not only does Whitehill's statement point to Cram's insistence that re-creation depended on studying the underlying motives and principles of a style rather than only its past forms, but also his analysis as a whole illustrates how keenly sensitive Cram was to where and with what materials he was working.

In the town of Westborough, for instance, when he converted a barn into a church in 1900, he insisted the painted red boarding of the exterior be left alone, refused to introduce pointed windows or even stained glass, and installed Venetian blinds only to filter the light. Yet he more than rose to the opportunity offered him in the same year by the dramatic site on which he built St. Stephen's Church in Cohasset (Figure 166), the massive Gothic tower of which rises majestically from a great crag overlooking the ocean. Similarly, the stone and half-timbered Atwood House (1917) and the nearby playhouse and art gallery (1916) Cram designed in Gloucester are built on great weatherbeaten rocky ledges and of the same rock. In the case of the house, entrance is gained through a kind of porte cochere that tunnels through the rocky foundations and the first floor of the house, from the middle of which a stone staircase leads up through the stone ledges to the main living floor, where the same rough stone is used for the fireplace. On Beacon Street in Brookline, however, near Richmond

166

167

Three parish churches in Boston by Cram and his partners.

FIGURE 166. St. Stephen's Church, Cohasset, 1899–1906.

FIGURE 167. All Saints' Church, Brookline, 1894–1926. Perspective by Goodhue showing the tower, which was never built.

FIGURE 168. Second Unitarian Church of Boston (now Ruggles Street Church), Audubon Circle, the Fenway, 1913–1917.

168

Court, his Gothic design of 1894 for All Saints' Church (Figure 167) at the corner of Dean Road is decidedly less robust and far more delicately conceived, and at nearby Audubon Circle, Cram reacted to that urbane red-brick apartment house square by making his Second Unitarian Church there (1913) the handsomest Georgian church in twentieth-century Boston (Figure 168).

This sensitivity to both site and materials proceeded as well from yet another controlling principle, without which all these buildings would have seemed only a kind of mimicry to Cram: his buildings are what they seem to be. If they possess vaults, they are *real* vaults of self-supporting masonry — as surely as Cram made no attempt to disguise the barn wall, he made no attempt to disguise construction generally. His great timber truss roofs, his vaults, everything in his work reflected his conviction that false construction could only be "ostentation," that the beauty of a thing was what it *did* beautifully. "The foundation of good architecture," Cram asserted, "is structural integrity." Anything else, he thought, was "scenepainting." A splendid illustration of this principle is St. Anne's Chapel at the Anglican convent of that order in Arlington (Figure 169), where the evocative character of the chapel derives in large measure from the rough but carefully designed random-coursed stonework, both within and without. But Cram's constructional honesty was not any more archaeological than his design. He was grateful for steel, and there *is* steel in some of his churches. But it is frankly used *as steel*, in the same way stone is used as stone. No material was unacceptable to Cram; he invariably used whatever material, ancient or modern, could honestly best serve his purpose. For example: he often wanted vaults, but he wanted also to answer the new need of his own time for better acoustics. Thus he stimulated

Wallace Sabine and Rafael Guastavino to undertake their pioneering acoustical experiments, which resulted in the first patent on an acoustical ceramic tile.

Another and crucial idea undergirded all Cram's work from the earliest rendering of a Gothic church we possess by Cram himself, dated 1888. This rendering, which established the fundamental design concept of his firm's first decade (including that of All Saints, Ashmont), shows an architecture of mass and proportion, simply composed and articulated. It documents Cram's assertion that "the trouble with most architects is that they do not know how to stop when they get through." This is perhaps the particular principle that triggered his creativity. Like Richardson, Cram had no faculty for designing detail; that was Goodhue's task. But he was a master of mass and scale, the quality that is most evident in the rough elevations by Cram himself — which contain as it were the genetic code of his buildings — from which Cram's designing partners developed the detail. The towers of All Saints, Ashmont, and St. Stephen's, Cohasset, are evidence of this. So also is his strikingly simple Ellingwood Chapel at Nahant (Figures 170, 171).

On a grander scale he only enlarged upon the same principles. The notion that Gothic must be characterized by great height is never found in his writings. Rather, he knew that its invariable characteristic was the varied organization of "perspective through perspective," as Kingsley Porter put it. This was accomplished best, Cram wrote, by a nave and chancel of "utmost simplicity of design, gravity of massing, refinement of proportion [and] classicism of composition," set within a larger space enclosed by "bounding walls following varied lines, giving space, distance [and] variety." This manipulation of space, he went on, should coincide with an analogous distribution of "clear, diffused light

169

Two suburban chapels by Cram and Ferguson that are among their most admired work.

FIGURE 169. St. Anne's Convent Chapel, Arlington, 1914–1916.

FIGURES 170, 171. Ellingwood Mortuary Chapel, Nahant, 1917–1920. Both were inspired by Cram's own chapel in Sudbury (Figure 176).

170

171

FIGURE 172. Cram and Ferguson. Conventual Church of SS Mary and John,
Monastery of the Order of St. John the Evangelist, 980 Memorial Drive,
Cambridge, 1935–1938. Cram's last major work in Boston. The nave makes
an interesting comparison with his first nave, at All Saints, Ashmont, in
1892 (Figure 164).

St. Paul's Cathedral in Boston shows the nature of Cram's revolution of the visual image of American liturgical art.

FIGURE 173. The chancel as it appeared in the late nineteenth century.

FIGURE 174. The same chancel after Cram's remodeling, 1913–1927.

173

dying away into shadows" in the great central space and an "infinite variety of light and color" beyond the arcades or, perhaps, the reverse. All these factors of space, detail, light, and color must subtly develop toward a flowering, as it were, at the chancel arch — where the church must at one and the same time "draw in, concentrate, until it converges on the high altar," and yet "open out, expand, reveal vistas." It was the nave arcades, Cram pointed out, that organized this design concept. By continuing to the altar their main lines invariably converged there, while their voids disclosed the expanding variety of perspective beyond, whose "profound shadow and sudden lights" were for Cram the fundamental decoration of a Gothic church. His wonderfully strong interior, with its rugged stone walls, at the Chapel of the Cowley Fathers Monastery in Cambridge, one of his last major works, is a splendid illustration of his evocative manipulation of interior space (Figure 172).

For Cram this *was* architecture, and he once suggested that every architect should eschew even "one atom of detail" for five years in order to learn this lesson.

They would learn, too, he thought, other lessons: that while detail was not necessary it could greatly deepen a building's significance if still other principles were followed. "Richness," wrote Cram in 1899, "must be backed up by fine, solid and simple architecture. The finer and franker the lines [of the building], the more reserved and powerful the parts, the greater the richness of detail that may be allowed" — so long, that is, as such detail was absolutely subservient to the building that it decorated. Stained glass, he argued, should never utilize perspective or modeling: it must be entirely flat, entirely decorative, entirely architectural, never assertive; never a hole in the wall, but, rather, the wall rendered translucent. Finally, such detail, though reticent, must be allowed only if it were of superb quality. Thus, such was the Cowley Chapel's strength and large simplicity that Cram felt able to fill the windows with jewellike glass and to articulate the various interior volumes with exquisite wrought iron and finally to introduce into the sanctuary a magnificent marble baldachino over the high altar. His remodeling of St. Paul's Cathedral in Boston is as well a vivid example in the Classical tradition of how different was a Cram chancel from a Victorian chancel because of these principles (Figures 173, 174). Similarly at one of his most distinguished Gothic churches, the First Unitarian Church in West Newton, he designed a tower of great elaboration. But a close study will disclose that the exquisite cut-stone detail grows perceptibly out of a very strong and simple mass as the tower rises (Figure 175).

Inevitably, some of Cram's Boston work is not successful. His First Universalist Church in Somerville (1916–1923) is curiously bland. Several other churches, having never been finished, lack coherence. This is particularly true of St. Paul's in Malden, probably designed in 1905 and started ca. 1911. All Saints in Brookline (begun in 1894), like Christ Church in Hyde Park (1892), suffers also from the fact that its tower was never built. Even the few elevations Cram himself did for Boston University in the late 1930s (most of the design of Boston University was by Cram's partners) must be pronounced failures; Cram admitted himself he was sad to have left so large a mistake behind him in his home town, a mistake later rendered ridiculous by mock-Gothic towers. Cram's Boston skyscraper was also a disappointment (Figure 216); he complained that after he had signed the contract for the Federal Building of 1930–1931, he discovered that the government expected him only to design a masonry veneer for another architect's steel frame. But it is not true, as so many assume, that most of Cram's finest work is elsewhere: the Boston area parish churches we have discussed here are among his best work in a vein many scholars think prompted Cram's most convincing achievement. Of this type Greater Boston possesses two buildings by Cram that are unique.

One is St. Elizabeth's Chapel in Sudbury, built by Cram in 1914 on his own estate for his family, friends, and neighbors and now the local Episcopal parish church (Figure 176). It is a masterpiece of straightforward but remarkably evocative church design, where mass and proportion and simple materials, sensitively handled, disclose the root of Cram's genius. It is in fact in such simple churches that one sees why Cram could handle so superbly the great masses of St. John the Divine in New York, which is the largest cathedral in the world. The second of these two works is, again, All Saints, Ashmont, for this church leads, as it were, two lives: not only did it herald Cram's Gothic Revival in the 1890s, but because Oliver and Mary Lothrop Peabody dedicated their fortune to its embellishment and endowment, Cram was able to develop and expand All Saints over a forty-year period into a uniquely distinguished example of his work. In the first place he was able to add to the church (in 1912 and 1929) two chapels, evolving an ante-choir in between, and thus to endow what was already an unusually lofty suburban church with the spatial grandeur of a great city church. But it is the decorative splendor of All Saints that is chiefly notable, for one may see at Ashmont work by most of Cram's important artist-collaborators, including the two who developed most under Cram's patronage and direction: the sculptor Johannes Kirchmayer and the glassman Charles Connick, two Boston artists who dominated American architectural art in their fields in the early twentieth century and whose work is the climax in Boston of the decorative revival of the 1870s we first saw in the Back Bay.

Two important Cram churches in the western suburbs.

FIGURE 175. The tower of the First Unitarian Church in West Newton (1906) is among the most striking in Greater Boston. The church was also notable for its cloistered garth, until it was ruthlessly obliterated by an extension of the parish house.

FIGURE 176. Built as Cram's own chapel, St. Elizabeth's Church, Sudbury (1914), is of its type Cram's masterpiece.

Connick, whose studio Cram helped to establish in 1910, was a master of expressive line. Though his glass was entirely decorative and architectural, that quality only enhanced Connick's often distinguished portraiture. Stained glass, for Connick, was pure translucent color, whose function it was, through the filtration and radiation of light passing through color in its utmost purity, to yield what he called an "adventure in light and color" — in the "balancing of light and shadow in dissolving color as it functions in changing lights," the light vibrating through "eloquent spaces patterned in stone." Connick's work, which moved the poet Earl Marlatt to describe Connick glass as "darkly murmurous as stars or ships on gull-illuminated seas," can be seen throughout Greater Boston. His best local work is probably at the Cowley Fathers Monastery in Cambridge, and his first representative window is at All Saints, Brookline. But All Saints, Ashmont, is the best place to study his characteristic style because here one can see his glass as nowhere else alongside the earliest and largest of only a few American windows by Christopher Whall, the great English glassman whose vitality decisively influenced Connick.

Kirchmayer's work at Ashmont may be his masterpiece. As persuasive an artist in wood as was Connick in glass (though on its own Kirchmayer's work shows a difficulty with scale that only Cram seems to have been able to control), Kirchmayer was quite different from Connick. He wrote almost nothing. But his Lady Chapel triptych at Ashmont (Figure 177), like all his work the result of chisel and mallet on a solid balk of wood with no model (only the nude in charcoal and the drapery in crayon on the balk itself), is sufficient to document his reputation as the preeminent American architectural sculptor in wood in this century. Inspired by his Detroit Cathedral reredos

of 1910 — which was exhibited in the rotunda of the Museum of Fine Arts in Boston, such was its distinction — the All Saints triptych was itself exhibited in Boston, before its installation in 1912, at the St. Botolph Club Gallery on Newbury Street. Notice how in the central panel Kirchmayer quietly persuaded the Virgin's robe into two small praying angels. It is a small thing, but it knits the central figure even more closely into the whole composition. This triptych, an undoubted masterpiece of the American Gothic Revival, is easily overlooked, however, because it is the decoration of the chancel at Ashmont by these and other artists between 1897 and 1918 (under Cram's overall direction) for which the church became so notable in the early twentieth century. Some of the planned decoration was never carried out. Sir Edward Burne-Jones died before he was able to undertake the altarpiece; the pavement was never tiled; the murals and stained glass Cram wanted in the chancel have never been attempted. But one notices these things only when they are pointed out.

Within the chancel arch is a lofty rood of Byzantine splendor. Conceived by Cram as a great "icon" to dominate the interior, it caused almost as much controversy when it was installed in 1911 as had the *Bacchante* at the Public Library in 1896. But though strenuous efforts were made to remove it, this vivid crucifix, which marks the triumph of Medievalism in Puritan Boston, is still there today. Behind it opens out the best example anywhere of Goodhue's genius for decorative detail as restrained and integrated by Cram into architecture (Plate 7). The stone figure sculpture was modeled for John Evans by Domingo Mora — sculptors whose work we first saw at Trinity Church and at the Public Library — while the gold plate of the high altar (Figure 178) was modeled by Kirchmayer, who also executed the

For forty years after the erection of All Saints, Ashmont, Cram continued to lavish upon it some of his most distinguished architectural art.

FIGURE 177. Detail of altar and triptych in the Lady Chapel, 1912; one of the outstanding works of art of the American Gothic Revival, it has been called the masterpiece of Johannes Kirchmayer.

FIGURE 178. Detail of elevation by Goodhue of the high altar cross, modeled by Kirchmayer in 1899 and executed by Thomas McGann in gold plate on chiseled brass. For the entire chancel see Plate 7.

178

superb carvings of the oak paneling by Irving and Casson. The altarpiece, *The Enthronement of the Virgin,* was painted by George Hallowell and was exhibited in London to critical acclaim in 1904. The tabernacle is the work of the Boston goldsmith James Woolley.

This sumptuous detail, which was widely published in its own right, is conceived as an integral part of the Caen stone reredos. Inspired by the great medieval screen at Winchester Cathedral, it in turn inspired Goodhue's famous reredos at St. Thomas, Fifth Avenue, and is comparable with both. The provision for oil paintings within the cut stone and for free-standing pedestals flanking the altar gives an unusually multidimensional feeling to this ensemble, which is so faultlessly detailed and proportioned that it enhances and sets off the altar, rather than crushing it. Indeed, the overall decoration of the chancel shows the last of the major principles from which Cram's vitalization of Gothic design proceeded — that though a strongly designed interior might be endowed with very elaborate detail, such detail had not only to be well crafted, it had to be organic and functional. There is no better illustration of Cram's strict functionalism: All Saints was designed as a setting for liturgical worship in the Catholic tradition, which is essentially corporate in nature. Thus its architectural art reflected this function. It was designed to be visually corporate, each detail calling attention not to itself but to an overall and organic unity of design that Cram insisted must pervade not only the architectural setting but all the elements of what John Henry Newman called "the sacred dance" of the High Mass — including even such things as altar frontals and processional crosses, which Cram and Goodhue designed here as elsewhere.

Cram did not pioneer this concept at All Saints. It is evident in his and Goodhue's first important decorative work, their Lady Chapel interior (1894) at the Church of the Advent. It also animates Cram's much simpler chancels at St. Luke's Chapel, Roxbury (1900), and at St. Michael's Church, Milton (ca. 1914), and his interior remodeling (1910–1930) at St. John the Evangelist on Beacon Hill, where Cram, who was a parishioner there, formed a kind of partnership with the choirmaster, the well-known American composer Everett Titcomb, that yielded a standard of liturgical art for which St. John's was known throughout the country. But the Ashmont chancel became as much the national model for church interiors in the Catholic tradition as had the church itself for exteriors because Cram and Goodhue and their artist collaborators achieved at All Saints one of the most distinguished ensembles of Gothic Revival art in the world.

I T is a measure of how vital a center of explicit revivalism Boston remained until the 1930s that two other local firms specializing in both Gothic and Classical church design emerged in Cram's wake after 1900 and achieved a national reputation. The most remarkable was Maginnis and Walsh, whose senior partner, Charles Donagh Maginnis, became the leading Roman Catholic architect in this country.

Boston is fortunate to possess perhaps Maginnis's masterpiece: the Church of St. Catherine of Genoa on Spring Hill in Somerville (Figures 179, 180), built from 1907 to 1916 through the generosity of a son of Boston's first Irish and Roman Catholic mayor, Hugh O'Brien, to whom a chapel of St. Catherine's is dedicated. The fact that Maginnis himself had first come to Boston as an immigrant from Ireland underlines the increasing importance at this time of the Irish Catholic contribution to Boston's cultural as well as its political life. (Maginnis, who near the end of his life was awarded the Gold Medal of the American Institute of Architects, the highest award the institute confers, may in the long run be accounted a more important figure in Boston's history than Mayor O'Brien.) St. Catherine's is admittedly flawed in two respects: its marble columns hide steel and its lofty campanile was never built. Probably neither flaw is due to Maginnis, and it is in other respects so fine a church that Cram published it frequently and Sylvester Baxter called it "one of the most beautiful churches in America." Few would quarrel with that assertion. Though the exterior today has been disfigured with some kind of paint, the high barrel-arched nave leads still to a sanctuary splendid with Mexican onyx and gray and white marble whose somewhat silvered hue contrasts beautifully with the rich gold ground of the half-dome above the high altar. The two side chapels, St. Hugh's and St. Catherine's, have reliefs by Kirchmayer, and the high altar was almost certainly the inspiration for Maginnis's altar and chancel of 1938 at Trinity Church in Boston, which Hitchcock has pointed out completed Trinity much as Richardson wished to in the first place (see Plate 5). Nor did Trinity's magnificent new high altar occasion any controversy. Though in 1913 President Eliot of Harvard had been scandalized by Cram's "Catholic" chancel for the Second Unitarian Church in Boston, by the 1930s Cram was designing high altars for Protestant churches all over the United States.

Maginnis (who was also a fine illustrator; see Figures 197–200) endowed many parishes in the Boston archdiocese with singularly beautiful churches. These include Our Lady of the Presentation in Brighton (1913); St. Aidan's in Brookline (1911), Maginnis's own parish; St. Julia's in Weston (1920); and the chapel at St. John's Seminary in Brighton

(1899–1902). Particularly notable are three Gothic churches: St. Catherine of Siena, built in Norwood in 1909 and noted also for extensive stained glass by Connick; St. Paul's (1920) in Dorchester; and St. Theresa's in West Roxbury, designed in 1929 and graced with figure sculpture by George Aarons. What is now Emmanuel College in the Fenway was also designed by Maginnis in 1916. But even these seem to pale before the beautiful Gothic buildings he began to design for Boston College in 1909 (Figure 181). Somewhat unappreciated today, his work there constitutes the most dramatic Gothic Revival ensemble in Greater Boston and was a strong factor in his widening reputation. On the other hand, for all his skill as a Medievalist, Maginnis was most persuasive as a Classicist. His design for the Jesuit chapel in Weston, assured, regal, and filled with splendid stained glass by Earl Sanborn, is the most distinguished example of twentieth-century Classicism in Greater Boston (Figure 182).

The other major Gothic firm in Boston was Allen and Collens. Like Maginnis and Walsh, whose work ranged from a much admired Carmelite convent in California to the sumptuous high altar of St. Patrick's Cathedral in New York City, Allen and Collens enjoyed a national reputation. They designed, for example, Riverside Church in New York City. As they were much given to compromising the structural integrity Cram insisted upon by using hidden steel framing, one is grateful that they did not do this in Boston at their Lindsey Chapel at Emmanuel Church on Newbury Street (Figure 183). This chapel, with its ornamental ironwork by F. Koralewski and its fine high altar and stained glass by Sir Ninian Comper, is exquisite. Other local work by Allen and Collens includes what is now St. Clement's Church (ca. 1920) in the Back Bay (which has lost its handsome tower) and the Second Church in

Newton (1909–1916). Nor should one forget that Henry Vaughan, despite the demands of his work on the Washington Cathedral, continued to design parish churches around Boston, including St. John's Church in Newtonville (1902–1903) and the Church of the Redeemer in Chestnut Hill (1913–1915), the handsome tower of which was added in 1920, after Vaughan's death but from designs prepared by him. Other architects essayed important Gothic work in Greater Boston that included R. Clipston Sturgis's Perkins School for the Blind in Watertown (Figure 184), and Shaw and O'Connell's Immaculate Conception Convent in Malden (1930). Non-Gothic church work of merit by able local architects must also be noted: particularly fine is Charles Greco's Blessed Sacrament Church in Jamaica Plain (1910–1917), with a reredos by Henry H. Ahl and Stations of the Cross by Kirchmayer, and two churches by Edward T. P. Graham: St. Paul's (1915) near Harvard Square (see Figure 201) and the Church of the Holy Name (1938–1939) in West Roxbury.

Often suburban ecclesiastical architecture, however little known, is of considerable interest. For example, the Church of the Blessed Sacrament (1911–1913) in Walpole is one of the best of the "modernist Gothic" type in Greater Boston. St. Paul's, Natick (Brigham, Coveney and Bisbee, 1919), includes chancel carvings by Charles Pizanno and glass by both Joseph Reynolds and Earl Sanborn. Connick glass not already mentioned will be found at the Harmony Grove Chapel, Salem, and at St. John's Church, Hingham, where one may also see glass by Wilbur Burnham, another early twentieth-century Boston craftsman of national reputation, whose best local work is probably in two West Roxbury churches, Holy Name and St. Theresa's. Glass by Margaret Redmond is extant at St. Peter's, Beverly (as well as at Trinity

Church, Boston), and the only building in Greater Boston whose facade is honored by the work of the distinguished British sculptor John Angel is Archbishop Williams High School in Braintree.

All religious groups felt the force of this Boston school of church design, and not only Cram designed churches for widely differing groups. C. H. Blackall, for example, designed both Temple Israel (1907) on Commonwealth Avenue near Kenmore Square and Temple Ohabei Shalom (1928), a richly Byzantine synagogue on Beacon Street in Brookline, as well as the Episcopal Church of Our Saviour (1889) in Roslindale and the Baptist Tremont Temple on downtown Tremont Street in 1895. Cram's own influence was most keenly felt in the mushrooming early twentieth-century suburbs around Boston, where modern Gothic churches abound. Sometimes they are small, like St. Joseph's in Needham (1918) or Sacred Heart in Watertown (1913); quite large Gothic churches, however, such as the Church of the Immaculate Conception in Everett (completed in 1908) or St. Theresa's in Watertown, begun as late as 1939, were not exceptional. Particular examples of Cram's influence include two churches in Winchester — the Church of the Epiphany (Warren, Smith and Biscoe, 1904) and the Unitarian Church of Winchester (George Newton, 1898) — and the First Baptist Church in Melrose, also by George Newton (1907), and Edwin J. Lewis's All Souls Church (1901) in Braintree. Churches that were more Romanesque than Gothic continued to be built — St. Anthony's in Revere (1924), for example — and one can see in Wellesley (at Carrère and Hastings's Wellesley Congregational Church, 1921–1923) that Georgian continued to be popular; but the Cram-type Gothic parish church was far more widely favored: both the First Congregational Church of Wellesley

The Boston work of Maginnis and Walsh, the leading American Roman Catholic architects of the early twentieth century, includes three buildings of national importance.
FIGURE 179. Church of St. Catherine of Genoa, Somerville, 1907–1916.
FIGURE 180. Interior of St. Catherine's.
FIGURE 181. Boston College, Newton, 1909, the most dramatic and extensive collegiate Gothic in Greater Boston. The pond is now built over.
FIGURE 182. Chapel of the Jesuit Novitiate, Weston, 1929. Maginnis's design is surely the most distinguished example of twentieth-century Classicism in Boston. His chancel at Trinity Church, Copley Square, is shown in Plate 5.

181

182

FIGURE 183. Allen and Collens. Leslie Lindsey Memorial Chapel, Emmanuel Church, Back Bay, 1920–1924.
FIGURE 184. R. Clipston Sturgis. Perkins School for the Blind, Watertown, 1912.

183

184

Hills (George Newton, 1901) and St. Paul's Roman Catholic Church in Wellesley (Joseph Maginnis, 1917) are thus typical of this period in that they were closely modeled on All Saints, Ashmont.

One could go on indefinitely: nearly every town around Boston as everywhere else has its memorial to Cram's influence. One wonders, however, if there was any deeper meaning to this. Was there an idea behind All Saints, Ashmont, as far-reaching for America in its sphere as the idea that lay behind McKim's Public Library? Beyond architectural reform, when he began All Saints in 1892, Cram made no such claim. Yet one looks naturally for a larger meaning in this triumphant twentieth-century Medievalism centered in once-Puritan Boston. It may well be found in the fact that both a Congregational and a Roman Catholic church in Wellesley as well as a Unitarian church in Winchester and a Baptist church in Melrose are by no means exceptional in having all been inspired by Cram's church at Ashmont, it-self an attempt to re-create a pre-Reformation English Gothic style. And as we have seen, by the twenties, the interiors of such churches were likely to be as similar to one another as their exteriors. In retrospect, the fact that Cram (unlike Richard Upjohn, who in the mid-nineteenth century refused even a Gothic exterior to a Unitarian parish in Boston) ultimately persuaded almost everyone in America in the early twentieth century to a common Christian architecture is surely not unrelated to the enthusiasm with which Americans of so many different religious traditions ultimately welcomed the ecumenical movement after the Second World War.

CHARLES MAGINNIS observed once that "in the austere quality of his mind and the logical enterprize of his pencil one detects [in Cram] a resemblance to McKim as certainly as one perceives the analogy between Goodhue and Stanford White." For Boston the first analogy was more important: McKim was the partner in charge of all his firm's Boston work, including the Public Library, and it was Cram who decisively shaped the important work of his office in Boston, including All Saints, Ashmont. Designed and built simultaneously, the Copley Square library and the Ashmont church paralleled each other from the beginning. Both the outgrowth of Richardson's work, each was so distinguished an example of "recreating" a historical style that church and library shaped the dominant modes in American architecture until the Second World War.

That both these pivotal examples of "creative scholarship" should have been built in Boston is significant. That Boston's leading architect from the early 1900s to the 1930s was a man who did recreate a vital Gothic architecture is of even more importance. As Kenneth John Conant has pointed out, Gothic "trigger[ed] an inventive personal reaction in Cram as a designer. Under him the Gothic which he loved had an afterlife so vigorous that it is unfair to think of him as merely a revivalist." Conant, in fact, makes the same point about Cram's architecture that the *Times Literary Supplement* made of Cram's writings on Medieval Gothic: Cram succeeded. McKim had also succeeded. In a more personal way, so had Isabella Stewart Gardner. In a letter to Mrs. Gardner about a proposed visit by her to his Sudbury chapel, Cram emphasized that it was not only *his* chapel and that it was regularly open to the public. Indeed, Fenway Court and Cram's chapel are very comparable buildings: it was scarcely less outrageous for Cram to build a "twelfth-century chapel" on his estate than it was for Mrs. Gardner to

build a "Venetian Renaissance palace." It is perhaps more to the point that in the case of both chapel and palace, as also at the Public Library and at All Saints, sincerity and taste — genius, if you will — yielded convincing and distinguished results.

It was these characteristics that ennobled so much that might otherwise be thought ostentatious in the legacy of beauty left to Boston. In each case these buildings reinforced in Boston particularly an attitude toward art and architecture that had for centuries been taken for granted. In their distinct and several ways the Public Library, Fenway Court, All Saints, and Cram's chapel sought to advance a whole range of cultural values in a society newly pluralistic enough to make good use of all of them and vital enough to have nurtured men and women equal to the creation of the kind of beauty that would express those values in a distinguished way. Architecturally, this involved recalling the Renaissance palazzo and the Medieval church. But these were perceived as building types that could stimulate the creative architect to his own personal and timely achievement in the same way that the Renaissance attempt to recover the architecture of antiquity had stimulated Bramante. That this centuries-old tradition of revival and re-creation found such vital champions in the 1890–1930 period, and that one of these, Cram, was the Boston architect who exercised the widest national influence in his time, was a crucial factor in Boston's architectural history during this period. A vital Boston culture, secure at the turn of the century in the glories of the Renaissance and Medieval revivals, withstood easily the violence of Louis Sullivan's fierce attack on what has often since been called "historicism."

8

The Shadow of
Louis Sullivan

For boston, Louis Sullivan will always be the man that got away. Actually, as Sullivan entitled his memoirs *Autobiography of an Idea*, one might better say that he will always stand for the *idea* that got away, which is rather loosely called "Modernism." Like so many architectural terms, it is not luminous, but Whitehill is one of the few people who have had the courage to point out that "it is no good at all trying to describe a building as an example of 'modern architecture.' Modernity evaporates overnight." Because it still has a polemic meaning, the word has stuck, however, to a movement in architectural history that began nearly one hundred years ago.

The son of immigrant parents, Sullivan was Boston born and bred — in 1856 at 225 Bennet Street, as is announced by the plaque on this site, which is now a part of the Tufts New England Medical Center. Sullivan did not like Boston. Nor has Boston ever really claimed Sullivan, and there is no work at all by him in his birthplace. Sullivan in Boston recalls irresistibly Conan Doyle's famous lines in "Silver Blaze," when the inspector asks Sherlock Holmes:

"Is there any point to which you would wish to draw my attention?"
"To the curious incident of the dog in the night-time."
"The dog did nothing in the night-time."
"That was the curious incident," remarked Sherlock Holmes.

What Sullivan did do in Boston seems somehow unreal today. Imagine a young man, uniformed and hoisting a Springfield rifle with fixed bayonet, tramping Tremont Street the night after the Great Fire of 1872, a part of the M.I.T. Battalion charged with defending what was left of Boston's business district. Behold the prophet and genius of modern architecture in America, in Boston in 1872 — before Charles McKim or Ralph Adams Cram; before even H. H. Richardson had come to live in Boston.

In his autobiography, which is written in the third person, Sullivan's impressions, as a boy and as a young man, of Boston were set down with a startling vehemence. "As a conglomerate of buildings," he remembered, Boston had "depressed Louis Sullivan continuously since he became engulfed in it." Yet the one building that overwhelmed Sullivan was perhaps the least likely — the Gothic Revival Masonic Temple on the corner of Tremont and Boylston Streets, designed in 1867 by Merrill G. Wheelock (see Figure 51). Sullivan passionately loved it. It seemed to him, he recalled:

a message from an unseen power. Thus immersed, he returned again and again to his wonder-building, the single one that welcomed him, the solitary one that gave out a perfume of romance, that radiated joy, that seemed fresh and full of laughter. How it gleamed and glistened in the afternoon sunlight. How beautiful were its arches, how dainty its pinnacles; how graceful the tourelle on the corner, rising as if by itself, higher and higher, like a lily stem, to burst at last into a wondrous cluster of blowering pinnacles and a lovely, pointed finial.

That he should also have admired Richardson's tower at the Brattle Square Church is more understandable (Figure 64).

After attending the public schools, young Sullivan began the study of architecture at M.I.T., having formed, he later remembered, his ambition to be an architect while talking of architecture with a builder one day on Commonwealth Avenue. But he liked M.I.T. no better than Boston; the curriculum seemed to him a "misch-masch of architectural theology" and after a year he departed, unnoticed, ultimately for Chicago, where his family had previously moved. The Boston of Richardson and of McKim's library and then of Cram did not mourn the loss. But as Sullivan's fame spread, his work and that of his disciples continually shadowed both the Classical and Gothic Revivals and all the modes in between during the 1890–1940 period in Boston as elsewhere, for behind the diverse pomps of traditional design, a perhaps revolutionary new force was increasingly evident after the 1890s; whatever style was chosen, working underneath and behind style (which was becoming, as it were, a kind of skin, not always nourished by underlying structure), there was often to be found — the steel frame.

Except in very tall buildings, its presence was (and is) only vaguely felt. Indeed, structural innovations often went unnoticed. Who suspected then, or knows now, that in the Shepley office's Chamber of Commerce Building of 1890–1893 (since become the Grain and Flour Exchange) "the floors and ceilings of the offices in the sixth and seventh floors over the Board Room," according to Charles S. Damrell, "are suspended from [the] roof" (see Figure 195)? In fact,

the least distinguished buildings "architecturally" in Boston in 1890–1940 are often those most famous for innovative structure. The New England Mutual Life Insurance Company (1939) is a case in point. Its design by his partners drove Cram to near despair and David McCord to a scathing clerihew:

> Ralph Adams Cram
> One morning said damn,
> And designed the Urn Burial
> For a concern actuarial.

But underneath lurked a tour de force; the so-called floating foundation (occasioned by the fact that this is all made land) that William Le Messurier called "an example of brilliant engineering."

What effect such structural innovations ought to have on design was much disputed in the 1890–1940 period. Cram wrote in 1914:

The steel frame is the *enfant terrible* of architecture, but like so many of the same genus it may grow up to be a serious-minded citizen and a good father. . . . If we can make it realize that it is a new force, not a substitute, we shall do well. When it contents itself in its own proper sphere . . . then it may be a good servant. Like all good servants it makes the worst possible master; and when it claims as its chiefest virtue that it enables us to reproduce the Baths of Caracalla, vaults and all, at half the price, or build a second Chartres Cathedral with no danger from thrusting arches, and with flying buttresses that may be content beautifully to exist, since they will have no other work to do, then it is time to call a halt.

"A new force, not a substitute" — Boston's leading "traditionalist" seems to have understood very well the driving force behind Sullivan's determination to break out of the historical circle of revivalism and eclecticism and create instead the steel frame's own aesthetic. But Boston as well as Chicago had a great fire in the early 1870s, which, as we have seen, Sullivan saw the effects of at first hand;

FIGURE 185. Proposed interior treatment (1895) of the Boston subway system, the first in the United States. The designer is unknown, but Peabody and Stearns, Alexander W. Longfellow, Jr., and Edmund Wheelwright are all known to have designed rapid-transit stations in the early 1900s. Nonetheless, *The Brickbuilder* complained in 1898 that architecturally the new subway was "about as enlivening and cheerful as a second century catacomb."

Boston as much as Chicago was bursting its narrow confines. Why then did Boston's vitality in the late nineteenth century — which is seen in its tremendous landfill operations and in such revolutionary new developments as America's first subway (Figure 185) — seem so uncongenial to Sullivan? Why was the Chicago Style of the 1880s and 1890s not, instead, the Boston Style? Was it, perhaps, for the same reason that in Scully's view the New England Shingle Style was left to Frank Lloyd Wright to develop? It is not quite so simple.

Quite aside from our new appreciation of the work of McKim and Cram, William Jordy has observed:

For those who would take an overly provincial view of the Chicago achievement, for instance, how puzzling that two of the principal clients for Chicago commercial buildings were the Boston financiers, Peter and Shepard Brooks, who seem to have been exceptionally forceful in instructing their architects (through their Chicago real estate agent,

Owen Aldis) on the virtues of architectural austerity. The Brooks brothers not only financed the Portland and Montauk, but the Monadnock, Rockery, and Marquette buildings, among others, all of them key buildings in conditioning what is conventionally tagged as the "Chicago" point of view. Yet the Brooks' exhortations seem to have been powerless to effect anything in Boston comparable to the Chicago achievement.

This is all the more interesting because, as Thomas Hines has pointed out, in their rationale for the Monadnock's severity — that it was "for use not ornament" and that "its beauty will be in its adaption to use" — these two Boston financiers unconsciously formulated the Chicago aesthetic. Moreover, it has long been argued that Richardson's work was a crucial influence on Louis Sullivan: Richardson's Ames Estate Store on Harrison Avenue (1886; demolished), for example, suggested a treatment Sullivan was to develop for the expression of the steel-skeleton skyscraper. Wheaton Holden has also documented an important inspiration for the Ames Store in Peabody and Stearns's R. H. White Boston Warehouse Store of four years earlier. He notes that Peabody and Stearns's design, "a milestone of its time" and the most widely published of their buildings, almost certainly was known to John Root when he designed his very similar McCormick Office and Warehouse Building in Chicago in 1885–1886 and that "Louis Sullivan may even have owed a lingering debt of thanks to Robert Peabody in his Walker Warehouse in Chicago [1888–1889]."

Still another new factor appears in Margaret Henderson Floyd's recent study of the Copley Square Museum of Fine Arts (Figure 53), where, as we have seen, Sturgis and Brigham introduced into this country the large-scale use of terra-cotta. Mrs. Floyd observes:

The importance of iron and steel construction to nineteenth-century architecture has long been known, yet the revival of ceramics plays a more important role than is generally recognized. Louis Sullivan's terra-cotta sheathing of the Wainwright Building in St. Louis (1890–1891) or his Guaranty Building in Buffalo (1894–1895) are acknowledged today as the finest designs of their time. They would hardly have reached reality, however, without the prior development of a terra-cotta industry in America for the reproduction of the material, or continuous experiment to perfect the relatively sophisticated technology of its application.

"Technologically," she concludes, "the [Copley Square] Museum of Fine Arts, Boston, was the bridge between London and Chicago."

To root these things in an even more venerable past, here are two further examples of what is increasingly surfacing. Cynthia Zaitzevsky recently discovered a long-overlooked building by Richardson (Figure 186), which because of its post and lintel construction on the upper floors suggests a relationship between Richardson's work and the mid-nine-teenth-century Boston Granite Style. Moreover, Winston Weisman has pointed out that a number of mid-century Philadelphia buildings may well have been important sources for the principles Sullivan applied to the tall metal-frame skyscraper. One building is thought by Weisman to be especially significant: the Jayne Building, whose front — "conceived as a stone skeleton with glass panels stretched between the ribs" — Weisman traces back to Isaiah Rogers's Boston work. He notes:

Isaiah Rogers seems to have first suggested the solution in his Merchants' Exchange of 1842, setting four monumental four-story Corinthian piers in antis as an ornamental screen for the business spaces behind. These are tied together at the various levels by deeply recessed floor strips. Windows fill the space between the vertical and horizontal elements. In the Brazer's Building [Figure 206], erected at the same time, Rogers transforms this ornamental scheme into a structural one while preserving its vertical character. In this instance, the granite piers of the ground story carry a lintel and then continue on through the second and third stories without interruption as a result of the way in which the spandrels are recessed between the piers.

Weisman goes on to point out that Sullivan, who worked in the vicinity of the Jayne Building when employed by Furness and Hewitt in 1873, is likely to have seen this and other buildings and he asserts that two early Sullivan buildings are "more or less identical" to the Philadelphia buildings. As such evidence accumulates, it surely bears out Jordy's observation.

On the other hand, now that the Modern movement has floundered somewhat, it will doubtless occur to many that Boston and not Chicago was building the better and more humane city in the 1880s and 1890s and that the 125-foot limit restricting the growth of the skyscraper in Boston was wise; that Boston was correct to draw back from the skyscraper. Norris K. Smith, for example, has written disparagingly of one scholar who,

like most historians, accepts the conventional notion that the tall building was somehow made necessary in Chicago (but not, for some reason, in Paris or London or Vienna)[or Boston], by economic and utilitarian considerations; yet I think it reasonably clear that the one motivating force behind the invention was simply greed. The skyscraper, with its fabulous multiplication of rents, was made for those same greedy exploiters who were slashing down the magnificent forest of Michigan and Wisconsin, all but exterminating the buffalo and the Indians, and polluting the rivers and the air (as Burnham outspokenly declared) in their heedless and headlong pursuit of wealth. William Jordy has taken the time to ascertain that the invention of the tall building was the work of uneducated architects — men who, to a man, had had a high school education at best, together with some instruction in engineering, and had little or no grasp of the traditions in support of which the art of architecture had long functioned.

In his recent and provocative *Form Follows Fiasco,* a play on Sullivan's famous dictum "form follows function," Boston architect and critic Peter Blake has concluded that Modernism after all was "a religion as irrational as all others, from snake-handling to psychoanalysis." But here again, it is not so simple a matter.

In the first place it is significant that Bostonians tunneled America's first subway under the sacred sod of the Common but nonetheless restricted the height of skyscrapers: one could not *see* the subway; it did not intrude visually on the streetscape. Skyscrapers did. And there is a strong tradition that the erection of a Haddon Hall type of tall apartment building (A. H. Vinal's twelve-story building of 1903 at 48 Beacon Street) precipitated the height restriction formulated finally in 1904. Strongly contested, the legislation had to be upheld by the United States Supreme Court. But it was thought then — as it would be now — to be highly progressive legislation in that it was "preservationist" in its point and also distinguished between the business district, where buildings 125 feet high were allowed, and residential areas, where the limit was 80 feet. The first such comprehensive height-of-building law in the country, it had actually more than anything else to do with zoning. As we shall see, it was altered when the 125-foot limit proved a hindrance to the growth of the business district. Furthermore, the steel frame — and even a reflection of its aesthetic expression — appeared in Boston in the same year that the Classical Revival heralded by the Public Library went west with a vengeance and overwhelmed Chicago — indeed, the whole country — at the Chicago World's Columbian Exposition of 1893. In that year, while the Boston Public Library and All Saints at Ashmont were nearing completion, Boston was endowed with the Winthrop Building.

WITHOUT at all suggesting that Boston got the better of the exchange, it is nonetheless true that however much the city lost to Chicago with Sullivan's departure, Boston gained not a little back when Clarence H. Blackall of Chicago, who had not only taken both his B.S. and M.S. degrees at the University of Illinois but also studied at the Ecole des Beaux Arts, decided to settle in Boston. He is said to have taken a walk down Washington Street and been scarcely more impressed than Sullivan. Unlike Sullivan, however, Blackall saw opportunity; he became a draftsman for Peabody and Stearns. The first Rotch Scholar (in 1884), he was also the first president of the Boston Architectural Club and ultimately enjoyed a national distinction.

Blackall's work has not subsequently been given the attention it deserves. Few know that it was Blackall who carved out

FIGURE 186. H. H. Richardson. Hayden Building, Washington at La Grange streets, Downtown, 1875–1876.
FIGURE 187. Clarence H. Blackall. The Carter (later the Winthrop) Building, 7 Water Street, between Washington and Devonshire streets, Boston's first entirely steel-framed office building, 1893–1894; looking from the lavish tripartite glazing of the second floor to the rich, overhanging cornice.

of several Beacon Hill tenements in the 1920s the imaginative Primus Avenue Apartments off Phillips Street, that he was in fact a leading apartment house and hotel architect (among the first, at Oxford Court in Cambridge in 1926, to provide a parking garage integral to an apartment house), and even fewer realize the great number of innovative theaters he designed (discussed in Chapter 9). Even less is known about his early years in Boston. Yet Blackall in the 1880s and nineties was a conduit of sorts between Boston and Chicago. He continued to work there (he designed several buildings for the University of Illinois at Urbana in the early 1900s) and in 1888 he was explaining Boston to Chicago in a series of articles in *Inland Architect* while at the same time explaining the Chicago innovations to Boston in a similar series of articles in Boston's periodical, *American Architect.* Nor was he content merely to explain: it was Blackall who in 1893–1894 startled Boston by designing and erecting the city's first steel-frame building, the Carter (now the Winthrop) Building, between Washington and Devonshire streets (Figure 187).

It seems quite clear that this is *the* first such Boston building. When the subject of steel framing has come up in the past it has only been in passing, and perhaps for that reason the terminology employed has not been exact. Hitchcock, in *The Architecture of H. H. Richardson and His Times,* observed that Richardson's successors, "in building the Ames Building on Washington Street [the still extant skyscraper of 1889, not to be confused with Richardson's own earlier Ames Estate Store of 1886 on Harrison Avenue], were the first to bring the new skyscraper construction to [Boston]. This was in the same year, 1889, in which Bradford Lee Gilbert first used skeleton construction in New York for the Tower Building on Broadway." Some years later, in his *Guide to Boston Architecture,*

Hitchcock noted the Ames Building's "bearing walls of solid masonry," but he still overlooked the Winthrop Building and pointed instead to the Iver Johnson Building of 1908 as "almost the only example of early skyscraper design in Boston." Of course, "skyscraper construction" and "skyscraper design" can mean many things. The Sears Building of 1868 on the corner of Washington and Court streets appears to have been the first office building to have possessed an elevator in Boston, and both Peabody and Stearns's Fiske Building (1887), now destroyed, and the fourteen-story Ames Building of 1889, which has survived to challenge in distinction of design every subsequent tall office building in Boston, can certainly be called skyscrapers in the sense of having been dependent on the elevator (Figure 188). But insofar as steel framing is concerned, only two buildings have been advanced as possibly predating the Winthrop Building: the Exchange Building of 1887 by Peabody and Stearns (for whom it should be remembered Blackall was a draftsman) and the second Brazer Building by Cass Gilbert. But Colonel W. Cornell Appleton, Peabody and Stearns's last chief designer (who told Wheaton Holden of the steel framing in the Exchange Building), insisted it was only used in part and that the Winthrop Building marked the first time in Boston steel framing had been used throughout a building. And Walter Kilham, who suggested the second Brazer Building, also noted that the Winthrop Building could have been erected first. In fact, an examination of the respective building permits shows the date of Gilbert's design to have been 1896, three years after the Winthrop Building.

This is reflected in extant correspondence at the Building Department between Blackall and the city engineer, with whom Blackall argued a number of technical questions about the proposed

188

189

The skyscraper in Boston before and after
Blackall's Winthrop Building (see also Figure
46).
FIGURE 188. Shepley, Rutan and Coolidge.
The Ames Building, 1889. The fourteen-story
Ames Building dominated the Boston skyline
until 1914. To its left is the Sears Building
(1868; Cummings and Sears), later enlarged;
probably the first office building in Boston to
have been dependent upon the elevator.
FIGURE 189. Carl Fehmer. The Worthington
Building, 33 State Street, 1894; this was
among the first steel-framed office buildings
in Boston to follow the Winthrop Building's
lead.
FIGURE 190. Julius Schweinfurth. The Garden
Building, 248 Boylston Street, 1911.

190

steel-frame construction. Interestingly, Blackall's first application (dated 1892 and later abandoned) was for a masonry structure, while the second application, which for the first time shows that Blackall was the owner as well as the architect, is conclusively for a steel-frame structure. This second permit specifies steel under "external walls," "floor timbers," "headers and trimmers," and "rafters," while under "materials of front" the specification is "steel frame, brick and terra cotta covering." That this is the historic document, recording as it does the first use in Boston of the steel frame, is also substantiated by statements made only two years after the building's erection by the second-in-command at the Building Department, Charles S. Damrell. In his *A Half Century of Boston Building*, in this case surely the best testimony, Damrell wrote:

Few Boston buildings have received the attention that has been given to the structure upon the irregular tract of land bounded by Washington, Water, Devonshire Streets and Spring Lane . . . the first structure to be erected in Boston in which the skeleton system of steel construction has been used. . . . It consists, in brief, of a steel frame with brick and terra cotta simply as a filling or skin. Supporting columns are made of four pieces of steel, the cross section of one of which is like the letter Z, all riveted to a center plate. These columns extend through the walls and are joined rigidly by beams in each story, and are also connected by horizontal trusses on the floors and vertical trusses in the partitions in such manner that the whole structure is rigid. . . .

Damrell's attitude also documents the fact that the innovative Winthrop Building by no means "snuck in" Boston's "back door"; its significance was at once appreciated. Damrell not only illustrated the building in his book; he devoted his longest article to it. It was also published in *Inland Architect* in 1893. And Cram remembered forty-three years later in his memoirs that the Winthrop Building had been in the 1890s in Boston "the source

of curiosity and doubting amazement."

Today the Winthrop Building is no longer amazing, though it is still handsome, with its pale golden buff brick and terra-cotta "about the color of slightly burned toast," to quote from a mid-nineties description. More importantly, its exterior design is as interesting as its steel frame, for the two *are* related, and in a way that illustrates nicely the extent to which Blackall both agreed and disagreed with Louis Sullivan's steel-frame aesthetic. Blackall discussed this question at some length in his "The Legitimate Design of the Architectural Casing for Steel Skeleton Structures" in *American Architect and Building News* in 1899, where he rejected what he called the "post-and-girder" mode, as well as the "aqueduct style," and argued instead for a frankly Classical casing such as one sees in the Winthrop Building. He did conclude that steel-frame buildings should be expressed through a strong base, a plain shaft, and a rich, crowning cornice, but he made precisely the analogy to the base, shaft, and capital of the Classical column that Sullivan rejected. Yet there is about the Winthrop Building as a whole, particularly in its lavish first- and second-floor glazing, a striking expression of its steel-frame construction. This is all the more evident if one compares the Winthrop Building with Carl Fehmer's 1894 design for the Worthington Building at 33 State Street (Figure 189), for although the clean-cut window and door openings (as well as the building's overall profile) show that Blackall was not the only Boston architect of the period alive to the challenge of the Chicago School, at 33 State Street the steel frame is not so noticeably expressed as at the Winthrop Building.

Each of these buildings — two of many similar Boston buildings of the late 1890s — ought, however, to be compared with the Garden Building of 1911 (Figure 190), designed by Julius

Schweinfurth, who, like Blackall, had been employed in the office of Peabody and Stearns in the 1880s. Stephen Neitz and Wheaton Holden have pointed out that the glass panes of the Garden Building's first-floor showcase windows were joined at the building's corners without any intervening structural member and that it was in the same year, 1911, that Walter Gropius featured the "glass corner" in his famous Fagus Factory at Alfeld on the Leine. It would be easy to exaggerate the importance of this fact. None of these buildings exercised the national influence in the 1890–1930 period of the Boston Public Library or All Saints, Ashmont. But the Winthrop, Worthington, and Garden buildings illustrate very clearly that in the year the Classicism heralded by the Public Library achieved its triumph in Chicago, and throughout the next two decades, the historic architectural innovations of the period were felt in Boston with greater force than most have suspected.

I F very few Bostonians remember that Louis Sullivan was born and grew up in Boston, probably even fewer realize that in the mid-1870s Frank Lloyd Wright, who would become Sullivan's most famous disciple, was playing with his "Froebel blocks" in the Boston suburb of Weymouth, where his father was minister of the First Baptist Church from 1874 to 1878. Wright departed the Boston area at age eleven, however, and it is not too much to say that however much his early domestic work may have been rooted in the New England Shingle Style, he was scarcely ever heard of in Boston again until the 1930s. A few weak echoes of the Prairie Style exist; there are a few of what can only be called "Stucco Style" houses, and it is interesting that some of the best of such houses, characterized by straightforward

geometric forms, uncluttered by ornament, were built by architects for themselves: in Cambridge, for example, H. Langford Warren's home at 6 Garden Terrace, built in 1904, and Charles Greco's home of six years later at 36 Fresh Pond Parkway. All sought a more modern idiom. One Cambridge stucco house — 16 Berkeley Street, designed by Harley Dennett in 1905 — does reflect more clearly some of the same design elements one sees in the Prairie Style — the blocky, geometric form, the horizontal quality strongly reinforced by low, lidlike, and wide projecting roofs, the banked windows, while flat stucco wall surfaces avoid "historic" style or detail (Figure 191). Also in Cambridge, at 114 Irving Street, built in 1911, is a cement-walled house of the "Craftsman" type, so called because such houses were popularized by the magazine of that name, edited between 1901 and 1916 by Gustav Stickley, who argued for a greater emphasis on well-crafted practicality and simplicity in residential design. There are also some early examples of the low-sloping "California Style" bungalows that were perhaps the Prairie Style's chief competitors. Boston's Building Commissioner Patrick O'Hearn designed one for himself in 1904 on Melville Avenue in Dorchester. Another of this type was built eight years later, at 71 Avon Hill Street in Cambridge. In the Back Bay, perhaps the most "progressive" design of this period was the facade of 395 Commonwealth Avenue (Figure 192) by A. J. Manning in association with Louis Comfort Tiffany, who designed the mosaic work of the facade and also decorated the staircase hall.

Concrete was also used increasingly at this time. Harvard Stadium was, in fact, one of the earliest large-scale buildings of reinforced concrete. A number of concrete warehouses and a fine concrete viaduct and train barn (see caption to Figure 201) were also built in the early 1900s and

191

192

New directions in domestic and commercial design in the 1900s.

FIGURE 191. Hartley Dennett. 16 Berkeley Street, Cambridge, 1905.

FIGURE 192. A. J. Manning in association with Louis Comfort Tiffany. Frederick Ayer House (now the Bayridge Residence for Women), 395 Commonwealth Avenue, 1899–1900.

FIGURE 193. Coolidge and Carlson. Store front, 1304 Massachusetts Avenue, near Harvard Square, Cambridge, 1907.

193

Modern construction did not necessarily imply what we should today call "modern" design.

FIGURE 194. Coolidge and Carlson. The Colonial filling station (now a fruit market), Massachusetts Avenue at Northampton Street, South End, 1922, is more "traditional" than Boston's only surviving nineteenth-century gasholder (right).

FIGURE 195. Peabody and Stearns. Custom House Tower, 1911–1915, built on top of the original Custom House (Figure 18). In the right foreground is Shepley, Rutan and Coolidge's Grain and Flour Exchange, 1890–1893.

FIGURE 196. Daniel Burnham and Company. Architect's perspective of Filene's Boston Store, Summer and Washington streets, 1912, the last major work of one of the architects of the Monadnock Building in Chicago.

195

196

even a few concrete block churches (stylistically Gothic) were built, an innovation pioneered in the Boston area by Frank Bourne. His first such experiment was at St. Luke's Church in Chelsea in 1907. The idea did not, however, achieve any wide currency.

Nor did Boston rally particularly in the early years of this century to the latest European import. Tiffany's popularity notwithstanding, the full-fledged curvilinear forms of the Art Nouveau style occur seldom: the best example is Coolidge and Carlson's altogether charming Art Nouveau storefront near Harvard Square (Figure 193), surely one of the few of its type to have survived in this country. But one has to search hard for such "progressive" currents; and like the curiously Sullivanesque entrance arch to the Hotel Somerset (Arthur Bowditch, 1897), these things mean more now than they did then. Even distinctly new building types sought traditional forms: one has only to discover, unbelievingly, the delightful old gas station (Figure 194) that still stands at the junction of Massachusetts Avenue and Northampton Street in the South End to see how tenacious what is now called "traditionalism" was in Boston. Designed by Coolidge and Carlson in 1922, this Classical pavilion is of cement block construction, its eye-catching red dome supported by concrete columns. But the best example is Peabody and Stearns's Custom House Tower, dedicated in 1915 (Figure 195). (The 125-foot limit on Boston buildings did not pertain, the property being owned by the federal government.) Boston's first really startlingly tall skyscraper, nearly five hundred feet high, the tower took the form of a granite Classical campanile that Burchard and Bush-Brown complain looks like "a vast chimney stack rising from a Roman temple."

The Custom House, like the gas station, is representative. Aside from office buildings, and even in that building

type more and more discreetly, Boston's architectural vitality at the turn of the century diverged from the Classical and Gothic norms only to seek an increasing eclecticism. Admittedly, critics like Dean Edgell thought they saw in some few local buildings — such as Coolidge and Shattuck's Boston Lying-In Hospital of 1923 — "something of the modernist expression that we associate with the work of Sullivan and Wright," but Edgell admitted that the architects of the hospital would probably have denied any such intent "indignantly."

Even in Chicago, traditionalism remained rampant, and it had more to do with local pride than any devotion to Modernism that when Shepley, Rutan and Coolidge designed the monumental Classical Art Institute of Chicago in 1892, that city's architects retaliated by renaming the Boston firm "Simply, Rotten and Foolish." Twenty years later the same attitude surfaced in Boston when one of the architects of the Monadnock Building, Daniel Burnham, was commissioned to design Filene's Boston store. R. Clipston Sturgis went even to the length of writing a letter to the Boston *Herald* to protest not the Filene design but the choice of Burnham.

One of a series of five major stores by Burnham — Marshall Field's in Chicago, Gimbel's in New York, Wanamaker's in Philadelphia, and Selfridges's in London — Filene's Boston store (Figure 196) was significantly more advanced technically than stylistically. A frame of light-gray terra-cotta encloses on each of the principal facades a generous olive-green terra-cotta grid of windows that does emphasize (as Burnham intended it should) the importance of light and air to the building's function. The color contrast is also handsome. But the gray outer frame is richly detailed Italian Renaissance stylistically, and the fact that it was characterized in *The Brickbuilder* in 1912 as "a frank expression of modern ideas" says much for how many meanings the word "modern" may have. Actually it was an example, all the more striking for Boston given its designer, of modern technology endowed with traditional Classical pomp. In our meaning of the word, Filene's stands not for Modernism, but for the traditionalism that through an increasing eclecticism would continue to dominate Boston architecture for the next twenty or more years.

In the early years of the twentieth century the Classical of McKim and the Gothic of Cram were only the dominant strands of many in Boston, which in a sense was beginning as a whole to look like the Bayley House at 16 Fairmount Avenue in Newton, designed in 1883–1884. Each of the ground-floor reception rooms of the Bayley House was in a different period style and by 1920 the same could be said of Boston's buildings generally. Cram himself, as we have seen, designed buildings in every style under the sun. Indeed, most of Cram's collegiate work in Massachusetts — at Wheaton College and Williams College — was in the Classical tradition. And any one work is likely to disclose its own eclecticism: Talbot Hamlin noted that Cram's Second Church of Boston in Audubon Circle (Figure 168) was as "distinctly English" to one side of its tower (the church) as it was "distinctly American" on the other side (the parish house).

How eclectic Boston was becoming in the 1890s and 1900s is perhaps best illustrated by the work of one important local architect in a very short period of time: Edmund March Wheelwright, the then city architect, whose *Reports of City of Boston Architect Department* for 1891–1894 include designs of his that range from redbrick Georgian to full-fledged half-timbered Medieval villages and Oriental temples (Figures 197–200). Although municipal architecture might be expected to be rather conservative, hardly any historical style was safe from Wheelwright, or, indeed, any one building; his admiration for the Palazzo Vecchio in Florence is evident, for example, in his Fire Department Headquarters (Figure 197). The Oriental shelter and duck house he proposed for the Fenway was never built; but a similar building by Charles Austin (The Bird House) exists in Franklin Park. Nor was Wheelwright, whose work was then and still is much admired, any less eclectic in his private practice. His splendid Longfellow Bridge (1907) was inspired by one he had admired in the then Russian capital of St. Petersburg, while his Horticultural Hall (1901) may be the handsomest English Baroque building in the city. And though he was more than capable of stately masses (he designed the New England Conservatory, the Massachusetts Historical Society, and the Opera House), he was also able to rise to the only occasion I know of in the history of Boston's architecture when an architect was asked to design a building that would be something of a joke: the Lampoon Building on Mount Auburn Street near Harvard Square (Figure 201). This "jolly brick midget of a building," in William Germain Dooley's words, "smiles at you like a caricature of a face — circular windows for eyes, hanging lantern for a nose, a domed roof for a hat with a birdcage tassel, Gothic windows for ears, classical pilasters, gargoyles and what have you." For all this, it is by no means a silly building; although it is more ingenious than beautiful, it sits jauntily astride a flatiron-shaped island in the middle of Mount Auburn Street, mediating elegantly between the huge Jacobean and Georgian piles that surround it and tying together the streetscapes into one of the most charming urban vistas in Greater Boston.

One might illustrate a similar variety

CITY · OF · BOSTON
HEADQUARTERS ·
· FIRE · DEPARTMENT ·
Edmund M. Wheelwright · City Arch't

Edmund M. Wheelwright's work illustrates vividly the breadth of his eclecticism.

FIGURE 197. Boston Fire Department Headquarters, South End, 1894, now the Pine Street Inn.

FIGURE 198. Ferry head house proposed for East Boston, 1893.

FIGURE 199. Lunatic asylum at Pierce Farm, West Roxbury, 1893.

FIGURE 200. Shelter and duck house proposed for the Fenway, 1895. The sketches are all by C. Maginnis, then Wheelwright's draftsman.

FIGURE 201. The Lampoon Building, Mount Auburn Street, Cambridge, 1909. In the background is the campanile of E. T. P. Graham's St. Paul's Church, 1915. It would be unfair to forget, however, that Wheelwright was concerned with much more than style. He was an authority on schoolhouse design (his Brighton High School of 1894 was nationally influential), and he designed the robust reinforced concrete and iron viaduct and train barn at Forest Hills Elevated Station, West Roxbury, in 1909.

197

198

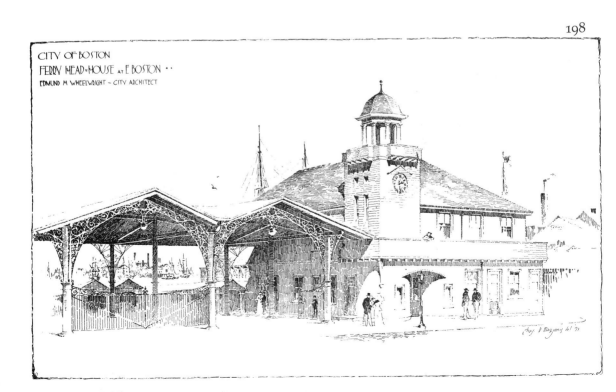

CITY OF BOSTON
FERRY HEAD-HOUSE at E BOSTON · ·
EDMUND M WHEELWRIGHT ~ CITY ARCHITECT

CITY OF BOSTON ≈ PVBLIC INSTITVTIONS DEPᵗ
LVNATIC ASYLVM ᴀᴛ PIERCE FARM. WEST ROXBVRY.
EDMVND M.WHEELWRIGHT CITY ARCHITECT..

CITY OF BOSTON   SHELTER ᴀɴᴅ DVCK HOVSE   BACK BAY FENS
EDMVND M. WHEELWRIGHT   CITY ARCHITECT

in the work of almost any of the leading Boston architects of the period. A recently discovered full-fledged High Georgian mansion of 1895 on Jones Hill in Dorchester by William G. Preston strikingly contrasts with his forbiddingly Medieval First Cadet Corps Armory of the same year in Park Square. Looking at these contrasts in the work of the same architects, one thinks of Walter Kidney's observation that after 1900

a house-was usually Georgian, Tudor, or Cotswold (Anglo-Saxon home atmosphere), unless it was a mansion and intended to look like one, in which case it might have been Jacobean or one of the Louis (aristocracy of wealth). A church — if not Colonial — would, for an old and ritualistic sect, be Gothic (Christian heritage); if it was for some new sect, like the Christian Scientists, it might be decently but non-committally wrapped in something classical. A synagogue, in absence of a true Hebraic architecture, was usually Byzantine or Moorish. A school was Tudor or Jacobean (Oxford, Eton). A theatre was either Louis XV (courtly diversions) or — especially if a movie house — something utterly fantastic, with some sort of high-pressure Mediterranean Baroque providing the norm (palace of illusions). For the center city, classicism was long the near-universal solution; a cluster of styles, rather than a single style, it clothed the museum, the library, the memorial structure in cool eternal beauty, but broke into rustications, ressauts, and swags, giant orders and Renaissance cornices for the more worldly office buildings, the bank, the apartment house, the theatre, the clubhouse, and the town mansion.

Quite distinguished architects even went so far as to essay one style on the exterior and another on the interior. Arthur Bowditch's extremely sparse exterior and vaguely Sullivanesque entrance arch at the Hotel Somerset does not prepare one for Little and Browne's opulent gilt Louis XIV ballroom within. Nor does the red-brick Georgian exterior of the second Fogg Art Museum, designed by the Shepley office in 1925, hint at the sixteenth-century Italian courtyard inside. To us this may seem incongruous,

but we vastly enjoy it. The truth is that the eclectics' creed is by no means dead.

Kidney's parenthetical asides — "Anglo-Saxon home atmosphere," "Christian heritage," "courtly diversions" — are the key to understanding the eclectics' creed. It is true that during this period well-traveled and well-educated architects, with well-stocked libraries of measured drawings and photographs of seemingly everything ever built and an endless supply of excellent immigrant craftsmen, coincided with clients equally well-traveled and well-educated and (until 1930) with more money than they often knew what to do with. It is also true that building beauty, as it were, was the high goal of many dedicated architects whose clients, insecure nouveaux riches, sought to build a kind of instant baronial heritage. But all these factors do not explain the stylistic diversity we are discussing. Kidney's asides do, for in Boston as elsewhere, just as the pervasive stylistic unity of the Greek Revival, for example, had reflected a homogeneous culture, so architectural eclecticism reflected the increasingly pluralistic culture that emerged at the end of the nineteenth century. Within the context of this cultural pluralism eclectic architects —meaning, substantially, all architects between 1890 and 1930 — argued that no one style could possibly be expressive and thus functional in every case for every building. One might continue to design Classical government buildings for the same reason Bulfinch had, because of Classicism's associations with Athens and the Roman Republic. Gothic churches were another example. But the eclectics pointed out that the country was far too diffuse culturally to rally as a whole in every case to any one style —including Sullivan's or Wright's. They did so because until the 1930s most continued to believe that the historical associations of a style were crucial to a building's functional expression, provided all the modern conveniences were worked into it. That was the eclectics' creed, and it proved an extraordinarily resilient idea: Everyman's definition of form follows function for many years, it was abandoned by architects only amid the financial trauma of the Depression and it has not been entirely abandoned yet — as numberless "Tudor" motels and "Colonial" restaurants attest — by the general public.

Only recently, however, have critics and scholars begun to take this controversial assertion seriously again and to try to judge eclecticism by its own standards. There are signs that the results may be startling. Some argue, for instance, that many of the innovations of the Shingle Style survived after all into the 1920s in the much maligned eclectic "Period House" in the suburbs. Jonathan Lane has asserted: "the early Period House took over with little modification the most advanced planning of the shingled houses of the eighties" and that between 1890 and 1930 the design of the Period House was marked by a gradual development from which

emerged three concepts in residential planning which survived the reaction against Eclecticism in the early thirties to influence profoundly the further evolution of domestic architecture in the United States — the open plan, the use of rambling, one-story designs [the horizontal dwelling unit whose development was also traced in Chapter 5], and the provision of outdoor living areas. The introduction of these ideas has been generally associated with the work of those architects who rejected eclecticism in the early thirties and who, at least initially, drew much of their inspiration from contemporary European architecture. It has not been fully recognized that these innovations first achieved considerable currency here at a time when the influence of eclecticism was paramount . . . !

A factor that contributed strongly to the integrity of this eclectic architecture was the remarkable contribution made by the artists' crafts (the Boston Society of Arts and Crafts, founded in 1897, was the first such society in the country). The superb quality of craftsmanship and of the artistry of the Public Library (Figures 140–142); of the chancel and Lady Chapel of All Saints at Ashmont (Figure 177); of Little and Browne's interiors at the Somerset Club, the Brandegee House at Faulkner Farm, and the Hotel Somerset; the finish of the Lindsey Chapel (Figure 183); the decoration of the Colonial Theatre (Plate 3) and the cut-stone detail of the west porch of Trinity Church (with figure sculpture for the Shepley office by Hugh Cairns and Domingo Mora under John Evans) — such things were seen then as they are coming to be seen again as very beautiful. Nor were such splendors restricted to great civic and religious buildings. Evans did superb cut-stone detail for the Ames Building. Such architects as Carrère and Hastings, McKim, Mead and White, and Cram and Ferguson designed a number of elaborate mansions on Boston's North Shore, discreetly hidden at the ends of private roads (particularly in Beverly, Manchester, and Gloucester). Hitchcock divulged a well-kept Boston secret when he remarked of these houses that "together they almost rival Newport." C. Howard Walker's interiors on the tenth floor of the Ditson Building (1916) at 178–179 Tremont Street include architectural carving by Kirchmayer himself. Henry Wilson, whose doors at St. John the Divine in New York have been so much admired, modeled a set of bronze doors (Figure 202) made by Gorham in 1929 — showing the history of the tea trade — for the Salada Tea Building near Park Square in Boston, designed by Densmore, Le Clear and Robbins. Overlooked by most today, these doors earned a Silver Medal at the Paris Salon in 1927. Undeniably the most magnificent of their type in Boston, they are among the major works of a distin-

FIGURE 202. The great bronze doors of the Salada Tea Building on Stuart Street near Park Square are the work of British sculptor Henry Wilson and were cast by the Gorham Company in 1929. The panels depict the Ceylonese tea trade, and the framing figures represent Indian deities. The cut-stone detail around the doors, the work of French sculptor Caesar Caira, is dominated by statues of Demeter, Triptolemus, and Persephone. FIGURE 203. Allen and Collens. Newton City Hall, 1932.

guished British sculptor who did very little work in the United States.

Thus between 1890 and 1930 Boston accumulated many variations of many things: ranging from the Classical dome of the Pantheon at M.I.T. (Figure 153) to the Romanesque Church of St. Trophîme at Arles that was the inspiration for the Shepley firm's west porch at Trinity Church. Nor was any secret made of such things — though sometimes the aptness of the model might be questioned. There is in the January 1916 issue of the *Boston Society of Architects Journal* a solemn protest against the convenience station newly erected on Boston Common, and judged to be "a fairly close copy of the Music Pavilion in the Gardens of the Petit Trianon at Versailles." Several architects protested that it was "an impropriety to copy one of the most elegant architectural monuments of the

past for a public urinal." (Just which historical model might have been more appropriate does not seem to have been considered; Osbert Lancaster points out that the ecclesiastical baptistry was a widespread model for British convenience stations — but not approvingly.) Usually, however, the historical association of a style was a clear guide. The Georgian Revival, for example, reached its climax in Boston not in domestic work but in public and collegiate design in the 1920s and 1930s.

The patriotic associations of Georgian naturally made that style particularly popular for civic buildings, especially in suburbs that wished to avoid monumental urban Classicism. Boston's suburbs abound in such buildings: two particularly fine Georgian examples of this period are the Weston Town Hall (1917) designed by Bigelow and Wadsworth, and that of Needham (1930) by Winslow and Bigelow. One of the most extensive is the Newton City Hall and War Memorial Building (Figure 203). It was designed by Allen and Collens and includes a spacious Aldermanic Chamber modeled on Independence Hall in Philadelphia. Indeed, the passion for things Colonial peaked in the 1920s in a number of remarkable ways. Henry Ford's much publicized restoration in the mid-1920s of the Wayside Inn in the Boston suburb of Sudbury was one local repercussion of a national movement Boston strongly influenced. It was a Boston architectural firm, Perry, Shaw and Hepburn (the designers in 1926–1928 of the Roxbury Latin School in West Roxbury and also in 1929 of Longfellow Hall at Radcliffe in Cambridge), who began in the 1920s the restoration at Williamsburg that has subsequently exercised so wide an influence on American taste. Both the Henry Francis du Pont Winterthur Museum at Winterthur, Delaware, and the American Wing at the Metropolitan Museum of Art in New York, which opened in 1924, were decisively influenced by Henry Davis Sleeper's remarkable ensemble of period rooms and artifacts at Beauport, his Gloucester home. In Boston this Colonial enthusiasm also coalesced with a similar passion for things maritime in the really extraordinary new "counting house" opened on State Street in 1928 by the State Street Trust Company, where one may yet transact one's affairs, in a building where oak and pine paneling, antique lanterns, and ship models combine to create an environment virtually unique in Boston business. The building itself was designed by Parker, Thomas and Rice; the interiors by Richardson, Barott and Richardson.

Greater Boston also possesses a Medieval reconstruction, Hammond Castle (1928) in Gloucester, designed by Allen and Collens, who also built The Cloisters in New York. But it is for its Colonial enthusiasms that the 1920s are best known, and their effect has been long-lasting; so much so that the chaste Colonialisms of Royal Barry Wills remained popular into the post–World War II period. Work in this vein by Wills and others (including many by the Shepley office) may be seen throughout Greater Boston: in Wilmington, Hanover, Bedford, Dover, Randolph, Medfield, the Bridgewaters, Abington, and particularly in Scituate, Lynnfield, Sharon, and Needham. No "period house" was as popular as the "Colonial" house, and this was especially so in the famous old Colonial towns-become-suburbs such as Lexington. More buildings in such towns than many visitors realize — for example, Frohman, Robb and Little's Trinitarian Congregational Church in Concord — date from the twentieth and not the eighteenth century. Vivid commercial variations on a Colonial theme have also survived the war, and some of these have become almost indelible images of vernacular America in the twentieth century. Perhaps the best-known such image to have originated in Boston during the twenties and thirties is Joseph Morgan's Colonial Revival design for the roadside restaurants of Howard Johnson; one of the earliest of these (ca. 1938) to feature the now ubiquitous orange roof (originally the idea of the designer Maurice Gianni) still stands at 2790 Washington Street in Canton. But throughout this period the most distinguished Georgian venture in Boston was undertaken at Harvard, so much so that this work is a excellent case study in the methods and mores of eclecticism.

H ARVARD YARD, venerable even in 1900, by which time it had served America's oldest college for nearly 270 years, was distinctly imperiled at the turn of the twentieth century. The once peaceful enclave was increasingly surrounded by noise and bustle. And more had fled, a great many thought, than just peace and quiet. No one regretted the fact that Eliot had by his pioneering emphasis on postgraduate study transformed Harvard from a small college into a great university; the foundation, in fact, of Boston's new greatness. But many, including Eliot's successor, Abbott Lawrence Lowell, regretted deeply that the more continental university tradition (which offered students only lectures, otherwise encouraging them to fend for themselves) was undermining what was left of Harvard's British collegiate tradition of communal living and learning. A crucial factor in a liberal arts education, which sought to instill values as well as facts and to encourage a broad cultural awareness, this tradition had languished under Eliot. At the same time many others felt, as the Overseers noted in 1894, that Eliot's rather erratic architectural development of the university had resulted in buildings so "inharmonious in style" that it was destroying Harvard's character. A number of people concluded that the two problems were not unrelated; that the haphazard character of the school's architectural development was closely related to Harvard's increasing diffusiveness as the collegiate tradition languished.

It was in this context that Charles McKim introduced the Georgian Revival into Harvard in his design of 1889 for the Johnston Gate. The gate's location, between Massachusetts Hall (1718) and Harvard Hall (1764), seemed to McKim to invite a Georgian design, and he endowed the new gate (and several more in the Yard he designed thereafter) not only with his usual excellence of design but with the same concern for materials that is characteristic of the Boston Public Library. Charles Moore noted that the "color and texture and form on the New Hampshire brick were the subject of experiment and repeated trials, with results so satisfactory that the term 'Harvard Brick' came to be applied to them." Nor did McKim make any secret of his desire to "bring Harvard back to bricks and mortar" and to just appreciation of her oldest Colonial work, where "simplicity, appropriateness and proportions were cardinal features." It was this lead that the Shepley office followed four years later in its design of two dormitories, Perkins and Conant halls to the north of the Yard on either side of Oxford Street in 1893. These were Harvard's first Georgian Revival buildings. The new mode reached a climax, however, in 1900 in McKim's Harvard Union, where the goal of restoring the "collegiate way" first coincided with a full-blooded, lavishly detailed Georgian Revival.

Again, an important new idea lay behind the Union: the second such facility to be built in this country and the first actually to be called a "union," McKim's huge and elaborate dining hall (which clearly inspired Parker, Thomas and Rice's dining room of 1912 at the Harvard Club of Boston on Commonwealth Avenue) was intended to revive the collegiate way at Harvard. One gets a keen sense of how important a role the Union's architecture played in its function from Santayana's remark (not suprising in view of his dislike of Queen Anne design) in a letter to a friend about "the chorus of praise we are raising about the big new room at the Union. It is the only noble room in the college and will give many people here their first notion of what good architecture means." The movements in aid of "Harvard Brick" and Harvard College seemed thus to coincide perfectly, and whichever may have begat the other, the results, both social and architectural, doubtless seemed too felicitous to be only coincidence. The adherents of the collegiate way, pining for the cohesion of the eighteenth-century Yard, did not resist

Coolidge, Shepley, Bulfinch and Abbott. The Houses of Harvard College, Cambridge.
FIGURE 204. The Great Court of Lowell House, 1929.
FIGURE 205. Right to left: Dunster (1929), Leverett (1925–1930), and Winthrop (1913–1930) Houses as seen from the Charles River. To the right of the bridge is McKinlock Hall at Leverett House.

McKim's admiration for the Yard's eighteenth-century architecture; once, that is, he had demonstrated at the Union that the spirit of the old work could be plausibly caught on the much larger scale required by twentieth-century Harvard.

Henceforth, for three and more decades, Harvard Brick and Harvard College became synonymous, almost sacramental; the former the outward and visible sign of the inward and spiritual grace. The Yard itself was closed to traffic and screened from the noisy streets around it by long rows of harmonious Georgian dormitories and gates erected in 1924–1930 by the Shepley office. When Lowell determined that the only way to preserve the collegiate way was to build a series of freshman halls (in 1913) along the Charles River and was then able to develop around these halls a whole new series of "colleges within the college," he commissioned Charles A. Coolidge of the Shepley firm virtually to re-create the eighteenth-century Yard all over again along the river, but on a much grander scale and around a series of Georgian quads, the architectural harmony of which he hoped would exhibit a "dignity and grace of a kind to impress and refine those who enter [its] courts, dining halls and libraries." Yet there was more to the new Houses than gracious communal living. Again, as at McKim's Public Library there was a new and vital idea behind it all, for the "Houses," as these small colleges within Harvard College are called, were an integral part of radical academic innovations by Lowell, built around a new tutorial system. Similarly, Coolidge did more than re-create the old Yard.

It is not hard to see that the river Houses not only recall the Yard, but often relate as well quite clearly to specific buildings there. The elaborate mantling on Dunster House is similar to that of Holden Chapel (1742); the Lowell House Dining Room is reminiscent of the Faculty Room in University Hall, designed by Bulfinch in 1813. Precedents from further afield are also evident: the Old State House (Figure 206) in Boston is startlingly apparent (see Figure 205) at McKinlock Hall; Lowell's tower seems to have been modeled on that of Independence Hall in Philadelphia; Eliot's cupola derives from that of the New York City Hall; and the river front of Gore Hall will seem very familiar to anyone who has even briefly seen Wren's seventeenth-century palace front at Hampton Court. Despite this, Bainbridge Bunting and Robert Nylander note that "the remarkable thing is how individualistic yet how harmonious" the whole range of houses seem and how hard it is to believe that they were built within sixteen years by one firm. Their analysis of Lowell House (Figure 204), for example, justly conveys the quality of Coolidge's work.

Since Lowell House consists of two quadrangles completely enclosed by massive buildings, the result could have been confining and monotonous. Such a feeling is skilful exploitation of natural irregularities in the topography and by the masterful way the massing of buildings on different sides of the quadrangles are varied. The entrance under the tower is at the highest elevation, and here also the block of buildings is at its greatest height: four stories, a raised cornice, and a high basement. . . . The dining hall and [common room] on the opposite (south) side of the court not only rise from lower ground but are of a single story in height. In this manner one seems to look over the roof of these lower buildings when entering the enclosure. Units on the east and west sides of the court are placed at intermediate levels so that there is constant variation in floor heights, and the wing on the east is lower than the other because it forms one side of the smaller quadrangle. The master's house in the southwest corner is also differentiated in massing. Furthermore, the two courts are connected by interesting vaulted passageways which change levels; thus the spaces of these quadrangles are varied and flowing rather than static and restrictive.

Eliot House, with its great hexagonal

court, is also distinguished. Nor do we pay enough attention to the fact that Hicks House at Kirkland (now the House library) and Apthorp House at Adams (the Master's Residence) are early and significant examples of not only saving eighteenth-century structures but using them in new and imaginative ways. At Adams House the Shepley office also sensitively incorporated not only Apthorp House but — what is remarkable for the 1930s — two rather exotic late Victorian apartment buildings as well as their own new Georgian work into a most improbable but in the end very successful ensemble. Adams House, all the Houses, are a notable architectural achievement. Not only did the Shepley office improve on the old Yard; they referred to one of the Yard's own models and H. A. Yeomans did not exaggerate when he wrote that "anyone who stands today on the Western Avenue Bridge and looks upstream will see something that may not unfitly be compared to the spires of Oxford." Indeed, the gathering Houses of Harvard, their towers lifting among the trees and reflected in the long sweep of the river, form the most magnificent architectural vista that Greater Boston affords (Figure 205).

The parallel vista along the Allston side is in no sense comparable, for the Harvard Business School (1924) by McKim's successor office (still under the name of McKim, Mead and White), though beautiful in the effect of its great court, does not possess the character and distinction of the Shepley Houses. The eclectic creed, that the successful building needed to be couched in a style whose historical associations expressed the building's function, was like all architectural creeds dependent in the event on the skill and vitality of the designer. The Shepley office simply designed the better ensemble. And from the eclectic point of view their reminiscences of eighteenth-century buildings were not disappointing. For the shapes one recognizes are quite differently organized; the details one has seen before are quite differently dispersed; and both are only a part of volumes and voids, of spaces and of plans that are the architect's own. The Harvard Houses are a singularly beautiful adaptation whose quality remains important to Harvard College today. And they reflect the fact, now often overlooked, that though the eclectic considered himself heir to an accumulated architectural vocabulary of many centuries, it was in his own mind his vocation to be the master and not the slave of that accumulated treasury of forms and details. Thus he saw no more need to invent a new vocabulary than does the poet, who does not invent new words or even necessarily new forms in order to write new poetry. For the eclectic, all the varying modes of the architectural vocabulary he had inherited, whether Classical or Gothic, were fundamentally timeless.

9

THE BOSTON RIALTO

THE EXPANDING METROPOLIS had yielded Boston by the early twentieth century two dramatic new "built environments": vast sprawling streetcar suburbs such as Dorchester and Jamaica Plain and densely built-up apartment districts such as on Commonwealth Avenue in Brighton, Park Drive in the Back Bay Fens, and Beacon Street in Brookline. In response to these, a third new "built environment" emerged in the heart of the old city, the scale of which would have astonished any previous generation; for by 1900, from Tremont Street toward State Street, Boston had transformed itself into a great metropolitan rialto. On Beacon Hill, in the Back Bay, in the South End, the old scale remained. But downtown, what remained after the Great Fire of 1872 of Boston's eighteenth- and nineteenth-century buildings no longer seemed quite the same. The elegant Old State House of 1711–1747, for example, began in the 1880s to be dwarfed on every side by great ranges of office buildings that by 1900 towered over it menacingly (Figures 206, 207).

The result was a network of canyons whose real style was "downtown." Some of the consequences of this we will touch on in our discussion in the next chapter of the ways in which the skyscraper sought sunlight. At this point it is simply the sheer size and radical new scale that concerns us. Peabody and Stearns's Exchange Building on State Street, for example, was built to include 1100 offices in 1887 — more offices in one building in 1887 than there had been brick houses in all of Boston 165 years earlier. Many such buildings were built to be little towns of sorts: the Old South Building, on Washington Street between Milk and Water streets, designed by Arthur Bowditch in 1902, and the Little Building, on the corner of Tremont and Boylston streets, the work of C. H. Blackall in 1916, are excellent examples. Each was designed with lavishly detailed exterior shops and extensive interior arcades on the lower two floors: filled with small shops then as they still are now, these and such later examples as the Park Square Building (1923), designed by Densmore, Le Clear and Robbins, are among the most successful and exciting urban spaces in Boston. It is to be hoped they will survive long enough to be restored one day — now that the Quincy Market has revived our interest in this time-honored urban amenity.

Other building types that illustrate the tremendous new scale of intown are the railroad station (Figure 208), the department store, and the hotel. R. H. White's store, designed by Peabody and Stearns in 1877, and Jordan Marsh, whose main store was the work of S. J. F. Thayer in 1880, are gone, but something of their pomp survives in Filene's (Figure 196) and in the R. H. Stearns Building, designed by Parker, Thomas and Rice in 1908, and in the Paine Furniture Company Building at

Park Square, the work of Densmore and Le Clear in 1912. (Even less remains of the elegant street-floor shops of this period, more of which are obliterated each year. Only one original shop survives at the Little Building. It is to be hoped that the nearby shop fronts on Boylston Street of what was lately the Wurlitzer Store and of the Boston Music Company will survive, and every effort should be made to preserve the handsome Victorian shop fronts — one including protruding glass display windows enhanced with stained glass — at the Old South Building.) Boston's late nineteenth- and early twentieth-century hotels have fared somewhat better. This is particularly fortuitous because Boston has a long tradition of distinction in hotel design reaching back to Isaiah Rogers, "the father of the American hotel," whose Tremont House of 1828 (it stood opposite the Parker House; see Figure 1) was credited by Jefferson Williamson with being "indisputably the first definitely recognized example of the modern first class hotel." It amazed Charles Dickens, who thought it possessed "more galleries, colonnades, piazzas and passages than he could remember or the reader believe."

In the late nineteenth and early twentieth centuries there followed a series of magnificent hotels, the most important of which — the Vendome (1871, 1881), the Touraine (1897–1898), the Somerset (1897), the Copley Plaza (1912) — have all been touched on previously. These, in turn, were then in some sense surpassed by Blackall's Hotel Kenmore of 1915 and by the three major hotels that opened between March and May of 1927: the new Parker House, designed by Desmond and Lord; the 1100-room Statler Hotel (now the Park Plaza), the work of the noted New York firm G. B. Post and Sons; and the Ritz-Carlton Hotel. Not only have all these survived, but also, in the case of the Copley Plaza and the

Parker House, so have their splendid interiors. Both have lately been compromised in places by spurious "restorations" (which included at the Parker House *removing* the crystal chandeliers of the main dining room), but one can at least be grateful that so much of each hotel has survived. Victorian interiors also endure in several Boston restaurants and shops unconnected with hotels: the most important is the lavishly detailed mahogany dining room of 1886 at Locke-Ober on Winter Place, but Wirth's on Stuart Street also possesses some handsome late nineteenth-century woodwork. Other nineteenth- and early twentieth-century interiors include the Marliave, on Bosworth Place, which still retains many original features, and Slagle's, an almost perfectly preserved Victorian lunchroom on Spring Lane, established in 1877 as Wyman's. Its present interior dates from 1902. (Another interior and front of note survive at Little and Rogers's Singer Sewing Machine store at 55 Temple Place.)

Other intown building types one might explore are the massive bank buildings so characteristic of the financial district, such as York and Sawyer's now demolished First National Bank (1924) and McKim, Mead and White's New England Trust Company (1905), and the distinctive "downtown" church type, built in office-building fashion right upon the sidewalk, often with stores on the ground floor. Tremont Temple, designed by Blackall in 1895, is the best example. But the building type that perhaps best illustrates the new function of "downtown" as a metropolitan rialto is the theater. Focusing on theaters is also an excellent way to conclude this discussion of revivalism by touching on the exuberant Baroque manner characteristic of theater design, an aspect of Boston's architectural history that was nationally influential and has for too long been overlooked.

A dramatic illustration of the changing scale
of nineteenth-century Boston: the Old State
House and its environs.
FIGURE 206. About 1870. The second building
from the left is the Brazer's Building.
FIGURE 207. About 1900, looking down State
Street from Broad Street.

FIGURE 208. Another example of the city's rapid growth in the late
nineteenth century: the great Union Station on Causeway Street. The three-
turreted structure to the left, behind which stretched a 700-foot-long
train shed, was designed by E. A. P. Newcomb in 1871–1878 as the Lowell
Station. To the right is the enlargement of 1894 by Shepley, Rutan and
Coolidge, which created the Union Station by linking the old Lowell Station
with yet another station to the far right. The entire Union Station was
demolished in 1927, when North Station and Boston Garden were erected.

Boston's first theaters, including the famous halls touched on in Chapter 2, invariably reflected the dominant style of their period. Bulfinch's Boston Theatre of 1794 (Figure 9), the first American theater designed by a native professional architect, was, as we saw in Chapter 1, a splendid Neoclassical landmark. The Tremont Theatre of 1827 by Isaiah Rogers was Greek Revival, with the full temple front characteristic of that style. The Howard of 1847, also by Rogers, was a notable theater long before it became (as the Old Howard) perhaps the most famous burlesque theater in the world. Though its Gothic facade was probably unique in the history of American theater architecture, it also reflected the fashion of the period. And the Boston Museum (Figure 22), designed in 1846 by Hammatt and Joseph Billings, was one of the most elegant Italianate buildings of its time. Even the High Victorian period left its mark on theater building in Sanders Theatre. A part of Ware and Van Brunt's Memorial Hall at Harvard (Figure 57), Sanders was modeled freely on the Sheldonian at Oxford, and has been called the "finest Shakespearean theatre in the world." By 1900, however, eclecticism was characteristic of theaters as of all building types in Boston.

Between 1900 and 1935, twenty-four major theaters and concert halls (leaving aside dozens of minor theaters and halls) were built along the intown rialto — startling evidence of how the theater district and "downtown" generally were growing during this period. Thirteen of these were clustered in the new Theatre District that emerged during this period on lower Tremont and Washington streets. Another concentration of halls appeared uptown, revolving around the Symphony Hall–Jordan Hall–Opera House cluster of 1900–1910. Two of the handsomest of the new playhouses were chiefly Georgian in inspiration — the

Wilbur on Tremont Street, designed by Blackall in 1914, and the Repertory (now the Boston University Theatre) on Huntington Avenue, designed in 1925 by J. Williams Beal's Sons. The Wilbur (Figure 209) is itself, however, a fine example of discreet eclecticism: its three well-proportioned portals and the scheme of two engaged columns framed in pilasters and pediments often seem familiar to Bostonians — who can be forgiven for not realizing why: the portals derive from a well-known Beacon Hill landmark, the Thomas Bailey Aldrich House of 1837 at 59 Mount Vernon Street (Figure 15). (Perhaps Blackall knew that Aldrich was one of Edwin Booth's closest friends.) Yet the Wilbur's facade is not merely derivative. One critic observed that the blind windows, for instance, were "something between cleverness and inspiration." The interior is as fine; the auditorium is in its chaste way the handsomest of any Boston playhouse. Steinert Hall, on the other hand, built on Boylston Street in 1896 from the designs of Winslow and Wetherell, is more monumental in its Classicism, while many of the forms and details of the Shubert on Tremont Street, designed in 1910 by Thomas M. James, reflect that architect's admiration for the Petit Trianon at Versailles. But the flamboyant and opulent Classicism so characteristic of theater design was early essayed at those two remarkable theaters built within three years of each other on either side of the corner of Tremont and Boylston — Blackall's Colonial Theatre and John Galen Howard's Majestic Theatre.

The erection of the Colonial, in 1899–1900, was enough of an architectural event to have been marked by a long series of articles by Blackall in *American Architect* and by a special tour of the new theater by Blackall for the Boston Society of Architects. After the tour, according to *The British Architect* in London, which reported the event, both

Two distinguished Downtown playhouses.
FIGURE 209. Clarence H. Blackall.
Architect's perspective of the Wilbur Theatre,
252 Tremont Street, 1914.
FIGURE 210. John Galen Howard and J. M.
Wood. Majestic (now Saxon) Theatre, 219
Tremont Street, 1903. Proscenium
boxes show original and no longer
extant lambrequins.

Blackall and H. B. Pennell (who decorated the interior) gave papers on the Colonial's design at a meeting of the society. The oldest theater of any sort in Boston continuously operated under the same name, was ever a name less apt? Far from evoking Boston's venerable Colonial architecture, this now richly storied playhouse, celebrated for its associations with Irving Berlin and Sigmund Romberg, where Ziegfeld launched his Follies and where Rodgers and Hammerstein opened so many triumphs, is as sumptuous and elegant as any of the productions that have played there (Plate 3). Its lavish carved detail is the work of the John Evans Company, whose other Boston work includes the cut-stone detail at Trinity Church and much of the exterior and interior detail of the Boston Public Library and All Saints, Ashmont. The extensive sequence of murals is in type and period unique in any Boston theater or concert hall and represents an attempt to introduce into theater building in Boston the integral architectural art of the Bos-ton Public Library. It includes three paintings in the lobby after the style of Boucher by Newton Wells and a series of landscapes above the door-heads by Victor Durando. Another and better-known artist, Marian Peabody, executed the work over the door-head in the ladies' room, where an otherwise unknown B. Tojetti did the ceiling panel. The great frieze in the dome of the auditorium (the three standing figures represent Tradition, Truth, and Inspiration, between pairs of figures representing the dances) was painted by Herman Schladermundt, who is perhaps best known for his mosaic vaults at the Library of Congress in Washington. Schladermundt and his assistants also executed the four seated female figures in the adjoining circles, which are entitled "Epic Poetry," "History," "Tragedy," and "Comic or Pastoral Verse." Pennell himself painted the act-drop. The effect of all this, amid satinwood paneling, blue-green satin wall hangings, and delicately toned and subdued gold, must have been stunning in 1900. It still is. And since the Colonial is the oldest Boston theater to survive intact, as splendid now as it was nearly eighty years ago, it would be hard to exaggerate its architectural importance. It was, incidentally, at a performance of the Ziegfeld Follies at the Colonial that John Singer Sargent selected three chorus girls to pose for the Danaïdes, who carry water jars in his lunette above the entrance to the library in the great staircase hall of the second Museum of Fine Arts.

Around the corner on Tremont Street, the Majestic Theatre (now the Saxon) is by no means as well preserved, for the Numidian marble lobby (with murals by the well-known New York painter William de Leftwich Dodge) has been covered over by a modern veneer. Enough survives, however, to make the Majestic (Figure 210) unique. The second of three benefactions to Boston (the others were Jordan Hall and the Opera House) by Eben Jordan, the owner of Jordan Marsh, the Majestic is the only known local work of John Galen Howard, who, after M.I.T., the Ecole des Beaux Arts, and an apprenticeship with H. H. Richardson, sought his opportunity out West, where he became professor of advanced design and head of the School of Architecture at the University of California at Berkeley. Howard was already well-known when he designed the Majestic, and it cannot have hurt his growing reputation. He did not attempt the refined elegance of the Colonial. Instead, behind a florid, monumental facade, he designed a playhouse Elliot Norton once called a theater of artifice and exaggeration; a theater whose lavish rococo auditorium, unmatched in Boston, was also in its day innovative in its exploitation of electricity. Rather than simulating older forms of illumination (candelabra, for instance), the electric fixtures are integrated into the architectural fabric, anticipating the movie palace genre of some years later. The interior is chiefly lit (as originally designed) by softly

glowing glass globes set into garlanded arches that bend sensuously over the auditorium, which for this reason seems to resemble an inverted bowl — an effect that is all the more intimate for its lavish detail. In a very real sense the Colonial and the Majestic were sufficiently sumptuous that nothing else of the same scale could have surpassed them. But another and much grander scale became necessary as Boston grew and it was on this scale that flamboyant Classicism — "Mediterranean Baroque" as Walter Kidney called it — erupted in the 1920s into the astounding architecture of the movie palace, the building type above all that illustrates most vividly the growth and importance of the downtown rialto.

The huge hall of several thousand seats was by no means new to Boston in the early twentieth century. As we saw in Chapter 2, in the mid-nineteenth century Boston was endowed with two huge halls: the 2000-seat Music Hall (now the Orpheum) of 1852 and the 3000-seat second Boston Theatre (now destroyed) of 1854 (Figure 25). At the Music Hall Bostonians thronged to see such notables as Oscar Wilde (in 1882) and to hear such important musical events as the world premiere of Tchaikovsky's Piano Concerto no. 1 in 1875. It was at a concert in this hall that Henry Lee Higginson discovered what Walter Muir Whitehill has called "the key to his great design," the founding of the Boston Symphony Orchestra, which played its first concert at the Music Hall in 1881. The New England Conservatory of Music, the first college of music founded in the United States, was started at the Music Hall in 1867.

In terms of drama and opera, the same significance attaches to the Boston Theatre, the grand staircase of which on opening night was once described as "a confusion of beauty, splendor and fashion." Virtually every important star of the time played the Boston, including Sarah Bernhardt, Maurice Barrymore, Lillie Langtry, James O'Neill (Eugene O'Neill's father, and Edwin Booth, who was appearing at the Boston, in fact, the night his brother shot Lincoln. Paderewski also played there, and Victor Herbert in some of his earliest appearances. It was, however, for opera that the Boston is chiefly remembered. In size and splendor it was an opera house and it was at the Boston Theatre that Bostonians first heard *Die Walküre,* in 1877; Massenet's *Manon,* in 1886, only one year after its American premiere in New York; *La Bohème,* in 1899, three years after its world premiere; the complete *Ring of the Nibelung,* in 1899; and in 1910, *Tosca,* ten years after its world premiere in Rome. The Metropolitan Opera first played the Boston Theatre in 1883, in the year of the Met's founding, and in subsequent years under this and other companies' auspices all the legendary divas, including Calvé, Melba, Gadski, and Lehman, sang at the Boston. Gustav Mahler conducted *Don Giovanni* there, and Caruso made his local debut on the Boston's stage. Memorable civic events also occurred at the Boston, including the Grand Ball given for the future King Edward VII during his visit to Boston in 1860 while still Prince of Wales.

The man who more than anyone else brought the whole of Greater Boston flocking downtown in the 1880s and 1890s was Benjamin Keith. A door or two away from the Boston on Washington Street, in 1883, he and another young man, Edward Albee, started a storefront "museum" of curiosities that eventually revolutionized American entertainment. The only eyewitness account of Keith's storefront museum is that of George Upham, who remembered that "Keith himself introduced the acts in this house and Mrs. Keith kept it clean." The underlying reason for Keith's increasing success was that he seized upon the pref-

erence of most Bostonians for family variety shows no minister or priest could object to and at the same time insisted upon first-quality acts that were not only decent but exciting. Moreover, because of his revolutionary concept of "continuous performances" he was able to do so at low prices. It was a winning combination, and in 1894 Keith was able to build right next to the Boston the B. F. Keith Theatre that would become known in later years as "the mother house of American vaudeville."

Conventional enough in appearance, the new Keith was revolutionary in concept. The first attempt (much ridiculed at the time) to appropriate the splendors of the opera house for "lowly, despised variety entertainment," the new theater (only a part of the lobby of which survives today) was designed by the New York architect J. B. McElfatrick, whose remodeling of the Metropolitan Opera House had been so much admired. A stunning success, the Keith was a landmark in the history of American theater building. Such palatial theaters became a crucial part of the Keith vaudeville formulas, and a phenomenon that in its own right and in terms of its later effect on movie design exercised an enormous influence on American vernacular culture in the first decades of the twentieth century. Eventually, there were nearly four hundred, including the famous Palace in New York — and one of these was the proud old Boston Theatre, which finally surrendered to Keith in 1909. At the same time Keith endowed the Bijou (a second-floor theater that was between the Keith and the Boston) with its famous "crystal staircase" made of glass. Underneath, lit by multicolored electric bulbs, was a cascading waterfall. Thus he created a three-theater complex that seated 7000 people. It seems today to have been the immediate prototype of the movie palace.

The first of these movie palaces to be

FIGURE 211. Clarence H. Blackall. Modern (later the Mayflower) Theatre, 523 Washington Street, Downtown, 1914. The theater, including the facade shown here, is a remodeling of the lower floors of an earlier building designed by Levi Newcomb.

FIGURE 212. Thomas Lamb. B. F. Keith Memorial (now the Savoy) Theatre, between Washington and Tremont streets, Downtown, 1928. This theater is built in part upon the foundations of the famous Boston Theatre of 1854 (Figure 25) and largely follows the plan of the Boston, itself a successor to Bulfinch's original playhouse of 1793–1794 (Figure 9), which was Boston's first theater.

created was the old Music Hall. When a plan to cut a street through seemed to threaten its existence, no one rushed to its defense; instead, the chance was seized to build Symphony Hall. The projected street was never built, however, and doubtless to the embarrassment of many, the old Music Hall survived and prospered, as a vaudeville theater, of all things, complete with an elaborate new stage and two new deep balconies, designed by Little and Browne in 1900, that incorporated the long, shallow concert-hall balconies into rows of boxes. In 1904 Arthur Vinal undertook another remodeling, enclosing the boxes in elaborate enframements, and the following year he designed the still extant Washington Street entrance and lobby to mark the Music Hall's new name — the Empire. In 1906 the present name was adopted, and it remained the Orpheum even after it had caught the eye of Marcus Loew, who bought the theater and commissioned Thomas Lamb in 1915 to remodel it into a movie palace. The result, though stylistically Adamesque, nonetheless included a crystal proscenium arch lit by hundreds of electric lights that has survived to this day. Boston's first concert hall is thus also her first movie palace, and its occasional exuberance — particularly in the imaginative use of electricity — can now be seen as early indications of how enormously movie palace architects would enlarge Keith's concept of a palace for Everyman. Other and smaller movie houses of the time — Blackall's Modern Theatre of 1914 on Washington Street (Figure 211), Lamb's Fenway Theatre of 1915 on Massachusetts Avenue, and Funk and Wilcox's Strand Theatre (1918) at Upham's Corner in Dorchester (probably the city's first movie palace built from the ground up as opposed to a remodeling) — sought a chaste Classical elegance. So too had the first downtown "deluxers," the Washington Street and

Scollay Square Olympias (1912 and 1915). But their sensuously undulating marquees, the more exotic for their introduction to the Boston rialto of electricity as a part of exterior design, were significant. In the early 1920s another Adamesque movie palace, Loew's State, was designed by Thomas Lamb. Then, in the "roaring Twenties," the rialto erupted into a rich "Movie Palace Baroque" splendor, unprecedented in Boston and comparable with that of any other American city, in the Metropolitan Theatre of 1925 and the B. F. Keith Memorial Theatre of 1928 (Figure 212).

Keith not only influenced, even dominated, American entertainment, he was also a much beloved civic benefactor; his legacies to the Boston Archdiocese, for instance, were enormous. It was thus not surprising that after Keith's death, Albee and Joseph Kennedy (who had become chairman of the board of the Keith successor firm) announced in 1925 a memorial that was astonishing even for the 1920s. They would build across the street from the Boston Theatre a new Boston Theatre of substantial impressiveness (now the Essex) that would keep the Keith shows running in Boston while they closed the Keith Theatre *and* the Boston Theatre and erected in their stead a magnificent new B. F. Keith Memorial Theatre. There was much dismay. What could honor all the accumulated and venerable associations of these two theaters more fittingly than the two as they stood? Albee, a showman, answered simply: "The most beautiful playhouse in the world."

Designed by Thomas Lamb, the B. F. Keith Memorial Theatre (now the Savoy) was built in 1928 in part on the granite foundations of the Boston Theatre and with the same floor plan. Its Baroque opulence is still intact. Certainly, it is one of the most beautiful movie palaces in the world. Unlike so many, it is what it seems to be: the sixteen great marble columns of the lobby *are* marble; they were quarried in Italy and polished in Vermont, and each weighs seven tons. The walnut paneling is by C. H. Rugg, whose interiors at the Parker House are so admirable. The molded plaster detail was executed by the John Evans Company. Frederick Bucher, the Newport art dealer, recalled in 1957 that one of the paintings in the lobby, Josef Israels's *The Young Mariner*, had cost Albee $27,000 and that he had had to outbid William Randolph Hearst to get it. And as for the immense auditorium, A. J. Philpott of the *Herald* did not exaggerate the morning after the opening: it was, he asserted, "a dazzling, architectural dream in ivory and gold." It is that still.

THE Boston rialto — and flamboyant Classicism — reached its extravagant climax at the immense and storied Metropolitan Theatre (Figure 213). Then as now one of the largest theaters in the world, the Metropolitan (now the Music Hall but soon to revert, one hopes, to its old name) is not the most refined theater in Boston in detail nor the most distinguished in finish. But these distinctions are overwhelmed by its grandeur of space and line and its splendid scale. Every American metropolis had something of the sort by 1930, but only the great cities were endowed with huge flagships like the Metropolitan, which it was no exaggeration to call "cathedrals of the motion picture." Blackall's last Boston theater (designed with several lesser-known associated architects), the Metropolitan is historically the most important Boston landmark of the roaring Twenties; of that astonishing era when Adolph Zukor, in town for the Met's opening, could promise Bostonians a 5000-seat theater of "mountainous splendor; a movie palace of fabulous grandeur and stupendous stage

presentations" — for 35¢ a ticket and no more than 75¢ on weekend evenings. Nor did first-nighters notice that there were only 4407 seats. Like so much about the age of exaggeration, the exaggeration was so slight as to be unimportant. The *Globe* the morning after the Met's opening (attended by some 20,000 people) willingly conceded on page one that the Met was an "Architectural Marvel." Bostonians, said the *Advertiser* some days later, were still "rubbing their eyes and wondering if it was all a dream."

It wasn't. The Metropolitan was the closest thing to a sort of dignified Disneyland Boston had ever seen. Not one but four lavishly detailed marble lobbies opened out behind the marcelled blondes in the box office — a block-long parade of marbled halls that Blackall handled superbly, drawing the audience through a first and second and then a third lobby, each elaborate but low-ceilinged, and then through even lower entries that yielded, suddenly, to a dramatic Grand Lobby, five stories high and dazzling, encircled by three tiers of promenades, the gold, marble, and crimson decor scintillating in the light of huge crystal chandeliers. Brilliant ceremonial and social planning is the chief characteristic of these lobbies, which in the best Beaux Arts manner unfold in a supremely logical way. One can never lose one's way at the Met. And even today, after many years of neglect, the mezzanine promenade of the Met's Grand Lobby discloses one of the great spaces of Boston, the view of which during any intermission is in itself worth the price of a ticket to almost any show.

The Met was overwhelming; yet it was not *only* designed to overwhelm. These huge lobbies and promenades could hold thousands of people because it was an essential component of the Met's continuous performance policy of lavish stage reviews alternating with first-run movies every few hours every day of the week that the auditorium be emptied of 4407 people and filled with 4407 more twice each afternoon and evening during relatively short intermissions. While the first show was on, the audience for the second had to be filling up the lobbies and lounges — the Grand Lobby alone is nearly a block long — which were intended not only to hold but to fascinate. There were fresh flowers every day; bridge hostesses sought to arrange card parties; there were Ping-Pong tables; a telephone room; an outdoor promenade and loggia; a wood-paneled smoking room for gentlemen, six sumptuous lounges for ladies; five checkrooms for coats and packages; and after 1932 there was a chic Art Deco restaurant as well — the Platinum Salon. There was a regular Met radio show, broadcast from the theater on WEEI. There were two orchestras: one played on the balcony overlooking the Grand Lobby; another, the Met Collegians, played nightly for dancing in the Grand Lounge. There was a "Taxi Room" at the Hollis Street door, from which cabs could be summoned, and if you became ill, no need to leave: there was a Red Cross room off the lobby, staffed by a professional nurse. Nothing like the Met had ever been seen in Boston (the manager's office even boasted a small private theater for screening films). The sumptuous decor of the theater's lounges and their varied activities and solicitous attendants were, so to speak, the first act. Just getting from lounge or restaurant to the auditorium was another; particularly if one's seats were in the balcony, for Blackall took care to make this usually dismal prospect the best adventure of them all. Balcony patrons at the Met never saw a staircase until they departed. Instead, they were whisked effortlessly up five stories by large passenger elevators — then as now unique in any Boston theater — to the highest promenade of all, where the view down seventy-five feet through the

great chandeliers to the Grand Lobby below was (and still is) stunning.

Movie palaces today, like Newport palaces yesterday, are not often taken very seriously. It is the immense and not easily duplicated seating capacity of the Met's auditorium that now fuels most of the plans to restore it. Yet the Metropolitan was in its day a serious architectural achievement. (Today it would be an impossible one.) Its handsome bronze details were the work of the Gorham Company, and the auditorium murals were perhaps the major work of Edmund Kellogg, a student of Frank Duveneck and well-known in his day. The Met itself was also widely and admiringly published, not only in contemporary architectural journals, but in R. W. Sexton's *American Theatres of Today* and in G. H. Edgell's *American Architecture of Today*, where the former dean of the School of Architecture at Harvard devoted a page to this latest work by the country's leading theater architect. While he thought the Met's Grand Lobby "as impressive as Versailles," he observed pointedly:

There is something jarring in the sight of commonplace crowds in overshoes hurrying across a lobby which, despite its occasional use of spurious materials, is worthy of Mansart, while the elegantly dressed visitors to the Boston Opera-House stroll during the entr'actes along a corridor scarcely more imposing than that of the city jail. None the less, this is typical of America and perhaps not an unhealthy phenomenon.

Blackall, who had achieved as successful an effect in the chaste auditorium of the Wilbur as in the opulent Colonial, really knew very well how to manage Movie Palace Baroque in Boston. "Atmospheric" theaters (with ceilings that simulated moving clouds) never got any closer to the downtown rialto than East Boston (where the Seville Theatre indulged in Moorish mystery) or Malden (where the Alhambra attempted the same thing) or Mattapan (where the Ori-

FIGURE 213. Blackall, Clapp and Whittemore, et al. Metropolitan Theatre, 268 Tremont Street, Downtown, 1925. Auditorium, with murals by Edmund Kellogg. One of the largest theaters in the world, the Met has recently been renamed the Music Hall, but when it is restored as a successor to the now destroyed Boston Opera House, the old and historic name will almost certainly be revived.

ental essayed the Chinese type) or Brighton (where the Egyptian only slightly varied the formula). Boston's rather staid Opera House (Figure 152) was simply another illustration that Boston would rather be dull than ostentatious. It is doubtless for this reason that the Met's Grand Lobby is not as voluptuous as similar movie palaces in other cities; the New York Paramount, for example. Blackall nonetheless took as his model for the Met not the Boston Opera House but the extravagant and opulent Paris Opera House (1861–1875) by Charles Garnier. And when the Met becomes Boston's opera house (the first one having been torn down) Boston will — by accident — have saved perhaps the handsomer interior.

The auditorium of the Metropolitan is not as stately as the Grand Lobby, but it possesses its own and comparable character. Though it is one of the largest auditoriums in the world, it is surprisingly warm and inviting. There is to be sure a wonderful amplitude as one moves down the orchestra floor, which achieves a distinct grandeur closer to the proscenium and its colossal flanking portals with their enormous reclining nymphs. But the scale of these portals also mitigates the sense of vastness, even as the horseshoe of loge boxes — an operatic touch unique in any Boston theater — gives a sense of enclosure rather than of limitless size. And when one mounts to the balcony, the side walls of the auditorium are now seen to bend generously toward each other to create something like the enclosing "inverted bowl" of the Majestic. Here, though, the enclosing feeling does not oppress the balcony, for the proscenium and overhanging sounding board bend too and all coalesce high above in an ample dome that breaks through the top of the "inverted bowl" to create an open and almost airy feeling above the immense balcony. The soft, burnished gold detail,

the rich hangings and the dull sheen of the black glass mirrors, all enlivened by the lambent polychromy of electrical color effects that glowed from the thousands of lights hidden throughout the dome and along the arched mirrors and from behind shadowed niches, created a stunning setting for the great stage and the silver screen it was the Met's function to glorify.

Both were worth glorifying. The Met's Grand Orchestra was conducted by Fabian Sevitsky. The corps de ballet and the 100-voice chorus were thoroughly professional. The organ was an immense Wurlitzer. The stage shows were spectacular. The Met produced its own shows; John Murray Anderson, a brilliant producer whose reviews appeared also at the Alhambra and the Hippodrome in London and at Radio City Music Hall in New York, staged many of them. Moscow once burned to the ground on the Met's stage, which of its type was then quite a flexible facility, incorporating, for instance, no fewer than four elevators. No wonder that when the banks of spotlights flooded down through the glowing auditorium to the gold curtain there was a perceptible hush before the Met's Grand Orchestra rose majestically into view on its forty-foot-wide elevator, signaling with the thundering Wurlitzer the start of still another spectacular stage show. These were so spectacular that the Met's management leased the Wilbur next door for additional rehearsal and scenery areas.

By 1930, Boston's intown theaters altogether seated nearly 50,000 people — and many a night they were all filled. So extensive were the amenities of the Boston rialto that two underground networks of luxurious tunnels and lobbies were built between 1890 and 1920 to facilitate access to several of the more important theaters. Robert Shackleton was rather amazed to report in 1916 that the Boston Theatre on Washington Street could be reached from Tremont Street "through a long tunnel-like foot-passage, and then an actual under-ground passage beneath a building; and another theatre, close by, has an en-trance even more interesting, this being a hundred yards or so of subterranean passage, lined with mirrors, not only under buildings but underneath a nar-row street." Similarly, in 1918 C. H. Blackall designed another network of tunnels and underground lobbies, still extant though unused, which connected the Boylston Street subway station and the Little Building with the Majestic and Plymouth theaters.

Thus the exuberant Classicism of the Paris Opera House proved as adaptable in the case of the movie palace as had the Georgian Revival at Harvard — an odd comparison, but perhaps each environ-ment is a striking evidence of the success of the eclectic creed. Behind style, there was, however, much invention along the Boston rialto. Quite aside from Keith's revolutionary concept of a palace for Everyman, Boston was very nearly the leading center of theater design in the early twentieth century in the United States.

C. H. Blackall, whose work at the Winthrop Building documents his ad-venturesomeness and whose Colonial, Wilbur, Modern, and Metropolitan the-aters document his eclecticism, was widely regarded as the most experi-enced theater architect in the United States. It is also often overlooked that Wallace Sabine of Harvard "found the solution of a difficulty thousands of years old" (to quote from the Harvard faculty's minutes at the time of his death) when his work with McKim, Mead and White on Symphony Hall in 1900 yielded the first concert hall in the world built ac-cording to a definite acoustical formula; even today Symphony Hall is in this re-

FIGURE 214. Arthur Bowditch. Paramount Theater, 549 Washington Street, Downtown, 1932. The magnificent "moderne" marquee and upright are extant but covered over.

spect internationally distinguished. Though Blackall clearly knew little or nothing of Sabine when in 1900 he wrote the long series of articles on the Colonial in which he insisted acoustics were a matter about which one could only guess, Blackall subsequently collabo-rated with Sabine on several Boston the-aters, including the Scollay Square Olympia and the Modern. Both men also embarked on a most creative collabo-ration with a third Bostonian of note, George Pierce Baker of Harvard. Few re-alize that Baker, who is best known for his "47 Workshop" at Harvard (Eugene O'Neill and Thomas Wolfe were among

219

his students), was as interested in the perfect playhouse as in the perfect play. Indeed, the "47 Workshop," an outgrowth of a number of ideas in local theater circles catalyzed by the American premiere in Boston in 1911 of *The Playboy of the Western World* by the Abbey Theatre, mounted productions at both the Brattle and Agassiz theaters in Cambridge and led Baker to study a number of downtown Boston and Cambridge playhouses carefully. His idea was to build *the* perfect playhouse at Harvard, and, naturally, Blackall and Sabine collaborated with him on this project. Though their ideal theater (designed by Baker and Blackall; Sabine was then dead) was not built until 1925 and then at Yale (whither Baker had gone), this creative Boston school of theater design ought not to be lost sight of in any discussion of Boston architecture.

It was, of course, precisely that the results of such innovative thinking were regularly cloaked in "historical" styles that so infuriated the early Modernists. But even in the 1930s the only concession Boston theater design made to this view was to take up the Art Deco style we will discuss in the next chapter, in which vogue the last of Boston's movie palaces, the Paramount, was designed by Arthur Bowditch in 1931–1932 (Figure 214). At the Paramount, however, the significant factor from our point of view in this chapter is the marquee and its upright sign. An integral part of the theater's "moderne" facade, as signs and graphics of all kinds were in that period, the Paramount marquee and upright (which survive today, though the marquee has been covered over with an ugly new veneer) are really better symbols than any skyscraper of the excitement of "downtown" in the early twentieth century. Marquee and upright alike were magnificent multicolored electrical extravaganzas whose thousands upon thousands of dancing light bulbs endowed Boston's theater district with a kind of incandescent splendor that typified "downtown." By the 1930s many such marquees lit the Boston rialto. Like fireworks, they bedazzled the metropolis.

10

TOWARD GROPIUS

ECLECTICISM AND MODERNISM appeared by the late 1920s and early
thirties to have achieved in buildings like the Paramount a kind of truce,
the terms of which were Art Deco. Actually, this new vogue only expanded the
range of styles available to the eclectic
architect, who continued to believe that
a building should be couched in a style
whose associations expressed its function but was increasingly faced with
buildings whose function was without
precedent and that seemed, therefore, to
require a style whose associations were
simply new — or, in the vocabulary of
the time, "moderne."

This appears to have been more a theoretical than a practical matter. Baroque
opulence had proved more than expressive of the movie palace because that
building type was really something old
— an opera house — called something
new — a movie palace. On the other
hand, once the houselights dimmed
to disclose the flickering images
of the silver screen, *that* was so incredibly new that the architectural setting
seemed to some perhaps by contrast too
old. No doubt the streamlined automobile pulling up in front of the Classical domed gas station (Figure 194) set
up similar vibrations; though one could
presumably service a car under a dome
as well as under anything, there was a
sense of incongruity in doing so. Significantly, though it could flower into an exotic decoration, Art Deco was chiefly
characterized by a sleek, streamlined,

machine-age geometry and it was thus
particularly useful to architects like
George Bartlett when faced, for example,
with the task of designing something
like the Colonial Air Transport Hangar
and Depot Building, ca. 1928, in East
Boston, where Boston Airport (now
Logan International Airport) opened
in 1923. Another new building type of
the 1930s was the drive-in movie theater.
The first of these in the Boston area (and
probably in New England) was the
Weymouth Drive-in Theatre in the suburb of that name; terraced so as to allow
each car a better view, it was built in
1936 by Thomas Domara.

Although very often understated in
Boston, Art Deco was not only widespread, ranging from Washington Street
shops to movie palaces, but important
for its chic, fashionable connotations:
some of *the* fashionable places in Boston — the Ritz-Carlton Hotel, the Junior
League Building, Shreve Crump and
Low — were by 1930 discreetly Art
Deco. And in 1929 the style sufficiently
intrigued Boston's architects that the entire Boston Architectural Club yearbook
of that year was given over to Art Deco
design.

A fair amount of it was in Boston
proper, including four dramatic new
skyscrapers, all four of which survive:
the Public Services Building at 60 Batterymarch Street (now the Batterymarch
Building) of 1928 by Harold Field Kellogg; the United Shoe Machinery Building of Parker, Thomas and Rice at

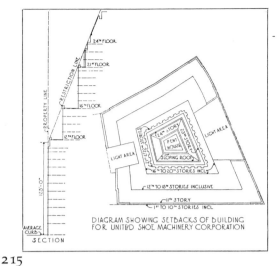

DIAGRAM SHOWING SETBACKS OF BUILDING
FOR UNITED SHOE MACHINERY CORPORATION

215

The Art Deco skyscraper in Boston.
FIGURE 215. Parker, Thomas and Rice. United Shoe Machinery Building, 138–164 Federal Street, 1929. Exterior perspective and diagram showing setbacks.
FIGURE 216. Cram and Ferguson and James A. Wetmore. Boston Post Office and Federal Building, Post Office Square, 1929–1931. The United Shoe Machinery Building is 24 stories and 298 feet high; the Federal Building is 22 stories and 345 feet high.

216

138–164 Federal Street (Figure 215); the State Street Trust Building at 70–75 Federal Street by Thomas M. James; and the Post Office Building by James A. Wetmore and Cram and Ferguson in Post Office Square (Figure 216). Of these four the United Shoe Machinery Building made the most important contribution to the skyline: its strong vertical ribbons of recessed windows and majestic stepped-back massing endowed Boston with a fine example of the characteristic skyscraper of the period, which took advantage of a 1928 revision of the Boston height restriction law that allowed much taller buildings if these were "stepped back" sufficiently to admit more sun into increasingly dark downtown canyons. The Batterymarch Building, on the other hand, was one of the first buildings in this country to seek an illusion of constant sunlight in the way Kellogg shaded the color of the bricks from dark heather brown at the bottom to lighter (and sunnier!) buff at the top. Whatever the differences in design concept, all four buildings virtually doubled the scale of downtown Boston, with some distinction; and it has thus always been something of a mystery to me why so many in dealing with the skyscraper in Boston pass at once from the Custom House Tower, completed in 1915, to the post–World War II John Hancock Building by Cram's successors.

Of all Boston's architects, Strickland, Blodget and Law were perhaps the most adept at Art Deco. In addition to quite large buildings such as the blatantly Art Deco Junior League Building of 1929 (now the Katharine Gibbs School) on the corner of Arlington and Marlborough streets and the nearby and more understated Art Deco-cum-Federal Ritz-Carlton Hotel, which opened in 1927, they did a number of fashionable Newbury Street storefronts. Two that survive more or less intact today are Mam'selle (1927) at 83 and the Kidder, Peabody office (ca.

1928) at 69, the polished black granite facade of which now announces Roberts Furs. Their most exquisite detail, including silver-gray and emerald-green murals by Jacques Carlu of M.I.T. and his wife, Natacha, was at the Ritz (Figure 217), the famous dining room of which was endowed with silvered detailing on the columns and huge silvered circles containing the signs of the zodiac on the ceiling.

Nearby, at Shreve Crump and Low, on the corner of Arlington and Boylston streets, William T. Aldrich, who remodeled this building in 1930, also used a silvered ceiling. But at Shreve's the exterior detail is what is important: the "pilasters" and "capitals" of the facade — flat, streamlined, stylized, and quite unlike the Classical forms they derive from — are superb examples of the inventiveness characteristic of Art Deco (Figure 218). But perhaps the most elaborate and characteristic Art Deco detail still visible in Boston is the metal work in the United Shoe Machinery Building lobby and in the Franklin Street foyer of the State Street Bank and, most of all, the exotic inlaid ebony and walnut chevron woodwork of the Paramount Theatre; highlighted by aluminum and gold decorations, this woodwork and the sleek, streamlined geometry of the Paramount interior generally are now unique in Boston.

The most important single Art Deco ornament in the city, the famous Bigelow Kennard clock (Figure 219), is no longer, alas, where it should be (protruding from a facade), though it has at least been preserved and is now in the Museum of Fine Arts. Nor is there, unfortunately, any work in Boston in this mode (though there are, as we have noted, earlier works) by Lee Lawrie, the American sculptor who was so influenced by Art Deco. There is, however, quite fine modernistic sculptural work at the East Cambridge Savings Bank (Figure 220) by the

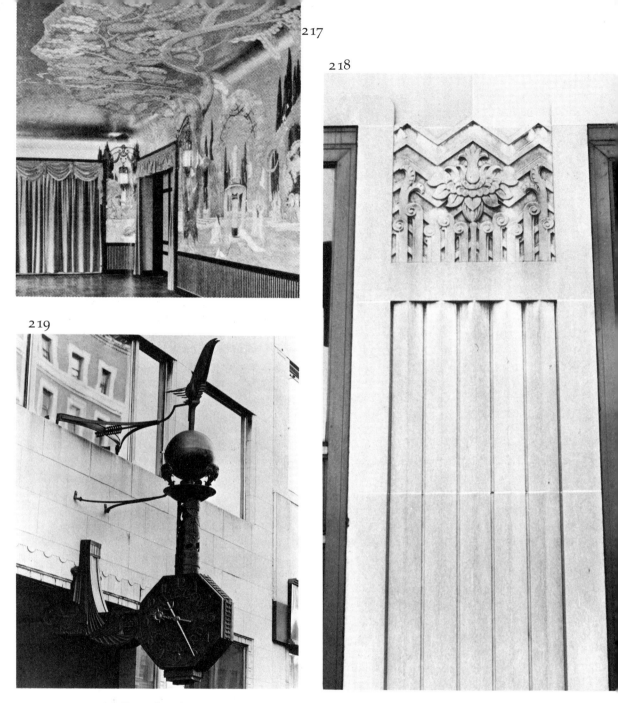

217

218

219

Art Deco details.

FIGURE 217. Strickland, Blodget and Law. Ritz-Carlton Hotel, 15 Arlington Street, Back Bay, 1926–1927. Interior of function room showing murals (now destroyed) by Jacques and Natacha Carlu.

FIGURE 218. William T. Aldrich. Remodeled store for Shreve Crump and Low, 330 Boylston Street, Back Bay, 1930. Detail of facade.

FIGURE 219. Cast bronze and aluminum clock designed by Roland Baldrey and installed in 1933 over the entrance of the Boston jewelers and metal-workers Bigelow Kennard and Company, and now in the collection of the Museum of Fine Arts, Boston. Apollo, the sun god, is depicted riding across the heavens, the waters of time beneath. The passage of time is sym-bolized by the "wings of time" in flight at the top of the structure, while the swiftness of time is suggested by the bent bow and raised arrow that connect the structure to the facade.

well-known New York sculptor Paul Fjelde. The bank itself, Italian Romanesque in feeling but with strong Byzantine overtones, was designed by Thomas M. James in 1931 and its modernistic detail well illustrates how the newer mode could be combined with more traditional forms in the same building and by an architect whose earlier Classicism we have noted at the Shubert Theatre.

James's Cambridge work points up as well the fact that the "moderne" was not restricted to intown, though it chiefly flourished there. In Cambridge, one may see in the Sears, Roebuck store at Porter Square, designed in 1928 by George C. Nimmons and Company, a more modest version of Nimmons's huge Boston store in the Fenway (Figure 221), which opened in the same year. Probably the finest of several suburban buildings of this sort is the miniature skyscraper J. Williams Beal's Sons designed in the mid-1920s for the Granite Trust Company at Quincy Center. One may also see in both city and suburbs fine examples of a characteristic new element of design in this period, the use of stylized lettering (usually the name of the firm or of the building) as an integral element in the design of the facade. Aside from the Paramount, the most splendid example in Boston was Shephard and Stearns's I. J. Fox Company facade on Washington Street (1934), recently devastated, first, by a new street canopy that ruins the front, and, secondly, by new owners who have removed the lettering of the facade. In Cambridge, along the Charles River on Memorial Drive, the BB Chemical Company building (Figure 222), by the Shepley office, has been much more fortunate: Polaroid Corporation, which recently bought the building, has shown great sensitivity in the way it carefully substituted its own name on the facade.

Sparser versions of more traditional styles paralleled Art Deco work in Boston. At Wellesley College, Charles Z.

Klauder designed an extensive modernistic Gothic complex in 1927–1931. A kind of stripped-down Classicism is also evident in Ralph Harrington Doane's Motor Mart (1927) in Park Square (Figure 223) and even more so in his Rindge Technical High School (1932) in Cambridge. But in hindsight the firm whose work during the 1930s was perhaps most progressive was the Shepley office, Richardson's successors, who have turned their hands to everything over the years from Romanesque churches to Logan International Airport. In 1930, while at work on Harvard's Georgian houses, they designed the first "modern" building at Harvard and perhaps the first really distinguished building in Greater Boston that sought to shed completely traditional "historical" ornament — the Biological Laboratory at Harvard (Figure 224).

Built of reinforced concrete, though it is finished in brick to honor its older brick neighbors and retains as well the basic Classical mass of colonnade and entablature, the building has crisply cut vertical panels of windows very much in the new spirit. So also is the architectural carving, which is inspired: a great herd of elephants sweeps across the topmost part of the building, carved in the brick by Katherine Ward Lane, who also modeled the rhinoceroses that flank the main entrance. It is really this carving that still gives this building distinction. How much it was admired in the thirties is evident in the fact that in 1936 Henry-Russell Hitchcock (who thought Shepley's Harvard Houses "parodies" of the eighteenth century) compared the Biological Laboratory with Sever Hall in its attempt to catch the spirit of older work nearby while striking out in a distinctly modern way. The laboratory was "certainly not the best example of contemporary style in America," Hitchcock wrote. "But there was," he continued, in 1930 "in the field of college architecture

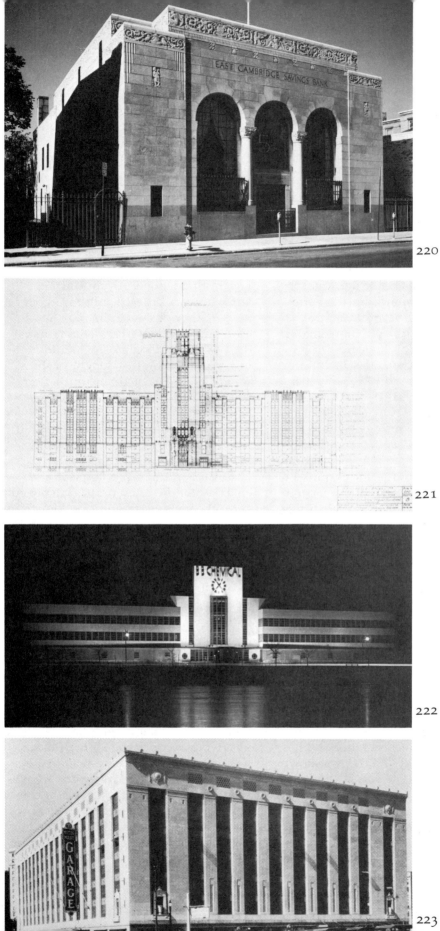

220

221

222

223

"Moderne" design in the 1920s and 1930s.

FIGURE 220. Thomas M. James. East Cambridge Savings Bank, 1931.

FIGURE 221. George C. Nimmons and Company. Sears, Roebuck store, the Fenway, 1928. Elevation of principal facade.

FIGURE 222. Coolidge, Shepley, Bulfinch and Abbott. BB Chemical Building (now Polaroid Building), 780 Memorial Drive, Cambridge, 1937.

FIGURE 223. Ralph Harrington Doane. Motor Mart Garage, Park Square, Back Bay, 1927.

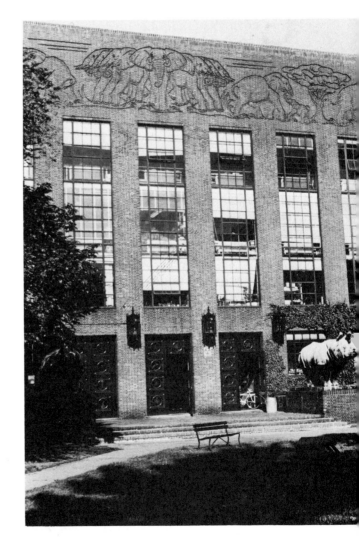

FIGURE 224. Coolidge, Shepley, Bulfinch and Abbott. Biological Laboratories, Harvard University, Cambridge, 1930.

in America no building of comparable significance, just as there was none at the time of Sever."

The Shepley office attempted more or less the same effect, on a much larger scale and this time in white brick, at Northeastern University, the competition for which work they won in 1934. On the other hand, they did not abandon traditional forms: the Littauer Center at Harvard (1938) is a full-fledged adaption of the Bulfinch Building of 1818–1823 at the Massachusetts General Hospital. It was the first building erected by Harvard after the appointment of Walter Gropius to the faculty of the Graduate School of Design in 1937.

GROPIUS's appointment, which has been called "an epoch-making event," brought to Boston one of the outstanding figures in modern architecture and design. Until the rise of Hitler had driven him first to England and then to America, Gropius had at the famous German school of architecture, the Bauhaus, led in formulating what is called the International Style. Characterized by flat-roofed and blocklike masses with no ornamentation of any kind, how revolutionary the "machine aesthetic" of this style must have seemed in Boston is evident if one considers the series of buildings Gropius and others of similar conviction embarked upon in the Boston area in the late 1930s. Among the earliest and most influential was a house Carl Koch designed (nominally with Edward Durrell Stone) at 4 Buckingham Street (Figure 225) in Cambridge in 1937. Bunting and Nylander describe it thus:

When first occupied, the house was a great curiosity, and the many people who came to see it were generously received by the owners. Tastefully furnished with contemporary furniture and fabrics, in large part imported from Sweden, the visual effect it created was warm and inviting, and it proved to many skeptics beyond a doubt that modern architecture was not necessarily cold and impersonal. Indeed, the Koch house played an important role in converting a whole generation of architectural students at Harvard and MIT to the cause of modern architecture.

Two years later M.I.T. possessed its own example of the International Style in the Alumni Swimming Pool of 1939, designed by Anderson and Beckwith, two alumni of M.I.T. (Figure 226) and during the same period Boston was endowed with several innovative buildings by Hugh Stubbins. These include the Troy House at 11 Wyoming Avenue in Needham (1936) and a dental office at 775 Main Street in Melrose (1936), both designed in association with Royal Barry Wills; and a 1939 remodeling, with Marc Peter, Jr., of the Telepix Cinema in Park Square, which John McAndrew described in 1940 as "the most thoroughly modern design for any movie theatre in the country."

It was, however, the work of Gropius himself, who formed a partnership with a former Bauhaus colleague, Marcel Breuer, in 1937, and of Walter Bogner, an associate of Gropius at the Harvard Graduate School of Design, that naturally attracted the widest attention in Boston in the late thirties. Bogner designed two houses: 45 Fayerweather Street (1940) in Cambridge and his own house (1939) on Wood's End Road in Lincoln. Gropius's own house of 1938 is on Baker Bridge Road in the same town (Figure 227). With Breuer, Gropius also designed the Haggerty House (1939) on Jerusalem Road in Cohasset (their first work in this country); the small Chamberlain cottage (1940) in Wayland; and the former Ford House (1939) in Lincoln, which like Bogner's own house and Breuer's own (1939) stands on Wood's End Road in Lincoln, a quiet suburban lane whose importance in Boston's architectural history in this period is seldom suspected.

226

225

227

Early landmarks of the International Style in Greater Boston.
FIGURE 225. Carl Koch and Edward Durrell Stone. 4 Buckingham Street, Cambridge, 1937.
FIGURE 226. Anderson and Beckwith. Alumni Swimming Pool, M.I.T., Cambridge, 1939.
FIGURE 227. Walter Gropius. Gropius House, Baker Bridge Road, Lincoln, 1938.

Significantly, the Chamberlain cottage sought to state the International Style in New England terms (by using wood) as did Bogner's 45 Fayerweather Street, which was built of bricks recovered from the destruction of a Back Bay house. And Carl Koch made a similar effort — using not only wood but also pitched roofs — in a group of five houses (the Gordon, Cushman, Hartshorne, Wissmann, and Koch houses) on Snake Hill Road near Pleasant Street in Belmont, that he designed in 1940. None of the modernists proposed tearing down Boston — as Le Corbusier had once considered leveling Paris. But the stark cubes of the International Style announced a revolution nonetheless: in 1948 Gropius would write of the need for an architecture that was "radiant and naked, unencumbered by lying facades and trickeries . . . an architecture adapted to our world of machines, radio and fast motor cars." The Gropius House, in Ada Louise Huxtable's words, "was a clarion call to the future."

Boston's response was uncertain. The fact that such leading modernists as Walter Bogner, Louis Skidmore, and Edward Durrell Stone had all been Rotch Fellows in the late twenties; indeed, that Gropius, whom Burchard and Bush-Brown would call "the most influential single man in planting modern architecture firmly in America," should have been asked to teach at Harvard, shows the lively intellectual climate of Boston during this period, echoed, for example, in the great amount of modern music premiered by Serge Koussevitsky and the Boston Symphony Orchestra in the thirties. Curiosity, however, does not always imply enthusiasm, as Burchard and Bush-Brown point out:

Gropius's appointment to Harvard in 1937 excited derision among many older architects, such as Charles Killam, Professor of Architecture Emeritus at Harvard, who wrote bitterly against the appointment of "social reform-

ers," "mere critics," "specialists in domestic work of low-cost housing," "extreme modernists." . . . Conservative communities such as Lexington, Massachusetts, thought that all the modernists who were settling on Six Moon Hill or in nearby Lincoln in modern houses must be liberals, even radicals, probably intent on violent reform.

The same authors, noting that Cram was perhaps "the most outspoken critic" of modernism, admitted, however, that "there was much folly Cram could point to in the modern movement" and that "an exhibitionist like Salvador Dali did not help matters when, on his arrival in New York in 1936, he announced his desire to live in a 'fur-lined uterus.'"

But there had also been much folly in the Gothic movement; few of Cram's "disciples" honored his ideal of constructional honesty, for instance. Moreover, Cram's response to Modernism, earnestly sought not just in Boston but throughout the country (for Cram by the 1930s was the last of the great traditionalists), was more subtle than strident, though consistent. He had warned as early as 1914 that when criticizing new forms American architects were on uncertain ground because "as a matter of fact, we are bound hand and foot to a traditionalism that is Byzantine in its rigidity and mounts often to the level of an historic superstition." He wondered repeatedly in his writings how one could "build a gymnasium like a medieval abbey," for example, or design a "Gothic" skyscraper, and despite the fact that Raymond Hood (who had been apprenticed to Cram) was a close friend, he once compared such anomalies to a "Byzantine motor car." In fact, no one attacked traditional architecture more fiercely than did Cram: "the astute archeology of some of our best modern work, Classic or Gothic," he wrote in 1914, "is stupefying and leads nowhere." What had happened, of course, was that Cram saw his own disciples and

FIGURE 228. Richard Shaw. St. Clement's Church, Somerville, 1946 remodeling.

FIGURE 229. Alvar Aalto. Baker House, M.I.T., Cambridge, 1947.

FIGURE 230. The Architects Collaborative (Walter Gropius). Harvard Graduate Center, Cambridge, 1949.

McKim's increasingly perpetuating the same sort of bloodless clichés Richardson's disciples had been guilty of in the 1880s. All Cram could do was to point out that it was natural that a "technological civilization . . . should show itself in an adequate art" and that if that art was ugly, as he frequently found it, it was because technological civilization was itself ugly. He did protest vehemently that only at great peril to their identities and values could the church or the home embrace the new technological aesthetic. But when he cautioned Modernists that "the force that destroys can never under any circumstances rebuild," Cram admitted too much for the traditionalists. Just as conservatives despaired of him when he publicly supported Franklin Delano Roosevelt, Cram really offered neither side much comfort. He was always his own man, prophet or crank according to one's view. The traditionalists were at least spared the knowledge that when Cram and Gropius, having expressed a desire to meet, commandeered the library of a mutual friend for a chat of several hours at a Sunday house party in suburban Boston in the late thirties, all that the curious guests overheard through the closed door was hearty laughter.

Charles Maginnis, who outlived Cram (who died in 1942) by over a decade, ultimately mounted a more vigorous attack on Modernism, but though persuasive he too was damning the age as much as its architectural expression when he wrote in 1945:

The mathematical system that is being proposed to us is superbly adequate to the challenges of realism, but it has yet to rise convincingly above the topicalities. Simplicity might well have been its largest gift, but it is presented to us, not as a gracious excellence, but as a by-product of a biting logic, a harsh and defiant emptiness. Its content is too thin, its temper too immediate. It is fitting for the things that end tomorrow. Why shake off the tyranny of history to take on the tyranny of the passing hour? . . . It is needful that architecture have the gift to express our ideals no less than our realistic habit. What is utility but an end that can be seen by the shortsighted? All the great ends lie further. . . . In a dramatic detachment we are expected to find our gratifications henceforth in the atmosphere of our machinery. The idea is too violent.

Maginnis's eloquence, however, was not matched by the architecture of his fellow traditionalists. The history of the J. Harleston Parker Gold Medal in the late thirties and early forties is ample evidence of what was happening. In 1939 it was awarded to Cram's Cowley Fathers Monastery in Cambridge (Figure 172); in 1943 it was given to Perry, Shaw and Hepburn for their Houghton Library at Harvard. Yet these were virtually the last buildings of distinction in Boston to earn this award in either the Gothic or Classical mode. The next award, in 1946, to Richard Shaw's St. Clement's Church in Somerville (Figure 228), represented a startling descent, and shows how under the pressure of Modernism, the traditionalists were driven to fatal compromises that were more violent by any traditional rubric than Modernism. A similar building, which essayed an absurd "Modernistic" Federal Revival style, was designed by Perry, Shaw, Hepburn and Dean for Jordan Marsh on Summer Street in 1948–1951. How striking by comparison were Gropius's Harvard Graduate Center (Figure 230) of 1949 in the North Yard or Alvar Aalto's Baker House (1947) along the Charles River at M.I.T., the serpentine plan of which allows every room a river view (Figure 229). About St. Clement's and Jordan Marsh there was a sense not only of compromise and uncertainty, but of apology and decline, even of decay. The Gropius and Aalto buildings, on the other hand, though more shocking in form, made no apology; indeed, they exuded a sense of confidence that this was to be the future. Whatever one's tastes, the sense of what was decaying and what was beginning must have been irresistible. In another sense, the same thing must have seemed true of another retail complex of the late forties — Shoppers World in Framingham, a pioneering suburban shopping center by Ketchum, Gina and Sharp (1949–1951). Perhaps even more startling was the technologically innovative house for Amelia Peabody in Dover designed by Eleanor Raymond in 1948; described then as a "sun-heated house," today it would be called a solar house.

Thus did the ground begin to shift under architecture; after the Second World War with the force of an earthquake. In the event, Boston not only accepted Modernism, but with open arms: Martin Myerson and Edward Banfield pointed out in their *Boston: The Job Ahead* that the post–World War II work in and around the city by Aalto, Belluschi, Gropius, Koch, Le Corbusier, Pei, Rudolph, Saarinen, Sert, Stubbins, and Yamasaki constituted "a greater concen-tration of work by outstanding living architects than is to be found anywhere else in the world." But that is another book. And if in the seventies we are again somewhat unsure of our footing, today we are all preservationists! Indeed, the planned preservation of the Gropius House by the Society for the Preservation of New England Antiquities prompted Ada Louise Huxtable to reach what is perhaps the only conclusion of this survey of what has been built in Boston until the eve of our own era:

There is first, the lovely, subtle paradox of the Gropius House, that clarion call to the future, as an authenticated antiquity. How inexorably time turns the avant-garde into history! And how much delicate irony can be obtained from the fact that this house marked the conscious rejection of history in terms of emulations of past styles (indigenous tradition was a superbly rationalized substitute) and the declaration of a new esthetic and a brave new world. The new esthetic is the norm, and the brave new world grows old. The landmark takes its place as part of the history that it spurned, and the movement that rewrote history becomes history. Always history wins.

Ultimately, the post-World War II architectural revolution has yielded a new respect for the architecture of the past.
FIGURE 231. Restored town houses, Monument Square, Charlestown.

BIBLIOGRAPHY

THIS BIBLIOGRAPHY consists primarily of sources consulted and quoted from in the preparation of this study. It has been broken down into the following several sections so as to make it easier for the reader to find the principal sources for particular areas, buildings, building types, or architects discussed in the text.

A. Boston: Metropolitan, City, and Boston Proper
B. Cities and Towns of Metropolitan Boston (including those annexed)
C. Sections of Boston Proper
D. Individual Buildings throughout Metropolitan Boston
E. Building Types
F. Architects Who Worked in Boston
G. Boston Artists and Craftsmen and Architectural Art
H. General Sources and Suggested Further Reading

The following abbreviations and short titles are used in the bibliography and picture credits:

AABN	*American Architect and Building News* (so titled from 1876 to 1908; thereafter, until it ceased publication in 1938, known under various titles: 1909–1921, *American Architect*; 1921–1924, *American Architect and Architectural Review*; 1925–1936, *The American Architect*; 1936–1938, *American Architect and Architecture*)
A.I.A.	American Institute of Architects
Arch. Forum	*Architectural Forum*
Arch. Record	*Architectural Record*
Arch. Review	*Architectural Review*
Inland Architect	*Inland Architect and News Record*
JSAH	*Journal of the Society of Architectural Historians*
OTNE	*Old-Time New England*
Proc. Bost. Soc.	*Proceedings of the Bostonian Society*
SPNEA	Society for the Preservation of New England Antiquities

(Note: city of publication is listed in references only when it is other than Boston.)

A. BOSTON: METROPOLITAN, CITY, AND BOSTON PROPER

The area each source deals with is indicated by the words Metropolitan, City, or Boston Proper. For the definitions of these areas see caption to Map 1, page iv.

1   Bacon, Edwin M., ed. *Bacon's Dictionary of Boston.* 1883. *City*
      An invaluable source. Includes brief but highly informative articles not only on such general subjects as "Architecture and Architects" and "Painters and Sculptors" but also on the different neighborhoods of the city (except for Hyde Park, not yet annexed) and on specific buildings and monuments, which are often described in great detail. Articles pertinent to this study are listed separately.

2   ————. *Boston: A Guide Book.* 1903. *Metropolitan*
      The only extensive and dependable guidebook ever issued for Greater Boston; covers Boston Proper and 45 suburban communities.

3   Beale, Joseph H. "Metropolitan Boston." In no. *13*, pp. 116–127. *Metropolitan*

4   Boston Architectural Club. *Year Books:* 1907, 1911, 1913, 1918, 1923, 1924, 1925, 1928, 1929. *Metropolitan*
      The 1929 volume deals entirely with Art Deco and contemporary work of that period, much of it in and around Boston.

5   Boston Board of Commissioners of the Department of Parks. *Annual Reports* and *Special Reports.* 1876–1937. *City*

6   *Boston [Street] Directories.* 1850–1940. *City*
      These list the occupations and business addresses (and residential addresses if they lived in the city) of all persons in business in the city of Boston. Used in conjunction with real estate atlases and such directories as *Clark's Boston Blue Book* (no. *736*), the street directories are the chief aids in reconstructing the social character of residential areas.

7   Boston Elevated Railway Company. *Fifty Years of Unified Transportation in Metropolitan Boston.* 1938. *Metropolitan*

8   Boston Public Library. Boston Architecture Reference File. Fine Arts Department (Research). *Metropolitan*
      This card index is divided into three sections: architects (more than 250), buildings by building type, and buildings by name (if any) and/or address.

9   ————. Boston Pictorial Archive, Print Department. *Metropolitan*

10   ————. "Boston Views: An Index Recording Views of Boston in the Library's Collections . . ." Typescript. 1963. *Metropolitan*

11   Boston Society of Architects. *Boston Architecture.* Intro. by John Coolidge. Cambridge, 1970. *Boston Proper*

12   Boston Street Commissioners. *Record of Streets, Alleys, Places, etc., in the City of Boston.* 1910. 2d ed. *City*
      Authoritatively traces the history of every street in the city.

13   Boston Tercentenary Committee. *Fifty Years of Boston,* ed. Elizabeth Herlihy. 1930. *City*
      Anthology of authoritative articles on all aspects of life in the city from 1880 to 1930; intended as a continuation of no. *65*. Articles pertinent to this study are listed separately.

14   Bromley, George W. and Walter S. *Atlas of the City of Boston.* 7 vols. Philadelphia, 1883–1928, with periodic revisions. *City*
      This source and no. *34* are invaluable in reconstructing the history of the city and all the annexed cities and towns. Each volume documents the location and size of every parcel of land on every street; its owner; and the size, outline, and materials of any building thereon. Although absolutely dependable in these respects, any additional information (such as dates of erection) given under major landmarks must be treated very carefully, since errors are frequent.

15   Bureau for Research in Municipal Government, Harvard Graduate School of Public Administration. *Metropolis in Maps: Graphic References for the Boston Area.* Cambridge, 1946. *Metropolitan*

16   Bushee, Frederick A. "Ethnic Factors in the Population of Boston." *Publications of the American Economic Association,* 3d series. New York, 1903. *City*

17   Bynner, Edwin L., and Edwin Stanwood. "Topography [and Landmarks]." In no. *65*, 1:521–556; 2:491–532; 4:25–63. *Boston Proper*

18   *Church Militant.* 1898–1940. *Metropolitan*
      This journal is an authoritative source for dates and attributions of all Episcopal churches and institutions in Greater Boston. An index by parish exists at the Diocesan Library, 1 Joy Street, Boston.

19   City of Boston Building Department. Records. *City*
      A most important source for this study. Photocopies of building permits and other records relating to buildings discussed have been given to the Fine Arts Department (Research) of the Boston Public Library. Eventually such data will be added to the Boston Architecture Reference File (no. *8*).

20   Cram, Ralph Adams. "Architecture." In no. *13*, pp. 340–346. *City*

21   Cummings, Charles A. "Architecture." In no. *65*, 4:465–489. *Boston Proper*

22   Damrell, Charles S. *A Half Century of Boston Building.* 1895. *City*
      A generally dependable work that discusses in detail all major buildings and many minor buildings, particularly those erected between 1875 and 1895. Articles pertinent to this study are listed separately.

23   Eldredge, Joseph. *Architecture, Boston.* 1976. *Boston Proper*
      Includes three sections beyond Boston Proper: Charlestown, Roxbury, and Cambridge.

24   Eliot, Charles W., II. "The Boston Park System." In no. *13*, pp. 657–671. *City*

25   Engelhardt, George W. *Boston Illustrated.* 1897. *Metropolitan*
      Invaluable illustrations of office interiors and of private homes in city and suburbs.

26   Estabrook, Harold K. *Some Slums of Boston.* 1898. *City*

27   Fay, Frederick H. "The Planning of a City." In no. *13*, pp. 41–61. *City*

28   Federal Writers' Project. *Massachusetts: A Guide to Its Places and People.* 1937. *Metropolitan and beyond*
      A part of the American Guide Series, this dependable source includes a surprising amount of architectural material as well as a general history of architecture in Massachusetts.

29   Firey, Walter. *Land Use in Central Boston.* Cambridge, 1947. *Boston Proper*

30   Forbes, Allan. *Towns of New England and Old England, Part I.* 1920. *Metropolitan and beyond*

31 Goody, Joan E. *New Architecture in Boston.* Cambridge, 1965. *Metropolitan*
32 Herndon, Richard. *Boston of Today.* 1892. *City*
      In addition to articles on Boston proper and on all the annexed cities and towns, there are short biographical notices of many prominent Bostonians, including a great many architects, for which see Section F.
33 Hitchcock, Henry Russell. *A Guide to Boston Architecture, 1637–1954.* New York, 1954. *Metropolitan*
      The only architectural survey of Metropolitan Boston; informative but occasionally unreliable, it also reflects the strong bias of its period against late Victorian and early twentieth-century architecture.
34 Hopkins, G. Morgan. *Atlas of the County of Suffolk, Massachusetts.* 7 vols. Philadelphia, 1873–1874. *City* (See also no. *14.*)
35 Howe, M. A. De Wolfe. *Boston: The Place and the People.* 1903. *Boston Proper*
36 Hubbard, Henry V. "Landscape Architecture." In no. *13,* pp. 347–352. *Metropolitan*
37 Keach, Leon. "Recent Architecture in Boston." *Pencil Points* 18 (1937): 277–284. *Metropolitan*
38 Kilham, Walter. *Boston after Bulfinch . . . 1800–1900.* Cambridge, 1946. *Metropolitan*
      An invaluable source but sometimes misleading.
39 King, Moses. *King's Handbook of Boston.* Cambridge, 1883, 1885. *Metropolitan*
      Reliable and detailed articles on all aspects of Boston in the late nineteenth century, including many lengthy descriptions of major buildings. Articles pertinent to this study are listed separately.
40 Langtry, Albert P. *Metropolitan Boston: A Modern History.* 4 vols. New York, 1929. *Metropolitan*
41 Lankevich, George J., ed. *Boston: A Chronological and Documentary History, 1602–1970.* Dobbs Ferry, N.Y., 1974. *Boston Proper*
42 Lord, Robert, et al. *A History of the Archdiocese of Boston.* 3 vols. 1929. *Metropolitan*
      While maddeningly silent on architects and artists, this work nonetheless records the construction dates of all Roman Catholic churches and institutions in and beyond Greater Boston. It is also excellent background material for the whole period of this study.
43 McCord, David. *About Boston.* 1948. *Metropolitan*
44 McNamara, Katherine. *The Boston Metropolitan District.* Cambridge, 1946. *Metropolitan*
      A bibliography of pamphlet literature on this subject.
45 "Metropolitan Boston." *AABN* 134 (1928): 632–716. *Metropolitan*
46 *Official Chronicle and Tribute Book.* 1930. *Metropolitan*
      An anthology of articles on Massachusetts and particularly on Greater Boston, issued for the 1930 Tercentenary of the state's settlement.
47 Rettig, Robert Bell, ed. *The Architecture of H. H. Richardson and His Contemporaries in Boston and Vicinity.* 1972. *Metropolitan*
      An excellent compendium of the latest scholarship on Victorian Boston architecture. Articles pertinent to this study are listed separately.
48 Rodwin, Lloyd. "Middle Income Housing Problems in Boston." Ph.D. diss., Harvard, 1949. *City*
49 Seaburg, Carl. *Boston Observed.* 1971. *Metropolitan*
      Sections pertinent to this study are listed separately.
50 Selig, J. Daniel. "The History of the Harleston Parker Medal." In no. *725,* pp. 133–140. *Metropolitan*
51 ———. "Traditional Architecture." In no. *714,* pp. 84–97. *Boston Proper*
52 Shackleton, Robert. *The Book of Boston.* Philadelphia, 1916. *Metropolitan*
      Interesting chiefly for the comparisons of Richardsonian and Classical architecture, reflecting the taste of its period.
53 Shaw, Charles. *A Topographical and Historical Description of Boston.* 1817. *Boston Proper*
54 Smith, Margaret Supplee. "Italianate Architecture in Mid-Nineteenth Century Boston." *JSAH* 34 (1975): 312–313. *Boston Proper*
55 Stanley, E. O. *Boston and Its Suburbs.* 1888. *Metropolitan*
      An excellent guide and one of the earliest to define Boston in larger terms than the city.
56 Stanwood, Edward. *Boston Illustrated.* 1872. *Metropolitan*
      Valuable for descriptive articles on the suburbs.
57 State Street Trust Co. *Boston's Growth.* 1910. *Boston Proper*
58 "Suburbs of Boston." In no. *1,* pp. 389–391. *Metropolitan*
59 Suffolk County Registry of Deeds, County Courthouse, Boston. *City*
      Boston's deeds are indexed from 1630 to the present and often include subdivision plans that can be studied in conjunction with street atlases.
60 Thwing, Annie Haven. *The Crooked and Narrow Streets of the Town of Boston, 1630–1822.* 1920. *Boston Proper*
61 Tucci, Douglass Shand. *Church Building in Boston.* 1974. *Metropolitan*
      The photographic archive deals with Boston Proper and 20 suburbs. The checklist of selected late nineteenth- and early twentieth-century church work includes all of Greater Boston.
62 Whitehill, Walter Muir. *Boston: A Topographical History.* 2d ed. Cambridge, 1968. *Boston Proper*
      The definitive study; touches also on most major Boston buildings.
63 ———. *Boston: Distinguished Buildings and Sites within the City and Its Orbit . . .* 1975. *Metropolitan*
64 ———. "Boston Society of Architects, 1867–1967: A Centennial Sketch." In no. *725,* pp. 15–70. *Metropolitan*
65 Winsor, Justin, ed. *Memorial History of Boston.* 4 vols. 1881–1883. *City*
      The standard and authoritative history of Boston to 1880. Articles pertinent to this study are listed separately.
66 Zaitzevsky, Cynthia. "Boston Park System." In no. *47,* p. 22. *City*

B. CITIES AND TOWNS OF METROPOLITAN BOSTON

Only sources that cover, at least in part, the 1850–1940 period are included. An asterisk (*) indicates that the city or town was subsequently annexed to the town or city of Boston.

In this section and the next, the entry following each city, town, or area indicates the pages on which its history and architecture are discussed in nine works of reference that cover metropolitan Boston. These sources range in date of publication from 1883 to 1972, and if read in chronological sequence will yield some sense of the area's relative importance throughout the period during which it became a suburb of Boston in the modern sense. The works are short-titled as follows, in order of publication:

Bacon's Dict.	Edwin M. Bacon, ed. *Bacon's Dictionary of Boston*. 1883. (No. 1)
Stanley	E. O. Stanley. *Boston and Its Suburbs*. 1888. (No. 55)
Bacon	Edwin M. Bacon. *Boston: A Guide Book*. 1903. (No. 2)
Forbes	Allan Forbes. *Towns of New England and Old England; Part I*. 1920. (No. 30)
OCTB	*Official Chronicle and Tribute Book*. 1930. (No. 46)
Mass.	Federal Writers' Project. *Massachusetts: A Guide to Its Places and People*. 1937. (No. 28)
Hitchcock	Henry-Russell Hitchcock. *A Guide to Boston Architecture, 1637–1954*. 1954. (No. 33)
Seaburg	Carl Seaburg. *Boston Observed*. 1971. (No. 49)
Rettig	Robert Bell Rettig, ed. *The Architecture of H. H. Richardson and His Contemporaries in Boston and Vicinity*. 1972. (No. 47)

ABINGTON. Mass., 626–627.
67 Hobart, Benjamin. *History of the Town of Abington*. 1866.
*ALLSTON. See BRIGHTON/ALLSTON.
ARLINGTON. Stanley, 127–128; Bacon, 152–153; Mass., 130–135; Seaburg, 302–303.
68 Cutter, Benjamin and William. *History of the Town of Arlington*. 1880.
AVON. Mass., 588–589.
BEDFORD. Mass., 434.
69 Brown, Abram E. *History of the Town of Bedford*. 1891.
BELMONT. Mass., 444–445; Hitchcock, 36; Rettig, 36–37.
70 Baldwin, Francis B. *The Story of Belmont*. Belmont, 1953.
BEVERLY. Bacon, 161; Forbes, 62–67; Mass., 421–422; Hitchcock, 55; Rettig, 45–46.
*BOSTON HIGHLANDS. See ROXBURY.
BRAINTREE. Stanley, 139; Bacon, 2; Mass., 587; Seaburg, 304–305.
BRIDGEWATER. Mass., 589.
*BRIGHTON/ALLSTON. Annexed 1874. Bacon's Dict., 70–71; Bacon, 97.
71 Drake, Francis S. "Brighton." In no. 65, 1:439–444, 2:369–374, 3:601–610.
BROCKTON. Stanley, 105–106; Mass., 176–178.
72 Kingman, Bradford. *History of Brockton, 1656–1894*. Syracuse, N.Y., 1895.
BROOKLINE. Stanley, 103–105; Bacon, 109–115; Mass., 179–183; Hitchcock, 33–34; Seaburg, 305.
73 Bolton, Charles K. *Brookline: The History of a Favored Town*. Brookline, 1897.
74 Brookline Historical Commission. *Brookline Village Walking Tours*. Brookline, 1977.
75 Chandler, Alfred D. *Annexation of Brookline to Boston*. Brookline, 1880.
76 Curtis, J. G. *History of the Town of Brookline*. 1933.
77 Wardwell, Anne. " 'Longwood' and 'Cottage Farm' in Brookline." In no. 807, pp. 57–69.
78 Woods, H. F. *Historical Sketches of Brookline*. 1874.
BURLINGTON. Mass., 465–466; Seaburg, 305.
CAMBRIDGE. Stanley, 112–120; Bacon, 98–109; Forbes, 74–81; OCTB, 386; Hitchcock, 24–33; Seaburg, 306; Rettig, 32–35.
79 Batchelder, Samuel F. *Bits of Cambridge History*. Cambridge, 1930.
80 Cambridge Historical Commission. Survey files.
81 ———. *A Survey of Architectural History in Cambridge*. 5 vols. Cambridge, 1965–1977. Vol. 1 [no author], *East Cambridge*; vol. 2, Antoinette F. Downing, Elizabeth MacDougall, and Eleanor Pearson, *Mid Cambridge*; vol. 3 [no author], *Cambridgeport*; vol. 4, Bainbridge Bunting and Robert H. Nylander, *Old Cambridge*; vol. 5, Arthur J. Krim, *Northwest Cambridge and Survey Index*.
82 Davies, Walter G., ed. *Cambridge: Fifty Years a City*. Cambridge, 1897.
83 Eliot, Samuel. *A History of Cambridge, Massachusetts*. Cambridge, 1913.
84 Rettig, Robert Bell. *Guide to Cambridge Architecture: Ten Walking Tours*. Cambridge, 1969.
CANTON. Stanley, 149–150; Mass., 614–615; Seaburg, 306.
*CHARLESTOWN. Annexed 1874. Bacon's Dict., 91, 263; Stanley, 97–100; Bacon, 65–68; Mass., 173–174, 270–271; Hitchcock, 23.
85 Bartlett, Joseph. *Historical Sketch of Charlestown*. 1813.
86 *Considerations Respectfully Submitted to the Citizens of Boston and Charlestown on the Proposed Annexation of the Two Cities*. 1854.
87 Edes, Henry H. "Charlestown." In no. 65, 1:383–401, 2:311–330, 3:547–570.
88 Frothingham, Richard. *History of Charlestown*. 1845.
89 Hunnewell, James F. *A Century of Town Life: A History of Charlestown, . . . 1775–1887*, 1888.
CHELSEA. Stanley, 100–101; Bacon, 142–143; Mass., 205–208; Seaburg, 307.
90 Chamberlain, Mellen. "Chelsea, Revere and Winthrop . . ." In no. 65, 3:611–617. See also Chamberlain's *A Documentary History of Chelsea*. 2 vols. 1908.
COHASSET. Stanley, 137, 141; Bacon, 167; Mass., 623; Hitchcock, 37; Seaburg, 307.
91 Howe, Oliver H. "A Brief History of Cohasset . . ." *OTNE* 32 (1941): 43–51.
CONCORD. Bacon, 156–159; OCTB, 379; Mass., 25, 210–217; Hitchcock, 37–38; Seaburg, 308.
DANVERS. Bacon, 161; Hitchcock, 38; Mass., 430–431.
DEDHAM. Stanley, 145, 149; Bacon 137–139; Forbes, 104–110; Mass., 217–222; Hitchcock, 38; Rettig, 27; Seaburg, 308.
*DORCHESTER. Annexed 1870. Bacon's Dict., 131–134; Stanley, 122–124; Bacon, 97, 134; Forbes, 111–123; OCTB, 364; Mass., 217–222; Hitchcock, 34.
92 American Series of Biographies, *Massachusetts Volume*. Micah Dyer, biographical notice. 1901.
93 Bellows, Samuel F. "Dorchester." In no. 65, 1:423–438, 2:357–368, 3:589–600.

94 Clapp, David. *The Ancient Proprietors of Jones's Hill.* 1883.

95 Coffin, Nathaniel W. *A Few Reasons in Favor of the Annexation of a Part of the Town of Dorchester to the City of Boston.* 1867.

96 *Dorchester Blue Books.* Vols. 1885–86, 1898, 1902, 1908. Dorchester is also included in nos. 724 and 736 below.

97 Dorchester Tercentenary Committee. *Dorchester . . . 1630–1930.* Dorchester, 1930.

98 Orcutt, William Dana. *Good Old Dorchester: A Narrative History . . . 1630–1893.* Cambridge, 1893.

99 Tucci, Douglass Shand. *The Gothic Churches of Dorchester.* 2 vols. Ann Arbor, Mich., 1974. 2d ed.

100 ——. *The Second Settlement: A Case Study in the Development of Victorian Boston.* 1974.

101 Warner, Sam B., Jr. "The Residential Development of Roxbury, West Roxbury and Dorchester . . . 1870–1900." Ph.D. diss., Harvard, 1959.

102 ——. *Streetcar Suburbs: The Process of Growth in Boston, 1870–1900.* Cambridge, 1962.
    This work, the foundation of all studies of Boston's streetcar suburbs, derives from no. 101.

DOVER. Mass., 440–441; Seaburg, 308.

*EAST BOSTON. Annexed 1635–1637. Bacon's Dict., 138–139; Stanley, 101–102; Bacon, 94; *OCTB*, 366; Mass., 175; Hitchcock, 23.

103 Boston City Planning Board. *East Boston: A Survey and a Comprehensive Plan.* 1916.

104 Summer, William H. *A History of East Boston.* 1858.

105 Woods, Robert, and Albert J. Kennedy. *The Zone of Emergence.* Ed. Sam B. Warner, Jr. Cambridge, 1962. 2d ed. 1969.

EAST BRIDGEWATER. Mass., 628–629.

EASTON. Mass., 616.

EVERETT. Mass., 227–229, 270; Seaburg, 308.

FOXBOROUGH. Mass., 612.

FRAMINGHAM. Stanley, 151; Mass., 435–436; Hitchcock, 39.

GLOUCESTER. Stanley, 165–166; Bacon, 161; *OCTB*, 130–143; Mass., 435–436; Hitchcock, 39; Seaburg, 309.

106 O'Gorman, James F. *This Other Gloucester.* 1976.

HANOVER. Mass., 619.

HINGHAM. Stanley, 137–138; Bacon, 167; Forbes, 162–169; Mass., 622; Hitchcock, 40–41; Seaburg, 309.

107 Town of Hingham. *History of the Town of Hingham.* 3 vols. Hingham, 1893.

HOLBROOK. Stanley, 139; Mass., 588; Seaburg, 310.

HULL. Stanley, 135–136; Bacon, 171; Mass., 623; Seaburg, 310.

*HYDE PARK. Annexed 1912. Stanley, 145.

108 Knight, Joseph, et al. *Memorial Sketch of Hyde Park . . .* 1888.

*JAMAICA PLAIN. See WEST ROXBURY/JAMAICA PLAIN/ROSLINDALE.

LEXINGTON. Bacon, 152–156; *OCTB*, 380; Mass., 255–260; Hitchcock, 43; Seaburg, 310.

LINCOLN. Stanley, 159; Mass., 445; Hitchcock, 43–44; Seaburg, 310.

LYNN. Stanley, 163–164; Bacon, 159; Mass., 266–270, 424; Seaburg, 311; Rettig, 44.

LYNNFIELD. Mass., 412; Seaburg, 312.

MALDEN. Bacon, 143; *OCTB*, 384; Mass., 270–273; Hitchcock, 46; Seaburg, 312.

MANCHESTER-BY-THE-SEA. Stanley, 165; Hitchcock, 55; Mass., 422; Rettig, 46–49.

MANSFIELD. Mass., 616.

MARBLEHEAD. Stanley, 164–165; Bacon, 160; Mass., 273–279; Hitchcock, 45.

109 Cord, Priscilla S., and Virginia C. Gamage. *Marblehead.* Philadelphia, 1972.

MEDFIELD. Mass., 441.

110 Tilden, William S. *History of the Town of Medfield, 1650–1886.* 1887.

MEDFORD. Stanley, 129, 154–155; Bacon, 144–145; *OCTB*, 371; Mass., 279–284; Seaburg, 312.

111 Brooks, Charles. *The History of the Town of Medford.* Rev. ed., 1886. Reprint, 1975.

MELROSE. Forbes, 170–174; Mass., 489–490; Hitchcock, 55; Seaburg, 313.

112 Goss, Eldridge H. *The History of Melrose.* Melrose, 1880.

113 Kemp, Edwin C. *Melrose, Massachusetts, 1900–1950.* Melrose, 1950.

MILTON. Stanley, 124–125; Bacon, 130–134; Mass., 586–587; Hitchcock, 46; Seaburg, 313; Rettig, 31.

114 Hamilton, Edward P. *A History of Milton.* Milton, 1957.

115 Teele, A. K. *A History of Milton.* 1887.

NAHANT. Stanley, 164; Bacon, 159, 171; Mass., 424; Seaburg, 314.

NATICK. Stanley, 150–151; Bacon, 123; Mass., 23, 25, 519; Hitchcock, 59; Seaburg, 315.

NEEDHAM. Bacon, 123–124; Mass., 518–519; Seaburg, 315.

NEWTON. Stanley, 106; Bacon, 116–120; *OCTB*, 368–369; Mass., 295–301; Hitchcock, 48–49; Rettig, 42–43.

116 King, Moses. *King's Handbook of Newton.* 1889.

117 [City of] *Newton Centennial, 1873–1973.* Newton, 1973.

118 Town of Newton. *Tercentenary of Newton, 1630–1930.* Newton, 1930.

NORWELL. Mass., 618–619.

NORWOOD. Stanley, 146; Mass., 426–427; Seaburg, 316.

PEABODY. Bacon, 161; Mass., 119, 422–423.

QUINCY. Stanley, 125–126; Bacon, 134–136; *OCTB*, 365; Mass., 335–340; Hitchcock, 51–52; Seaburg, 316–317.

RANDOLPH. Stanley, 142; Mass., 588; Seaburg, 317.

READING. Mass., 490; Seaburg, 317.

REVERE. Bacon, 141–142; Mass., 341–343; Seaburg, 317–318.

119 Chamberlain, Mellen. "Chelsea, Revere and Winthrop . . ." In no. 65, 3:611–617.

120 Shurtleff, Benjamin. *The History of the Town of Revere.* 1937.

ROCKLAND. Mass., 627.

ROCKPORT. Stanley, 166; Bacon, 161; Mass., 235–244.

*ROSLINDALE. See WEST ROXBURY/JAMAICA PLAIN/ROSLINDALE.

*ROXBURY. Annexed 1868. Bacon's Dict., 351–353; Stanley, 121–122; Bacon, 95–96; Mass., 172–173; Hitchcock, 34. See also nos. 101, 102.

239

121 Boston City Council and Roxbury City Council. *Reports in Relation to the Annexation of Roxbury . . .* Roxbury City Doc., no. 3, 1967.
122 Clifford, John H. *Argument on the Question of the Annexation of Roxbury to Boston before the Legislative Committee, Thursday, February 23, 1865.* 1867.
123 Committee in Favor of the Union of Boston and Roxbury. *Report.* 1851.
124 Drake, Francis S. "Roxbury." In no. *65*, 3:571–588.
125 ———. *The Town of Roxbury.* Roxbury, 1878.
126 Quincy, Josiah. *Annexation of Roxbury and Boston: Remonstrance of Bostonians against the Measure.* 1865.
127 Roxbury Committee Opposed to the Annexation to Boston. *A Word for Old Roxbury.* Roxbury, 1851.
SALEM. Stanley, 165; Bacon, 160–166; *OCTB*, 374; Mass., 32, 343–352; Hitchcock, 52–55.
SAUGUS. Bacon, 159–160; Mass., 413; Seaburg, 318.
SCITUATE. Stanley, 140; Bacon, 167; Mass., 624; Hitchcock, 51.
SHARON. Stanley, 150; Mass., 615.
SOMERVILLE. Stanley, 154; Bacon, 143–144; *OCTB*, 378; Mass., 353–356; Seaburg, 318–319.
*SOUTH BOSTON. Annexed 1804. Bacon's Dict., 373; Stanley, 93–96; Bacon, 95; *OCTB*, 387; Mass., 167–169.
128 Gillespie, Charles B. *Illustrated History of South Boston.* 1900.
129 Severy, Robert B. "South Boston." In no. *807*, pp. 27–40.
130 Simmonds, Thomas C. *History of South Boston . . .* 1857.
131 Toomey, John J., and Edward P. P. Rankin. *History of South Boston . . .* 1901.
STONEHAM. Stanley, 155; Mass., 489–490; Seaburg, 319.
STOUGHTON. Stanley, 142; Mass., 615; Rettig, 27.
SUDBURY. Mass., 470–471.
SWAMPSCOTT. Stanley, 164; Mass., 423–424; Hitchcock, 55; Seaburg, 319–320.
WAKEFIELD. Stanley, 162; Mass., 490; Seaburg, 320.
WALPOLE. Stanley, 162; Mass., 490.
WALTHAM. Stanley, 159; Bacon, 126–128; Mass., 370–373; Hitchcock, 56–58; Seaburg, 320; Rettig, 37–38.
WATERTOWN. Stanley, 159; Bacon, 126, 128–129; *OCTB*, 370; Mass., 374–378; Hitchcock, 48; Seaburg, 321.
WAYLAND. Stanley, 157; Mass., 435, 469–470; Hitchcock, 62; Seaburg, 321.
WELLESLEY. Bacon, 120–122; Mass., 379–382; Hitchcock, 58–59; Seaburg, 322; Rettig, 38–41.
132 Fiske, Joseph E. *History of the Town of Wellesley.* 1917.
133 *Town of Wellesley, 1881–1931.* Wellesley, 1931.
WEST BRIDGEWATER. Mass., 589.
WESTON. Stanley, 159; Bacon, 117; Mass., 469; Seaburg, 322; Rettig, 38.
*WEST ROXBURY/JAMAICA PLAIN/ROSLINDALE. Annexed 1874. Bacon's Dict., 219, 436; Stanley, 107–111; Bacon, 96–97; Hitchcock, 34. See also nos. *101, 102.*
134 Austin, Arthur, W. *Address at the Dedication of the Town House at Jamaica Plain, . . .* 1860.
135 *West Roxbury Magazine.* Hudson, Mass., 1900.
136 Whitcomb, Harriet M. *Annals and Reminiscences of Jamaica Plain.* Cambridge, 1897.
137 Zaitzevsky, Cynthia. "Victorian Jamaica Plain." In no. *807*, pp. 71–86.
WESTWOOD. Mass., 440–441; Seaburg, 322.
WEYMOUTH. Stanley, 140; Mass., 31, 382–385; Seaburg, 322–323.
WINCHESTER. Stanley, 128–129; Bacon, 145; Mass., 465; Seaburg, 323.
138 Chapman, Henry S. *History of Winchester, Massachusetts.* Winchester, 1936.
WINTHROP. Bacon, 139–141; Mass., 425; Seaburg, 323.
139 Chamberlain, Mellen. "Chelsea, Revere and Winthrop . . ." In no. *65*, 3:611–617.
WILMINGTON. Mass., 433.
WOBURN. Stanley, 155; Mass., 389–392; Hitchcock, 63; Seaburg, 325.
140 Sewall, Samuel. *The History of Woburn.* 1868.

C. SECTIONS OF BOSTON PROPER

BACK BAY/FENWAY. Bacon's Dict., 31–32, 90, 119; Stanley, 3–34; Bacon, 74–92; Hitchcock, 15–22; Rettig, 16–21.
141 Baxter, Sylvester. "Boston's Fenway . . ." Undentified magazine, ca. 1908, pp. 894–908. Author's collection.
142 Bruce, James L. "Filling In of the Back Bay and the Charles River Development." *Proc. Bost. Soc.* (1940), pp. 25–38.
143 Bunting, Bainbridge. *Houses of Boston's Back Bay . . . 1840–1917.* Cambridge, 1967.
144 Eliot, Christopher R. "The Boston Public Garden." *Proc. Bost. Soc.* (1939), pp. 27–45.
145 Floyd, Margaret Henderson. "Copley Square and Dartmouth Street: A Showcase for Architectural Terra Cotta, Sculpture and Mural Painting." In no. *807*, pp. 40–55.
146 Forbes, Allan. *Copley Square.* 1941.
147 Mumford, Lewis. "The Significance of Back Bay Boston." In no. *148*, pp. 18–35.
148 Museum of Fine Arts, Boston. *Back Bay Boston: The City as a Work of Art.* 1969.
149 Whitehill, Walter Muir. "Back Bay Churches and Public Buildings." *Proc. Bost. Soc.* (1967), n.p.
BEACON HILL. Bacon's Dict., 38–39; Stanley, 61–72, 75; Bacon, 37–47, 68–73; Hitchcock, 6–10. See also no. *169.*
150 Boston Historic Conservation Committee. *Beacon Hill: The North Slope.* 1963.
151 Chamberlain, Allen. *Beacon Hill: Its Ancient Pastures and Early Mansions.* 1955.
152 Lawrence, Robert M. *Old Park Street and Its Vicinity.* 1922.
153 McIntyre, A. McVoy. *Beacon Hill: A Walking Tour.* 1975.
154 Warren, William M. "Beacon Hill and Boston University." *Bostonia* 4 (1930): 3–21.
155 Weinhardt, Carl, Jr. "The Domestic Architecture of Beacon Hill, 1800–1850." *Proc. Bost. Soc.* (1958), pp. 11–32.
156 Whitehill, Walter Muir. "A Corner of Louisburg Square . . ." In no. *63*, pp. 14–17.
DOWNTOWN COMMERCIAL DISTRICT. Stanley, 35–60, 74, 83–86; Bacon, 4–36, 48–54; Hitchcock, 3–4, 10–14. See also no. *517.*
157 Boston Redevelopment Authority. *Broad Street.* 1974.

158 "The Boston Theatre District." *Drumlin* 3 (Jan. 1978). Entire issue.
159 McKay, Robert. "Downtown Boston: The Waterfront and Commercial Districts." In no. *807*, pp. 1–11.
160 "Some Noteworthy Buildings." In no. 32, pp. 27–54.
161 *Washington Street, Old and New.* 1913.
162 Whitehill, Walter Muir. "The Metamorphoses of Scollay and Bowdoin Squares." *Proc. Bost. Soc.* (1972), n.p.
163 ———. *The Neighborhood of the Tavern Club.* 1971.
HARBOR AND WATERFRONT. See also no. *159*.
164 King, Moses. *King's Handbook of Boston Harbor.* Cambridge, 1882.
165 Payson, Gilbert R. "Long Wharf and the Old Waterfront." *Proc. Bost. Soc.* (1926), pp. 23–40.
166 Snow, Edward Rowe. *The Romance of Boston Bay.* 1944.
NORTH AND WEST ENDS. Bacon's Dict., 275, 435–436; Stanley, 72, 78–83; Bacon, 54–65, 73–74; Hitchcock, 2–3, 4–5.
167 Cummings, Abbott Lowell. "Charles Bulfinch and Boston's Vanishing West End." *OTNE* 52 (1961): 46–47.
168 Flower, Benjamin O. *Civilization's Inferno, or Studies in the Social Cellar.* 1893.
169 "North and Old West Ends." In no. 32, pp. 81–85.
170 Woods, Robert A., ed. *Americans in Process: A Settlement House Study.* 1903.
171 Wieder, Arnold A. *The Early Jewish Community of Boston's North End.* Waltham, 1962.
SOUTH END. Bacon's Dict., 374–375; Stanley, 87–93; Bacon, 92–94; Hitchcock, 14.
172 Smith, Margaret Supplee. "Boston's South End: Mid-Century Urban Planning and Architecture." In no. *807*, pp. 13–26.
173 "The South End." In no. 32, pp. 73–80.
174 Van Meter, Mary. *Bay Village, or the Church Street District.* 1970.
175 Whitehill, Walter Muir. "Worcester Square . . ." In no. *63*, pp. 50–53.
176 Wolfe, Albert B. *The Lodging House Problem in Boston.* Cambridge, 1913.
177 Woods, Robert A., ed. *The City Wilderness: A Settlement House Study.* 1899.

D. INDIVIDUAL BUILDINGS THROUGHOUT METROPOLITAN BOSTON

Books or articles devoted entirely to one building are rare, and a number of significant buildings that are worthy of such attention are as yet untreated except in general works. For such major buildings not listed here, see under their architects (Section F); under the city, town, or area in which they are located (Section B); or under the appropriate building type (Section E). Institutional histories have been included here only when the institution's building is discussed. Only in the case of a few major works has any attempt been made to list illustrations published without accompanying text. Collegiate buildings will be found under their respective colleges or universities. Except for theaters, buildings are listed by present-day name; for example, for the Museum of Natural History in the Back Bay, see Bonwit Teller. Note also that descriptions cited in *AABN* are often untitled.

ADVENT, CHURCH OF THE (BEACON HILL). See also nos. *259, 444, 643, 664, 665.*
178 Goodrich, Wallace. *The Parish of the Advent in the City of Boston.* 1944.
179 Tucci, Douglass Shand. "Liturgical Art at the Church of the Advent in Boston, 1850–1950." Typescript. Fine Arts Dept. (Research), Boston Public Library. 1973.
180 Wright, John. "The High Altar Reredos of the Church of the Advent." In no. 682, pp. 310–311.
181 Wuonola, Mark. *Church of the Advent, Boston: A Guidebook.* 1975.
ALL SAINTS' CHURCH (ASHMONT). See also nos. *436, 542, 547, 552, 661, 703, 767, 768.*
182 Brown, Robert. "All Saints' Church . . ." *Arch. Record* 7 (1900): 101–104.
183 Cram, Ralph Adams. "All Saints' Church . . ." *Churchman* 79 (1899): 559–564.
184 ———. "Architecture." In *The New Parish Church of All Saints.* 1892.
185 Floyd, A. P. *The History of the Parish of All Saints . . .* 1945.
186 Tucci, Douglass Shand. *All Saints', Ashmont: A Centennial History.* 1974.
187 ———. *All Saints' Church, Boston: An Introduction to the Architecture of Ralph Adams Cram.* Ann Arbor, Mich., 1975. (vol. 2 of no. *99*).
188 ———. "Articles, Exhibition Reviews and Published Plates in American and British Books and Periodicals on the Architectural Art of the Chancel and Lady Chapel of All Saints', Ashmont: A Checklist, 1897–1920." Typescript. Cram Collection, Print Dept., Boston Public Library.
189 Wright, John. "The High Altar Reredos of All Saints' Church, Boston." In no. 682, pp. 313–314.
ALL SAINTS' CHURCH (BROOKLINE). See also nos. *436, 547, 686.*
190 *A Tour of All Saints' Church.* 1954.
AMES BUILDING (DOWNTOWN; WASHINGTON STREET). See also nos. *493, 616, 747.*
191 *AABN* 26 (1889): 18.
AMES ESTATE STORE (demolished; Harrison Avenue). See nos. *605, 611.*
AMES-WEBSTER HOUSE (BACK BAY). See also no. *143.*
192 Floyd, Margaret Henderson. "Another French Connection for American Mural Painting: *The Justinian Cycle* by Benjamin Constant for a Back Bay Queen Anne Palace." *JSAH* 34 (1975): 312.
ARLINGTON STREET CHURCH (BACK BAY). See also no. *684.*
193 Gilman, Arthur. "A Return to Solid and Classical Principles . . ." (1859). *JSAH* 20 (1961): 191–193.
ATWOOD HOUSE (DORCHESTER)
194 Tucci, Douglass Shand. "The Most Curious House in Dorchester." *Dorchester Argus-Citizen,* 1 June 1972, p. 3.
AYER HOUSE (BACK BAY)
195 *AABN* 74 (1901): 94.
BATTERYMARCH BUILDING (DOWNTOWN; formerly Public Services Building)
196 Kellogg, Harold F. "The Use of Color — The Part It Plays in the Design of the Public Services Building, Boston." *AABN* 134 (1928): 211–216.

BONWIT TELLER (BAY BAY; originally Museum of Natural History). See also no. 39.
197 "Exit Taxidermist . . ." *Interiors* 107 (1947): 82–87.
BOSTON ATHENAEUM (BEACON HILL). See also nos. 38, 54.
198 *Change and Continuity: A Pictorial History of the Boston Athenaeum.* 1976.
199 Whitehill, Walter Muir. "Portrait Busts in . . . the Boston Athenaeum." *Antiques* 103 (1973): 1141–1156.
BOSTON CITY HALL, OLD (DOWNTOWN). See also no. 38.
200 "Uses of the Past . . ." *Arch. Forum* 137 (1972): 24–33.
201 Wren, George L. "The Boston City Hall, Bryant and Gilman, Architects, 1862–1865." *JSAH* 21 (1962): 188–192.
BOSTON CITY HALL ANNEX (DOWNTOWN)
202 *Architecture and Building* 47 (1915): 265–267.
BOSTON CITY HOSPITAL (SOUTH END; partially demolished). See also no. 1.
203 *Documents of the City of Boston*, doc. 34, 11:31.
BOSTON COLLEGE (NEWTON). See also nos. 42, 592, 686.
204 "Boston College." In no. 712, pp. 70–71.
205 *Boston College Library: History and Description.* 1933.
206 Cram, Ralph Adams. "The New Boston College." *AABN* 119 (1921): 615–618.
207 Dunigan, David R. *A History of Boston College.* Milwaukee, 1947.
BOSTON EVENING CLINIC (BACK BAY; originally Burrage House). See also no. 143.
208 *AABN* 74 (1901): 56.
BOSTON LYING-IN HOSPITAL (THE FENWAY). See also nos. 37, 50, 461.
209 "Boston Lying-In Hospital." In no. 712, pp. 64–65.
BOSTON NAVAL SHIPYARD BUILDINGS (CHARLESTOWN)
210 Norton, Bettina A. "The Boston Naval Shipyard." *Proc. Bost. Soc.* (1974), n.p.
BOSTON OPERA HOUSE (demolished). See also nos. 510, 741.
211 Jackson, Frank H. *Monograph of the Boston Opera House . . .* 1909.
BOSTON PARK PLAZA HOTEL (BACK BAY; originally Statler Hotel)
212 *AABN* 132 (1927): 14–16.
BOSTON PUBLIC LIBRARY (BACK BAY). See also nos. 696, 697, 704, 763, 767, 768.
213 "Boston Public Library." *Brickbuilder* 19 (1910): 32–37.
214 Burke, Doreen Bolger. "*Astarte*: Sargent's Study for *The Pagan Gods* Mural in the Boston Public Library." *Fenway Court* (1977), pp. 9–20.
215 *Edwin Austin Abbey, 1852–1911.* Intros. by Kathleen A. Foster and Michael Quick. New Haven, 1973.
216 Fenollosa, Ernest F. *Mural Painting in the Boston Public Library.* New York, 1896.
217 *Handbook of the New Public Library of the City of Boston.* 1895.
218 Jordy, William H. "The Beaux-Arts Renaissance: Charles McKim's Boston Public Library." In no. 765, pp. 314–375, 392–396.
219 Kingsbury, Martha. "Sargent's Murals in the Boston Public Library." *Winterthur Portfolio* 11 (1976): 153–172.
220 Moloney, Francis. *Tour of the Boston Public Library, Copley Square.* 1966.
221 Moore, Charles. "The Boston Public Library: A Manifestation of Civic Consciousness" and "Charles McKim Summons Saint-Gaudens . . . and Other Artists." In no. 586, pp. 62–95.
222 *Thirty-Seventh Annual Report of the Trustees* (of the Boston Public Library). 1888.
223 Whitehill, Walter Muir. *Boston Public Library: A Centennial History.* Cambridge, 1956.
224 ———. "The Making of an Architectural Masterpiece: The Boston Public Library." *American Art Journal* 11 (1970): 13–35.
225 ———. "The Vicissitudes of *Bacchante* in Boston." *New England Quarterly* 27 (1954): 435–454.
BOSTON PUBLIC LIBRARY, OLD (demolished). See nos. 39, 163.
BOSTON THEATRE, FIRST (demolished). See also nos. 516, 530.
226 Brown, Frank C. "The First Boston Theatre . . ." *OTNE* 36 (1945): 1–7.
BOSTON THEATRE, SECOND (demolished). See also no. 516.
227 Kavanaugh, Joseph. "Three American Opera Houses." M.A. thesis, University of Delaware. 1967.
228 Tompkins, Eugene. *The History of the Boston Theatre, 1854–1901.* 1908.
BOSTON SUB-TREASURY AND POST OFFICE (demolished). See nos. 38, 39.
BRAZER BUILDING (DOWNTOWN). See also no. 38.
229 *AABN* 56 (1897): 64.
CARTER BUILDING. See WINTHROP BUILDING
CHADWICK HOUSE (DORCHESTER). See also no. 100.
230 Tucci, Douglass Shand. "A Discovery . . . of the Plans of 20 Cushing Avenue . . ." *Dorchester Day Magazine*, *Dorchester Argus-Citizen*, June 1972, pp. 12–13.
CHARLESGATE, THE (BACK BAY). See also no. 22.
231 *AABN* 32 (1891): 14.
CHARLES PLAYHOUSE (DOWNTOWN; originally Fifth Universalist Church). See also no. 38.
232 Van Meter, Mary. "A New Asher Benjamin Building in Boston." *Drumlin* 3 (Jan. 1978): 1–2.
CHARLES STREET MEETING HOUSE (BEACON HILL)
233 Greene, Joseph G. "The Charles Street Meeting House." *OTNE* 30 (1946): 87–93.
234 Whitehill, Walter Muir. "A View of the Charles Street Church . . ." In no. 63, pp. 22–25.
CHRIST CHURCH (NORTH END)
235 Bolton, Charles K. *Christ Church.* 1912.
236 Foley, Suzanne. "Christ Church, Boston." *OTNE* 51 (1961): 67–85.
CLUNY, HOTEL (demolished)
237 *AABN* 4 (1878): 40.
COLONNADE ROW (demolished). See also no. 470.
238 Brent, Samuel A. "Colonnade Row." *Bostonian Society Publications* 40 (1914): 11–13.
239 Kirker, Harold. "The Colonnade, Boston." In no. 530, pp. 258–260.
COLONIAL THEATRE (DOWNTOWN)
240 Blackall, C. H. "The Colonial Theatre and Building." *AABN* 72 (1901): 11–12, 27–28, 44–45, 51–52, 67–69.

CONGREGATIONAL HOUSE (BEACON HILL)
241 AABN 64 (1899): 16.
CONVERSE MEMORIAL LIBRARY (MALDEN). See nos. *611, 614, 659*.
COVENANT, CHURCH OF THE (BACK BAY; originally Central Church). See also nos. *446, 630, 684*.
242 Koch, Robert. *The Tiffany Windows and Lantern at the Church of the Covenant.* 1966.
COWLEY FATHERS MONASTERY (CAMBRIDGE). See nos. *81, 703*.
CRANE MEMORIAL LIBRARY (QUINCY). See nos. *659, 662*.
CUSHING-ENDICOTT HOUSE (BACK BAY). See also no. *143*.
243 Laing, Diana Whitehill. "Cushing Endicott House, 463 Marlborough Street." *Proc. Bost. Soc.* (1960), pp. 15–52.
CUSTOM HOUSE (DOWNTOWN). See also no. *752*.
244 Smith, Margaret S. "The Custom House Controversy." *19th Century* 3 (1977): 99–105.
DAVENPORT HOUSE (MALDEN). See no. *659*.
DEWEY HOUSE (THE FENWAY). See no. *411*.
ELLINGWOOD MEMORIAL CHAPEL (NAHANT). See no. *353*.
EMMANUEL CHURCH (BACK BAY). See no. *682*. See also under LINDSEY MEMORIAL CHAPEL.
EXCHANGE BUILDING (DOWNTOWN). See no. *22*.
EXETER STREET THEATRE (BACK BAY; originally First Spiritualist Temple). See no. *567*.
FAIRBANKS HOUSE (DEDHAM). See no. *793*.
FANEUIL HALL (DOWNTOWN). See also no. *530*.
245 Whitehill, Walter Muir. "A View of Faneuil Hall." In no. *63*, pp. 6–9.
FANEUIL HALL MARKETS (DOWNTOWN). See also no. *787*.
246 Brown, Abram E. *Faneuil Hall and the Faneuil Hall Market.* 1901.
247 Monkhouse, Christopher P. "Consideration of Faneuil Hall Market and the Architect, Alexander Parris." *JSAH* 28 (1969): 212.
248 SPNEA and Architectural Heritage, Inc. *Faneuil Hall Markets: Historical Study.* 1958.
249 Webb, Roger S. "The History and Restoration of Boston's Faneuil Hall Markets." *JSAH* 28 (1969): 225.
250 Whitehill, Walter Muir. "Historical Continuity versus Synthetic Reconstruction." *Athenaeum Items* 67 (Jan. 1958): 1–3.
FEDERAL BUILDING (DOWNTOWN). See also nos. *542, 716*.
251 Loring, Charles G. "The Boston Federal Building." *AABN* 143 (1933): 15–19.
FENWAY COURT (ISABELLA STEWART GARDNER MUSEUM; THE FENWAY)
252 Baxter, Sylvester. *An American Palace of Art, Fenway Court . . .* 1904.
253 Carter, Morris. *Isabella Stewart Gardner and Fenway Court.* 1925.
254 *Guide to the Collection: Gardner Museum.* 1976.
255 O'Haggan, Anne. "The Treasures of Fenway Court." *Munsey's Magazine* 34 (1906): 655–678.
256 Saarinen, Aline B. *The Proud Possessors.* New York, 1958.
257 Stout, George L. *Treasures from the Isabella Stewart Gardner Museum.* New York, 1969.
258 Tharp, Louise Hall. *Mrs. Jack.* 1965.
259 Tucci, Douglass Shand. "Ralph Adams Cram and Mrs. Gardner: The Movement toward a Liturgical Art." *Fenway Court* (1975), pp. 27–34.
FILENE BOSTON STORE (DOWNTOWN). See also no. *534*.
260 "The New Filene Store." *Brickbuilder* 21 (1912): 247–250.
FIRST BAPTIST CHURCH (BACK BAY; formerly Brattle Square Church). See nos. *47, 611, 614*.
FIRST CHURCH OF BOSTON (BACK BAY; partially demolished). See also nos. *47, 149, 446*.
261 Ellis, Arthur E. *History of the First Church . . .* 1881.
FIRST CHURCH OF CHRIST, SCIENTIST, EXTENSION (BACK BAY)
262 Armstrong, Joseph. *The Mother Church.* 1911 and later eds.
263 Williamson, Margaret. *The Mother Church Extension.* 1939.
FISKE BUILDING (demolished). See no. *22*.
FORT INDEPENDENCE (CASTLE ISLAND; SOUTH BOSTON)
264 Whitehill, Walter Muir. "A View of Fort Independence." In no. *63*, pp. 62–65.
GALLERY ON THE MOORS AND ATWOOD HOUSE (GLOUCESTER). See also no. *320*.
265 O'Gorman, James F. "Parnassus on Ledge Road." In no. *106*, pp. 77–96.
GARDNER MUSEUM. See FENWAY COURT.
GATE OF HEAVEN CHURCH (SOUTH BOSTON). See also nos. *42, 686*.
266 *AABN* 55 (1897): 15.
GORE PLACE (WALTHAM). See also no. *63*.
267 Wick, Peter A. "Gore Place: . . ." *Antiques* 110 (1976): 1250–1261.
GRAIN AND FLOUR EXCHANGE (DOWNTOWN; originally Chamber of Commerce Building). See no. *22*.
GROPIUS HOUSE (LINCOLN). See also nos. *31, 33, 774*.
268 Huxtable, Ada Louise. "Gropius House . . ." *The New York Times*, 18 May 1975, p. 36.
269 "Tomorrow's Antiquity Today . . ." *Architecture: New England* 1 (1975): 16–19.
HADDON HALL (BACK BAY)
270 *AABN* 49 (1895): 42.
HAMILTON, HOTEL (demolished)
271 *AABN* 1 (1876): 373.
HAMMOND CASTLE (GLOUCESTER)
272 Witham, Corinne B. *The Hammond Museum Guide Book.* Gloucester, 1966.
HANCOCK HOUSE (demolished)
273 Millar, Donald. "Notes on the Hancock House, Boston." *OTNE* 17 (1927): 121–124.
274 Watkins, Walter K. "The Hancock House and Its Builder." *OTNE* 17 (1926): 3–19.
HARRIS WOOD CRESCENT (ROXBURY). For a discussion of Townsend Street see nos. *101–102*.
275 *AABN* 29 (1890): 74.
HARVARD UNIVERSITY BUILDINGS (CAMBRIDGE; THE FENWAY; BRIGHTON). See also nos. *47, 141, 616, 686, 782*.
276 Barton, George E. "Harvard University." *AABN* 112 (1917): 31.

277 Bunting, Bainbridge, and Robert H. Nylander. "Harvard University Architecture." In no. *81*, 2:149–203.
278 "Fogg Art Museum." *Arch. Record* 61 (1927): 465–477.
279 *Harvard College Yearbook, 1932.* Cambridge, 1932. The first yearbook to treat in some detail all the new Houses, which are lavishly illustrated.
280 "Harvard University Business School Competition." *Architecture* 51 (1925): 131 et seq.
281 *Harvard University: Education, Bricks and Mortar.* Cambridge, 1949.
282 Moore, Charles. "Puritan Liberalism and Pagan Austerity in New England Architecture." In no. *586*, pp. 95–112. This chapter deals almost entirely with McKim, Mead and White's Georgian Revival work at Harvard.
283 Parsons, David McI., and Douglass Shand Tucci. "The Idea of the House." Typescript. Harvard University Archives, Harvard College Library. 1971.
284 "Recent Collegiate Architecture as Exemplified by the Work of Messrs. Shepley, Rutan and Coolidge at Harvard . . ." *Brickbuilder* 23 (1914): 259–273.
285 Reiff, Daniel D. "[Memorial Hall:] Splendor beneath the Dust." *Harvard Bulletin* 74 (1972): 28–42.
286 Schuyler, Montgomery. "Harvard University." *Arch. Record* 26 (1909): 243–269.
287 Ticknor and Company. "Austin Hall." Monographs on American Architecture, no. 1 (*Arch. Record*, 1886).
288 Whitehill, Walter Muir, "Noble, Neglected Memorial Hall Turns 100." *Harvard Bulletin* 74 (1972): 22–27.
289 ———. "A View of Gore Hall . . ." In no. *63*, pp. 70–73, 74–77.
290 Yeomans, Henry. *Abbott Lawrence Lowell.* Cambridge, 1948. The chapters on the freshman dormitories and the Houses contain all the pertinent background material from Lowell's Annual Reports after the announcement of these projects.

HOLY CROSS, CATHEDRAL OF THE (SOUTH END). See also nos. *39, 446, 571.*
291 Murphy, Francis. *Centennial of Holy Cross Cathedral.* 1975.

HORTICULTURAL HALL (BACK BAY)
292 *AABN* 74 (1901): 71.
293 Benson, Albert E. *History of the Massachusetts Horticultural Society.* 1929.

HOWARD ANTHENAEUM (demolished). See nos. *1, 516.*

HUNNEWELL ESTATES (WELLESLEY). See no. *47.*

IMMACULATE CONCEPTION, CHURCH AND CONVENT OF (MALDEN). See nos. *37, 50.*

IMMACULATE CONCEPTION, CHURCH OF THE (SOUTH END). See also nos. *39, 446, 571.*
294 "Dedication of the Church of the Immaculate Conception." *Boston Journal,* 10 March 1861.
295 Murray, Thomas, and Douglass Shand Tucci. "The South End's Neglected Treasures . . ." *Drumlin* 1 (Sept. 1976): 45.
296 Santayana, George. "The Church of the Immaculate Conception." In *Persons and Places,* pp. 163–177. New York, 1944.

INTERNATIONAL TRUST BUILDING (DOWNTOWN). See also no. *22.*
297 *AABN* 39 (1893): 14.

JESUIT NOVITIATE (WESTON). See also no. *703.*
298 "Jesuit Novitiate." In no. *434,* pp. 37–38.

KEITH MEMORIAL THEATRE, B. F. (DOWNTOWN; now Savoy Theatre). See also no. *517.*
299 *The B. F. Keith Memorial Theatre. Boston Sunday Herald,* 28 Oct. 1928. Special rotogravure section.

KEITH'S THEATRE, B. F. (DOWNTOWN; partially demolished)
300 Birkmire, William. "The Gaiety Theatre." In no. *508.* For some reason this chapter on Keith's Theatre is mistitled.

KENNEDY HOUSE (BROOKLINE)
301 Cameron, Gail. *Rose: A Biography of Rose Kennedy.* New York, 1971.

KINGMAN HOUSE (BROCKTON).
302 Floyd, Margaret Henderson. *309 Main Street . . .* Brockton, 1973.

KING'S CHAPEL (DOWNTOWN). See also no. *566.*
303 Metcalf, Priscilla. "Boston before Bulfinch: Harrison's King's Chapel." *JSAH* 13 (1954): 11–14.

KOCH HOUSE (CAMBRIDGE). See nos. *81, 618.*

KRAGSYDE (MANCHESTER-BY-THE-SEA). See nos. *604, 605, 793.*

LINDSEY MEMORIAL CHAPEL OF EMMANUEL CHURCH (BACK BAY). See also no. *37.*
304 *The Leslie Lindsey Chapel.* 1966.
305 "The Lindsey Chapel." *Architecture* 50 (1924): 393–398.

LONGWOOD TOWERS (BROOKLINE)
306 "Alden Park Manor [Longwood Towers]." In no. *712,* pp. 210–211.

MAJESTIC THEATRE (DOWNTOWN; now Saxon Theatre). See also no. *509.*
307 *AABN* 80 (1903): 24 et seq.
308 "The Majestic." *Boston Sunday Globe,* 15 Feb. 1903, p. 44.

MASONIC TEMPLE (DOWNTOWN; 1867 building). See nos. *39, 628.*

MASSACHUSETTS HISTORICAL SOCIETY BUILDING (THE FENWAY)
309 *Handbook of the Massachusetts Historical Society.* 1949.

MASSACHUSETTS INSTITUTE OF TECHNOLOGY BUILDING, OLD (demolished). See no. *1.*

MASSACHUSETTS INSTITUTE OF TECHNOLOGY (CAMBRIDGE). See also nos. *31, 81, 448.*
310 Kebbon, H. E. "Building the 'New Technology.' " *Arch. Review* 4 (1916): 85–92.

MERCANTILE WHARF (WATERFRONT). See also no. *730.*
311 Huxtable, Ada Louise. "Progressive Architecture in America." *Progressive Architecture* 39 (1958): 117–118.

METROPOLITAN THEATRE (DOWNTOWN; originally Music Hall). See nos. *510, 515, 708.*
312 Boston Redevelopment Authority. *The Metropolitan Theatre.* 1975.
313 "Metropolitan Theatre." In no. *712,* pp. 136–137.
314 "The Metropolitan Theatre." Scrapbook of newspaper clippings of the theater's history. Fine Arts Dept. (Research), Boston Public Library.

MOTOR MART GARAGE (BACK BAY). See nos. *37, 50.*

MUSEUM OF FINE ARTS (FIRST BUILDING; demolished). See also nos. *321, 480.*
315 Floyd, Margaret Henderson. "A Terra-Cotta Cornerstone for Copley Square: Museum of Fine Arts, Boston, 1870–1876, by Sturgis and Brigham." *JSAH* 32 (1973): 83–103.

MUSEUM OF FINE ARTS (SECOND BUILDING; BACK BAY)

316 Addison, Julia de Wolf. *The Boston Museum of Fine Arts.* 1910.

317 Blackall, C. H. "The Sargent Decorations . . ." *American Architecture* 121 (1922): 241–244.

318 Brown, Frank Chouteau. "The Boston Museum's New Wing." *Architecture* 58 (1928): 315–320.

319 Coburn, F. W. "The New Art Museum . . ." *International Studio* 33 (1907–1908): 57–62.

320 Tucci, Douglass Shand. "Three New England Art Galleries by Ralph Adams Cram: The Japanese Department of the Museum of Fine Arts, Boston; the Currier Gallery in Manchester, N.H., and the Gallery on the Moors in Glouces-ter, Massachusetts." *Currier Gallery Bulletin*, forthcoming issue.

321 Whitehill, Walter Muir. *Museum of Fine Arts, Boston: A Centennial History.* 2 vols. Cambridge, 1970.

MUTUAL LIFE INSURANCE BUILDING (demolished). See also no. 22.

322 *AABN* 3 (1878): 84.

NEW ENGLAND CONSERVATORY OF MUSIC (BACK BAY)

323 *The Conservatory Building.* 1928.

NEW ENGLAND MUTUAL BUILDING (demolished). See no. 22.

NEW ENGLAND MUTUAL BUILDING (BACK BAY). See no. 770.

NEW OLD SOUTH CHURCH (BACK BAY). See also nos. 22, 64, 145, 446.

324 Hill, A. Hamilton. *History of The Old South Church (Third Church), 1869–1884.* 1890.

NEWTON CITY HALL (NEWTON). See also nos. 37, 50.

325 *The Official Dedication Program of the Newton City Hall . . .* Newton, 1932.

OLD SOUTH CHURCH (DOWNTOWN). See no. 1.

OLD STATE HOUSE (DOWNTOWN)

326 Bruce, James L. *The Old State House.* 1965.

327 Whitehill, Walter Muir. "A View of the Old State House . . ." In no. 63, pp. 2–5.

OLD WEST CHURCH (BEACON HILL)

328 Voye, Nancy S. "Asher Benjamin's West Church: A Model for Change." *OTNE* 67 (1976): 7–15.

329 Whitehill, Walter Muir. "A View of the Old West Church." In no. 63, pp. 10–13.

OTIS, HARRISON GRAY, FIRST HOUSE (WEST END). See also nos. 530, 779.

330 Cummings, Abbott Lowell. "The First Harrison Gray Otis House in Boston: A Study in Pictorial Evidence." *OTNE* 60 (1970): 105–108.

331 Nylander, Richard. *The First Harrison Gray Otis House.* 1975.

OTIS, HARRISON GRAY, SECOND HOUSE (BEACON HILL). See also nos. 530, 787.

332 Parsons, Susan, and Wendell D. Garrett. "The Second Harrison Gray Otis House." *Antiques* 92 (1967): 536–541.

OTIS, HARRISON GRAY, THIRD HOUSE (BEACON HILL). See nos. 530, 787.

OUR SAVIOUR, CHURCH OF (BROOKLINE). See also no. 686.

333 Fletcher, Herbert H. *The Church of Our Saviour.* Brookline, 1936.

PAINE HOUSE (WALTHAM). See nos. 47, 611, 793.

PARK STREET CHURCH (DOWNTOWN)

334 Whitehill, Walter Muir. "A View of the Granary Burying Ground . . . and Park Street Church." In no. 63, pp. 30–33.

PARKER HOUSE (DOWNTOWN)

335 "Parker House." In no. 712, pp. 126–127.

336 Spring, James W. *Boston and the Parker House.* 1927.

PARSHLEY HOUSES (DORCHESTER). See also no. 100.

337 Tucci, Douglass Shand. *The Master Builders.* Parts V–VIII of this series appeared in *Dorchester Argus-Citizen*, 15 June–6 July 1972, pp. 3 et seq.

PEABODY, THE (DORCHESTER). See also no. 186.

338 *AABN* 58 (1897): 43.

339 *Brickbuilder* 9 (1900): Plate 72.

PERKINS SCHOOL FOR THE BLIND (WATERTOWN, originally Perkins Institution for the Blind)

340 Perkins Institute. *Eighty-first Annual Report of the Trustees.* 1913. Includes Sturgis's plans.

341 "The Perkins Institute . . ." *Brickbuilder* 22 (1913): 154–156.

PERPETUAL HELP, BASILICA OF OUR LADY OF (MISSION CHURCH; ROXBURY). See also no 42.

342 *AABN* 12 (1877): 240.

343 Byrne, John. *The Glories of Mary in Boston.* 1921.

344 Currier, Charles W. "History of the Church of Our Lady of Perpetual Succor in Boston." *American Catholic Histori-cal Society Report* 2 (1886–1888): 206–224.

PIERCE, S. S., STORE (BROOKLINE)

345 *AABN* 62 (1898): 92.

PINEBANK (JAMAICA PLAIN)

346 Floyd, Margaret Henderson. "Pinebank: Another Conservation Challenge for Boston." *Drumlin* 1 (July 1976): 4–5.

RADCLIFFE COLLEGE. See HARVARD UNIVERSITY BUILDINGS

REDEEMER, CHURCH OF THE (CHESTNUT HILL). See also no. 632.

347 Morgan, William D., and Douglass Shand Tucci. "A Guide to the Church of the Redeemer." Typescript. Church of the Redeemer. 1974.

REVERE, PAUL, HOUSE (NORTH END)

348 *Handbook of the Paul Revere Memorial Association.* 1950.

349 "Restoration of the Paul Revere House." *Arch. Record* 36 (1914): 80.

RICHMOND COURT (BROOKLINE). See also no. 542.

350 Cram, Ralph Adams. *Richmond Court Apartments.* 1899. The only known extant copy of this booklet is in the Boston Athenaeum. Plans and exterior photographs were also published in *Brickbuilder* 9 (1900), Plates 40 et seq.

RITZ-CARLTON HOTEL (BACK BAY)

351 "Mural Decorations for the Ritz Carlton Hotel in Boston." *Arch. Record* 63 (1926): 178–179.

352 "Ritz-Carlton Hotel." In no. 712, pp. 134–135.

ROXBURY LATIN SCHOOL (WEST ROXBURY). See no. 37.

ST. ANNE'S CONVENT CHAPEL (ARLINGTON)

353   Cram, Ralph Adams. "Three Small Chapels." *Architecture* 46 (1922): 363–369.
ST. CATHERINE OF GENOA (SOMERVILLE). See nos. *42, 592.*
ST. CATHERINE OF SIENA (NORWOOD). See nos. *42, 686.*
ST. CLEMENT'S CHURCH (CHURCH OF THE REDEEMER; BACK BAY). See also no. *42.*
354   "Church of the Redeemer." In no. *434*, pp. 16–50.
ST. CLEMENT'S CHURCH (SOMERVILLE). See also nos. *42, 50.*
355   "St. Clement's Church, . . ." *Liturgical Arts* 12 (1943): 15–16, 17–20.
ST. ELIZABETH'S CHAPEL (SUDBURY). See no. *353.*
ST. JAMES CHURCH (SOUTH END). See nos. *42, 446.*
ST. JOHN THE EVANGELIST, CHURCH OF (BEACON HILL; originally Beecher Congregational Church). See also nos. *446, 542.*
356   Smith, Robert C. *The Shrine on Bowdoin Street.* 1958.
ST. JOHN'S SEMINARY (BRIGHTON). See also no. *42.*
357   Sexton, John E., and Arthur J. Riley. *History of Saint John's Seminary.* 1945.
ST. LUKE'S CHURCH (CHELSEA)
358   Bourne, Frank. "The Possibilities of Concrete in Building Churches." *Church Militant* (March 1907), p. 6.
ST. PAUL'S CHURCH (BROOKLINE; partially demolished). See also nos. *74, 154, 442, 630.*
359   Bigelow, Robert Payne. "Movements and Men in the Early History of St. Paul's Church . . ." Manuscript in parish archives, 1951.
ST. PAUL'S CHURCH (DEDHAM)
360   Worthington, Arthur M. *History of St. Paul's Episcopal Church . . . 1758–1958.* Dedham, 1958.
ST. PAUL'S CHURCH (DORCHESTER). See nos. *37, 42.*
ST. PETER'S CHURCH (DORCHESTER). See also *no. 42.*
361   Marnell, William, and Douglass Shand Tucci. *Saint Peter's Centennial.* 1974.
ST. STEPHEN'S CHURCH (NORTH END). See also nos. *42, 530.*
362   *Saint Stephen's Church, Boston, Massachusetts.* 1966.
363   Whitehill, Walter Muir. "Saint Stephen's Church . . ." In no. *63*, pp. 38–41.
ST. THERESA'S CHURCH (WEST ROXBURY). See nos. *37, 42.*
SALADA TEA BUILDING (BACK BAY). See also no. *707.*
364   Cowell, Mark S. "Echoes of the Tea Trade." *Boston Globe Magazine*, 3 Nov. 1974, pp. 28–32.
365   "Salada Building." In no. *712*, pp. 180–181.
366   Société des Artistes Français. *Salon de 1927.* Paris, 1927.
SECOND CHURCH IN NEWTON (CONGREGATIONAL). See also no. *686.*
367   *Our Church.* Newton, 1926.
SECOND UNIVERSALIST CHURCH (SOUTH END). See no. *446.*
SOMERSET CLUB (BEACON HILL; originally Sears House). See also no. *752.*
368   Whitney, Hugh, and Walter Muir Whitehill. "The Somerset Club." In *The Somerset Club, 1851–1951*, pp. 18–20. 1951.
STATE HOUSE, NEW (BEACON HILL). See also no. *787.*
369   Burrill, Ellen M. *The State House.* 1914.
370   Hitchings, Sinclair, and Caroline H. Farlow. *The Massachusetts State House.* 1964.
371   Kirker, Harold. "The Massachusetts State House." In no. *530*, pp. 101–114.
372   ——— and James Kirker. "Bulfinch's Design for the Massachusetts State House." *OTNE* 55 (1964): 43–45.
373   Pickens, Bufford. "Wyatt's Pantheon, the State House in Boston and a New View of Bulfinch." *JSAH* 29 (1970): 124–131.
374   Thwing, Leroy. "The Bulfinch State House." *OTNE* 43 (1952): 63–67.
STOUGHTON HOUSE (CAMBRIDGE). See nos. *475, 611, 793.*
SUFFOLK COUNTY COURT HOUSE (1886 BUILDING; BEACON HILL). See no. *22.*
SUFFOLK COUNTY JAIL (WEST END). See No. *1.*
"SUNFLOWER CASTLE" (BEACON HILL)
375   *AABN* 4 (1878): 85.
SYMPHONY HALL (BACK BAY). See also no. *586.*
376   Johnson, H. Earle. *Symphony Hall, Boston,* 1950.
TEMPLE ISRAEL (BACK BAY)
377   Blackall, C. H. "The Symbolism of Temple Israel." In no. *379*, pp. 28–31.
378   Mann, Arthur. *Growth and Achievement: Temple Israel, 1854–1954.* Cambridge, 1953.
379   Obst, S. D. *The Story of Adath Israel.* 1917.
TEMPLE OHABEI SHALOM (BROOKLINE)
380   *American Architecture* 134 (1928): 707–711.
TONTINE CRESCENT (demolished). See also nos. *470, 530.*
381   Waite, Emma F. "The Tontine Crescent and Its Architecture." *OTNE* 43 (1953): 74–77.
TORREY HOUSE (demolished)
382   *AABN* 7 (1880): 141.
TOURAINE HOTEL (DOWNTOWN)
383   *AABN* 58 (1897): 35.
TREMONT HOUSE (demolished). See also nos. *467, 739, 752.*
384   Eliot, William Howard. *Description of the Tremont House . . . 1830?*
385   Lee, Henry. "Boston's Greatest Hotel." *OTNE* 55 (1965): 97–106.
TREMONT TEMPLE (DOWNTOWN)
386   Blackall, C. H. "Tremont Temple." In *Tremont Temple Sketch Book*, pp. 45–64. 1896.
TRINITY CHURCH (BACK BAY). See also nos. *47, 64, 145, 611, 684, 768.*
387   "A Boston Basilica." *Architect* 18 (1877): 274.
388   Chester, Arthur H. *Trinity Church.* Cambridge, 1888.
389   Graff, Myrtle S. *Guidebook to Trinity Church . . .* 1924.
390   Richardson, Henry Hobson. *A Description of Trinity Church.* 1877.

391   Romig, Edgar D. *The Story of Trinity Church . . .* 1952.
392   Sergeant, Perry T. "Colour Decoration in America." *Architect* 18 (1877): 210–211.
393   Stebbins, Theodore E., Jr. "Richardson and Trinity Church . . ." *JSAH* 27 (1968): 181–198.
394   Ticknor and Co. "Trinity Church." Monographs on American Architecture, no. 5 (*Arch. Record*, 1888).
395   Weinberg, Helene B. "John La Farge and the Decoration of Trinity Church, Boston." *JSAH* 33 (1974): 323–353.
TRINITY CHURCH RECTORY (BACK BAY). See nos. *143, 611.*
UNITED SHOE MACHINERY CORPORATION BUILDING (DOWNTOWN). See also no. *489.*
396   *AABN* 134 (1928): 270.
UNION CONGREGATIONAL CHURCH (SOUTH END). See no. *446.*
UNION STATION (demolished). See no. *22.*
VENDOME HOTEL (BACK BAY). See also no. *1.*
397   "Uses of the Past . . ." *Arch. Forum* 137 (1972): 24–33.
VINAL HOUSE (DORCHESTER)
398   Tucci, Douglass Shand. "Dorchester Sinecure at City Hall." *Dorchester Argus-Citizen,* 25 May 1972, p. 2.
WARREN, THE (demolished)
399   *AABN* 20 (1886): 231.
WELLESLEY COLLEGE (WELLESLEY). See also nos. *449, 615, 686.*
400   Clements, Lee Ann. "A New Light on College Hall." *Wellesley Alumnae Magazine* 62 (Spring 1978): 4–7.
401   Poindexter, Jean, and Louise Sander. *The New Wellesley.* 1931.
402   Schuyler, Montgomery. "Three Women's Colleges . . ." *Arch. Record* 31 (1912): 513–537.
WELLESLEY TOWN HALL. See no. *47.*
WESTMINSTER CHAMBERS HOTEL (demolished)
403   *AABN* 71 (1901): 40.
WILBUR THEATRE (DOWNTOWN)
404   "Georgian Architecture in Business." *Boston Evening Transcript,* 2 May 1914, p. 3.
WINN MEMORIAL LIBRARY (WOBURN). See nos. *611, 613, 614.*
WINTHROP (CARTER) BUILDING (DOWNTOWN). See also nos. *38, 486, 542.*
405   Damrell, Charles. "The Carter Building." In no. *22,* pp. 70–71.
406   "The Carter Building." *Inland Architect* 22 (1893): 31.
WOMEN'S CITY CLUB (BEACON HILL; originally Appleton and Parker houses). See no. *752.*
WORTHINGTON BUILDING (DOWNTOWN)
407   "The Worthington Building . . ." *Brickbuilder* 3 (1895): 33–34.

E. BUILDING TYPES

APARTMENT HOUSES AND APARTMENT HOTELS
408   Apartment House Number. *AABN* 110 (29 Nov. 1916): 332–350.
409   Apartment House Number. *Arch. Forum* 43 (1925): 121–184.
410   Bacon, Edwin M. "Apartment Houses and Family Hotels." In no. *1,* pp. 16–17.
411   "Boston Flats." *Brickbuilder* 14 (1905): 119–123.
412   Boston Redevelopment Authority, and the Boston Urban Observatory. *Three Decker Housing in the City of Boston: A Reconnaissance.* 1974.
413   Boston *Transcript.* Real Estate pages, 1870–1925.
414   Brown, Frank Chouteau. "Some Recent Apartment Buildings." *Arch. Record* 63 (1928): 193–278.
415   Comstock, William T. *Two Family and Twin Houses.* New York, 1908.
416   Edgell, G. H. Section on apartment houses in no. *744,* pp. 144–150.
417   Hall, Prescott F. "The Menace of the Three-Decker," and discussion by Edwin H. Marble. In no. *760* (1917), pp. 133–152, 321–327.
418   Hill, George. "Apartment House" and "Tenement House." In no. *802,* cols. 82–89, 777–781.
419   Kilham, Walter H. "The Planning of Apartment Houses." *Brickbuilder* 13 (1904): 2–8.
420   Krim, Arthur J. "The Three Decker as Urban Architecture in New England." *The Monadnock* 44 (1970): 45–55.
421   Logue, Charles. "How It Strikes a Bostonian." In no. *760* (1919), pp. 342–348.
422   May, Charles C. "The Group House — Its Advantages and Possibilities." In no. *760* (1919), pp. 308–311.
423   Newman, Bernard J. "Shall We Encourage or Discourage the Apartment House," and discussion by James H. Hurley, et al. In no. *760* (1917), pp. 153–166, 328–348.
424   Peters, Andrew J. "The City's Obligation in Housing." In no. *760* (1919), pp. 329–335.
425   Sexton, R. W. *American Apartment Houses of Today.* New York, 1926.
BANKS
426   Bank Number. *Arch. Forum* 38 (1923): 253–312.
427   Edgell, G. H. Section on banks in no. *744,* pp. 345–348.
BRIDGES. See also no. *613.*
428   Schweinfurth, Julius. "Some Bridges of Boston's Park System." *AABN* 116 (1919): 329–333.
CHURCHES AND SYNAGOGUES. For a complete checklist of Boston area churches, see no. *61.* See also nos. *18, 42, 99, 149.*
429   Anson, Peter. *Fashions in Church Furnishings, 1840–1940.* London, 1960.
430   Blackall, C. H. "Boston Sketches — Churches." *Inland Architect* 12 (1888): 77–78.
431   Brandeis University, Rose Art Museum. *Two Hundred Years of Synagogue Architecture.* Waltham, Mass., 1976.
432   Coolidge, John P. "Gothic Revival Churches in New England and New York." B.A. thesis, Harvard, 1935.
433   Cram, Ralph Adams. *American Church Architecture of Today.* New York, 1929.
434   ——. *American Churches.* 2 vols. New York, 1915.
435   ——. *The Catholic Church and Art.* New York, 1930.
436   ——. *Church Building.* 1899.

437   ———. "The Philosophy of the Gothic Restoration" and "The Artist and the World." In no. *544*, pp. 19–63, 105–139.
438   Edgell, G. H. Section on churches and synagogues in no. *744*, pp. 197–226.
439   Kervick, Francis. *Architects in America of Catholic Tradition.* Rutland, Vt., 1962.
440   Maginnis, Charles. "Catholic Church Architecture." *Brickbuilder* 15 (1906): 25–28, 46–52.
441   ———. "The Movement for a Vital Christian Architecture and the Obstacles — The Roman Catholic View." *Christian Art* 1 (1917): 22–26.
442   Shinn, George W. *King's Handbook of Notable Episcopal Churches in the United States.* 1889.
443   Short, Ernest H. *A History of Religious Architecture.* New York, 1936.
444   Stanton, Phoebe B. *The Gothic Revival and American Church Architecture.* Baltimore, 1968.
445   Taylor, Walter. "Protestant Churches." In *Forms and Functions of Twentieth-Century Architecture,* ed. Talbot Hamlin, 3:335–336. 3 vols. New York, 1952.
446   Willard, A. R. "Recent Church Architecture in Boston," *New England Magazine* (Feb. 1890), pp. 641–662.

COLLEGIATE AND SCHOOL DESIGN. See also no. *141*.
447   Cram, Ralph Adams. "American University Architecture." In no. *544*, pp. 169–211.
448   Edgell, G. H. Section on academic architecture in no. *744*, pp. 156–163.
449   Klauder, Charles Z., and Herbert C. Wise. *College Architecture in America.* New York, 1929.
450   Schuyler, Montgomery. "Architecture of American Colleges." *Arch. Record* 26 (1909): 243–269.
451   Tolles, Bryant Franklin, Jr. "College Architecture in New England before 1860 . . ." *Antiques* 103 (1973): 502–509.
452   Wheelwright, Edmund M. "The School House." In no. *802*, cols. 422–434. A series by Wheelwright on the same subject appeared in *Brickbuilder* throughout 1897, beginning in 6 (1897): 244–247.

GARAGES AND SERVICE STATIONS. See also no. *81*.
453   Automotive Buildings Number. *Arch. Forum* 46 (1927): 201–312.
454   Blanchard, Harold. "Ramp Design in Public Garages." *Arch. Forum* 35 (1921): 169–175.
455   Guth, Alexander G. "The Automobile Service Station." *Arch. Forum* 45 (1926): 33–56.
       Several early Boston service stations are discussed and illustrated, including a no longer extant duplicate in Dorchester of the South End service station shown in Figure 194.

GOVERNMENT BUILDINGS. See also LIBRARIES AND MUSEUMS; no. *149*.
456   Edgell, G. H. Section on civic architecture in no. *744*, pp. 226–241.
457   Loring, Charles G. "The Small Town Hall: Plattsburgh, N. Y.; Arlington, Mass.; Tewksbury, Mass.; Weston, Mass., etc. . . ." *Arch. Forum* 47 (1927): 193–204.
458   Sexton, R. W. *American Public Buildings of Today.* New York, 1928.
459   Wheelwright, Edmund M. *Annual Reports of City of Boston Architect Department.* 1891–1894.
460   ———. *Municipal Architecture in Boston.* 1898.

HOSPITALS
461   Edgell, G. H. Section on hospitals in no. *744*, pp. 314–322.
462   Hospital Number. *Arch. Forum* 37 (1922): 245–314.
463   Stevens, Edward F. *The American Hospital of the 20th Century.* New York, 1921. Rev. ed.

HOTELS
464   Edgell, G. H. Section on hotels in no. *744*, pp. 334–345.
465   Hardenburgh, H. J. "Hotel." In no. *802*, cols. 400–414.
466   Hotel Number. *Arch. Forum* 39 (1923): 195–274.
467   Williamson, Jefferson. *The American Hotel.* New York, 1930.

HOUSES (SINGLE-FAMILY). For a checklist of Back Bay town houses, see no. *143*. For a checklist of representative streetcar-suburb houses, see no. *100*. See also nos. *81, 150–156, 167, 172, 174*.
468   Blackall, C. H. "Boston Sketches — Suburban Work." *Inland Architect* 13 (1889): 40–41, 53–54.
469   Brown, Frank Chouteau. "Boston Suburban Architecture." *Arch. Record* 21 (1907): 245–280.
470   ———. "The First Residential 'Row Houses' in Boston." *OTNE* 37 (1947): 60–69.
471   Edgell, G. H. Section on domestic architecture in no. *744*, pp. 87–144, 149–154.
472   Kocher, A. Lawrence. "The American Country House." *Arch. Record* 58 (1925): 401–512.
473   Lancaster, Clay. "The American Bungalow." *Art Bulletin* 40 (1958): 239–253.
474   Seale, William. *The Tasteful Interlude.* New York, 1975.
475   Sheldon, George. *Artistic Country Seats . . .* New York, 1886.
476   "The Narrowness of City House Fronts and the Abuses That Have Arisen in Their Treatment." *AABN* 4 (1878): 51.
477   Wharton, Edith, and Ogden Codman, Jr. *The Decoration of Houses.* New York, 1897.

INDUSTRIAL BUILDINGS. See also no. *81*.
478   Edgell, G. H. Section on factories in no. *744*, pp. 289–294.
479   Industrial Building Number. *Arch. Forum* 39 (1923): 83–151.

LIBRARIES AND MUSEUMS
480   Burt, Nathaniel. *Palaces for the People.* 1977.
481   Edgell, G. H. Section on libraries and museums in no. *744*, pp. 241–271.
482   Harris, Neil. "The Gilded Age Revisited: Boston and the Museum Movement." *American Quarterly* 14 (1962): 545–566.
483   Library and Museum Number. *Arch. Forum* 47 (1927): 497–608.

OFFICE BUILDINGS. See also nos. *27, 32, 157–162, 534, 611, 623–629*.
484   Birkmire, William H. *The Planning and Construction of High Office Buildings.* New York, 1898.
485   Blackall, Clarence H. "Boston Sketches — Business Buildings." *Inland Architect* 12 (1889): 94–96.
486   ———. "The Legitimate Design of the Architectural Casing for Steel Skeleton Structures." *AABN* 66 (1899): 78–80.
487   Corbett, Harvey. "High Buildings on Narrow Streets." *AABN* 119 (1921): 603–608, 617.
488   Edgell, G. H. Section on commercial architecture in no. *744*, pp. 350–375.
489   Fay, Frederick. Section on heights in "The Planning of a City." In no. *13*, pp. 41–61.
490   Jordy, William H. "Masonry Block and Metal Skeleton . . ." and "Functionalism as Fact and Symbol . . ." In no. *765*, pp. 1–180.
491   Nimmons, George C. "Skyscrapers in America." *A.I.A. Journal* 11 (1923): 370–372.

492 Office Building Number. *Arch. Forum* 41 (1924): 89–160.
493 Ripley, Hubert G. "Office Buildings of the '90s." *Architecture* 59, 60 (1926): 583–585, 275–278.
494 Sexton, R. W. *American Commercial Buildings of Today.* New York, 1928.
495 "Skyscrapers: Prophecy in Steel: Houston, Philadelphia, Miami, Cleveland, Hollywood, New York, Chicago, Detroit, Boston, Minneapolis." *Fortune* 2 (1930): 84–88.
496 Sullivan, Louis. "The Tall Building, Artistically Considered." *Lippincott's Magazine* 57 (1896): 403–409.
497 Weisman, Winston. "New York and the Problem of the First Skyscraper." *JSAH* 12 (1953): 13–21. Weisman later reorganized and somewhat modified his views in his "A New View of Skyscraper History" in Edgar Kaufmann, Jr., ed., *The Rise of an American Architecture,* New York, 1970, pp. 113–160.

STORES AND SHOPS
498 Edgell, G. H. Section on stores and shops in no. *744,* pp. 306–314.
499 French, Leigh, Jr. "Show Windows and Shop Fronts." *Arch. Forum* 46 (1927): 177–192.
500 "Innovations in Small Store Design . . . Three Candy Stores in Boston." *Arch. Forum* 34 (1921): 135–138.
501 Marnell, William. *Once Upon a Store: A Biography of the World's First Supermarket.* New York, 1971.
502 Shop and Store Number. *Arch. Forum* 40 (1924): 233–287.
503 Soames, Dana. "Recent Shop Fronts in New England." *Arch. Forum* 40 (1924): 249–257.

SUBWAY AND ELEVATED SYSTEM
504 "The Boston Subway . . ." *Brickbuilder* 7 (1898): 133–134.
505 Cudahy, Brian J. *Change at Park Street Under . . . Boston's Subways.* Brattleboro, Vt., 1972.
506 "Enameled Brick Treatment of Subway Construction." *Brickbuilder* 9 (1900): 262. The still-extant kiosks of Park Street Station were illustrated in *AABN* 56 (1897): 47.
507 Smith, H. McKelden, III. "The 'El': Boston's Elevated Railroad Stations." In no. *807,* pp. 133–139.

THEATERS AND HALLS. For a complete checklist of Boston theaters, see no. *517.* See also nos. *158, 162.*
508 Birkmire, William. *The Planning and Construction of American Theatres.* New York, 1896.
509 Blackall, Clarence H. "The American Theatre." *Brickbuilder* 17 (1908): 2–8 et seq.
510 Edgell, G. H. Section on theaters and halls in no. *744,* pp. 322–333.
511 Hall, B. M. *The Best Remaining Seats.* New York, 1961.
512 Mullin, Donald C. *The Development of the Playhouse: A Survey of Theatre Architecture from the Renaissance to the Present.* Berkeley, Calif., 1970.
513 Motion Picture [Theater] Number. *Arch. Forum* 42 (1925): 361–432.
514 Pichel, Irving. *Modern Theatres.* New York, 1925.
515 Sexton, R. W. *American Theatres of Today.* New York, 1930.
516 Stoddard, Richard. "The Architecture and Technology of Boston Theatres, 1794–1854." Ph.D. diss., Yale, 1971.
517 Tucci, Douglass Shand. *The Boston Rialto: Playhouses, Concert Halls and Movie Palaces.* 1977.
518 Young, William C. *Famous American Playhouses.* Chicago, 1973.

F. ARCHITECTS WHO WORKED IN BOSTON

Architects who practiced chiefly elsewhere are included if they worked also in Boston, as are one or two who briefly lived in the Boston area. For specific buildings by the architects below, see Section D.

ARCHITECTS COLLABORATIVE, THE. See GROPIUS, WALTER.
ATWOOD, HARRISON. See no. *32,* pp. 130–131; no. *811,* p. 32.
BACON, WILLARD M. See no. *32,* p. 401.
BANNER, PETER. See also no. *38.*
519 Keith, Elmer D., and William L. Warren. "Peter Banner, Architect, . . ." *OTNE* 57 (1967): 57–76.
BATEMAN, CHARLES J. See no. *32,* p. 139.
BEAL, J. WILLIAMS. See no. *811,* pp. 61–62.
BENJAMIN, ASHER
520 Benjamin, Asher. *The Works of . . .* 7 vols. 1806–1853. Reprint, New York, 1973.
521 Howe, Florence T. "More about Asher Benjamin." *JSAH* 13 (1954): 16–19.
BESARICK, JOHN H. See no. *32,* p. 144.
BLACKALL, CLARENCE H. See also nos. *32, 64, 810.*
522 Blackall, C. H. "American Architecture Since the War." *AABN* 133 (1928): 1–11.
523 ———. "Fifty Years Ago." *AABN* 129 (1926): 7–9.
524 ———. "Looking Back on Fifty Years of Architecture." *AABN* 132 (1930): 38–41, 86, 88, 90.
525 ———. "Notes on Travel — Chicago." *AABN* 23 (1888): 90–94.
526 ———. "Notes on Travel — [Adler and Sullivan's] McVickers Theatre [in Chicago]." *AABN* 22 (1887): 299–300, 313–315.
BRADLEE, N. J. See no. *64.*
BRIGHAM, CHARLES W. See no. *32,* pp. 156–157. See also no. *47.*
BROWN, FRANK C. See no. *811,* pp. 113–114.
BROWN, J. MERRILL. See no. *32,* p. 160.
BRYANT, GRIDLEY J. FOX. See also no. *38.*
527 Bailey, Henry T. "An Architect of the Old School." *New England Magazine* 25 (1901): 326–349.
BULFINCH, CHARLES. See also nos. *150–156, 167.*
528 Bulfinch, Ellen Susan. *The Life and Letters of Charles Bulfinch.* 1896.
529 Hudnut, Joseph. "The Romantic Architecture of Boston." In no. *725,* pp. 6–11.
530 Kirker, Harold. *The Architecture of Charles Bulfinch.* Cambridge, 1969.
531 Kirker, Harold and James. *Bulfinch's Boston 1787–1817.* New York, 1964.
532 Place, Charles A. *Charles Bulfinch, Architect and Citizen.* 1925.

533 Stanley, William H., ed. *Mr. Bulfinch's Boston.* 1963.
BURNHAM, DANIEL H. See also no. *497.*
534 Hines, Thomas S. *Burnham of Chicago.* New York, 1974.
535 Moore, Charles. *Daniel H. Burnham, Architect, Planner of Cities.* 2 vols. 1921. Reprint, New York, 1968.
536 Schuyler, Montgomery. "D. H. Burnham and Co." Great American Architects Series, no. 2 (*Arch. Record,* 1896), pp. 49–71.
CABOT, EDWARD. See no. *38,* pp. 53–54, no. *64,* pp. 17–18.
CARRÈRE AND HASTINGS
537 "The Work of Carrère and Hastings." *Arch. Record* 27 (1910): 1–120.
538 Gray, David. *Thomas Hastings, Architect.* 1933.
CLOUGH, GEORGE A. See no. *32,* p. 186.
COOLIDGE, CHARLES A. See SHEPLEY FIRM
COOLIDGE, CORNELIUS
539 Bernstein, Allen. "Cornelius Coolidge, Architect of Beacon Hill Row Houses, 1810–1840." *OTNE* 39 (1948): 45–46.
CRAM, RALPH ADAMS. For a complete bibliography of Cram's writings, which run into the hundreds, see no. *554.*
540 Allen, George H. "Yankee Medievalist." *Arch. Forum* 55 (1931): 79–80.
541 Cram, Ralph Adams. *Impressions of Japanese Architecture and the Allied Arts.* New York, 1906. Reprint, New York, 1916–1917.
542 ———. *My Life in Architecture.* 1936.
543 ———. "The Architecture of Japan" and "The Architecture of China." In no. *802,* cols. 541–547.
544 ———. *The Ministry of Art.* 1914.
545 ———. *The Substance of Gothic.* 1917.
546 The Cram Collection of Drawings and Memorabilia in the Boston Public Library.
547 Daniel, Ann Miner. "The Early Architecture of Ralph Adams Cram, 1889–1902." Ph.D. diss., University of North Carolina. Chapel Hill, 1978.
548 Hamlin, A. D. F. *A Study of the Designs for the Cathedral of St. John the Divine.* New York, 1925.
549 Muccigrosso, Robert. "American Gothic: Ralph Adams Cram." *Thought* 47 (1972): 102–118.
550 North, Arthur T. *Ralph Adams Cram.* New York, 1931.
551 Porter, Kingsley. Letter of 22 June 1926 to Dr. Cram printed in no. *554.*
552 Schuyler, Montgomery. "The Work of Cram, Goodhue and Ferguson." *Arch. Record* 29 (1911): 4–112.
553 *Times Literary Supplement,* 30 March 1916, p. 141.
554 Tucci, Douglass Shand. *Ralph Adams Cram, American Medievalist.* 1974.
555 ———. "Ralph Adams Cram: America's Foremost Gothic Scholar-Architect." *American Art Review* 111 (1976): 125–136.
556 ———. "Ralph Adams Cram and the Boston Gothicists: A Reappraisal." *JSAH* 34 (1975): 311–312.
557 *The Work of Cram and Ferguson, including Cram, Goodhue and Ferguson.* New York, 1929.
DOANE, RALPH HARRINGTON. See no. *811,* p. 233.
EMERSON, WILLIAM RALPH. See also no. *793.*
558 Zaitzevsky, Cynthia. *The Architecture of William Ralph Emerson, 1837–1917.* Cambridge, 1969.
FOX, JOHN A. See no. *32,* p. 230.
GILBERT, CASS
559 Gilbert, Julia, ed. *Cass Gilbert: Reminiscences and Addresses.* New York, 1935.
GILMAN, ARTHUR. See also nos. *444, 497, 793.*
560 Gilman, Arthur. "Architecture in the U.S." *National Review* 58 (1844): 436–480.
561 ———. *The Story of Boston.* New York, 1889.
GOODHUE, BERTRAM. See also under CRAM, RALPH ADAMS
562 Whitaker, Charles H., ed. *Bertram Grosvenor Goodhue: Architect and Master of Many Arts.* New York, 1925.
GRECO, CHARLES R. See no. *811,* p. 335.
GROPIUS, WALTER (THE ARCHITECTS COLLABORATIVE)
563 Giedion, Sigfried. *Walter Gropius: Work and Teamwork.* New York, 1954.
564 Gropius, Walter. *The New Architecture and the Bauhaus.* New York, 1937.
565 ———, ed. *The Architects Collaborative, 1945–1965.* New York, 1966.
HARRISON, PETER
566 Bridenbaugh, Carl. *Peter Harrison: First American Architect.* Chapel Hill, N.C., 1949.
HARTWELL, HENRY W.
567 Vogel, Susan Maycock. "Hartwell and Richardson: An Introduction to Their Work." *JSAH* 32 (1973): 132–146.
HASTY, JOHN. See no. *32,* p. 255. See also no. *81.*
HOWARD, JOHN GALEN
568 Hays, William C. "Some Architectural Work of John Galen Howard." *Architect and Engineer* 40 (Jan. 1915): 47–92.
HUNT, RICHARD MORRIS
569 Gass, John B. "American Architects . . . Richard Morris Hunt and Henry Hobson Richardson." *Journal of the Royal Institute of British Architects* 3 (1896): 229–232.
570 Schuyler, Montgomery. "A Review of the Works of the Late Richard M. Hunt." *Arch. Record* 5 (1895): 97–108.
KEELEY, PATRICK C.
571 Kervick, Francis. *Patrick Charles Keeley.* South Bend, Ind. 1953.
572 Tucci, Douglass Shand. "The *Other* Gothic Revival: The Work of P. C. Keeley and Maginnis and Walsh." *Drumlin* 1 (March 1976): 4–5.
KILHAM, WALTER. See also no. *38.*
573 Croly, Herbert. "The Work of Kilham and Hopkins." *Arch. Record* 31 (1912): 97–128.
LEMOULNIER, JEAN
574 Kirker, Harold, and David Van Zanten. "Jean Lemoulnier in Boston." *JSAH* 31 (1972): 204–208.
LEWIS, EDWIN J., JR. See no. *32,* p. 290; no. *810,* p. 1408.
LEWIS, W. WHITNEY. See no. *32,* p. 291.
LITTLE, ARTHUR. See also no. *32.*

575 Little, Arthur. *Early New England Interiors.* 1878.

576 Sturges, Walter Knight. "Arthur Little and the Colonial Revival." *JSAH* 32 (1973): 147–163.

LONGFELLOW, ALEXANDER W. See no. *32,* p. 295; no. *810,* p. 1441.

LORING, GEORGE F. See no. *32,* p. 296.

LOWELL, GUY

577 "The Works of Guy Lowell." *Arch. Record* 13 (1906): 13–40.

MCINTIRE, SAMUEL

578 Cousins, Frank, and P. M. Riplcy. *The Woodcarver of Salem.* 1916.

579 Kimball, Fiske. *Mr. Samuel McIntire, Carver: The Architect of Salem.* Salem, Mass. 1940.

MCKAY, HENRY S. See no. *32,* p. 307.

MCKIM, CHARLES FOLLEN

580 Bacon, Henry. "Charles Follen McKim . . ." *Brickbuilder* 19 (1910): 38–47.

581 Cortissoz, Royal. "Some Critical Reflections on the Architectural Genius of Charles Follen McKim." *Brickbuilder* 19 (1910): 23–37.

582 Desmond, Henry W. "The Work of McKim, Mead and White." *Arch. Record* 20 (1906): 153–268.

583 Granger, Alfred H. *Charles Follen McKim.* 1913.

584 Hudnut, Joseph. "The Romantic Architecture of Boston." In no. *725,* pp. 11–13.

585 *Monograph of the Work of McKim, Mead and White, 1879–1915.* New York, 1915. Rev. ed., New York, 1973. Intro. by Leland Roth.

586 Moore, Charles. *The Life and Times of Charles Follen McKim.* 1929. Reprint, New York, 1969.

587 Moses, Lionel. "McKim, Mead and White . . ." *AABN* 121 (1922): 413–424.

588 Peabody, Robert S. "A Tribute." *Brickbuilder* 19 (1910): 55–56.

589 Ramsey, Stanley. "The Work of McKim, Mead and White." *Journal of the Royal Institute of British Architects* 25 (1917): 25–29.

590 Reilly, C. H. *McKim, Mead and White.* London, 1924.

591 Sturgis, Russell. "McKim, Mead and White." Great American Architects Series, no. 1 (*Arch. Record,* 1895): 1–111.

MAGINNIS, CHARLES DONAGH. See also nos. *434, 436.*

592 Baxter, Sylvester. "The Works of Maginnis and Walsh." *Arch. Record* 53 (1923): 93–115.

593 Dooley, William Germain. "Charles Donagh Maginnis." In no. *725,* pp. 83–84.

594 Maginnis, Charles. Introduction to no. *557.*

595 Maginnis and Walsh Collection of Drawings in the Boston Public Library.

596 Walsh, Robert, and Andrew W. Roberts, eds. *Charles Donagh Maginnis: A Selection of His Essays and Addresses.* New Haven, Conn., 1956.

MOSELEY, HERBERT. See no. *32,* p. 319.

NEWCOMB, E. A. P. See no. *32,* p. 323.

OLMSTED, FREDERICK LAW. See also no. *613.*

597 Broadus, Mitchell. *Frederick Law Olmsted.* Baltimore, 1924.

598 Olmsted, Frederick L., Jr., and Theodora Kimball. *Frederick Law Olmsted.* New York, 1922.

599 Roper, Laura Wood. *FLO.* Baltimore, 1973.

600 Zaitzevsky, Cynthia. "Frederick Law Olmstead and the Boston Park System." In *Boston's Uncommon Parks.* 1976.

PARKER, THOMAS AND RICE

601 "Notes on the Work of Parker, Thomas and Rice of Boston and Baltimore." *Arch. Record* 34 (1913): 97–184.

PARRIS, ALEXANDER. See also no. *752.*

602 "Parris' Perusal." *OTNE* 58 (1967): 51–59.

PEABODY, ROBERT SWAIN. See also nos. *64, 793.*

603 Dooley, William Germain. "Robert Swain Peabody." In no. *725,* pp. 72–74.

604 Holden, Wheaton. "Robert Swain Peabody of Peabody and Stearns in Boston — The Early Years (1870–1886)." Ph.D. diss., Boston University, 1969.

605 ———. "The Peabody Touch: Peabody and Stearns of Boston, 1870–1917." *JSAH* 32 (1973): 114–131.

606 Peabody, Robert S. "Georgian Houses of New England." *AABN* 2 (1877): 338–339; 3 (1878): 54–55.

607 The Peabody and Stearns Collection of Drawings in the Boston Public Library.

608 Sturgis, Russell. "The Work of Peabody and Stearns." Great American Architects Series, no. 6 (*Arch. Record,* 1896), pp. 53–97.

PERRY, SHAW AND HEPBURN. See no. *811,* pp. 376, 608. See also no. *37.*

PRESTON, WILLIAM G. See also no. *32.*

609 The William Preston Collection of Drawings in the Boston Public Library.

PUTNAM, J. PICKERING. See no. *32,* p. 363.

RICHARDSON, HENRY HOBSON. See also nos. *783, 793.*

610 Bosworth, Welles. "I Knew Richardson." *Journal of the A.I.A.* 16 (1951): 115–127.

611 Hitchcock, Henry-Russell. *The Architecture of H. H. Richardson and His Times.* New York, 1936, Rev. ed., Cambridge, 1961.

612 Langton, W. A. "The Method of H. H. Richardson." *Architect and Contract Reporter* 63 (1900): 156–158.

613 O'Gorman, James F. "Henry Hobson Richardson and Frank Lloyd Wright." *Art Quarterly* 32 (1969): 308–311.

614 Van Rensselaer, M. Griswold. *Henry Hobson Richardson and His Works.* New York, 1969.

RINN, J. PHILIP. See no. *32,* p. 371.

ROGERS, ISAIAH. See no. *752,* pp. 111–117.

ROTCH AND TILDEN. See no. *32,* pp. 375, 423. See also no. *542.*

SCHWEINFURTH, JULIUS

615 Neitz, Stephen J. *Julius A. Schweinfurth: Master Designer, 1858–1931.* Ed. Wheaton Holden. 1975.

SEARS, WILLARD. See no. *810,* p. 2091.

SHEPLEY FIRM. See also nos. *32, 810, 811.*

616 Forbes, J. D. "Shepley, Bulfinch, Richardson and Abbott, . . ." *JSAH* 17 (1958): 19–31.

617 Sturgis, Russell. "The Work of Shepley, Rutan and Coolidge." Great American Architects Series, no. 3 (*Arch. Record,* 1896), pp. 1–51.

SPOFFORD, JOHN C. See no. 32, p. 401.
STONE, EDWARD DURELL
618   Stone, Edward Durell. *The Evolution of An Architect.* New York, 1962.
STRICKLAND, BLODGET AND LAW. See no. *618*, p. 21.
STURGIS, JOHN HUBBARD. See also no. *143*.
619   Floyd, Margaret Henderson. "Sturgis and Brigham." In no. *47*, pp. 8–10.
STURGIS, R. CLIPSTON. See also nos. *32, 810*.
620   Dooley, William Germain. "R. Clipston Sturgis." In no. *725*, pp. 79–80.
621   Sturgis, R. Clipston. "Architecture in England." In no. *802*, cols. 886–914.
622   ———. Collection of Notebooks at the Boston Athenaeum.
SULLIVAN, LOUIS. See also nos. *47, 490, 497, 534.*
623   Bush-Brown, Albert. *Louis Sullivan.* New York, 1960.
624   Connely, Willard. *Louis Sullivan As He Lived.* New York, 1960.
625   Hoffman, Donald. "The Set-back City of 1891: An Unknown Essay by Louis H. Sullivan." *JSAH* 29 (1970): 181–187.
626   Morrison, Hugh. *Louis Sullivan: Prophet of Modern Architecture.* New York, 1935.
627   Schuyler, Montgomery. "Adler and Sullivan." Great American Architects Series, no. 2 (*Arch. Record*, 1896), pp. 3–48.
628   Sullivan, Louis. *Autobiography of an Idea.* New York, 1924. Reprint, New York, 1956.
629   Weisman, Winston. "Philadelphia Functionalism and Sullivan." *JSAH* 20 (1961): 3–19.
THAYER, S. J. F. See no. *32*, p. 421.
UPJOHN, RICHARD. See also no. *444*.
630   Upjohn, Everard. *Richard Upjohn: Architect and Churchman.* New York, 1939. Reprint, New York, 1968.
VAN BRUNT, HENRY
631   Coles, William A., ed. *Architecture and Society: Essays of Henry van Brunt.* Cambridge, 1969.
VAUGHAN, HENRY. See also nos. *436, 554.*
632   Morgan, William. *The Architecture of Henry Vaughan.* Ann Arbor, Mich., 1972.
WALKER, C. HOWARD. See no. *32*, p. 431.
WARE, WILLIAM R. See also no. *38.*
633   Bunting, Bainbridge. "Ware and Van Brunt." In no. *47*, pp. 6–7.
634   Ware, William R. "Eclecticism." In no. *802*, cols. 846–848.
WARREN, H. LANGFORD. See no. *32*, p. 437.
WETHERELL, GEORGE H. See no. *32, p.* 444; no. *810*, p. 2462.
WHEELWRIGHT, EDMUND M.
635   Dooley, William Germain. "Edmund M. Wheelwright." In no. *725*, pp. 75–78.
WILLARD, SOLOMON. See also nos. *38, 752.*
636   Wheildon, William W. *Memoir of Solomon Willard* . . . Ca. 1865.
WILLS, ROYAL BARRY. See also no. *811.*
637   Wills, Royal Barry. *Houses for Homemakers.* New York, 1945.
WRIGHT, FRANK LLOYD. See also nos. *585, 768, 793.*
638   Hitchcock, Henry-Russell. "Frank Lloyd Wright and the 'Academic Tradition.' " *Journal of the Warburg and Courtauld Institutes* 7 (1944): 46–53.
YOUNG, AMMI B. See also no. *752.*
639   Woodhouse, Lawrence. "Ammi Burnham Young, 1798–1874." *JSAH* 25 (1966): 268–280.
640   ———. "Architectural Projects in the Greek Revival Style by Ammi B. Young." *OTNE* 60 (1970): 73–85.

G. BOSTON ARTISTS AND CRAFTSMEN
AND ARCHITECTURAL ART

GENERAL
641   American Federation of Arts. *Art in Our Country.* Washington, D.C., 1923.
642   Boston Society of Arts and Crafts. *Annual Reports.* 1901, 1908, 1909, 1912, 1914, 1917, 1918, 1919, 1920.
643   Cleveland, Frank. "The Arts and Crafts." *Christian Art* 2 (1907): 72–80.
644   Code, Grant H. "The Decorative Arts." In no. *13*, pp. 379–390.
645   Cram, Ralph Adams. "The Artist Crafts." In no. *436*, pp. 217–238.
646   ———. "The Craftsman and the Architect." In no. *544*, pp. 143–166.
647   Dexter, Arthur. "The Fine Arts in Boston." In no. *65*, 4:383–444.
648   Downes, William H. "General Progress in the Fine Arts." In no. *13*, pp. 335–339.
649   Gordon, Jean. *The Fine Arts in Boston.* Ann Arbor, Mich., 1965.
650   Fielding, Mantle. *Dictionary of American Painters, Sculptors and Engravers.* New York, 1926. Reprint, 1965.
     Lists many of the artists and craftsmen mentioned in the text. No. *655*, however, often contains fuller entries.
651   Marlat, Earl. "Transfiguration." In no. *686.*
652   Ritter, Richard H. *The Arts of the Church.* 1947.
653   Society of Arts and Crafts, Boston and New York. *Annual Reports,* 1925, 1927.
654   Whitehill, Walter Muir. "Boston Artists and Craftsmen at the Opening of the Twentieth Century." Unpublished paper given in 1976 to the Art-Workers' Guild, London.
655   "Who's Who in Art." *American Art Annual* 24 (1927): 465–802.
ARCHITECTURAL SCULPTURE (WOOD) INCLUDING CARVING AND JOINERY. See also nos. *181, 186.*
656   Blake, Channing. "Architects as Furniture Designers." *Antiques* (1976): 1042–1047.
657   Coburn, Frank W. "Wood Carving and Architecture." *The Studio* 41 (1910): lxiv.
658   Cram, Ralph Adams. "John Kirchmayer, Master Craftsman." *Architecture* 63 (1931): 87–92.
659   Farnam, Anne. "A. H. Davenport and Company, Boston Furniture Makers." *Antiques* 109 (1976): 1048–1055.

660 Gibson, Katharine. "A Wood-Carver of Today: I. Kirchmayer." In *The Goldsmith of Florence,* pp. 171–186. New York, 1929.
661 Karnagahn, A. W. "Ecclesiastical Wood Carving in America." *International Studio* 85 (1926): 50–53.
662 Museum of Fine Arts, Boston. *The Furniture of H. H. Richardson.* 1962.
663 O'Gorman, James F. "Decorative Arts." In no. *613,* pp. 203–210.
664 Sturgis, R. Clipston. "On Certain Carvings of I. Kirchmayer." *Christian Art* 4 (1908): 131–144.
665 Tower, L. Leslie. "The Wood Carvings of I. Kirchmayer." Reprint, ca. 1910, from unidentified journal. Cram Collection, Boston Public Library.

ARCHITECTURAL SCULPTURE (STONE AND CUT-STONE DETAIL). See also nos. *145, 181, 186.*
666 Adams, Adeline. *Daniel Chester French: Sculptor.* 1932.
667 Cresson, Margaret. *Journey into Fame: The Life of Daniel Chester French.* Cambridge, 1947.
668 Forbes, Allan. *Some Statues of Boston.* 1946.
669 ———. *Other Statues of Boston.* 1947.
670 Gardner, Albert TenEyck. *American Sculpture.* New York, 1965.
671 Geranio, Silvio. "Domingo Mora." *Revisto de la Sociedad Amigos de la Argueologia* (Montevideo, 1924), pp. 247–268.
672 John Evans Collection. Print Dept., Boston Public Library.
673 Laroche, Ernest. "Domingo Mora." In *Alqunos: Pintores y Escultorres,* pp. 151–156. Montevideo, 1939.
674 Maginnis, Charles D. "Sculpture." In no. *13,* pp. 365–378.
675 Metropolitan Museum of Art. *American Sculpture.* New York, 1965.
676 Saint-Gaudens, Augustus. *Reminiscences . . .* 2 vols. New York, 1913.
677 Taft, Lorado. *The History of American Sculpture.* New York, 1903.
678 Tharp, Louise Hall. *Saint-Gaudens and the Gilded Era.* 1970.
679 *The Sculpture of Joseph Coletti.* Intro. by Allan Priest. New York, 1968.
680 Whitney Museum of American Art. *200 Years of American Sculpture.* 1976.
681 Whitehill, Walter Muir. *Boston Statues.* Barre, Mass., 1970.
682 Wright, John. *Some Notable Altars in the Church of England and in the American Episcopal Church.* New York, 1908.

STAINED GLASS AND MURAL DECORATION. See also nos. *145, 186, 215, 216, 219, 242, 392, 395.*
683 "Belligerent Gothicist, Patron of Glass — Cram." *Fortune* 2 (1930): 77.
684 Berkon, Susan F. "Stained Glass in Back Bay Churches." In no. *807,* pp. 121–131.
685 Brown, R. Walter. "Singer in Light — Charles J. Connick." Reprint, ca. 1940, from unidentified journal. Cram Collection, Boston Public Library.
686 Connick, Charles J. *Adventures in Light and Colour.* New York, 1937.
       The appendices include a discussion of Boston glassmen and a list, for the most part accurate, of stained glass by well-known studios in the Boston area.
687 ———. "Boston Stained Glass Craftsmen." *Stained Glass* 28 (1933): 84–93.
688 ———. "Stained Glass Windows: The Craft." *Technology Monthly and Harvard Engineering Journal* 3 (1916): 3–7.
689 "Connick, Charles J." *Cowley* 19 (1946): 25–28.
690 Charles Connick Collection. Print Dept., Boston Public Library.
691 Cortissoz, Royal. *John La Farge: A Memoir and a Study.* 1911.
692 Cram, Ralph Adams. "Stained Glass and Decoration." In no. *436,* pp. 127–150.
693 Goodhue, Harry Eldridge. "Church Windows in America." *Arch. Review* 12 (1905): 196–199.
694 Harrison, Martin. "Victorian Stained Glass." *Connoisseur* 182 (1973): 251–254.
       The author discusses only English glass, but by several makers (Westlake; Clayton and Bell) whose work is extant in Boston and is not generally well documented.
695 Koch, Robert. *Louis C. Tiffany: Rebel in Glass.* New York, 1966.
696 Lucas, E. V. *Edwin Austin Abbey: Royal Academician.* 1921.
697 McKibbin, David. *Sargent's Boston.* 1965.
698 Mount, Charles. *John Singer Sargent: A Biography.* New York, 1955.
699 Museum of Fine Arts, Boston. "Augustus Saint-Gaudens," "John La Farge," and "John Singer Sargent." In no. *148,* pp. 122–133.
700 Purtell, Joseph. *The Tiffany Touch.* New York, 1971.
701 Skinner, Orin. "Stained Glass Tours: Boston." *Stained Glass* 60 (1965): 7–17.
702 Tiffany, Louis C. "American Art Supreme in Colored Glass." *The Forum* 15 (1893): 621–628.
703 Tucci, Douglass Shand. "Yankee Stained Glass: Windows as Architecture in Four Boston Churches." *American Art Review,* forthcoming issue.
704 Wattenmaker, Richard J. *Puvis de Chavannes and the Modern Tradition.* Toronto, 1975.
705 Weinberg, Helene. "The Early Stained Glass Work of John LaFarge (1835–1910)." *Stained Glass* 77 (Summer 1972): 4–16.
706 ———. "A Note on the Chronology of LaFarge's Early Windows." *Stained Glass* 77 (Winter 1972–1973): 13–15.

METALWORK
707 Cram, Ralph Adams. "The Work of Henry Wilson." *Christian Art* 2 (1907–1908): 261–273.
708 Geerlings, Gerald K. *Metal Crafts in Architecture.* New York, 1929. Reprint, 1957.
709 ———. *Wrought Iron in Architecture.* New York, 1929.
710 Gibson, Katharine. "Master Smith: Frank Koralewsky." In *The Goldsmith of Florence,* pp. 187–206. New York, 1929.
711 Glendenning, Herman W. "Arthur J. Stone, Master Craftsman." *Silver* (Sept. 1973), pp. 27–28.

H. GENERAL SOURCES AND SUGGESTED FURTHER READING

This is a highly selective bibliography. See also "Suggested Reading" in no. *63,* pp. 195–200.

712 *Achievements of New England Architects.* 1923.
       A collection of plates, with text, of then-prominent buildings erected throughout New England.

713 Adams, Adeline. *Childe Hassam*. New York, 1938.
714 American Federation of Arts and Institute of Contemporary Art. *The Cultural Resources of Boston*. New York, 1965.
715 *American Victorian Architecture*. Intro. by Arnold Lewis. New York, 1975. Republication of *L'Architecture Américaine*. Paris, 1886.
716 Appleton, Jane. "Theatrical Art Deco Swayed Bulfinch Boston." *Boston Sunday Globe Magazine*, 30 Nov. 1975, pp. 15–62.
717 Austin, William D. "A History of the Boston Society of Architects in the Nineteenth Century." 3 vols. 1942. Typescript. Boston Athenaeum.
718 *Avery Index to Architectural Periodicals*. 1973. 2d ed.
719 *Avery Obituary Index of Architects and Artists*. 1963.
720 Bacon, Edwin M. *The Book of Boston*. 1916.
721 Bannister, Turpin C. "Bogardus Revisited . . . The Iron Fronts." *JSAH* 15 (1956): 12–22.
722 Berenson, Bernard. *Sunset and Twilight*. New York, 1963.
723 Blake, Peter. *Form Follows Fiasco: Why Modern Architecture Hasn't Worked*. 1977.
724 *Boston Blue Book*. 1931. See no. *736*.
725 *Boston Society of Architects: The First Hundred Years, 1867–1967*. Ed. Marvin E. Goody and Robert P. Walsh. 1967.
726 Boston Transcript. *Index to Obituaries*. 5 vols. 1875–1930.
      A chief source here for the biographical profiles of Cushing Avenue residents; a number of Boston architects are also included.
727 Bragdon, Claude. "The Gothic Spirit." *Christian Art* 2 (1908): 165–172.
728 Brooks, Van Wyck. *The Flowering of New England*. New York, 1936.
729 ———. *New England Indian Summer: 1865–1915*. New York, 1940.
730 Bryan, John. *Boston's Granite Architecture, c. 1810–60*. Ann Arbor, Mich., 1972.
731 Burchard, John, and Albert Bush-Brown. *The Architecture of America*. 1961.
732 Bush-Brown, Harold. *Beaux-Arts to Bauhaus and Beyond*. New York, 1976
733 Carrott, Richard C. "The Neo-Egyptian Style in American Architecture." *Antiques* 90 (1966): 482–488.
734 Chapman, John Jay. *Memories and Milestones*. New York, 1915.
735 Clark, Kenneth. *Civilisation*. New York, 1969.
736 *Clark's Boston Blue Book, 1913: The Elite Private Address and Club Directory and Ladies Visiting List*.
      Includes listings of upper and upper-middle-class residential streets in all parts of the city of Boston and in suburban Brookline and Cambridge; listed alphabetically by residents' name and also by street number, and including the residents of the principal apartment houses and hotels and the membership of the important social clubs. The 1931 volume (no. *724*) includes also Milton and Chestnut Hill.
737 Conant, Kenneth John. "The New Boston Architecture in an Historical Setting." In no. *725*, pp. 89–98.
738 Cook, Clarence. "Architecture in America." *North American Review* 135 (1882): 247–249.
739 Dickens, Charles. *American Notes*. London, 1855.
740 Downing, Andrew J. *The Architecture of Country Houses*. . . . New York, 1850.
741 Eaton, Quaintance. *The Boston Opera Company*. New York, 1965.
742 Economy Concrete Company. *Many Examples of The Use of Decorative Concrete Stone*. New Haven, 1915.
743 Edgell, George H. "The Development of American Architecture." In no. *744*, pp. 3–84.
744 ———. *American Architecture of Today*. New York, 1928. Sections pertinent to this study are listed separately.
745 Eliot, Charles W. *The Book of American Interiors*. 1876.
746 Emerson, Ralph Waldo. "The American Scholar: An Oration . . . 1837." In *Emerson's Essays*, pp. 113–154. New York, 1900.
747 Fergusson, James. *History of the Modern Styles of Architecture*. 3d ed. revised by Robert Kerr. London, 1891.
748 Girouard, Mark. *Sweetness and Light: The 'Queen Anne' Movement, 1860–1900*. London, 1978.
749 Green, Martin. *The Problem of Boston*. New York, 1966.
750 Hale, Edward Everett. *A New England Boyhood*. 1893.
751 Hamlin, A. D. F. "Twenty-five Years of American Architecture." *Arch. Record* 40 (1916): 1–4.
752 Hamlin, Talbot. "The Greek Revival in Boston." In *Greek Revival Architecture in America*. New York, 1944, pp. 90–118.
753 ———. *The American Spirit in Architecture*. New Haven, 1926.
754 Handlin, Oscar. *Boston's Immigrants*. Cambridge, 1959. Rev. ed.
755 "Highlights of American Architecture, 1776–1976." *A.I.A. Journal* 65 (1976): 88–158.
      The source of the survey of significant U.S. buildings discussed in the Introduction.
756 Historic American Buildings Survey. *Massachusetts Catalogue*. 1964.
757 Hitchcock, Henry-Russell. *Architecture; Nineteenth and Twentieth Centuries*. Baltimore, 1958.
758 ———, and Philip Johnson. *The International Style* . . . New York, 1932. 2d ed., New York, 1966.
759 Hobson, Barbara, and Paul M. Wright. *Boston, A State of Mind: An Exhibition Record*. 1977.
760 *Housing Problems in America*. New York, 1914–1920.
      A series of volumes issued every year. Articles pertinent to this study are listed separately throughout this bibliography with the year of the volume in parentheses after the identifying numbers.
761 Howe, Helen. *The Gentle Americans, 1864–1960*. New York, 1965.
762 Howells, John Mead. *Lost Examples of Colonial Architecture*. New York, 1931. Reprint, New York, 1963.
763 James, Henry. *The American Scene*. New York, 1907.
764 Jones, Howard Mumford and Bessie Zaban. *The Many Voices of Boston* . . . 1975.
      Includes selections from such classics as *The Late George Apley*, *The Last Hurrah*, etc.
765 Jordy, William H. *American Buildings and Their Architects: Progressive and Academic Ideals at the Turn of the Twentieth Century*. New York, 1976.
766 Kidney, Walter. *The Architecture of Choice: Eclecticism in America, 1880–1930*. New York, 1974.
767 Kimball, Fiske, and G. H. Edgell. *A History of Architecture*. New York, 1918.
768 Kimball, Fiske. "Eclecticism and Functionalism." *Arch. Forum* 29 (1918): 21–25.
769 Lancaster, Osbert. *Pillar to Post*. London, 1938.
770 LeMessurier, William J. "Architecture and Engineering in Boston." In no. *725*, pp. 119–120.

771 Logue, Charles. "How It Strikes a Bostonian." In no. *760* (1918): 342–348.
772 Loth, Calder, and Julius Trousdale Sadler, Jr. *The Only Proper Style: Gothic Architecture in America.* 1975.
773 Maass, John. *The Gingerbread Age.* New York, 1957.
774 McAndrew, John. "Massachusetts." In *Guide to Modern Architecture: Northeast States.* New York, 1940.
775 Madsen, Stephen Tschudi. *Art Nouveau.* New York, 1967.
776 Major, Howard. *The Domestic Architecture of the Early American Republic: The Greek Revival.* Philadelphia, 1926.
777 Mann, Arthur. *Yankee Reformers in an Urban Age.* Chicago, 1974.
778 Metropolitan Boston Number. *AABN* 134 (1928): 632–716.
779 Morison, Samuel Eliot. *The Life and Letters of Harrison Gray Otis . . .* 1913.
780 ———. *The Maritime History of Massachusetts, 1783–1860.* 1921.
781 ———. *One Boy's Boston.* Garden City, N.Y., 1948.
782 ———. *Three Centuries of Harvard, 1636–1936.* Cambridge, 1936.
783 Mumford, Lewis. *The Brown Decades.* New York, 1931.
784 ———. *Sticks and Stones.* New York, 1924. Reprint, with new preface, New York, 1955.
785 Myerson, Martin, and Edward C. Banfield. *Boston: The Job Ahead.* Cambridge, 1966.
786 Norton, Charles Eliot, ed. *The Letters of John Ruskin to Charles Eliot Norton.* 2 vols. 1904.
787 Pierson, William H., Jr. *American Buildings and Their Architects: The Colonial and Neo-Classical Styles.* New York, 1976.
788 *Rand McNally Guide to Boston.* 1911.
789 Ruskin, John. *The Seven Lamps of Architecture.* London, 1849. Reprint, New York, 1966.
790 Santayana, George. *The Letters of . . .* New York, 1955.
791 ———. *People and Places.* New York, 1944.
792 Schuyler, Montgomery. "The Romanesque Revival in America." *Arch. Record* 1 (1891): 151–198.
793 Scully, Vincent. *The Shingle Style . . .* New Haven, Conn., 1955.
794 Seale, William. *The Tasteful Interlude: American Interiors through the Camera's Eye, 1860–1917.* New York, 1975.
795 Selz, Peter. *Art Nouveau.* New York, 1959.
776 Shannon, Martha A. S. *Boston Days of William Morris Hunt.* 1923.
797 Smith, Norris Kelly. Review of nos. *534, 585,* and *766. JSAH* 34 (1975): 324–326.
798 Solomon, Barbara. *Ancestors and Immigrants: A Changing New England Tradition.* Chicago, 1956.
799 Stein, Roger. *John Ruskin and Aesthetic Thought in America, 1840–1900.* Cambridge, 1969.
800 Story, Grace Haskell. *Edward Howard Haskell: A Memoir.* Cambridge, 1927.
801 Sturges, Walter Knight. "The Long Shadow of Norman Shaw." *JSAH* 9 (1950): 15–20.
802 Sturgis, Russell, ed. *A Dictionary of Architecture and Building . . .* 3 vols. New York, 1901–1902.
    Articles pertinent to this study are listed separately.
803 Tallmadge, Thomas E. *The Story of Architecture in America.* New York, 1927.
804 Torre, Susana, ed. *Women in American Architecture: A Historical and Contemporary Perspective.* New York, 1977.
805 Tyron, W. S. *Parnassus Corner: A Life of James T. Fields, Publisher to the Victorians.* 1963.
806 Upjohn, Everard, et al. *History of World Art.* New York, 1949.
807 Victorian Society of America, New England Chapter. *Victorian Boston Today: Ten Walking Tours.* Ed. Pauline Chase Harrell and Margaret Supplee Smith. 1975.
808 Weston, George F., Jr. *Boston Ways: High, By, and Folk.* 1957 and later eds.
    Interesting enough to be worth reading despite a number of misleading statements and inaccuracies.
809 Whitehill, Walter Muir. *Boston in the Age of John Fitzgerald Kennedy.* Norman, Okla., 1966.
810 *Who's Who in America 1914–1915.* Vol. 8. Chicago, 1914.
811 *Who's Who in Massachusetts 1940–1941.* 1940.
812 [Wines, E. C.] *A Trip to Boston in a Series of Letters to the Editor of the Boston Gazette.* 1838.
813 Withey, Henry F. and Elsie. *Dictionary of American Architects, Deceased.* Los Angeles, 1957.

Index

Specific buildings and streets appear under their own names and not under their locales; location is given for all buildings and streets except in the case of Boston Proper. Harvard buildings not listed separately are under Harvard University. For further information on individual suburbs, the reader is referred to Section B of the Bibliography. Page numbers in italics indicate illustrations.

257

260

Picture Credits

Figure 14 is reproduced from *Charles Bulfinch: Architect and Citizen* by Charles A. Place. Copyright 1925 and renewed 1953. Reprinted by permission of the publisher, Houghton Mifflin Company. Figures 15 and 20 are reproduced from *The Domestic Architecture of the Early American Republic: The Greek Revival* by Howard Major. Copyright 1926 by J. B. Lippincott Company. Reproduced by permission of J. B. Lippincott Company. Figure 64 is reproduced from the second edition of *The Architecture of H. H. Richardson and His Times* by Henry-Russell Hitchcock. Copyright 1961 The Shoe String Press, Inc.

About the Author

Born and raised in Boston, where he still lives, Paul Douglass Shand-Tucci was educated at Ashbury College in Ottawa and at Harvard College, where he has since been Senior Affiliate in the History of Architecture in Eliot House. He has taught in the School of Architecture at the Massachusetts Institute of Technology and at the Boston Museum of Fine Arts and has appeared regularly on the Ten O'Clock News on WGBH, Channel 2, Boston's PBS station. The author of several books, including *Ralph Adams Cram, American Medievalist*, which Ada Louise Huxtable, writing in the *New York Times*, called "impressive and illuminating," Shand-Tucci has also published work in *Harvard Magazine* and *American Art Review* and in the journal of the Isabella Stewart Gardner Museum. Currently he is Special Advisor to the Trustees of the Boston Public Library for the restoration of the McKim Building.